THE CONCUBINE, THE PRINCESS, AND THE TEACHER

Kâğıthane

Eyüp

Beşiktaş

Y

C F

Beyoğlu

D

Galata

GOLDEN HORN

BOSPHORUS

EUROPE

Üsküdar

Stambul

T

B

ASIA

Haydarpasha

Kadıköy

SEA OF MARMARA

5 miles (8.3km)

THE PALACES OF ISTANBUL

B = Beylerbeyi   F = Fer'iye
C = Çırağan   T = Topkapı
D = Dolmabahçe   Y = Yıldız

THE
Concubine,
THE Princess,
AND THE
Teacher

VOICES FROM
THE OTTOMAN HAREM

TRANSLATED AND EDITED BY
DOUGLAS SCOTT BROOKES

University of Texas Press ◆ Austin

LIBRARY OF CONGRESS CATALOGING-IN-PUBLICATION DATA

Brookes, Douglas Scott, 1950–
    The concubine, the princess, and the teacher : voices from the
Ottoman harem / Douglas Scott Brookes. — 1st ed.
        p.   cm.
    Includes bibliographical references and index.
    ISBN 978-0-292-71842-5 (cloth : alk. paper)
    1. Harems—Turkey.   2. Women—Turkey—Biography.
    3. Women—Turkey—Social conditions.   I. Title.
    HQ1726.7.B758   2008
    306.84′23092249618—dc22
                                                    2008022634

In fond remembrance
of William B. Slottman
Professor of History,
University of California
at Berkeley

Yerden temenna ile

Contents

Acknowledgments

My sincere thanks to Hamid Algar and Selim Kuru for their generous assistance with particularly abstruse sections of the texts, to Hakan Karateke for his incisive comments on the manuscript, and to Hakan Erdem and Ehud Toledano for their insights into the nature of Ottoman concubinage. Very cordial thanks to Osman Osmanoğlu for the use of Ottoman family photographs to illustrate the text.

The National Endowment for the Humanities' Fellowship Award allowed these translations to reach timely completion, and for that I am especially grateful.

Typically enough, what began as a limited exercise morphed into a project far vaster than anything even remotely imagined at the outset. For this I am thankful, as the years spent in the world of the late Ottoman palace have been rich indeed. Nonetheless the long and wandering paths of this undertaking contained treacherous potholes. In many of them I undoubtedly still languish without knowing it. If so I take full responsibility for the errors that occur when attempting to convey the spirit of one culture to inhabitants of another, later, culture. My goal has been to replicate in English the sense of life in this era that is relatively recent in time but vastly different in spirit. If the translation succeeds in that, I shall be content.

And so a tip of the hat—no, surely a floor *temenna*—in heartfelt thanks to the three ladies who share their lives in these pages. Translating your writings has been a privilege and a delight. I wish I could have known you all.

THE CONCUBINE, THE PRINCESS, AND THE TEACHER

Introduction

The imperial harem of the Ottoman sultans has long fascinated outsiders as a mélange of sex, debauchery, slavery, power, riches, and sheer abandon—in short, the incarnation of the most attractive vices. Concealed behind its own veil of circumspection, the imperial harem formed an object of mystery even in Ottoman culture, as decorum demanded respect for the privacy of the institution whose name means "forbidden, prohibited, sacred" in its Arabic original.

Penetrating behind that veil, and beyond the image of the harem in the public's fancy, this book reveals everyday life in the Ottoman imperial harem through the memoirs of three women whose home it was between 1876 and the dispersal of the harem in 1924. The memoirs are those of the concubine Filizten in Ziya Şakir's biography *Çırağan Sarayında 28 Sene: Beşinci Murad'ın Hayatı* [Twenty-Eight Years in Çırağan Palace: The Life of Murad V]; Princess Ayşe Osmanoğlu in her reminiscences, *Babam Sultan Abdülhamid* [My Father, Sultan Abdülhamid]; and schoolteacher Safiye Ünüvar in her record of life in palace employment, *Saray Hatıralarım* [My Palace Memories]. These works were selected for this translation because of the rich detail each provides, but also because of the divergent positions in the harem the authors possessed, which allows us to construct a portrait of the harem from diverse yet complementary sources.

The importance of the memoirs lies in their revelations of life in an institution still largely misunderstood today. For the veil that insulated the imperial harem during its existence has survived nearly intact, despite the death of the harem six years after World War One. Exploring the origins and persistently robust health of the harem myths lies outside the purview of this book,[1] but surely an explanation of their persistence must cite the dearth

1 European writers probably played the lead role in creating and propagating the myths. For

of reliable accounts of life within the harem. For Ottoman women familiar with the institution, whether as residents or visitors, not one would have considered writing of her life as long as a sultan occupied the Ottoman throne. As a result, the few accounts of harem life by Ottoman females who knew it well appeared only after the fall of the empire and the concomitant destruction of the social system in which the harem thrived.

Then, of the exceedingly few foreign female visitors to the harem who wrote of their visits, to our knowledge none spoke Turkish or witnessed harem life for more than a short social call. This left them poorly positioned to reliably understand and interpret what they witnessed. For a similar reason, the accounts we have of the harem by male authors—all foreigners—may safely be treated with skepticism, or even discounted outright, since Ottoman court practice barred foreign men from entering the harem at all (with the possible exception of physicians). Their accounts are second-hand at best, and prone to fancy.

On quite the other hand, the memoirs translated here issue from ladies intimately familiar with the harem because they resided within it. Presented chronologically, each translation is an excerpt of the sections in the memoirs that directly recount life in the harem or that describe inhabitants of the palace. In order to provide as much detail of the harem as possible from all three ladies yet produce a book manageable in size, the translations omit sections of the memoirs that do not directly concern harem life, primarily personal opinions of political events or statesmen of the day and events that transpired after each author left the imperial harem.

THE STRUCTURE OF THE OTTOMAN PALACE HAREM OF THE LATE NINETEENTH AND EARLY TWENTIETH CENTURIES

Although any discussion of the Ottoman palace harem must acknowledge that our understanding of the institution is limited by the relative paucity of studies of it,[2] nevertheless certain conclusions can be drawn based on scholarly work to date as well as on the memoirs of our three ladies. To be sure, the brief analysis here applies to the imperial harem only in the last hundred

---

the "barbarous odalisque" in European letters see, for instance, the figure of Gulnare in Byron's *The Corsair* (1814), or Zarema in Pushkin's *The Fountain of Bakchisarai* (1823). For one Western writer's evocation of the harem's "primitive hot-house bred voluptuaries" (to use her phrase), see Dodd [1903] 2004, 140–150.

2   The veil enshrouding the harem began to be thrown back in the 1990s, thanks to the insightful scholarship of Leslie Peirce and Ehud Toledano, among others.

or so years of its existence, as an institution such as the harem that endured for centuries would certainly have evolved a very great deal indeed over the long course of its existence.

Seemingly authenticating the popular fantasy of harem life is that, in theory, the Ottoman sultan might choose any number of concubines from among the slave women in imperial service, the only restriction being the canonical injunction that he could name but four of them as his official wives. But in practice the prince's sexuality was restrained by the fact that each maiden he took to bed had to be provided a rank, her own suite of rooms and servants, and the right to advance in the concubine hierarchy. In other words, she had claims on the prince that he had to honor.

As a result of these restraints, as nearly as we can determine for the monarchs of the period of these memoirs, Sultan Murad V had sexual relations with nine ladies, Abdülhamid II with thirteen ladies, and Reşad and Vahideddin with five ladies each—more than the vast majority of their subjects, to be sure, who took one wife, but not the stuff of legend. From their multiple ladies, Murad sired seven children, Abdülhamid seventeen, Reşad and Vahideddin four each.

In consequence of the practical restraints on the number of concubines the sultan might take, combined with extremely high infant mortality rates, and the custom since the early seventeenth century of limiting contenders to the throne by forbidding a prince to father children until he became sultan, by November 1808 the Ottoman dynasty had dwindled to but one male, Sultan Mahmud II. And so the imperial family most assuredly did *not* number in the thousands by 1876, when our memoirs begin.

The restriction among male members of the dynasty that allowed only the monarch to sire children began to give way in the last years of the reign of Sultan Abdülmecid. In 1857 his brother and heir Prince Abdülaziz fathered a son, although the child's existence was kept secret until Abdülaziz ascended the throne in 1861.

The Entourage System

Given the presence of multiple concubines, royal children, and slaves resident in it, quite understandably court practice divided the Ottoman harem into entourages, or households.

The sultan oversaw the largest entourage. His serving women and eunuchs ranked as the most revered in the palace. Then, each adult prince and princess oversaw his or her own entourage, as did each concubine and

Prince Yusuf İzzeddin, eldest son of Sultan Abdülaziz, at age sixteen in 1873. Since the boy's birth contravened Ottoman court tradition, his existence had remained secret until his father came to the throne. Photographer: Abdullah Frères.

the highest-ranking officeholders in the harem. Special harem residents might receive their own small entourage—for example, our schoolteacher. Each entourage occupied its own set of apartments, physically separate from the other entourages. Each possessed its own cadre of female slaves and eunuchs in service to it.

If she were living, the sultan's mother constituted the chief authority over the harem, so that only the more senior and experienced slave women served in her entourage. If she were deceased, authority over the harem devolved to the sultan's Senior Consort, a position appointed by the monarch for life.

The entourage system flourished in miniature in the villas of the imperial family throughout Istanbul. Married princesses had always lived in their own villas with their husbands. As an innovation of the nineteenth century, in imitation of European practice, adult princes also received permission to move out of the palace to their own villas around the city.

The Imperial Family: Members and Adjuncts

In the Ottoman monarchy of our period, succession to the throne passed not to the monarch's eldest son but to the eldest male member of the dynasty. In order to limit claims to the throne, and to clarify rank and precedence, the House of Osman defined a member of the dynasty as the son or daughter of a sultan or of a prince. In other words, descent through males alone imparted royal rank. For this reason, children of princesses were not considered members of the dynasty but rather *mensuplar*, adjuncts of it. A princess's grandchildren were commoners, albeit prestigious ones.

Concubines too, even the mother of the sultan, were held to be but adjuncts of the dynasty, not members of it. In this way the imperial family distinguished itself from these slave women in service to it, even though these slaves provided the family with its future members. Thus a concubine's children outranked her. However, from the memoirs it is clear that, rather than slighted, these women felt vastly honored to attain the distinction of adjunct to the imperial house. The distinction worked in their favor in 1924, when the law exiling members of the imperial family excluded the adjuncts. The son or daughter had to leave, but the mother could stay, and several did, including the mother of our Princess Ayşe.

Concubines consisted of three ranks. The highest level belonged to the four consorts of the sultan, ranked in precedence as Senior Consort, Second Consort, Third Consort, and Fourth Consort. The ambiguous term *consort* rather than *wife* is deliberate here to translate their title of *Kadın* (Lady), for it is unclear whether an Ottoman prince underwent a wedding ceremony with a woman he took as a concubine or, if he acceded to the throne, whom he elevated to the rank of Kadın. The subject of weddings with imperial concubines requires further study, but given the present state of our knowledge we can say that until the mid-nineteenth century, such marriages formed the exceedingly rare exception in the House of Osman. For concubines were slaves, and Islamic religious law does not require a master to marry his slave in order to have sexual relations with her. Princess Ayşe's story that her grandfather Sultan Abdülmecid promised his aunt he would actually wed her servant girl Perestû if she presented the girl to him bears witness to this custom.

After the mid-nineteenth century, however, marriages with concubines became more frequent as part of the Ottoman monarchy's increasing adoption of European royal practice, and Princess Ayşe tells us that her father married her mother. Still, marriages that did occur remained brief and discreet events inside the harem, an expression of esteem on the part of the royal male. Not affairs of state, they went unreported in the press, unlike the lavish weddings of princesses, which very much served the state as a means to honor high-ranking men of the government and military by linking their families in loyalty to the imperial house.

Below the four consorts ranked the two levels of concubines who were in theory not limited in number. The higher-ranking bore the title İkbal (fortunate one), and like the consorts were ordered by seniority as "Senior İkbal, Second İkbal," etc. The lower-ranking bore the title Gözde (chosen one), but were not ordered by seniority.

The Female Slaves

Insofar as we can tell, nearly all the female slaves[3] in the imperial harem in the era of our memoirs were ethnically Circassian.

---

3   Although the harem women and eunuchs were indeed slaves, the term does not serve us well to convey the position these individuals occupied in Ottoman court life, since it conjures the image of a person without power at the bottom of society—i.e., a position of shame. But as the concubine Filizten and Princess Ayşe tell us, in the Ottoman case this purchased individual, if male, could serve as chief aide to the head of state, accumulate a vast fortune, and oversee a range of influential foundations. Ministers, generals, and wealthy men curried his favor. Or, as our schoolteacher makes clear, if female she might similarly manage a complex organization at the center of state power, accumulate riches, and supervise her own retinue of servants. Unhappily, however, unlike Turkish the English language lacks words that connote this status as owned indeed by master or mistress, yet wielding power, overseeing wealth, and commanding respect. Hence we are left with the unsatisfactory word *slave*.

Over the course of the nineteenth century the Russians had largely expelled the Circassian peoples, Muslims, from their native Caucasus. Most fled into the Ottoman Empire, at the time an impoverished society hardly in a position to absorb the large numbers of refugees streaming into it. One way in which uprooted Circassian families could realize a large sum of money, however, was to sell their daughters into slavery in the harems of the Ottoman elite. For Circassian girls, especially if blonde, blue-eyed, and fair of complexion, were considered highly desirable beauties. The fact that Islamic law forbade the enslavement of fellow Muslims was overlooked, given the economic and social advantages the trade offered for seller, buyer, and slave. Even after the imperial decree of 1854 that abolished slavery, the government turned a blind eye to the continued market in slaves, both for the revenue it generated and on the general principle that an institution as ingrained in Ottoman elite society as slavery could not realistically be banished overnight.[4]

And so the trade in females went on, in both white Caucasian and black African slaves destined for the mansions of the elite and the palaces and villas of the imperial family. While the black female slaves in general entered into manual labor, the Circassian girls were preferred for more genteel service in the harems and as potential sources of concubines for the male members of the family. Indeed, purchasing young Circassian girls, teaching them refined manners and accomplishments, and then reselling them to wealthy families or the imperial court when they reached adulthood, constituted an honored profession for a select number of women well placed for access to the upper reaches of Ottoman society.

Though the traffic in humans continued, the Ottoman slave trade began to collapse in the era of our memoirs. Reflecting prevailing tastes worldwide, Ottoman society had come to regard the old institution with disfavor, but the decisive factor in the decline of slavery was economic. As Circassian refugee families assimilated into society, the supply of their daughters diminished, causing steep price increases that few families in this chronically impoverished economy could afford. By the end of the era we are considering, 1924, practically the only household still engaging slave labor was the imperial palace itself.

Once in the palace, a novice slave girl received a new name from the sultan, by tradition a name Persian in origin that might describe her looks or

---

4 Toledano 1998, 122 ff. Professor Toledano's pioneering study of Ottoman slavery, especially pp. 30–52 on the female slaves and eunuchs in the Ottoman palace, has formed the basis for my comments on the institution here.

personality. As the concubine tells us, a novice girl underwent training under the supervision of her elders in service until she had mastered the Turkish language, the standards of comportment, and the skills of the job. Her training complete, she received assigned duties within her entourage. After years of service, a deserving novice could be elevated to the rank of *kalfa* (lit., master assistant; overseer). A prettier kalfa might be chosen as concubine to a prince. Even were she not so selected, however, if the prince she served succeeded to the throne, a kalfa could still hope to attain senior status in the harem through appointment by the monarch to the supervisory rank of *hazinedar*.

An unknown number of the senior female and male slaves in palace service were manumitted, as the schoolteacher mentions, but chose to remain in palace service. Nor were slave women who were unhappy in service forced to remain in the palace until the end of their days, for as both our Princess and the schoolteacher tell us, they possessed the right to ask to leave service for marriage to a man outside the palace. In the era of our memoirs this request appears to have been always granted.

The Eunuchs

We do not know a good deal about the origin of the black African eunuchs at the Ottoman court. Captured by slave raiders, they were castrated shortly afterward by removing, it would appear, both penis and testicles. For the few who survived this ordeal, the physical repercussions of their trauma included testosterone deficiency that resulted in misshapen bodies, high-pitched voices, and lack of a beard. The emotional repercussions await in-depth study, but at the time were considered to include eccentricity, meanness, and the potential desire to avenge oneself on society. Our memoirs include examples of this behavior, but also of kindness, trustworthiness, and loyalty on the part of the eunuchs in palace service.

Conveyed from Africa to the slave markets in Egypt, Arabia, and Yemen, the newly created eunuchs were purchased primarily by dealers from Istanbul. While the imperial family acquired some of these eunuchs directly from slave dealers, most eunuchs came to the palace as gifts from wealthy officials seeking to ingratiate themselves at court through this exceedingly costly act. Once registered at the palace, eunuchs entered training in their expected duties as well as in proper comportment and etiquette. Only after completing this training were they assigned to duty within one of the entourages in the palace.

Princess Ayşe notes in her memoir that the eunuchs' duties included the prosaic tasks of "locking the doors to the Imperial Harem each evening and unlocking them in the morning, standing watch at the doors, keeping an eye on those who entered and left, accompanying people to their carriages, escorting doctors in and out, and not leaving alone anyone who had come from outside the palace."[5] But the highest-ranking eunuchs, reporting directly to the Sultan, also came to wield vast power as administrators of the palace and supervisors of wealthy pious foundations.

In terms of numbers, we know that as of 1903 a total of 194 black eunuchs served the imperial family, 31 at the Sultan's residence of Yıldız Palace, and the remaining 163 distributed in service to the other princes and princesses in their villas in and around Istanbul.[6]

NORMS ADOPTED IN THE TRANSLATIONS

Because the British royal court lacked slaves and harems, the English language lacks words to precisely translate a good number of the ranks and titles at the Ottoman court. Where English bears no suitable equivalent the term is left in its Turkish original.

Equerry designates a eunuch who possessed the high rank *Musahib* (companion). Eunuchs who ranked below this position are simply "eunuch" in the translation, to render the venerable title *Ağa* that by the late nineteenth century at the Ottoman court nearly always denoted a eunuch.

The title of the monarch's mother, *Valide Sultan* (*valide* means "mother"), is translated as Princess Mother to approximate the Ottoman original, which sought to honor this lady as the only concubine at court permitted to bear the word *sultan* in her title. Apart from this lady, among women at court only princesses bore the title *sultan*, which in their case followed the given name. The title *sultana* that one encounters in European texts for Ottoman princesses is a strictly European invention, never used at the Ottoman court.

In Turkish, shortened versions of a monarch's name occur often; this variety has been retained. Thus Mecid, Aziz, and Hamid for the sultans Abdülmecid, Abdülaziz, and Abdülhamid, respectively.

Ottoman princes of this era usually received two given names, "Mehmed" followed by the personal name unique to that prince and by which he was commonly known. For instance, at his accession Prince Mehmed Reşad became

5 Osmanoğlu 1994, 94.
6 Toledano 1998, 41 ff.

commonly "Sultan Reşad," although formally he was "Sultan Mehmed V." In the memoirs one encounters these princes' names both with and without "Mehmed," and the translation follows this usage.

Calendar dates in the Islamic Hijri calendar or the Ottoman *mali* calendar have been converted to the Gregorian calendar.

For determining current-day values of sums of money mentioned in the text, the following comparison should prove most useful. At the time of our memoirs, the Ottoman *lira* or pound consisted of 100 *kuruş* or piasters. In 1914, during the period of our memoirs, the average daily wage of a worker in Istanbul amounted to ten to twelve *kuruş*, so that the average monthly wage of a worker in Istanbul totaled approximately three liras. The average annual income of a worker in Istanbul, then, came to around thirty-six liras.[7]

Foreign words not found in a good English dictionary are italicized. Exception is made for the titles *kadın, kadınefendi, kalfa, hazinedar,* and *usta,* which recur so frequently that to avoid maddening the reader they are italicized only at first appearance. Spelling of Turkish words generally follows Modern Turkish orthography as in the *New Redhouse Turkish-English Dictionary* (Istanbul, 1974). Pronunciation of Turkish letters is as in English with the following exceptions:

c = j
ç = ch
ğ = not pronounced, simply extends the length of the preceding vowel
ı (undotted i) = the "i" in *pick*
i (including capitalized dotted i) = "ee"
ö = the "er" in *her*; same as French *eu* or German ö
ş = sh
ü = "ee" pronounced with rounded lips; same as French *u* or German *ü*

Brackets indicate insertions by the translator, while parentheses indicate insertions by the authors in the original texts.

Footnotes followed by bracketed initials identify notes from the original Turkish texts that have been retained in the translation, as follows. Notes not followed by a bracketed initial are those of the translator.

1. Concubine Filizten
   [Ş] = Footnote by Ziya Şakir

---

7 The currency figures here are taken from Pamuk 2000.

2. Princess Ayşe
   [A] = Footnote by Princess Ayşe
   [ÖO] = Footnote by the Princess's sons Ömer and Osman in subsequent editions
3. Schoolteacher Safiye
   [Ü] = Footnote by Safiye Ünüvar

THE
Concubine Kilizten

THE MEMOIR OF THE CONCUBINE FİLİZTEN CONSTITUTES ONE OF ONLY three known memoirs by slave women in the Ottoman palace harem.[1] This alone makes her memoir noteworthy, but of additional interest is that this lady spent twenty-eight years confined in Çırağan Palace along with her deposed master, Sultan Murad V, and the other members of his entourage.

The biographical details we have on the life of the lady Filizten come entirely from the few clues she leaves in the memoir. She does not tell us her ethnic origin, but almost certainly she was Circassian, as was nearly every other slave woman in the Ottoman palace of her day. We know she was born around 1861–1862, since she tells us she had been presented at the age of fourteen or fifteen to the entourage of then-Prince Murad shortly before his accession to the throne, which occurred 30 May 1876. She was a gift to the palace from her mistress at the time, a lady formerly in palace service herself in Murad's entourage, but who had left the palace and married one Tayyar Pasha.[2] At the time she penned her memoir, Filizten was in her seventies, and she died in Istanbul probably around 1945.

From the name given her when she entered palace service, one might assume she was thin and wispy, since *filiz ten* means "tendril-bodied." But palace slave names could be ironic, and in fact she tells us she was somewhat heavy. Her hair was blonde and she was of medium height.

Filizten's memoir constitutes the majority of the biography of Murad compiled by the journalist and avocational historian Ziya Şakir under the

---

1   The others being that of the lady Nevzad Nimet, later consort of Sultan Mehmed VI Vahideddin, and Leyla (Açba), in service to that Sultan's consort, Nazikeda.
2   Filizten does not name her former mistress, and research has failed to further identify Tayyar Pasha.

title *Twenty-Eight Years in Çırağan Palace: The Life of Murad V.*[3] In his preface, Şakir describes the concubine as over seventy years of age but in excellent health, in complete command of her faculties, and aware of what he called her responsibility to history in retelling the events she witnessed in Çırağan Palace. In other words, we are to conclude, the concubine is dictating to the compiler from memory; the memoir is an oral history by one who witnessed the events of fifty years earlier. In fact the concubine states in her memoir that she did not keep a diary.

The pleasing flow of the narrative reveals the talented hand of the journalist Şakir, who surely reworked the concubine's words into a style suitable for publication. That style included long-ago conversations quoted verbatim. While the historical accuracy of these conversations may well be challenged, to say the least, nevertheless their value lies in furnishing the reader with the concubine's impression of an event, the same as the portions of her text that do not lie within quotation marks.

Possibly because the concubine herself wished to remain discreet, nowhere in the work does Şakir name Filizten with simple clarity, instead providing clues to her identity. Knowing that historians and generally educated readers would demand authentication of his source, however, Şakir informs us that he took the precaution of showing the concubine's words to the handful of survivors from the entourage of the ex-Sultan, all of whom corroborated her statements. That Şakir also interviewed these colleagues of Filizten's, and occasionally inserted their reminiscences into the text, becomes clear from the few but abrupt, and unattributed, references in the memoir to Filizten in the third person.

The compiler's idiosyncrasies notwithstanding, the authenticity of the memoir itself has never been in doubt. Immediately after publication it formed a primary source for the articles on Murad V published by the eminent historian İsmail Hakkı Uzunçarşılı, who directly identified the memoir's author as Filizten Hanım, *gözde* of Murad V.[4] Today it continues to form a primary source both for the life of this Sultan in particular, and for life in the late Ottoman palace harem in general.

---

3   *Çırağan Sarayında 28 Sene: Beşinci Murad'ın Hayatı.* Istanbul: Anadolu Türk Kitap Deposu, 1943, number ten in the series of his historical works published by Muallim Fuat Gücüyener. The prolific Şakir (1883–1959) published some 140 biographies and histories serialized in newspapers. Approximately 25 of these—including the biography of Murad V—appeared subsequently as books.

4   The first such citation appears in Uzunçarşılı 1944 "Ali," 81n4.

Prince Murad in court uniform in 1866, age twenty-six, ten years before he ascended the throne. At the Ottoman court princes could sport mustaches, but only the sultan could wear a full beard. Photographer: Abdullah Frères.

Eldest son of Sultan Abdülmecid, Murad was born to the Imperial Consort Şevkefza in Istanbul 21 September 1840. The young Prince's education included history, philosophy, and French, while early on he showed talent for drawing and music, especially piano.

At the age of twenty Murad became father to his first child, Prince Salâheddin. Five months later his own father was dead and Murad became heir to his uncle, the new Sultan Abdülaziz. In contrast to his uncle, Murad began receiving leading intellectuals in his villas—European visitors, but also Ottomans interested in discussing ways to advance their country.

Prince Murad accompanied his uncle on the imperial tours to Egypt in 1863 and Europe in 1867. While in London a friendship arose between Murad and Edward, Prince of Wales, his fellow Freemason. After returning to Istanbul, Murad increased his ties with liberals interested in introducing constitutional government as the means to resuscitate the Ottoman state, so that by 1870 the Heir to the Throne represented the hope of those frustrated with the autocratic rule of Sultan Abdülaziz. Unfortunately, as his brothers at least had come to realize, Murad was an alcoholic.

On the night of 29–30 May 1876, the committee led by the statesman Midhat Pasha and the Minister of War, Hüseyin Avni Pasha, deposed Abdülaziz and raised Murad to the throne. The new monarch struggled to appear normal in his new role, so at odds with his previously quiet life of dabbling in music, and evenings enveloped in a pleasant, alcohol-induced haze. But the suicide of his deposed uncle only days after his accession stunned him. Added to his struggle with alcoholism, the distress over the abrupt manner in which he was brought to the throne, and the demands besieging him as ruler was the anxiety that the world would assume he had ordered his uncle's murder.[5]

Murad began to manifest bizarre behavior that preceded his complete collapse. The government leaders called in the Viennese specialist in psychiatric disorders, Dr. Max Leidesdorf, who concluded that the new Sultan could make a complete recovery with three months' treatment in a clinic. This the government leaders were unwilling to attempt. A mentally competent prince on the throne formed an essential component of their plans to implement reforms with due legitimacy. Murad's younger brother and

5 Despite the widespread suspicion at home and in the foreign press that Abdülaziz had been murdered, the foreign and Ottoman physicians who examined the corpse and the room in which Abdülaziz died all concluded without any doubt that the Sultan had committed suicide. The report of the British Embassy physician thoroughly convinced even the skeptical British ambassador of the day. Elliot 1922, 236–241.

heir Prince Abdülhamid, however, appeared eminently healthy physically and mentally—moreover, a teetotaler—and supportive of the leaders' plans to introduce parliamentary government. Securing the Şeyhülislâm's ruling sanctioning Murad's dethronement, and Abdülhamid's promise to proclaim a constitution, on 30 August 1876 the government ministers declared Murad deposed. His reign had lasted ninety-three days, the shortest in Ottoman history.

The new Sultan ordered Murad and his entourage transferred to the vacant Çırağan Palace along the shore of the Bosphorus. Some nine months later, Murad regained his mental faculties. The first two years of Murad's confinement in Çırağan witnessed three attempts by supporters to free him and restore him to the throne, but all three resulted only in Abdülhamid's tightening the cordon that isolated Çırağan Palace from the city around it.

His mental faculties restored, Murad lived out a far more benign existence than that attributed to him by the Western press, as our concubine attests. Fanciful reports through the years claimed that the ex-Sultan languished in prison, or escaped and was hiding, or lectured his brother on the Armenian troubles.[6] At length, suffering from diabetes, Murad died at age sixty-three on 29 August 1904, one day short of the twenty-eighth anniversary of his confinement in Çırağan Palace.

6 All in *New York Times*: "Ex-Sultan Murad in Prison" (7 July 1877, p. 1); "Sultan Murad's Letter" (22 September 1895, p. 9); "Ex-Sultan Murad Escapes" (13 December 1896, p. 1); "Abdul's Imprisoned Brother" (9 April 1901, p. 1).

THE Memoir

This is a date I shall never forget as long as I live: the night of Tuesday, 30 May.[7] For some days a complete silence had fallen over the palace. Two of our master's serving women, the kalfas Aynıfer and Dilberengiz, had been coming and going from the room of the Lady Mother. Elderly kalfas were whispering to one another off in secluded corners, but fell silent and knitted their brows as soon as they caught sight of us young novice girls, newly arrived in palace service.

We sensed that something was afoot. But no one dared to ask what it was, for when we entered palace service the first admonition from the kalfa to whose retinue we were assigned for training was this: "Whatever you see, you will behave as if you hadn't seen. Whatever you hear, you will tell no one. You will make no attempt to learn about a matter that has been concealed from you. If you do not heed this warning..."

The threat was a terrible one. They showed us a round table in the middle of a dank room in the basement, and whispered in our ears: "The novice girls who fail to heed these words are strapped to this table. This table has a machine attached to it. It will start to spin, lowering itself down to the sea beneath, drowning the girl strapped onto it." This threat was enough for us. They had made their point, with no need to say more.

That evening, once the night prayers had been performed,[8] Enginaz Kalfa, in whose room we slept and who oversaw our training, came into the room. She said with an agitated voice, "Ah, but life is wicked! All right girls, tonight

---

7 The year was 1876, and the events the *gözde* is about to describe took place in the Heir's apartments at Dolmabahçe Palace.

8 The last of the five daily prayers, performed some one-and-one-half to two hours after sunset.

we shall go to bed early." But to turn in so early was not the custom; after prayers the fruit tray called *ekşilik* [tart platter] was brought in and we'd eat fruits and nuts before going to bed. So the kalfa's order struck us as odd, but it was imperative to obey her command without the slightest objection. And so the kalfa's order was carried out. We got into our beds without saying a word, pulling the blankets over our heads.

I shan't forget it, for truly the weather that night was terrible. A violent wind was howling off the Bosphorus and rain pelted the windows. I don't know if it was because the weather had me on edge or if I sensed something in my bones, but I tossed and turned and only dozed off after a few hours.

A sudden noise woke me up. I raised my head and listened. I had a feeling about something and simply couldn't bear it anymore, so I slipped out of bed silently so my kalfa wouldn't hear. Quietly, I stole through the door. When I entered the great hall beyond the vestibule outside our room, I came across one of the duty kalfas hurrying toward the Lady Mother's apartments. I couldn't ask her anything, but when I heard the clear sounds of running and weapons rattling, I realized something important was happening. Passing through the great hall dimly lit by chandeliers, I approached the other duty kalfas, who were looking out a window. I slipped in beside them and looked through the grillwork of the window, down to the courtyard, and froze.

It was raining. Soldiers were running about in the dark night. In their midst stood a ramrod-straight man with a short beard, ordering the two officers in front of him, "You, take your unit to this side. And you, over to this side. Have your men fix their bayonets. Allow no one in or out. If anyone disobeys your orders, bayonet them."

Half asleep, the aides and eunuchs on duty that night were gathering, their dress disheveled, trying to pull their jackets over their arms. The aides huddled together, talking with one another, while the eunuchs gathered around Abdülkerim Ağa. Once he finished giving orders to the other officers, the bearded officer came over to the door behind which the aides and eunuchs had gathered. In a stern voice he demanded, "Open the door. I want His Highness the Prince."

One of the aides began to speak. "The door may not be opened without His Highness's express order. State what your purpose is and we shall send word in. At any rate the keys are inside." But the bearded officer exploded in anger and shouted, "There is no time to waste! Have this door opened at once and bring His Highness out, or I shall hold all of you responsible!"

Abdülvahid Ağa, the keeper of the keys, opened the door with the keys he carried with him. Meanwhile Abdülkerim Ağa and Raşid Ağa ran inside to the foot of the stairway and called out to the duty kalfas, "Quickly, tell the Lady Mother and our master that a major is here with his men and wants to see our master."

Since the kalfa who was running toward the Lady Mother's apartments when I left my room had already alerted her to what was happening, the Lady Mother came into the hallway at that moment. She was terribly anxious, and there in her state of agitation the duty kalfas relayed Abdülkerim Ağa's message to her. She stood there hesitating, rubbing her hands together: "This is most irregular—make certain no one hears of this. Ask that major who it is who wants to see my son."

From the foot of the stairs angry shouts were coming, consisting mostly of the words, "Hurry up, hurry up." Abdülkerim Ağa and Hâfız Ağa ran up the stairs to the Lady Mother and whispered something in her ear. With that the Lady Mother assumed a bit more composure. "Go and let my son know what has happened. But be careful not to frighten him! Since he's been asleep he might feel unsteady."

While Emsalinur and Siranto, two of the Lady Mother's kalfas who had come in with her, were hurrying off to the apartments of our master, Raşid Ağa came bounding up the stairs two and three steps at a time. He brought this news: "Don't worry, Ma'am, these men have come to bring good news. Just now the Senior Doorkeeper took me aside and told me, 'Run and tell the Lady Mother. . . . I know what's happening. I opened the door myself and let the soldiers in. Tell her not to worry that something bad is happening. The palace is completely surrounded by troops.'" This news put the Lady Mother at ease, and her face relaxed into a wide smile.

Now our master came in. Over his nightshirt he had thrown a long fur coat trimmed with cinnamon-colored silk. He was practically in a daze, having awakened so suddenly. When the Lady Mother saw her son she went up to him and said, "Don't be afraid, my boy. God willing, this is auspicious."

"Mother, you say not to be afraid, but who are these people? Why have they come?"

"A major, apparently. He's come to fetch you quickly."

"There's something strange about this, Mother. A major wouldn't be the one to come and summon me if this were something favorable; surely someone prominent should be the one. And Seyyid Bey has always told me that this would happen during the day. Where is Seyyid Bey?"[9]

9 Seyyid Bey, courtier in Murad's household, as well as an intimate and friend, had sponsored Murad into his Freemason lodge in 1872.

Abdülkerim Ağa supplied the answer. "Sir, Seyyid Bey is on leave this evening."

Now Emin Ağa came leaping up the stairs. "Please, Sir. The officer is raising the devil downstairs. He wants to see Your Highness at once."

Our master was quite frightened and agitated. He seemed to implore help from the people around him, his eyes searching them as he answered, "No . . . no . . . I won't go down. Tell him so. Let *him* come *here*." The Lady Mother felt the same way, as did all the hazinedars and kalfas who had heard the commotion and flown from their beds, gathering there. Everyone was saying, "Yes, yes . . . whoever that officer is, let *him* come *here*."

Quietly I made my way over to the stairs. I stuck my head between the balusters and looked down. The motley view I saw in the darkness consisted of aides and eunuchs gathered around a rather tall, sallow-skinned officer with a somewhat curly beard. They were pleading with him, "Please remove your sword and revolver. If our master sees you armed like this he'll take fright." But the officer wouldn't budge, and bellowed, "My good fellows, I am a soldier! I always carry weapons wherever I go! This is not the time to remove weapons! Do not waste time! You proceed in front of me and take me to His Highness! You are harming both him and me!"

Süleyman Ağa, tutor of our master's eldest son, Prince Salâheddin, came hurrying in. When he saw the officer he made his way through the aides and eunuchs and put the officer off by saying, "Oh, my lord Pasha, is it you? This is good news, God willing," and then he came running up the stairs. At that point our master and the Lady Mother were standing at the top of the stairway and Süleyman Ağa said to them, "This officer waiting below is the Commandant of the War College, Süleyman Pasha. I used to stop by his office for chats on the days I took Prince Salâheddin to the College. He bears the utmost respect for Your Highness."

While the tutor Süleyman Ağa was speaking, Süleyman Pasha had hurried up the staircase as well. Halfway up the steps his sword tangled in his feet and he nearly tripped. His uniform was most strange—no silver braid at all at his shoulders or on his cuffs. And the sword belt at his waist was not like that worn by pashas; it was common black leather.

Now I too was so engrossed in everything that I forgot all palace rules and regulations and went right up and slipped into the group there. Seeing that a strange man had entered the premises, the kalfas had withdrawn to the background and were watching the proceedings from there. They had wrapped a delicate shawl around the head of the Lady Mother.

Süleyman Pasha performed a floor *temenna* before our master. In a loud voice he said, "Your Highness, please, the people are calling you. Soldiers are waiting outside. The ministers and the ulema also await you!"

Our master was still hesitating. He exchanged these words with Süleyman Pasha:

"And my uncle, what has happened to him?"

"He has been placed under guard."

"Is he aware of this business?"

"I do not know. My duty as your servant is to issue this summons to you. I beseech you, let us go quickly, let us not waste time."

Süleyman Ağa was standing beside the Lady Mother, whispering some things in her ear. At this point the lady interjected these words: "My son, since our Pasha is in such haste, why not just quickly make yourself ready and go with him."

With that our master came suddenly to life. He nearly ran to his apartments, got dressed, and came back in. In the meanwhile a colorful crowd of people filled the great hall. No one was sleeping anymore, all the kalfas and eunuchs had come in and the place hummed with their excited conversations. The old kalfas were reciting some things and then blowing toward our master.[10]

Our master had gone quite pale in the face and seemed bewildered as to what he should do. He had put on a thick-collared stambuline overcoat. Süleyman Pasha tucked the hilt of his sword under his arm and approached our master from the left. "Just this way, Sir," he said, gently taking him by the arm. "God willing, Sir, I dare say this is good news for you."

With that they descended the stairway. The gözdes and hazinedars were weeping with joy and offering thanks to God for showing them this day. The Lady Mother went to the head of the stairs and called out, "My dear Pasha, I have only one son in this world. I entrust him first into the hands of God, and then into your care!"

All the women hurried over to the windows to see how they would take our master out of the courtyard. I went over with them and heard a voice shouting, "Atten-TION!" Our master came out of the doorway, followed by Süleyman Pasha. The soldiers, lined up in two rows, raised their rifles in salute. Süleyman Pasha called out to a captain who was scurrying about, "Necib Bey, one of the units should stay here and one should come with us." Captain Necib then issued a brief order and soldiers lined up around our

---

10 This is the superstitious practice of wishing blessings upon others by reciting an incantation and then blowing in the direction of the intended beneficiary.

master and Süleyman Pasha. Some of the eunuchs and aides wanted to accompany our master, but once the soldiers lined up around him they were left out. Only the eunuch Hâfız Ağa managed to get next to him.

The hazinedars and older kalfas gathered in the Lady Mother's apartments and began praying loudly, reciting the Quran, fingering their prayer beads, and continuously blowing their breath in the direction of Istanbul. Everywhere there was a flurry of activity for reasons that weren't clear to us. The two kalfas Dilberengiz and Aynifer came flying out of the Lady Mother's apartments and hurried toward the door, one of them clutching a small white envelope. They were looking for a eunuch to send to the apartments of Prince Hamid. Later I learned that our master had taken the important precaution of scribbling a note when he had gone to his rooms to change: "Brother: they are taking me away, but I don't know where or why. I entrust my children and household first to God and then to you." He gave the note to Dilberengiz and advised her, "As soon as I go out the door, show this note to my mother. Have her read it and then send it to my brother without delay."

Let us pause to consider this extremely important point: at this moment, our master was acting entirely rationally and prudently. Later on I realized that he wrote this note and sent it to Prince Hamid out of fear. Nor was this fear without reason. Our master was so certain of the power and authority of his uncle that he could never imagine his uncle would be easily overthrown and he himself quickly raised to the throne in his stead. In fact as I heard it, it never occurred to him that he might ascend the throne while his uncle was still alive.

This is why our master quite naturally could not readily put faith in Süleyman Pasha's summons. And it is why he took the great precaution of writing that note to Prince Hamid. It gave him an alibi in case the plot to overthrow the Sultan failed. He could plead, "I knew absolutely nothing. These men came to my rooms and forced me to go with them."

The note our master wrote was sent immediately to Prince Hamid, but our entourage was in such a state that no one gave the matter serious thought. Anticipation had gripped every one of us. Within less than an hour, all these people who had spent long and gloomy years confined and restricted might find themselves embarking upon an entirely new life. They could abandon these stultifying rooms in order to move into the monarch's apartments and assume the mantle of sovereignty along with our master.

But this unnerving period of approximately one hour did not seem to bode well for a new and grand change in our lives. We had no idea what was happening outside, and we couldn't understand what was behind the first bit of news we heard. When Sultan Aziz's eunuchs and footmen were awakened by the sound of marching troops and dashed to the windows to see our master led away by columns of soldiers, they smiled and said, "It's for Prince Murad. They always said he was in league with the infidels! So it was true! No doubt he was involved with some treason against our master, so the soldiers have taken him away." This alarmed us dreadfully, but the Senior Doorkeeper, who had quietly opened the door for Süleyman Pasha and the soldiers who entered our quarters, reassured us. "Don't believe that talk. Within the hour you'll hear the cannons announcing a new reign. Necib Bey, the captain who came with Süleyman Pasha, is a friend of mine. He came by during the day and told me what was going to happen. That's why I opened the door so quietly for them, because I knew what was going on. Do you think I'd have opened the door if they were up to no good?"

While we were listening to the eunuch's story we heard the sound of running on the floor below. Raşid Ağa came bounding up the stairs. "Beg pardon, Süleyman Pasha is coming. He's bringing good news," he shouted as he ran off to the Lady Mother's apartments. And indeed Süleyman Pasha came in behind Raşid Ağa, grasping his sword in the middle of the blade. He was soaking wet from the rain and his fez had slipped down to his ears. The Lady Mother rushed out into the great hall when she heard Raşid Ağa, not even bothering to cover her head. There she met Süleyman Pasha, who said to her in a loud voice, "Ma'am, an aide-de-camp has just come from the city. His Highness has landed safely from the boat and has proceeded by carriage to the War Ministry. There is no more cause for the slightest concern. Please be so kind as to pass this news on to His Highness Prince Salâheddin."

The Lady Mother became quite excited. "Girls," she called out, "go fetch the Prince! Let him hear the Pasha's news from his own mouth! Quickly!" As it turned out, there was no need to search for Prince Salâheddin, as he was standing behind one of the nearby doors listening, and came out when he heard his grandmother shouting. He was frightened and approached Süleyman Pasha warily. The Pasha was about to say something to him when the boom of a cannon rattled the windows of the palace. Caught unawares, the girls and the kalfas screamed and scattered hither and yon. But Süleyman Pasha raised his hands and said, "Do not be afraid, everyone, do not be afraid," which stopped the commotion. Then he performed a floor *temenna* before the Lady Mother. "Ma'am, this cannon is the first salute to announce the new reign. Beginning with this moment, your son sits upon the throne. My congratulations to you! And now our real duty is about to begin. With your permission, I will leave to resume command of the troops."

Sultan Abdülaziz, wearing the distinctive low-cut fez he favored, around 1870
when he was forty years of age. Photographer unknown.

Down the stairs and out he hurried with his sword still in his left hand, accompanied by the prayers of the Lady Mother who had now become the Princess Mother.

With that our apartments turned as joyful as a bridal chamber. Everyone was thrilled, excited, delighted. The roars of the cannon continued to rattle the panes and the girls crowded around the seaward windows. Dawn had begun to break. The Bosphorus opposite the monarch's apartments had filled with oared boats and steam launches packed with sailors carrying rifles. Now and again flames burst from the guns of the patrol vessel just off the palace, sending black smoke up through her masts festooned with flags.

From the monarch's apartments we could hear women wailing in anguish, along with the appalling sound of breaking glass and chandeliers. The elderly kalfas bowed their heads in acceptance of what fate had decreed, signaling to one another with their eyebrows and eyes as if to say, "Ah, this world, for some it's heaven, for others it's hell. Yesterday they were happy and blessed with good fortune, today the world is their prison. Whatever they're doing now they have a perfect right to do. This should serve as a warning never to think one can achieve mastery over this fickle world."

Two royal barges, one behind the other, pulled away from the quay at the imperial apartments. Oared boats filled with soldiers swiftly took up position around them. Sultan Aziz and his sons the princes Yusuf İzzeddin and Mahmud Celâleddin sat in the first barge. Ten minutes ago he was the Padishah, now he was nothing. His magnificent physique had shrunk in those ten minutes; now it seemed almost the body of a child. The ex-Sultan was bending forward, as if he did not want to see the world anymore. It was the same with the Princess Mother and the other ladies in the second barge. One can guess the chaotic circumstances under which they had left, since they obviously hadn't had time to veil themselves properly but had only wrapped shawls around their heads. This painful scene, which served as a warning to us all, lasted not more than a few minutes.

As the caiques followed the patrol vessel down towards Palace Point, the mood in our apartments underwent a sudden transformation. The place erupted into a flurry of activity, with kalfas scurrying hither and yon, calling the new girls in their charge, then hurrying back to their rooms and shouting, "What are you standing around for, girls? You'd better pull yourselves together—at any moment we'll get the order to move our things." We threw ourselves so much into packing that we missed the procession that brought our master back to Dolmabahçe Palace following the proclamation of his accession at the Ministry of War.

While we were caught up in all this busyness an urgent message arrived from the imperial apartments. Our master had asked for a few girls to help with undergarment and clothing service. The kalfas Dilberengiz and Aynıfer prepared the bundles of clothing and undergarments, but since the senior kalfas couldn't really deal with the matter given everything that needed doing, they sent five of the younger girls, including me.

Just as we were about to go out the door we encountered Princess Fatma, the sister of our master and eldest of Sultan Abdülmecid's daughters. Of all his siblings, she loved our master the best. Princess Fatma had just stepped ashore from a caique and was hurrying—almost running—alongside the eunuchs who were escorting her by the arm. She was saying, "I thank God that we have lived to see this day." We didn't even have time to kiss the hem of her skirt.[11] The eunuchs with us were hurrying us along by saying, "Come girls, be quick," so we began to run over to the monarch's apartments.

Troops still occupied the imperial apartments. We passed rows of soldiers who had bayonets at the ready. The ground floor hall was jammed with people, and the eunuchs escorting us were constantly calling out, "Make way, make way," so they could get us through the crowd. We went upstairs and into a room adjoining the grand salon. The door along the right-hand wall was open. Our master was standing there with his brother Prince Hamid and his brother-in-law Nuri Pasha, the husband of Princess Fatma. Even though I was still just a youngster, the first thing I noticed was the remarkable change in our Prince's appearance. Until yesterday his gloomy face never smiled, and just the night before he was trembling with fear when Süleyman Pasha came to take him away, but now he seemed in fact as merry as a happy child, laughing as he said in a loud voice, "Oh well, there you have it. . . . such is the will of fate!" He came over when he spotted us and said the same thing to us. With the same beaming smile he promised us all new clothes, shoes, earrings, and rings. Then he seemed to come back to himself as he asked, "Oh, but how is Mother?"

At that age I was still a child and couldn't judge the situation properly, but now when I think about those moments I am sure our master's mental problems began that day. Other people who saw him acting like this might think his behavior quite normal, because they had not seen him live through the long and spiritually torturesome years in fear of his uncle, when for days on end not even the trace of a smile appeared on his lips. But we were with him every day. Even though we were ignorant and untrained young girls, we

---

11 The usual practice when greeting a woman of royal rank.

could sense the torments that gnawed at him from inside. When the torment suddenly ceased, and that fearful and melancholy life abruptly changed, of course he was affected adversely, of course his mind and nerves suffered a great shock.

However, the shock had not yet registered completely on his brain. At length, before starting to change his clothing, he went back and opened the connecting door, calling out, "My good brother-in-law Pasha! I am appointing you the marshal of my household. But I beg of you, please go and stop that racket, it's upsetting me terribly," while pointing his finger toward the harem of the imperial apartments.

And indeed, the harem was like a house visited by death. We could still hear things being smashed and shattered, not to mention deep, heart-rending sobs. But our master didn't keep us there long because the accession ceremony was about to begin, so as soon as he changed his clothes and undergarments he sent us back to our quarters.

The whole place was in a state of utter upheaval. Boxes, saddlebags, and chests being packed had been dragged out of the rooms and lined up in the halls. Footmen were to come and haul them over to the sovereign's apartments.

The young palace girls were ecstatic with joy. They had dressed themselves up, painted their lips and cheeks bright scarlet red, applied kohl around their eyes, adorned their heads with the *hotoz*, and put on their earrings, rings, brooches, and necklaces so that every one of them looked like a bride on her wedding day. A thousand chores needed doing, but these young girls, preparing themselves to greet their master as the Padishah, were thinking only of making themselves look as pretty as possible for him. This made the older kalfas quite cross: "Well now, don't they stink," they snapped. "Yesterday you could barely wash your faces, today you're all covered with mold and painted up like Easter eggs."

The Lady Mother's mood had quickly changed as well. Until an hour or two ago Sultan Abdülmecid's former beloved was living out a lackluster existence in a remote corner of these gloomy rooms, but as soon as she acquired the title of Princess Mother she took on an amazing kind of grandeur. Hands on hips, she promenaded about the hall imperiously and pridefully, giving orders right and left: "Let me think, where shall my son sleep tonight. . . . you, go tell those people to clear everything out of those rooms and clean them up. See that the Imperial Kalfas hurry over there and prepare my son's private rooms. Be quick!"

Little by little the noise increased. The sound of a military band was coming from the imperial apartments. We could hear shouts of "Long live the Sultan" from schoolboys, soldiers, and who knows whom else out on the street.

Princess Fatma gathered up her long skirts and stayed right on the heels of the new Princess Mother, for all the world acting in the role of a harem housekeeper or one of the head kalfas. Other princesses also began to call, alone or in pairs, including Princess Cemile. This very grand Princess was the wife of Mahmud Celâleddin Pasha, the imperial son-in-law known in court circles as *Şişko Damad* [Tubby]. On the great religious holidays she would appear last of all among the princes and princesses come to pay homage to our master, but today she came right after Princess Fatma.

The daughters of Sultan Mecid had gathered around the new Princess Mother. Yesterday they wouldn't even speak her name; today they were showering Şevkefza Kadın with praise and deference. Joyfully they called out, "Praise God, fate has restored the throne to the *Mecidîs*."[12]

After some time Prince Hamid also came and congratulated the new Princess Mother. Now, Şevkefza Kadın cared not at all for Prince Hamid and did not want him coming to the palace often. Nor was her coldness toward him without reason. Since he got along well with everybody, Prince Hamid always used to pay a call three times a week on Sultan Aziz's mother, the Princess Mother Pertevniyal. To be sure, our mistress did not at all take kindly to Prince Hamid's being on such close terms with the Princess Mother Pertevniyal. She would say, "Here's another sin of this Prince. No doubt he's telling tales to the Princess Mother all about what happens in our court." This is why she wasn't so indulgent toward Prince Hamid, and why she received him so frostily on this day as well. Nonetheless she showed him a bit of politeness by saying, "I congratulate you too, my boy; now you've become the Heir Apparent."

Anyway, the new Princess Mother was in no position to bother herself with petty emotions or affairs on this day. She was entirely preoccupied with moving into the imperial apartments as soon as possible. The harem eunuchs were continually going over to the imperial apartments and each time they came back they'd announce, "It's impossible to explain anything to anyone over there. They just shout nasty things at us. There's nothing they haven't said."

This news exasperated the new Princess Mother, who bellowed, "What is the meaning of this? Everyone must accept his fate! Go and tell my son,

12 Sultan Aziz himself coined this term when he named the sons and daughters of his brother, Sultan Mecid, the *Mecidîler* ["those of the Mecid line"]. They in turn called the sons and daughters of Sultan Aziz the *Azizîler* ["Azizîs"]. [Ş]

they should be removed by force! What are all these soldiers with their bayonets waiting for? I cannot go against palace tradition! My son will sleep there tonight!"

As fate had it, Prince Hamid had come in in the middle of all this uproar. Once they had congratulated each other, the new Princess Mother tried to put Prince Hamid in charge of immediately clearing out the imperial apartments. I shan't forget it; Prince Hamid threw up his hands and said, "Please, do not charge me with this task. I cannot insult my uncle's household in that way." This answer deeply offended our mistress and she retorted in barely suppressed indignation, "Very well, Prince Hamid, we know. You cannot allow anything to be done against your uncle. But mark my words, those days are over."

This brief exchange I have related to you is extremely important. I could even say that it was practically the declaration of war between the new Princess Mother and Prince Hamid. Henceforth a bitterness and rancor insinuated itself between these two important personages in the palace. Indeed, I have no doubt that the secret decision of a few days later to put all the adult princes to death was none other than the result of this brief run-in. But let us continue with this account so that we don't get events out of order.[13]

Not five or ten minutes after this little wrangle between the Princess Mother and Prince Hamid, Princess Cemile's husband, Mahmud Pasha, came in. He greeted the new Princess Mother with a great deal of respect and esteem. Since she was trying to line up someone to calm her concerns and carry out what she wished done, she said, "I know, Pasha. You certainly are most highly capable. Now what if you applied yourself. See to it that the imperial apartments are vacated right away. You can see with your own eyes that we are packed and ready to go. It's almost time for the afternoon prayer, but where will my son sleep this evening? I'd like you to take care of it."

Mahmud Pasha set off to accomplish the task.[14] He hadn't been gone

13 The concubine is referring to the unfounded rumor circulating at the time that the subsequent invitation to all of Sultan Murad's brothers to dine with him at the Nisbetiye Villa was a secret plot to murder them all. She returns to this episode in the following pages.

14 This is the imperial son-in-law Mahmud Celâleddin Pasha, who was put to death with Midhat Pasha in the fortress at Taif [Arabia]—not to be confused with Mahmud Pasha, the father of Prince Sabaheddin. [Ş]

Two Mahmud Celâleddin Pashas figured as members of the imperial family in this era, each having married a daughter of Sultan Abdülmecid. The pasha mentioned here was born circa 1836 and murdered in 1884 in Arabia, where he was exiled for his alleged role in overthrowing Sultan Abdülaziz. The other pasha, some seventeen years his junior (b. 1853), eventually fled to Europe with his two sons due to his opposition to the autocratic rule of Sultan Abdülhamid.

thirty minutes when a message came back that His Majesty's sleeping chambers were vacated and that kalfas should hurry over to clean them. Headed by Aynifer, Dilberengiz, İspantiyar, and Elâdil, who all henceforth bore the title Imperial Kalfas, a caravan of us harem kalfas including Emsalinur, Siranto, Teranedil, and others set off for the imperial apartments. There we found a small delegation of elderly gentlemen as well as the imperial sons-in-law Nuri and Mahmud Pashas. They were sealing the doors of some of the rooms, admonishing us, "There's a treasure in here. See to it these seals are not broken."

Sultan Aziz's mother and his ladies had left their apartments in such a hurry that morning that they hadn't been able to take anything with them; every item was just as they left it. We went through the lot and then rearranged things the way we thought our master would like them. In the midst of this cleaning, one thing in particular caught our attention: the lower drawers of every cabinet contained handfuls of talismans written on little notes, sealed sheets of paper, and strips of yellow and green satin.

The Princess Mother's apartments had the greatest number of these magic charms. One talisman in particular, located beneath some bundles right in the cabinet in the Princess Mother's bedroom chamber, astonished us all. This talisman was a very crude statuette made from a yellow wax candle about two palm-widths high. The name "Murad" was written in red across the chest, back, head, kneecaps, and arms of this statuette, while dozens of round-headed pins had been stuck into it from the top of its head to the soles of its feet.

Just as we thought, for we palace girls had always whispered amongst ourselves that the Princess Mother used witchcraft to control her son.

While we're on this subject, palace lore also told of the sheikh of a dervish lodge in the neighborhood of the Edirne Gate. Somehow, a clever palace girl by the name of Nakşifend went through a relative of hers in the city to introduce him to the Princess Mother. This sheikh possessed extremely sharp breath[15]—he could melt a stone just by reciting something. And his powers of divination and ability to work miracles were amply evident. For example, during Sultan Aziz's return from his journey to Egypt, the steamer transporting the Padishah ran into a great storm.[16] Even though the vessel had

---

15 I.e., his spells and incantations were extremely effective.

16 Sultan Abdülaziz departed Istanbul 3 April 1863 to tour the Ottoman province of Egypt—the first reigning Ottoman monarch to set foot in the province since Selim I conquered it in 1516—returning to Istanbul 1 May 1863. Contemporary descriptions of the return voy-

passed through the Dardanelles it could not make enough headway to reach Istanbul. The Princess Mother flew into a panic, grabbed Süreyya Hanım, jumped into an unmarked carriage, and set off for the Edirne Gate. Once in the sheikh's presence, she implored him, "O Sheikh, has something happened to my son? Why isn't he back yet? You can help, you must bring my son back to me at once."

The sheikh fell into a trance for some time, then raised his head and said, "Your Highness, our master was indeed in danger, but I have saved him. Now return to the imperial palace, and be at peace." With that he sent her back to the palace to be greeted with the good tidings, "Praise God, our master will arrive in two hours!"

As a result of this episode the Princess Mother believed more than ever in the powers of this sheikh. In fact she clung to him completely. She would make use of him in every furtive business of hers. She had Nakşifend take her son's undergarments to this sheikh, and after the sheikh had recited an incantation over the clothing she would see that Sultan Aziz put them on. If she had a wish that her son had not granted, she would dispatch some sugar to the sheikh, have him recite an incantation over it, then mix it into coffee she had brewed, and have her son drink it.

Stranger things than this happened. Now and again Sultan Aziz would fall into a rage and begin to shout and order people about, completely disrupting life in the harem. On these occasions the Princess Mother would hurriedly dispatch a sheep's tongue to the sheikh and have him recite an incantation over it, then find some excuse to feed it to her son. With that the infuriated Sultan would become as gentle and soft as the sheep's tongue itself.

I don't know how much truth there is in all these rumors. But one thing I know for certain because I saw it with my own eyes, and that is that both Sultan Aziz's mother and his harem dealt in magic and written charms. A couple of days after we moved into the imperial apartments, we had to change the mats. When we lifted them up we found all kinds of charms under them, all of which we threw into the Bosphorus.[17]

---

age do not mention a storm, but his return to Istanbul was delayed as Abdülaziz stopped at Izmir for some days of fetes and inspections there. This delay could account for his mother's anxiety, if indeed the account here is not simply anti-Aziz gossip current in the retinue of Prince Murad.

17 When Prince Hamid's entourage moved into the Heir Apparent's apartments [i.e., the rooms vacated by Prince Murad's entourage], they too found baskets full of charms and magic spells—a timeless tradition in the Ottoman palaces. [Ş]

THE FIRST DAYS OF THE NEW REIGN

The ceremonies that took place on accession day lasted until evening, so that our master could only get back to the harem quite late.

We had lined up to greet him in the hallway that ran from the doorway of the public wing of the palace to the monarch's apartments. But just as he entered, the eunuch Emin Ağa hurried over and warned us sternly, "Kalfas, as our master passes, all of you are to remain where you are. Do not by any means approach His Majesty in order to kiss his feet. And don't make too much movement when you greet him."

We were at a loss to understand these words, but of course we did as ordered. Our master came into the harem with an exhausted look on his face. He took a few steps past the doorway, then stopped abruptly and studied us all. Somehow he seemed almost fearful. His mother, the new Princess Mother, hurried to him and took his arm. "May your reign be blessed, my son," she said.

He seemed to take a step backwards. Nodding toward us, the first words he uttered were, "Are these our girls? Be sure none of Uncle's is among them."

The Princess Mother took one arm while Dilberengiz Kalfa took another. His *ikbals* Elâru, Reftarıdil, Şayan, and Meyliservet—who now each bore the title *Kadın* [Consort]—approached and kissed the hem of his coat. The Princess Mother was whispering something into our master's ear while gesturing toward us with her eyebrows and her eyes. Our master took a few more steps forward, then once again stopped abruptly and turned his head around. To the harem eunuchs following him along with the ladies he mumbled, "Tell Hüseyin Avni Pasha to stay here tonight."

We had thought that a magnificent ceremony of celebration would take place in the great hall. In anticipation of this we had lighted all the candles in the chandeliers and candlesticks. As it turned out, the Princess Mother led our master directly to his rooms. She stayed with him for half an hour, then returned to her own rooms and the doors were shut.

The fact that the Princess Mother shut herself in her rooms with the consorts Reftârıdil and Şayan made us all uneasy. We knew that something was wrong. So this was how this night would pass at the palace. Just as in the city, everyone was supposed to celebrate, games were supposed to take place, and at last we were supposed to bask in the long-awaited pleasure of ascending the throne. Here we were standing about, waiting for these things to occur, but instead a kind of pall descended over the palace.

At first, this state of affairs was explained away by claiming that the previous sovereign's entourage had not yet vacated the palace. To be sure, quite a few of Sultan Aziz's ferocious concubines and kalfas had not yet left. They hurled all kinds of foul oaths at the people sent over to get them out. At one point, some of them even came over to the top of the stairway and shouted insults at the new Princess Mother. I can't forget one of these women, who was so bold as to bellow out in a voice choked in sobs, "Yes, they deposed our red-blooded master, and then they brought that little milksop of a Prince to the throne! Just let the people see what he's worth! Now that stinking hag, that trash, that witch of a mother of his, going around calling herself 'the Princess Mother' and all, just let her try to rule. . . . This fickle world will dump them too!" Clearly, these furious palace women, having lost the sultanate, might do anything, so of course there could be no celebrations and festivities as long as they were still in the palace. Nor could our master be shown around the palace under these circumstances.

Various whispered rumors reached our ears while we were standing there talking. According to these rumors, our master was taken to the carriage of Hüseyin Avni Pasha.[18] Hüseyin Avni Pasha pulled out the pistol he kept in his belt and said, "If we get into a situation where you sense your life is in danger, kill me first." This really set our master off, what with the Minister of War suddenly pulling out a gun in his presence, then talking about killing. They made it to the shore of the Bosphorus in all this excitement. Our master was afraid to get into the caique, but with difficulty they got him in. He shouted, "Now I understand! My uncle is sending me into exile!" He tried to throw himself overboard, but fortunately at that moment they saw a steam launch in the darkness. They hailed the launch and got our Prince aboard it and down to Sirkeci, then up to the War Ministry Gate. All the roads and gates were crowded with soldiers toting bayoneted weapons, which only scared our master more. "It is the custom to bring a Prince to Topkapı Palace when he ascends the throne," he said anxiously. "Why have you brought me here?"

He was given assurances that the War Ministry was safer, so the homage ceremony would take place there. But by a most remarkable coincidence, or rather omen, these men who had carefully plotted and planned every step in deposing Sultan Aziz and in raising our master to the throne had quite forgotten to have the throne itself brought over from the imperial treasury. This detail only occurred to them now. But since there was no time to send over to

---

18 When Prince Murad was first escorted from the palace to be proclaimed Sultan, the night of the coup.

Topkapı Palace to have the throne brought round, they made do with seating our master in a gilded armchair. With that the homage ceremony began.

But what was truly astonishing was that the same thing happened again for the ceremony at Dolmabahçe Palace. First the throne could not be brought over to the palace what with all the confusion, then given the raging wind and rain it was thought too difficult to transport it, so here too once again the ceremony took place with just a large armchair instead of the great throne. And so, fate denied our master the privilege of sitting for even one moment upon the throne of the Ottomans.

Rapidly unfolding as they did within the space of an hour or two, all these alarming events wreaked havoc on our master's nerves. Henceforth he began to act most unnaturally.

The eunuchs said that when the homage ceremony got under way in the palace, our master's face went completely white. He began to tremble palpably and was utterly unable to retain his composure. His face plainly registered fear, but still his mouth was frozen in a smile.

What could be the verdict on our master, who returned to the harem after passing a day full of fright, anxiety, and agitation? At that time we were not in a position to know and understand. We simply had to content ourselves with what we heard. I myself could not make head or tails of why some concubines and hazinedars were shut up with the new Princess Mother in her rooms.

That night, as we all went to our rooms, got into bed, and pulled the blankets over our heads, I had no way of knowing what my harem sisters were thinking. But as a relatively clever and sensitive young girl I knew that what had happened was significant. It seemed to me there was something strange—or to put it more clearly, almost something malevolent—about this new life we had just begun in the court of the ruling monarch.

I remembered a curious tale that I heard from one of the elderly kalfas when I first came into the palace. Just before our master was born, there was a rumor circulating among some fortune-tellers and astrologers and others who read the stars, that a Prince was about to be born who would have a mole on his face. This Prince would be distinguished for his intelligence and acumen, and would make an exceptional sovereign who far outshone any Prince the Ottoman House had ever produced or ever would. Just when these rumors were at their height, our master was born. And how? With a rather prominent mole on the right side of his face, toward the bottom of his jaw.

Word spread that this was the Prince predicted by the astrologers. All kinds of praise and approval were lavished upon the infant, so much so that his father, Sultan Mecid, began to tire of it and even grow jealous of his son. Our Prince sensed his jealousy. He even heard that his father had decided to have the mole removed from his face, so he himself acted quickly and of his own accord underwent an operation to have the mole removed. It was after the mole was removed that our Prince began to experience ill-fortune.

At that time I was not capable of judging how much faith to put in this interpretation of events. I only knew that nothing good could come of the events that occurred on this very first day, when fate had finally brought our master to the throne after the long years he had suffered in fear of his uncle.

THE SCRAMBLE FOR HAPPINESS AND GOOD FORTUNE

We had no idea what was happening outside the palace, nor who was to be appointed to what high-ranking positions so newly opened up, but the harem was abuzz with the important business of reinventing itself as the Imperial Harem of the monarch.

First of all, the four Imperial Consorts of the monarch were appointed in accordance with procedure. Elâru became the new Senior Consort. Now, everyone thought this most unusual, because Elâru had not given birth to any children whatsoever, and in imperial practice and convention it was not the custom for a childless concubine to hold the rank of Imperial Consort. So our master demonstrated unusual behavior in this matter as well. He simply insisted that this old love of his, with whom he had grown up since they were both young, and who had entered the ranks of his concubines when he was still a prince, should become his Senior Consort.

Nonetheless, it was certainly true that Elâru possessed the talents and skills necessary to occupy the post of Senior Consort. First of all, she was extremely beautiful. Beneath her incomparably graceful black eyebrows, her flashing, kohl-tinged black eyes lent an irresistible enchantment to her clear white face, which warmed with a touch of gentle pink whenever she spoke. She was highly intelligent and perceptive. Anyone who met her or spoke with her could not help but fall under her bewitching spell. And she had long reconciled herself to her lot; throughout our imprisonment in Çırağan Palace, she remained completely loyal to her master. After the proclamation of the Constitution[19] she purchased a home in Şişli and retreated there to live a life in seclusion. She died one year ago.

Reftarıdil, the mother of Prince Salâheddin, obtained the post of Second

19 In 1908.

Consort. She too had been a concubine of our master's when he was a prince. She was a lovely lady with pink skin, large blue eyes, a straight nose, and a round face.

The Third Consort, Şayan, was one of those beauties one encounters but rarely. Her exquisite blue eyes, adorning her rose-pink face, made her a marvel in the art of feminine loveliness. After our master died she remained in Çırağan Palace even though everyone else had left.

Meyliservet, who received the post of Fourth Consort even though she had not been a purchased slave girl, came to the palace through a most unusual coincidence, and of her own volition.

The story of Meyliservet's life begins with her elder sister, the wife of the ambassador to Rome. The ambassador and his wife brought her sister, Meyliservet, to Italy, provided her with an excellent education, and saw to it that she learned several languages. After remaining in Italy for more than eight years, the two sisters returned to Istanbul where they lived a lonely life. Meyliservet's sister came to know our master's sister, Princess Refia, who would pay a call now and then. During one of these visits the sister complained that she couldn't live in a foreign country and for that reason she hadn't seen her husband for years.

Princess Refia was touched by her sadness and told her not to worry, she would speak to her uncle, Sultan Aziz, and see that her husband was brought back home. True to her word, she had the ambassador appointed to an important post in Istanbul. As soon as the ambassador returned to Istanbul, he presented himself at court to extend his thanks while his wife presented herself at the palace of Princess Refia on the same mission, taking Meyliservet along.

While there Meyliservet liked what she saw of palace life so much that she swore she would not leave, even if they put her to death for refusing to go. This astonished the senior kalfas, who tried to convince her to go home by telling her, "But my dear girl, how can this be? You're a city girl, and it's not the custom for city folk to remain in the palace except on a visit." But they failed to persuade her and finally had no recourse but to turn the matter over to the Princess.

Princess Refia considered the issue and decided, "Oh well, what of it. If someone wants to join us, we'll gladly take her in. It really doesn't matter if she's a city girl, let her stay. Give her a room." This is how she took Meyliservet into the palace.

Some months went by, the holidays came around, and our master, who at the time was still the Heir, called at his sister's villa in order to pay his respects. Now, at the holidays, when a prince came round to pay his respects to the princesses, he was not served by just any girl. Considerable thought was put into the matter in advance, and one girl was selected to serve him. If it became clear that the visiting prince took a fancy to the girl, she was instantly presented to him as a lady for his harem. She would be sent over to his palace after he left.

Conforming to this custom, Princess Refia, who knew that her brother liked blondes, selected a tall, yellow-haired girl and for a period of time had her provided with special training. When she saw her one day, the Princess said, "I am going to give you to my brother as a lady for his entourage. Mind you don't disgrace me." Of course the girl was delighted with this news and could hardly wait for the holidays.

At length the holidays arrived and, as I mentioned, Prince Murad came to the villa. The girl waited upon the Heir, during which her manners were absolutely faultless. But isn't life strange? While this was going on, Meyliservet caught Prince Murad's eye. When after dinner the orchestra struck up European music and dancing began, the Heir summoned Meyliservet and danced with her. During this dance he displayed an obvious interest in her. When Princess Refia noticed what was happening, she was reluctant to tell her brother that she had groomed the blonde girl for him, so she pulled her other brother Prince Kemaleddin aside and asked him to do so. Prince Kemaleddin approached Prince Murad on some pretext and relayed to him what their sister had said, but he received this reply from Prince Murad: "I don't care for that blonde girl. I'd like our sister to give me the girl I danced with." Of course Princess Refia could not refuse her brother's wish, and so she sent Meyliservet forthwith to the apartments of the Heir. After some time Meyliservet became pregnant and gave birth to Princess Fehime.

This is how Meyliservet, who joined the ranks of the Heir's concubines and even gave birth to a child, came to be betrothed, as she had not been a purchased slave girl. In this way this city girl entered the ranks of bona fide consorts of our Prince Murad. Such is the brief tale of Meyliservet, who now received the title of Fourth Consort.[20]

Once the Imperial Consorts had been appointed, it was the turn of the hazinedars and Imperial Kalfas. The rank of High Hazinedar was given to Aynifer, who had practically raised our master herself. This was the high-

20 From the story recounted here, it appears likely that Meyliservet and her sister were ethnic Circassians who had been groomed for marriage into the Ottoman elite. The unusual twist to her story is that she entered palace service of her own accord as a young adult, rather than as a child slave purchased or presented as a gift.

est rank in the palace below the Princess Mother and the Imperial Consorts, and the female equivalent of the Senior Chamberlain. The old and valued harem retainer Ispantiyar Kalfa received the post of Second Hazinedar, while the kalfas Renknaz, Elâdil, and Dilberengiz received the posts of Third, Fourth, and Fifth Hazinedar respectively. Apart from these, thirteen girls selected from among the well-trained young kalfas each received the title of hazinedar.

While these high ranks were being apportioned, a few girls were presented to our master as gifts commemorating his accession. Two of them were straightaway appointed Duty Kalfas on account of their refined manners and their high level of training.[21] Of these two young girls, the medium-tall, blonde, and incomparably beautiful kalfa by the name of Filistan or Filizten was the gift of one of the former palace ladies who had served as hazinedar to our master when he was Heir to the Throne and who later became the wife of a gentleman named Tayyar Pasha. The other girl was the tall and delicate Dilber Kalfa, who was assigned to assist our master's Coffee Server because she was a very clean girl.

The palace had come to resemble a house where a joyous wedding feast was taking place, everyone smiling with whatever amount of bliss and delight had come her way, according to her rank. No one thought at all that the darkest of nights would follow these happy days, despite the fact that all of us now so elated with our good fortune, from the Princess Mother on down to the newest girl, were witnessing plenty of events from which we should have taken warning.

Sultan Aziz's stubborn ladies and kalfas had not wanted to leave the palace at all, so they were grabbed by the arms and booted out. In the process they were searched from head to toe and everything of value was taken from them, even down to the silver Mecca rings on their fingers.[22] The mighty and proud Sultan Aziz himself, we heard, was sitting in Topkapı Palace, hungry, sobbing when the guards brought him coffee, and that in an old cracked cup. Then we heard that while his seriously ill Fourth Consort was carried on a stretcher to the caique that was to take her away to the Fer'iye Palaces, someone even snatched the shawl that had been wrapped around her. Yesterday

21 I.e., they did not have to undergo the lengthy instruction period required of novice girls who entered harem service without any prior training.
22 Keepsakes of Mecca, worn as a memento of the city even by those who had never performed the annual pilgrimage to it, such as these ladies. Only one Imperial Consort is known to have completed the pilgrimage, the lady Nevfidan, consort of Abdülaziz's father, Sultan Mahmud II, in 1842; perhaps she brought the souvenir rings back to the palace.

they were sauntering about these rooms and halls draped in gold and diamonds and brilliants; today they had nothing but the clothes on their backs and were thinking only of where they would lay their heads and from where their next morsel of food might come.

The sealed apartments of the Princess Mother Pertevniyal were opened and from them eight chests of gold and four chests of debentures were removed. Eight porters were needed to lift each one of the chests with gold. If I remember correctly, it was said these eight chests contained 5,120 *okkas* of gold.[23] This was the personal fortune of the Princess Mother, which according to the laws of the imperial house now devolved to the new Sultan. Since it was our master's mother who exercised complete authority over him, this fabulous fortune now fell entirely into the hands of the new Princess Mother.

The harem became a blinding swirl of gold and diamonds. The new Imperial Consorts and the new hazinedars, the concubines and the kalfas decked themselves out in the exquisite jewelry lavishly bestowed upon them, so that each of them looked for all the world like a bride on her wedding day.

The strange behavior that had overpowered our master on the day of his accession disappeared the next day. Once again he was himself and for two days everything went well. Anyway, everyone was so distracted with all the ceremonies going on that we took no notice of one another.

But on the third day, once again our master seemed grave and pensive. Before going over to the Palace Secretariat that morning he went to the Princess Mother's apartments, where he was heard complaining about Hüseyin Avni Pasha and his friends, "Here I've escaped from Uncle's iron rule, only to fall into their hands." What was this all about? Of course, there was no one we could ask, but one thing we knew for certain, something about Hüseyin Avni Pasha had unnerved our master. Whenever he was ready to make his way to the Secretariat, first he would have someone find out whether the Minister of War had come to the palace. If the answer was yes, the minister was there, he went pale and knit his eyebrows and did not want to leave the harem.

HOW DID THE ILLNESS BEGIN?

The next day we awoke at the usual hour. After morning prayers we had set about our first chores for the day when we heard the curious news that the

---

23 A total weight of 14,336 pounds.

sound of women wailing could be heard coming from the direction of the Fer'iye Palaces. Some of us attributed the racket to the continued rebelliousness of the self-indulgent and delirious women in Sultan Aziz's entourage, but others said, "Well, remember the Fourth Consort was sick? Something must have happened to the poor thing." No one told our master about this so that he wouldn't get upset.

Some time later our master got dressed and went over to his rooms in the *Mabeyin*, where he was going to take breakfast as usual. Not fifteen or twenty minutes later a message came that our master was feeling ill. The Princess Mother sent a man to the door of the *Mabeyin* in order to learn how bad this sudden indisposition was. In the meanwhile the High Hazinedar and the Imperial Kalfas gathered at the door, all anxious and wondering. For some time there was no answer from the *Mabeyin*, but then the equerries Anber Ağa and Raşid Ağa came out and announced, "There's nothing to be concerned about. He felt a little faint at breakfast. Dr. Capoleone is giving him some medicine and he's going to rest a bit. Go and let the Princess Mother know, but do not cause any alarm."

Not only did these words fail to quiet the concerns of the Princess Mother, they sent her into a frenzy. "Girls!" she shouted, "bring me a shawl, quickly! I must see my son!" With that she went up to the *Mabeyin* door, just as word came that they were bringing our master into the harem. Behind the door we could hear the eunuchs calling out, "Make way, make way."

They had removed our master's jacket and laid him onto a long sofa that eunuchs and footmen had lifted on all sides and were slowly carrying inside. Dr. Capoleone was leading them in. The Princess Mother cried out, "Oh dear God, what has happened to my son?" and tried to throw herself onto our master, but Dr. Capoleone prevented her. "Your Highness," he said, "if you have any love and pity for your son at all, you must remain calm. The slightest noise could cause the direst consequences." With that the room became very quiet.

Our master's face was drained of all color. His half-opened eyes stared at the ceiling and indeed he seemed in a state of semi-consciousness. In this state he was brought to the door of his bedchamber, when suddenly he opened his eyes. He looked desperate with fright at something and ready to flee, but Dr. Capoleone grabbed hold of him so that he couldn't throw himself from the sofa. They got him into his room and onto his bed and closed the doors at once. Of course this left all of us shaken, and alarmed.

They took the Princess Mother by the arms and led her back to her rooms. She was swaying her head and crying out, "What has happened to my son?

Have they done something bad to my boy?" All the eunuchs were summoned to her rooms and made to swear that they would tell the truth. Together, with one voice, those present at the moment when our master took ill related what had happened, as follows.

That morning, the former sovereign, Sultan Aziz, had died under mysterious conditions in which blood was shed. When he received the news, the Senior Chamberlain, Edhem Bey, ordered that our master should not be informed just yet, as the news would be too upsetting for him. However, after our master had gone from the harem into the *Mabeyin* and was eating his breakfast, the Head Butler Ali Ağa came into the dining room with a smile on his face. Thinking that it would please his master he blurted out, "Sire, what good news. And may you live long despite the death of your uncle."[24] Our master was puzzled by these unexpected words and muttered, "Have you lost your senses, Ali? Just last night my uncle was in perfect health."

But Ali insisted that what he had said was true. "I went over there and saw him with my own eyes," he said. "He's lying on a worn old mat, in the basement of the police station, all covered in blood."

At this our master jumped from his chair and shouted, "My God, now they'll think I did it." He threw his napkin onto the table and rushed toward the door, but there he fell to the floor in a faint.

The five days and nights of celebration and merriment ended at that moment as a mournful gloom and hush descended precipitously over every room in the harem. Colorful *hotozes* on our heads gave way to simple crepe, while our long, trailing skirts we exchanged for plain and loose robes.

Those who had bound up their lives and destinies with Sultan Murad's person now sensed that their lives had taken a turn after only five days of joy and merrymaking. This new period had begun with this debacle, and who knew how long it would last? No one could possibly guess. The girls who entered our master's room could only say that while just this morning our young master was striding down the halls to the *Mabeyin*, now he was lying in his bed, beside himself with fear and anxiety, staring at the ceiling, murmuring things in a hoarse voice that sounded barely human.

Dr. Capoleone sent for a golden bowl and drained blood from our master's arm, in the meanwhile sending a message to the Princess Mother telling her not to worry at all, that in half an hour His Majesty would be quite himself. But half an hour went by, in fact several hours went by, and still our master did not come around.

---

24 A standard manner of expressing condolences.

Toward evening Dr. Capoleone ordered fifty leeches brought in. With the help of the kalfas he applied these to our master's buttocks and the soles of his feet. After these fifty hungry leeches had finished sucking his blood with gusto, all that was left of his body on that magnificent bedstead was a heap of flesh and bones. And with that, our master completely lost consciousness.

THE REIGN OF THREE MONTHS AND THREE DAYS

I shan't say much about the events of our master's reign, which lasted three months and three days. The reason is that the government officials took such extreme measures to hide his illness that even we weren't able to see him.

I remember very well the situation in the first days of his illness. Our master was running an extremely high temperature. For hours on end he was out of his mind, but now and again he would suddenly sit up in the greatest panic and cry out that roaring flames of fire were blazing all around him, or that deep and violent seas were crashing about him.

His illness had begun on a Sunday. What with Dr. Capoleone having applied fifty leeches to him, our master had absolutely no strength left. As I mentioned, he began to have nightmarish visions. For this reason, the proposal to send him out in that state the following Friday for the Royal Mosque Procession was clearly a mistake. But the officials who had deposed Sultan Aziz on the grounds that he was insane knowingly decided upon this very mistake. They thought they had to get our master to the Friday prayer service, by force if necessary, so as to quell any potential rumors among the people. But the way we heard it, they could hardly get him up onto the horse from the mounting stoop.

That night our master made an unexpected attempt to throw himself into the Bosphorus, and was prevented from doing so only with great difficulty. After that Dolmabahçe Palace was thought no longer suitable for him and he was moved to Yıldız Palace.[25]

The situation grieved everyone in the harem, but none more so than the Princess Mother and Princess Fatma, our master's sister and the wife of Nuri Pasha. On the one hand, worry for her son tormented the Princess Mother; on the other hand, fear plagued her that his reign could end with disastrous consequences if his condition went on much longer. As for Princess Fatma, she simply could not bear to witness the sufferings of the brother she loved so dearly.

25 Uphill from the shoreside Dolmabahçe Palace, Yıldız Palace offered no access to the sea.

At length our master completely lost the strength to speak, which meant he suffered even more from terrors he could not articulate. Quite often he would go out of his mind for some twenty-four hours, during which periods his body shook violently now and again and he moaned dreadfully.

Led by Dr. Capoleone, the palace doctors Marko Pasha and Mehmed Bey as well as other physicians brought in from the city treated the patient. But the Princess Mother did not stop at this kind of treatment alone. She sought help from the most accomplished spellbinders among the pundits and sheikhs of Istanbul, having them send over written charms by the handful.

The Heir to the Throne, Prince Hamid, also came by often to visit his brother and clearly suffered a good deal of anguish at each visit. "Oh my brother," he would lament, "to think we would see you like this."

Days and even months passed by, with not the tiniest change for the better in our master's condition. The despairing and heartbroken palace staff worried terribly until gradually they came to abandon hope for his recovery. In the end, the bitter truth confronted us in all its nakedness.

IN ÇIRAĞAN PALACE

Our master's reign lasted three months and three days. But in fact both for him and for us his real reign had lasted but five days, from the day he ascended the throne until the day Sultan Aziz died and he himself fell ill. From that point forward he was confined to bed and the palace became a house of mourning. Bit by bit these sorrowful days prepared us to face catastrophe, which is why not a single untoward event occurred when our master was deposed, Prince Hamid was elevated to the throne, and we were moved into Çırağan Palace.

We had no inkling of what was happening on the day our master's reign ended. We learned that he had been deposed from the sound of the booming cannon around midday, announcing the accession of a new monarch. When we first heard the cannon we thought there must be a fire somewhere, but when the cannon kept firing after seven shots, we realized that the horrible truth we were dreading had come to pass.

The Princess Mother wailed, "Dear God, it has happened!" and collapsed. All the Imperial Consorts and the hazinedars gathered in her rooms but no one had the slightest idea what to do. Only the old and experienced kalfas resigned themselves, bowing to the will of fate: "In truth, these palaces are but pigeon lofts. They belong to no one! One group leaves, the next arrives. Come girls, start getting your things together."

Some fifteen minutes later the eunuch Raşid Ağa came running up. "A delegation of pashas is here," he announced. "They wish to see our master." "Our master" indeed. What master? To whose presence should they be admitted? He was still in his bedchamber, completely lost in his own world.

The Princess Mother came rushing out of her rooms to the head of the stairs, exclaiming, "Under no circumstances admit them to my son's presence! He might take fright and something bad could happen. Tell them to come and speak with me."

Later on we learned who they were. Two of the oldest ministers, Rıza and Namık Pashas, and the Chief Justice of Istanbul, Halid Efendi, followed by our master's Senior Secretary Sadullah Bey and the Princess Mother's Court Steward Salih Efendi, slowly trundled up the stairs and approached the Princess Mother. Each in turn kissed the hem of her garment, whereupon Şevkefza Kadın, who in one stroke had just lost her rank as the Princess Mother and was once again simply an Imperial Consort, nervously pulled her shawl to cover her face and in a trembling voice whispered, "Yes, gentlemen."

The judge Halid Efendi began by declaring, "May God be praised. Because all of us are honored to be Muslim, we must find consolation in contentment with what God has ordained, and we must seek to perpetrate meritorious actions." He tried to introduce the subject of our master's deposal gently by saying, "In this transitory world there can be no higher kingdom to rule than that of good health. Hopefully, His Majesty will soon be restored to good health ..." But the Lady could bear no more. She buried her face in her hands and began to sob, "Oh my son, my son, my unlucky Murad, you couldn't have the very thing you wanted most."

Her Ladyship wasn't the only one sobbing. The sound of weeping began to rise from nearly every corner of the great salon. The two pashas and the Chief Justice of Istanbul could not endure this heartbreaking scene and lowered their heads as they said, "May Almighty God grant you patience and endurance," and started down the stairs, repeating the phrase over and over. Sadullah Bey and Salih Efendi seemed turned to stone where they stood respectfully, their hands folded in front of them. With the dethronement of our master, they too had lost their positions.

As Emsalinur, one of the Lady Mother's kalfas, and the High Hazinedar took the Lady's arms in order to help her to her rooms, she turned to Sadullah Bey and Salih Efendi and said, "Well, there is nothing to be done. This is what fate has decreed. May God grant my son long life." Then she added, "And now, I wonder where we shall go?"

Salih Efendi performed a floor *temenna*. "My Lady, Çırağan Palace has been selected as the residence of His Imperial Highness. If you will give the order, we shall proceed there at once."

The Lady sighed and headed toward our master's apartments. "Well, at least let me go and get my son ready," she said. "Girls, you too make yourselves ready, but quietly. Don't start an uproar that could disturb my son."

The old kalfas hurried off in all directions, taking care to forestall any unseemly behavior by the young kalfas, such as breaking glass or mirrors. But nothing of the kind occurred, as they saw to it that everyone promptly gathered her things together in complete silence.

An unmarked imperial carriage for use of the sultans was brought round to the door of the harem. Servants supported our master under his arms and walked him in his nightclothes out onto the mounting stoop. Her Ladyship got into the carriage first, then invited her son in: "Come, my boy, we're going out for a ride," she said softly. Our master looked about him sadly and vacantly, hesitated slightly, then got into the carriage. In this way, quietly and placidly, he was transferred to Çırağan Palace.

Everyone exhibited the utmost gentleness and consideration toward us during our own transfer over to Çırağan Palace. It was all over by the time

The elegant seaward façade of Çırağan Palace, circa 1905. Photographer unknown.

of the afternoon prayer. Dolmabahçe Palace was given over to the new sovereign, Sultan Abdülhamid.

Let me say this as clearly as I can: at this most sorrowful time for us, not even the slightest hint of discourtesy transpired. No one in our entourage was offended or pained in any way.

Indeed, that evening Sultan Hamid's new Senior Equerry came over to Çırağan Palace and reported directly to Her Ladyship, after paying her his humble respects, "Madam, our master has commanded me to ascertain, has your comfort been attended to? Do you have any orders? No one in the entourage of His Highness the previous monarch will be removed from his service; those who wish to do so may remain in his service. Once the normal rush of activity has quieted down, His Majesty will personally pay a call to visit his exalted brother."

Abdülhamid kept his promise. Toward evening two days later he came to the palace and visited his brother quite simply, without the least ceremony or formality. The Lady Mother received him. To be sure, there was something rather reserved and dejected in the way she did so. Having just undergone three months of sorrow and agony over her son's illness, not to mention having just fallen from the highest position that good fortune could bestow upon her, the Consort adopted an almost irritated and nettled air as she greeted the new monarch. Abdülhamid, however, greeted her with deference, telling her, "God knows I am not at all pleased with the situation. If the people had not wished this to occur, I would never have accepted it."

As they made their way into our master's rooms, Abdülhamid stayed behind the Consort, and then stepped aside once they reached the door so that she could enter first. Once inside he made his way directly to the bedstead where our master was lying and took his hand. "How are you, Brother?" he asked, but our master was in no position to answer the question or even to recognize Sultan Hamid. He just kept staring into the new sovereign's face with a long and vacant look. The hazinedars brought an armchair over to the bedside so that Sultan Hamid could take a seat. He perched on the edge of the chair and tried to get our master to speak by asking him questions such as, "Do you want something? Do you need anything? What would you like?" but he answered none of them.

After sitting there for a quarter of an hour, Sultan Hamid said, "My poor brother!" and stood up. He told the Lady Mother, "Whatever you desire, send word at once. It is my duty to ensure that my brother lacks nothing and is in no distress." To the hazinedars he said, "I can see that my brother has been well cared for. I shall reward each of you individually."

Having thus won everyone's sympathy, he departed.

To tell the truth, we really were given everything we needed in those first few days. We were even rather glad to have made the move from Dolmabahçe to Çırağan because this new palace seemed cheerier to us. A very few of our colleagues left us, and that of their own accord; likewise, a few of the girls asked to leave harem service and marry. But none of the equerries, adjutants, or the officials of our master's court while he was the Sultan was dislodged; in fact, the only thing lacking in our palace was the title "Padishah."

Things might have remained this way for long years were it not for the bizarre episode that took place in the palace some five or ten days later and that brought decisive consequences in its wake, completely shattering our peace and comfort.

This opposition movement first made its appearance among us as a curious rumor. It ended by forcing us into an isolated existence for some twenty-eight years, cut off from a life lived in freedom, indeed cut off from the entire world.

As you know, a bloody event took place in the villa of Midhat Pasha on the thirteenth night after Sultan Aziz was deposed. A Circassian officer by the name of Hasan Bey shot dead the Minister of War Hüseyin Avni Pasha—the leader of the group that overthrew Sultan Aziz—and a few other persons.

Midhat Pasha and the other ministers interpreted Hasan Bey's deed as the beginning of a rebellion by supporters of Sultan Aziz. Since they presumed that the former monarch's mother was one of those behind the rebellion, they transferred her to Topkapı Palace and cut off all her communication with the outside. Poor Pertevniyal Kadın spent three full months moaning and wailing in the veritable prison of her rooms in Topkapı. A few times she sent word to our Lady Mother, hoping that she would help put an end to her anguish, but our Lady Mother was always afraid of anything that could stir up trouble and so she replied, "Your stay there is a matter of state business. I do not interfere in matters of state."

Most noteworthy of all this for us was that some members of our entourage took great pleasure in the sufferings of Sultan Aziz's mother. The leader of this faction was the kalfa Nakşifend, who had been in service for quite some time.

Let us pause for a moment on this name so that we can get to know this woman, whose intrigues more than once convulsed our lives with pandemonium, and who brought down upon us the tragedy that lasted for twenty-eight years.

Nakşifend had been one of the kalfas in Sultan Mecid's service. She served at first as one of the monarch's kalfas, but after some time she was given to our Lady Mother's entourage. She was of average height, with black eyes and eyebrows, olive skin, and a delightful personality. But these were not her most important qualities. Almighty God gave this woman boundless intelligence and eloquence, as well as a determination and perspicaciousness that could bring the most resolute of men to their knees. She could also cross her fingers and tell a thousand fibs. And if any of her friends in the palace had some problem or worry, she would instantly start issuing orders like a skilled attorney in order to solve them.

When Sultan Mecid died she remained in the palace, deciding not to leave palace service in order to get married. Quite the contrary, she spent long years in service to our Lady Mother in the villa at Kurbağalıdere as well as in the Heir's apartments at Dolmabahçe Palace.

She was a free thinker, never a fanatic. I never witnessed this, but those who did said that while at the Kurbağalıdere Villa, if our master were drinking with a group of his male friends and she wanted to say something to him, she would just throw a scarf over her head then and there and make her way right into his presence.

When our master was still the Heir, if he needed money or the like he would usually send this Nakşifend over to see Sultan Aziz's mother Pertevniyal about it. One day Nakşifend was at Dolmabahçe Palace on some mission, but because the Princess Mother was busy with something she had to wait. The kalfas gathered around Nakşifend in the room where she was waiting and soon enough were listening to the stories that flowed freely from her tongue. In the meanwhile the Princess Mother finished her business and heard these voices coming from the room where Nakşifend was holding forth. She made her way over and eavesdropped on the tales being recounted, then burst out in anger, "Get that foul-mouthed hag out of the palace this instant! And tell Prince Murad he is not to send such persons here again!"

Nakşifend took great offense at this treatment. From then on she nurtured a deep grudge against Pertevniyal Kadın, which led to her maligning Pertevniyal Kadın and Sultan Aziz to everyone she could. This resulted in quite a movement opposed to them. The adherents of this movement took quiet pleasure in Sultan Aziz's death, just as they did in the torment and anguish Pertevniyal Kadın suffered in the dank rooms where she was confined in Topkapı Palace. Nor did they refrain from revealing their true feelings when they would say, "The things they used to do to us—now let them get a good dose of it."

On quite the other hand, Prince Hamid had loved Pertevniyal Kadın since he was a little boy. He was more devoted to her than to the lady Perestû, who had raised him,[26] and so as soon as he became Sultan his mind turned to the days of torment that Pertevniyal had passed in Topkapı Palace. He sent men to move the lady and her entourage to one of the villas in Ortaköy, thereby delighting her and repairing the injustice done her. Of course, in doing so Sultan Hamid stirred up the ire of the clique opposed to Sultan Aziz's entourage—notably Nakşifend Kalfa, but our Lady Mother numbered among them as well—which led to the first opposition movements against the new Sultan.

An event still more important than this occurred a few days after the change of monarchs. Sultan Aziz's entourage appealed to Sultan Hamid, complaining, "The day that our master was deposed, we were kicked out of the palace lock, stock, and barrel. They wouldn't let us take even a piece of rubbish with us. We left everything in the palace, our diamonds, our money, all our things. And when we were leaving, they looted everything we had on. They stripped us clean, like brigands in the mountains!" They even went so far as to claim that on the night that Sultan Aziz had been deposed and his rooms sealed by an official delegation, someone had broken the seals and plundered all the diamonds and other valuables in them.

To be sure, such a claim could not be dismissed out of hand, and Sultan Hamid charged Midhat Pasha with investigating the matter. Upon his recommendation a commission was formed of state ministers including the imperial son-in-law Mahmud Celâleddin Pasha, the former army commander-in-chief Rıza Pasha, Namık Pasha, and others. They set about their investigations with all due seriousness.

Most likely they secretly recruited some informants among the servants in our entourage who would have confirmed during the investigations that quite a few of the diamonds of Sultan Aziz's entourage were now in our possession. All of these were repossessed, which also served to fuel the flames of the movement taking shape against Sultan Hamid. Before long our girls had decided that the new Sultan was their bitterest enemy.

In the meanwhile rumors were flying all over. In fact, some people in our entourage who had gotten wind of the impending elevation of Sultan Hamid to the throne and gone over to his side, now fanned the flames in the rumor mill in order to curry favor with him.

---

26 Sultan Abdülmecid's consort Perestû had raised Prince Abdülhamid after the death of his mother Tîrimüjgân in 1852, when the Prince was ten years of age.

The biggest rumor of all had to do with the Nisbetiye Villa episode.[27] As I remember it, this was on the third day after our master ascended the throne. Our Lady Mother, who was so carried away with being the new Princess Mother that she lost all sense of proportion in her words and deeds, came up with an idea; who knows who set her to it? She summoned our master's chamberlain Seyyid Bey as well as the imperial son-in-law Nuri Pasha and said to them, "Prince Hamid is on Sultan Aziz's side, and it's quite likely that he might try to stage a coup against my son in order to bring Sultan Aziz back to the throne. I want you to inform the pashas, confidentially, that they are to host a banquet for Prince Hamid and the other Princes at the Nisbetiye Villa; for whatever they do, they must prevent such a dangerous eventuality. I shall send my son to this banquet." That was as much as any of us knew. Table settings were even dispatched to the villa that day, for as she said, "Our master is giving a dinner in honor of his brothers, which he himself will attend."

But that evening Seyyid Bey came to the Lady and told her, "For whatever reason, Prince Hamid did not accept the invitation. He said, 'My brother has not yet received the ambassadors and other such people. Let him finish with the ceremonies of state he must perform; then we can have dinners and the like.' I have no idea what to make of this answer. Did Prince Hamid suspect something?"

And so this event that played out some three months earlier now came back to life as something entirely different. A new investigation surreptitiously started up in the palace, without doubt as a result of the revelations— who knows what they said—of those who left us and went over into the camp of the new ruler, as well as of outsiders who wanted to get into his good graces.

This investigation centered foremost on Seyyid Bey and Nuri Pasha. But as we heard it, the investigators tried to find out how much our master was involved in all of this since, as they said, "No sooner was Sultan Murad on the throne than his mother tried to have all his brothers poisoned so that her

27 To put an end to gossip about the health of the new Sultan Murad, his six brothers were invited to join him for dinner at the imperial villa of Nisbetiye on the evening of Friday, 2 June 1876. Having heard the rumor that the princes were to be murdered at the isolated villa that night, the suspicious Prince Abdülhamid declined to attend, giving birth to the "Nisbetiye Affair." No evidence has surfaced to corroborate the unfounded rumors of a plot to murder the princes, and indeed the concubine's soon-to-follow description of the Princess Mother Şevkefza's reaction to Prince Hamid's accusations also leads one to conclude this affair consisted entirely of rumor.

son would have no rivals—that was the reason for the banquet at Nisbetiye Villa. Now, was Sultan Murad aware of this or not?"

Seyyid Bey and Nuri Pasha vehemently denied the accusation of poisoning. "Our goal was simply to allow our master the opportunity to dine with his brothers," they answered. "Neither our master nor his mother is the sort of person capable of concocting and executing a crime such as that."

Sultan Hamid summoned them and made his opinion clear. "I am entirely certain that my brother is not capable of harming even a flea. But I know his mother to be an absolute witch, a rapacious snake. I am aware of many things, but at this moment I am not in a position to divulge them. I would investigate this matter fully, were it not for Princess Fatma and Prince Kemaleddin. They came to me and implored me to stop the investigation, which I am doing. For the sake of my brother, I am prepared to forget everything that has transpired."

Seyyid Bey came hurrying in that day to tell the Lady Mother what Sultan Hamid had said. Of course she flew into a rage at his words and began to wail, between her sobs, "What did I ever do to him that he should call me a witch? The real witch is Pertevniyal! She's behind all this mischief, mark my words! Dear God, may those who make trouble for us never find peace!"

And so the matter was closed, but not without kindling among those in service to our master a deep bitterness and resentment against Abdülhamid.

Two persons headed up this movement. Nakşifend Kalfa led affairs in the harem, while the harem steward Süleyman Efendi stoked the fires that erupted on the outside. The rumor as we heard it went like this: the murdered Hüseyin Avni Pasha and Midhat Pasha had secretly met a year earlier with then-Prince Hamid in the villa at Tarabya and concluded a pact with each other. According to its terms, they would depose Sultan Aziz on the grounds that he was insane. They would then get rid of our master and bring Prince Hamid to the throne. But they could find no other way to dethrone our master, who was as healthy as a horse, than to use some trifling illness as a pretext to confine him to the palace. They frightened him by threatening him with swords and guns. For three months they tormented him in this way, completely destroying his nerves, until finally they started calling him crazy. They deposed him from the throne that was legally his upon the death of Sultan Aziz, and tossed him into some corner of Çırağan Palace. Once they placed Prince Hamid on the throne, at last they achieved all their aims. As it was, our master was not even ill, let alone crazy, and make no mistake, he was still the rightful possessor of throne and sovereignty. Prince Hamid had usurped our master's rights.

This rumor made its first mark in the palace, whose residents, most of whom were simple and ignorant folk, came to the unflappable belief that our master was not sick. They concocted their own diagnosis for his illness: "Our master was delirious with fever, and when it passed a silence overcame him, like that of the angels. All of this is a gift of God, a mark of God's perfection." This bit of propaganda came to a boil on the small coffee stoves in the palace, spilled over from there in ripples into the city, and began to flow in waves among the people.

At that point the gates of Çırağan Palace had not yet been closed, so admirers and supporters of our master were coming to the palace in great numbers and extending their felicitations to the Lady Mother by saying, "What good news, our Prince has completely recovered."

Needless to say, this sort of talk caused consternation to Sultan Hamid as well as to his government ministers. One day aides-de-camp came over from Dolmabahçe Palace and took Dr. Capoleone away, which caused all sorts of alarm in our palace by the way he was led off so precipitously. The Lady Mother was particularly anxious for his return, and once he finally came back, summoned the doctor to her apartments for questioning. He told her that they took him straightaway to the palace and ushered him right into Sultan Hamid's presence without his speaking with anyone else at all. The imperial son-in-law Mahmud Pasha and Midhat Pasha were present. Sultan Hamid exchanged many pleasantries with him, and then, with a smile on his face, began to question him.

"I hear that a major change has come about in the state of my brother's health," he said. "And I am delighted to hear it. But I would have liked to have heard this good news from you personally. Tell me, why did you not inform me of it?"

Dr. Capoleone answered, "Had I noted the slightest success resulting from the treatment that my colleague Dr. Mongeri and I have administered, I would have informed Your Majesty immediately. Unfortunately, as of now we have had not the slightest good news to report to you."

At this Abdülhamid turned to Midhat Pasha and Damad Mahmud Pasha and said, "Did you hear? On the one hand we have the doctor's pronouncement, on the other hand my brother's ignorant and dissolute servants are throwing everyone into an uproar. This simply cannot continue, keeping me in suspense. Send a message to the embassies and have physicians brought round. Bring in the specialists in town as well and get them all together. I want them to examine my brother jointly."

Then he turned back to the doctor and added, "Bravo, Doctor! I offer you my felicitations on your excellent care of my brother, as well as on your devotion to the truth. You and Dr. Mongeri both shall be rewarded for your efforts. Tomorrow, remain in the palace, as I shall be sending over a delegation to examine my brother. But you must in no way involve yourself in their examinations. Do no more than describe the course of his illness."

Before leaving the palace, Dr. Capoleone was escorted to a room where he was offered coffee and sherbet drinks. After a time the Senior Chamberlain came in and informed him, "His Imperial Majesty has seen fit to grant you a lifetime income of 7,500 kuruş.[28] In addition, he awards this to you in recognition of your commitment to the truth," whereupon he handed the doctor a red velvet box containing a decoration. On his way back the doctor opened the box for a look. It contained the Order of the Ottoman Dynasty, Third Class.

The Lady Mother listened most attentively and anxiously to his words. Clearly, she was not pleased at what she was hearing. After Dr. Capoleone left she said, "I can place absolutely no more trust in this man. He was the only true friend my son had left, but now Sultan Hamid has bought him too. Now we have no more hope of regaining the throne."[29]

Consternation reigned in the palace that night. The great question everyone debated was, "If the delegation comes tomorrow, shall we show them our master or not?" Nakşifend Kalfa was beside herself with rage. She puffed herself up self-righteously and loudly declared, "My Lady! This is what I believe! All the doctors coming over here will be sweet-talked at Dolmabahçe Palace first! Of course they'll decide their diagnosis of our master before they even see him! What's the point of taking these Europeans in to our master and stirring up his nerves, all for nothing? If they come here tomorrow, kick the infidel pigs out!"

28 Ostensibly an annual figure, and if so a generous sum, approximately double the average worker's income in a year.

29 This ignorant woman failed to realize that Dr. Capoleone himself was the cause of Sultan Murad's disastrous condition. Dr. Mavroyeni Pasha [Spiridion Mavroyeni (1817–1902), personal physician and friend to Sultan Abdülhamid] took his patient Abdülhamid under his wings and shielded him from everything harmful, thus securing for Abdülhamid his long reign. On the other hand Dr. Capoleone introduced Sultan Murad while still a very young man to alcohol, then ensured that for years afterward he continued to lead his life of dissipation. On top of all this the doctor completely destroyed the unfortunate Sultan's health by prescribing fifty leeches at once, when his patient fell ill following the death of Sultan Aziz. [Ş]

So many of Murad's associates have been blamed for his alcoholism that to single out one or another is pointless. Murad had developed a taste for alcohol as a young man, even before he became Heir to the Throne at age twenty-one.

But in truth, our master was quite ill. He remained lost in his own world, extremely weak, and so frail that one could have said he was completely broken. He would eat or drink nothing. Once or twice each day he'd come to his senses for a few moments, but only enough to mumble, "I want to get up for a little while." The kalfas would take his arms and help him to the toilet, then wash his face. In order to humor the entreaties of the kalfas, he would take a spoonful or two of the chilled pudding on the table, suck the juice from a couple of chilled grapes, then say, "Put me back to bed now," and once again sink into unconsciousness.

He was still unable to speak coherently. Only with difficulty could one understand his words. He was as weak as a baby. Even though lost in unconsciousness he would still twitch continually with spasms. He would fix his eyes on something and stare in terror.

The Lady Mother held to the decision taken the previous night: she did not want to show our master to the delegation scheduled to arrive the following day. But Damad Mahmud Pasha somehow or other convinced her to change her mind.

It was not possible to dress our master, so he was brought into the great salon in his nightclothes. The examining delegation—physicians dispatched by the embassies of seven countries—examined him there. I don't know what their diagnosis was, but late in the morning of the next day the palace was turned upside down. Armed troops surrounded the gates and aides-de-camp came inside. They led away the chamberlain Seyyid Bey, who was in the men's wing of the palace, the entourage superintendent Süleyman Efendi, the secretary Raif Efendi, the undercover bodyguard Halil Ağa, and the equerries Abdülvahid, Anber, Emin, and Raşid Ağas, as well as a few other of the staff at court.

This threw us all into a state of fright. In fact it made some of us sick with fear. For days we fretted over the plight of those who had been taken into custody, and finally we learned their sad fate. It seems Sultan Hamid wanted to get these men out of Istanbul because they were spreading propaganda in support of our master, so he dispatched them forthwith to Mecca. For some reason he was particularly angry with our master's manservant Anber Ağa, and so he issued a special order to the ship captain: "This man was the ringleader behind this mess. You will set him down on an uninhabited island and let him die there of hunger and thirst."

From what we heard, the captain stopped the vessel at an uninhabited island on the way to the Hijaz and abandoned Anber Ağa there. But on the way back the captain began to wonder, "Well, how could that poor Negro

The lavish neo-Moorish interior of Çırağan Palace, circa 1905. Photographer unknown.

be faring? Suffering terribly, no doubt. Why not at least pick him up and drop him off on some inhabited island." But when he arrived at that deserted island he encountered a horrible sight, for ferocious animals had torn Anber Ağa to shreds. His bones were scattered everywhere, with one of his dismembered hands still clutching a white handkerchief.[30]

HOW DID OUR PRISON LIFE BEGIN?

We didn't take long to settle in. Our master was moved into the monarch's apartments, while his mother Şevkefza Kadın occupied the Princess Mother's apartments. The princes, princesses, consorts, and concubines moved into the apartments appropriate for them on the upper and lower floors.

---

30 This tale related by the *gözde* consists of what she heard at the time. The truth is that some of Sultan Murad's Privy Staff and persons propagandizing on his behalf outside the palace were indeed arrested, but all of them were dispatched to various localities in Anatolia, and to positions that accorded with their situations. The implicated harem eunuchs, for their part, were dispatched to the Hijaz, where they were set up in residence in Medina. Of course, they were allowed no communication with Istanbul. The manservant Anber Ağa lived in Medina for two years before he took ill and died of dysentery. [Ş]

Within a few days everyone was settled and the situation seemed back to normal. Even the Secretariat wing of the palace quieted down, following the banishment of those involved in spreading propaganda in support of our master. Courtiers no longer needed were let go, so that the only ones remaining were his aide-de-camp Ali Bey (son of Namık Pasha), who was devoted to our master, his wardrobe attendant Akif Bey, and other necessary persons.

Abdülhamid assigned the entire administration and oversight of Çırağan Palace to one of his most trusted equerries, Cevher Ağa. But because Cevher Ağa's duties at Yıldız Palace prevented him from spending all his time at our palace, he brought in a man by the name of Vanlı Mehmed Ağa to serve as his deputy under the title of "Palace Administrator."

At first this man carried out his duties quietly and modestly, but after a week or two he abruptly turned threatening and vicious, like a hideous snake, and practically set himself up as the dictator of the palace. Since the banishment of the propagandists, access to the palace had been somewhat restricted, although it wasn't yet so severe. In these conditions Vanlı Mehmed fancied himself "more royalist than the king," actually imposing rules and procedures for how he was to be treated.

Dr. Capoleone seldom called at the palace anymore. Quite often Abdülhamid sent over Rifat Pasha, one of his own doctors, to examine our master. But his examinations hardly constituted a course of treatment. Rifat Pasha would just come by, stay at our master's side for ten or fifteen minutes, note his condition, then leave without prescribing medications or recommending anything. From this it was clear that all attempts to cure the former monarch had been relinquished and that he had been abandoned to the condition in which he lay.

Things continued in this way for some time, with our master ceded completely to a certain state of peace and tranquility. As he lay in this repose, bit by bit one noticed a change in his condition. First, he began to sleep better. He was still unconscious for long periods, but the nervous twitching, the deep transfixing of his eyes on who knows what, staring in mortal terror at something—these things became far less frequent. He began to recognize the people around him and to smile at them, and he even began to talk a little.

Although the kalfas still had to help him, he became better able to get to the privy. He would wash his own face, and when he came back to his room he began to show an appetite for the pudding, grapes, and other food always laid out for him on the table.

This change in our master's condition altered the political situation for the palace. One day Cevher Ağa came by, along with the doctor Rifat

Pasha, and thoroughly examined our master with obvious apprehension. He seemed nearly overcome with alarm at the resulting prognosis. Clearly he was not pleased at our master's recovery. But of course not—because if our master's recovery became public knowledge outside the palace, all kinds of rumors would spread, perhaps even a movement might start to restore him to the throne.

Our master's return to health stirred Nakşifend Kalfa to action more than anyone. This wildly energetic and animated creature once again went to the Lady Mother and tried to instigate something: "My Lady, thank God our master is well again! God willing, today or tomorrow will see the last of his illness! We can't just sit here doing nothing, we've got to get ready now, we've got to get back our master's rightful position! It was stolen from him!"

Nor was Nakşifend the only one who felt this way. Princess Seniha, who had not yet married and had spent a great deal of time in our palace with our master, as well as Princess Fatma, who never set foot outside the palace, thought the same thing. For whatever reason Princess Seniha was not on good terms with Sultan Hamid, while Princess Fatma turned against Abdülhamid when her husband Nuri Pasha fell from grace after the plot against the princes at Nisbetiye Villa came to light. Furthermore, relations were sour between Sultan Hamid and Prince Kemaleddin, who resided in the First Fer'iye Palace just above Çırağan Palace, so that he too believed our master should be restored to the throne.[31]

As for the Lady Mother Şevkefza Kadın, more than anything she pined for the sultanate. "For years my son suffered and beat his breast bitterly in the forgotten corners of the palace and the apartments of the Heir," she would weep and moan, "trembling in fear of his uncle. Just as he sat on the throne, and before he could say so much as 'Oh!' this business came down upon him! Only four short days could he enjoy his reign! My poor, unlucky son!"

And so, when these factions came together, another venture against Sultan Hamid took shape in the palace.

New eunuchs selected by Cevher Ağa were brought over from Yıldız Palace to replace those banished as a result of the propaganda incident. Both these eunuchs and the Palace Administrator Vanlı Mehmed wasted no time

31 It is said that in the days when Abdülhamid was yet a Prince, Prince Kemaleddin once ran into pressing financial difficulties. He applied to the wealthy Abdülhamid for funds and even sent over valuable objects as security for a loan. But Abdülhamid replied, "I'm no petty moneychanger! Since he wants to pawn something for money, let him try the moneychangers in the Caviar Building!" Prince Kemaleddin took offense at this, and ever afterwards relations between the two were frosty. [Ş]

Princess Fatma, half-sister to Prince Murad, around 1870 when she was thirty years of age. Photographer unknown.

in informing Yıldız Palace of this venture once they got wind of it. Sultan Hamid was furious. "This sort of thing will end in no good," he informed the Lady Mother through Cevher Ağa. "I have nothing but the greatest respect for my brother, and I am trying to do everything I can to take care of him. Nor have I refused the palace staff anything whatsoever. What are they lacking? What have they asked for that I have not sent over? Why this ingratitude? Why do they believe what some person or other tells them, and come together against me? If matters continue like this, I shall be quite angry with them."

Sultan Hamid did more than just send this message, he tightened the security ring around the palace just a little bit more. Access to the palace was so severely curtailed that visitors were practically limited to the princes he trusted, such as Prince Reşad and Prince Burhaneddin.

One day around this time, Princess Fatma came by to pay another visit to her brother, but the gate guards, who had come from Yıldız Palace, refused her permission to enter. That led to quite a scene at the gates of the palace, with Princess Fatma defiantly exploding, "Indeed! And just who is preventing me from entering? Is it that miserable blackguard? Who does he think he is, trying to keep me from visiting my brother? I want to see my brother, and until I do, I am not moving! I shall spend the night here if I must!"

In the street a crowd gathered, which policemen from the Beşiktaş station dispersed as they cordoned off Princess Fatma's carriage. The Yıldız Palace officials went hysterical at what was happening. Up to the palace they ran and informed Sultan Hamid. After a while Cevher Ağa came down and said, "Begging Your Highness's pardon . . . the guards misunderstood their orders! His Majesty in no way restricts members of the imperial family from visiting one another!" This soothed Princess Fatma's rage, and into the palace she went, weeping all the way to our master's apartments, where brother and sister hugged and embraced one another and talked for hours until finally they took their leave of one another with more embraces.

As she left, Princess Fatma said she would come again soon, to which our master replied, "Do come visit, dear sister. I'd love to see you as often as possible." Their meeting had proven that the former sovereign's mental equilibrium was quite capable of returning to normal.

However, what Princess Fatma did that day resulted in nothing good for her. No sooner had she returned to her villa in Baltalimanı than soldiers and policemen surrounded it. The Princess was imprisoned in her own villa.[32]

---

32 Having incurred Abdülhamid's displeasure at her support of Murad, Princess Fatma retired to her shoreside villa at Baltalimanı from 1876 until her death in 1884. Throughout these years she kept up a secret correspondence with Murad.

With the passing of the days, our master's condition improved. He was able now to answer questions perfectly well and ask naturally for things he needed. He didn't care for his bedroom so he chose for himself the small salon overlooking the Bosphorus next to the place where tradition claimed the fourteen saints were resting.[33] He himself chose the location for his bedstead.

Later he had a piano brought into one of the rooms that opened onto this salon and sent for Tarzınevin,[34] who played the piano better than any of the girls. "You are to stay in this room," he told her, "and always play the piano for me." Indeed some days later, as Tarzınevin was playing the piano, our master got out of bed, came quietly into the room, and listened to her for a while, leaning one arm against the piano with the other arm behind his back. He became more and more animated while listening to the music until finally he leaned over to Tarzınevin and said softly, "Go bring me some music paper. Write down the notes for the arrangement I'm going to play." As soon as she got up he sat down on the piano stool and began to pick out a melody with one hand. Tarzınevin took down the notes to the piece, which our master then sent to Princess Fatma. As we later heard it, Princess Fatma was thrilled to receive the music. Through some means she sent it to the organ grinders, as though by having the air played by organ grinders she wanted to let the people know that our master had completely recovered his health.

Needless to say, it didn't take long for news of these events to reach Yıldız Palace. The screws were turned just that much more on Çırağan. Still fewer people were allowed access to the palace. Apparently even Dr. Rifat Pasha fell under suspicion, for he was replaced with Dr. Rıza Pasha.

The powers of the Palace Administrator, Vanlı Mehmed, increased— as did the impudence of this ignorant and crude man. Whenever the doctor called, the Administrator would come in with him, even exhibiting the effrontery to enter our master's bedroom. Thus under inspection himself, the doctor would ask one or two limited questions of our master, then be on his way, unable to spend time either with him or with anyone in the harem who might need medical attention.

One day Princess Seniha did something bold indeed. She took two kalfas

---

33 During the construction in 1834–1841 of the palace that occupied the site where Çırağan Palace was later built (in 1863–1872), the Mevlevî dervish lodge on the site had been demolished. Legend held that the graves of the dervish saints were disinterred and relocated beneath the palace.

In light of the tragic events that transpired within Çırağan before it burned in 1910, popular belief subsequently interpreted the reinterment as an act of desecration that brought a curse upon the palace. Akbayar 1998, 73.

34 One of the kalfas, and member of the harem musical ensemble.

Murad's dashing half-sister Princess Seniha around 1876, the year she turned twenty-four. The Princess's husband and sons became vocal opponents of her other half-brother, Sultan Abdülhamid. Photographer unknown.

with her and went out into town in an unmarked carriage, returning an hour or two later in the same way—but with one difference. The carriage stopped at the home of one of her own former serving girls who had left palace service. There she met up with a doctor, had him put on the veil of one of the kalfas, and in this manner smuggled the doctor into the palace. This doctor remained in the palace for twelve nights, treating our master and anyone who was sick. Twelve days later he was smuggled out of the palace in the same way.[35]

This sort of thing could not be kept secret for long. Soon enough the Yıldız spies found out about it and Princess Seniha was instantly expelled from the palace. Henceforth Çırağan was subjected to the strictest discipline and surveillance.

THE INMATES OF ÇIRAĞAN PALACE

At the time when the security cordon around Çırağan Palace really began to be tightened, our harem cadre consisted of the following persons: our master; the Lady Mother Şevkefza Kadın; the consorts Elâru, Reftarıdil, Şayan, and Meyliservet; Prince Salâheddin; and the princesses Hadice and Fehime.

The gözdes

RESAN HANIM
Resan and her foster sister Şayeste were presented by the Senior Kalfa to our master as a gift on the occasion of his accession to the throne. Shortly after we were imprisoned in Çırağan, she gave birth first to Princess Fatma and then some time later to Princess Aliye. Although his action was contrary to court convention, our master accorded her the title of *Hanım* [Lady].[36]

GEVHERRİZ
Gevherriz had been a *gözde* of our master's since before his accession to the throne. She spoke excellent French, and it was she who taught French to the young Princes and Princesses.

NEVDÜR
She too had been a *gözde* since before our master's accession to the throne.

35 Despite considerable research, I have been unable to determine the name of this doctor. [Ş]
36 A title usually reserved for a prince's consort, not granted a *gözde*.

REMİŞNAZ (REMZŞİNAS)[37]

FİLİSTİN (FİLİZTEN)

She is still living, and even though she has passed the age of seventy, she retains both the beauty of her youth and, in particular, a sound memory as well as all her mental faculties.[38]

The Hazinedars

The High Hazinedar, Aynifer; the Second Hazinedar, İspantiyar; the Third Hazinedar, Renginaz; the Fourth Hazinedar, Elâdil; and the Fifth Hazinedar, Dilberengiz.

Other hazinedars and Imperial Kalfas in our master's service included Navekendaz, Nazlı Alem, Evrengdil, Ferengiz (still living), Desteriz (still living), Niyazter, Dilber (still living and in excellent health), Nefidem (she is also still alive), Tarzınigâr (the pantrywoman), Nazikter, Dilbersima, and Şinasidil.[39] In addition to Melekrû, Perniyaz, and Dilagâh there were another ten or fifteen kalfas, whose names I cannot recall.

Kalfas to the Lady Mother

Emsalinur, Siranto, Nakşifend, Vasfıcihan, and Rûşen.

The Kalfa Musicians

Dürrünab Kalfa (the ensemble director) was presented to our master by Princess Refia. She played the violin and piano exquisitely.

Tarzınevin, who was extremely talented on the piano. She could write out the notes to any piece of music she heard, on the spot.

Lebriz, who played the flute.

Desteriz, who both played in the music ensemble and directed the dancing girls. She possessed the most wonderfully elegant figure and agile body.

---

37 The text contains no entry for this concubine. Properly her name was "Remzşinas" (Knower of Signs), transformed in colloquial speech to the more easily pronounced "Remişnaz."

38 The author of these memoirs, so that the flattering description of her is, one presumes, tongue in cheek, although one hopes that the assessment of her memory is accurate.

39 When Sultan Murad was henceforth compelled to eat only in the company of women, these three hazinedars waited on his table, each in turn. [Ş]

Teranedil, whose graceful movements distinguished her among the kalfa dancers.

Other kalfas both played in the music ensemble and numbered among the dancing girls, but I can't remember their names.

In addition, the kalfas of Prince Salâheddin and the Princesses, as well as these kalfas' young assistants, known as "novices," totaled at least some twenty or twenty-five in number.

The Equerries

After the banishment of Anber Ağa and the other eunuchs implicated in the propaganda incident, the palace eunuch staff of equerries and footmen consisted of Abdülkerim, Abdülvahid, Emin, Raşid, Said, Zülkifli, and Cafer. Also the butler Ali Ağa as well as Nazım and Sokrat, who formerly waited at table, did not forsake the palace; they too suffered through the long years at Çırağan, remaining loyal to our master until his death.

After Anber Ağa and the others had been banished, Sultan Hamid's Senior Equerry Cevher Ağa brought over from Yıldız Palace three eunuchs by the names of Sadık, Asım, and Cafer, and settled them in the places vacated by the three exiles. Ostensibly they were to carry out assigned duties just as the other eunuchs were, but in reality they were charged with reporting daily to Cevher Ağa any events that happened in the palace and whatever talk they might have overheard. But may God bless them for it, these eunuchs never did spy on anyone. Instead they exhibited the deepest respect toward each of us, from our master down to the lowliest kalfa, and became our true companions in palace service.

Asım Ağa had been the eunuch assigned to Sultan Aziz's laundry kalfa. He had come to love our master while our Prince was still the Heir, and demonstrated his affection by word and deed after he came to Çırağan. Not only did he not spy on us, as soon as he heard some bit of news from outside, he would come right in and pass it on to us. And every time he went out of the palace, he would come back full of news for us about what was happening in the world. When matters eventually reached the low point in which it was forbidden to bring pen and ink into Çırağan, this Asım Ağa somehow or other smuggled us pens, paper, envelopes, and the like.

Sadık Ağa also exhibited heartfelt devotion to our master. I shall never forget how bitterly he wept the day our master died.

In sum, such was the composition of the palace harem cadre, more or less, up until the time of the Ali Suavi incident.

My Position Changes

The persons plotting to restore Sultan Murad to the throne were secretly working away toward their goal, and with the greatest of finesse. First of all, they silenced Nakşifend's loose talk. Then they took care not to take our master on walks around the palace too much, so as not to attract Sultan Abdülhamid's attention. If Yıldız were to learn that our master had taken a turn towards recovering completely, of course they would have tightened the surveillance net around the palace even more and cut off our contact with the outside world completely. That is why it was thought preferable to keep our master out of sight as much as possible.

As it was, however, since our master had entirely recovered his powers of perception and thought, he wanted to explore every cranny of the palace and learn who was in his service. This desire on our master's part led to quite an important event for me and brought about a change in my position in the palace.

I shan't forget that day. I was sitting on the floor, playing dominos with Zatıgül Kalfa, who later on became the Senior Consort of Prince Salâheddin. Suddenly Zatıgül cried out, "Our master!" and raced off through a side door into another room. I, however, was overweight and couldn't make an escape. I scooped up the dominos and threw them under the sofa just in time to stand up and clasp my hands together over my chest, then just stood there, frozen.

Our master was standing in the doorway, looking at me with a smile on his face, the eunuch Abdülvahid and the kalfas Dilberengiz and Dürrünab beside him. Dürrünab was signaling me with her head and her eyes, trying to say, "What are you standing there for? Kiss his feet!" Suddenly I came to my senses, ran over to our master and threw myself at his feet. They patted my back, then took me under the arms and helped me up. As I was backing away I heard him say, "Who is this?" Dilberengiz answered our master's question. "Your Highness, this is F——, Tayyar Pasha's little one."[40] Then our master addressed me. "Oh yes, you were a little girl. Now look how you've grown."

The fact that he said this proved that his comprehension and his memory had completely returned, because he had seen me when he was still the Heir and I was about fourteen or fifteen years old. I had come to the palace just shortly before he ascended the throne. Now at this point I was still a novice,

40 Here our author is confirming that she was presented to Murad by one Tayyar Pasha, who had married a former hazinedar of Murad.

and novices didn't go around much, so their masters rarely saw them. That meant that he remembered the first time he saw me, and he recognized me.

This incident changed my position from that moment forward. All my friends congratulated me on my release from the position of novice and my promotion to that of Senior Foot,[41] and the senior kalfas and hazinedars expressed their approval of me. The Lady Mother even summoned me to her presence and expressed her pleasure with me, while my kalfa promised me then and there a new dress.

A COURAGEOUS BRITISH DOCTOR

Around this time another clandestine operation took place in the Lady Mother's retinue. Led by Nakşifend, she and Gevherriz, one of our master's most loyal gözdes, as well as the hazinedar Dilberengiz, began meeting together with the Lady Mother, excitedly concocting all sorts of plans. Throughout these meetings, Dilberengiz Kalfa would regularly relay news back and forth to our master's rooms.

After three days of these hush-hush plottings, Nakşifend Kalfa suddenly took ill. Some two or three days later, as Cevher Ağa came to the palace to ascertain her needs, the Lady Mother said what she was to say and then added, "Our Nakşifend keeps saying she is sick, and she asks to be sent out for convalescence.[42] Please convey this request and secure the order for it." Three days later the order arrived allowing Nakşifend to be sent out for convalescence. With that the kalfa took her small wickerwork basket out to the home of one of our master's retired tray bearers, the eunuch Hüseyin Ağa, in the Kılıç Ali District.

Not two days later, a rumor began circulating among the girls that notes tied to stones were being thrown at night over the wall into the little garden off the sitting room next to the grand salon. Gevherriz wasted no time in pulling these girls aside and warning them, "If you say one more thing about this,

---

41 *Ayak eskisi.* "Senior Foot" is one of the amusing palace customs. A young girl, new in palace service, could only hope to become "old" or "senior," that is to say, a kalfa, after waiting for many years. Alternatively, convention had it that she could also become a kalfa if she chose the degradation of kissing the foot of her master. Those presented with the rare opportunity to kiss his foot became at that moment "Senior Foot" and hence entered into the ranks of the kalfas. [Ş]

42 Members of the palace household suffering from illnesses such as nervous conditions or other afflictions were sent out to the homes of trusted palace officials for a change of air and environment lasting perhaps five or ten days. This was called *tımara çıkmak* [to go out for care and attention]. [Ş]

I will rip the lips off your face." She also had the senior kalfas make rounds in the garden at night and declared it off-limits to the younger kalfas.

Things continued this way for several days, during which time a thick veil of silence descended over the palace. In the midst of this stillness the kalfas of our master and the Lady Mother went to work. They formed a veritable guard, by turns, between the apartments of the Prince and the Lady Mother, forbade the other kalfas to enter the area at all, and in fact prevented anyone from coming anywhere near the Prince's apartments. We all sensed perfectly well that mysterious things were happening in our master's apartments, but each of us buried that realization so deeply within herself, under such a thick layer of discretion, that none of us mentioned even a single word of it amongst ourselves, even though we were dying to find out what was going on.

As it turned out, days, months, and finally years passed before we learned the truth of what was happening. It seems that the heir to the British throne had sent a personal note to the ambassador asking him to determine whether our master was indeed mad. The ambassador at once assigned the task to the dragoman at the embassy. The brother of the dragoman[43] was both a freemason and by repute a close friend and supporter of our master. He in turn informed the head of the freemasons,[44] who then summoned their fellow freemason Hüsnü Bey, who had at one time served as our master's Second Secretary, and told him to find some sound means for them to communicate with the palace harem.

Hüsnü Bey, who knew the harem and the palace staff inside out, dispatched a secret note to the tray bearer Hüseyin Ağa, who was one of the

---

43 In a footnote at this juncture, Şakir states this was the dragoman himself, not his brother; however, Uzunçarşılı (1944 "Kaçırmak," 590) and others identify the veiled visitor as the brother. In these years the dragoman at the British Embassy was the Ottoman-Greek Stavrides.

44 This is the Greek Cleanthi Scalieri, Grand Master of the Proodos Lodge. The investigative reports concerning this incident in the Yıldız Palace Archives mistakenly record this person's name as İskalari Gırlandi. [Ş]

    The Proodos ("Progress" in Greek) Masonic Lodge was founded in the Beyoğlu district of Istanbul in 1867, as an associate of the French lodge "Grand Orient." The lodge's rituals were conducted in both Turkish and Greek. In 1872 the Istanbul-born Ottoman-Greek Cleanthi Scalieri became Grand Master, and on 20 October of that year Prince Murad was clandestinely inducted into the lodge, sponsored by his chamberlain Seyyid Bey. Murad rose through the ranks in the lodge. At one point he proposed establishing an independent Ottoman lodge to be named Envar-ı Şarkiye, "Eastern Lights," with its ritual conducted in Turkish, but the plan was never realized. In 1873 and 1875 respectively, his brothers Prince Nureddin and Prince Kemaleddin also joined the Proodos Lodge. Erginsoy 1996, 15–16.

most loyal of the palace staff, as well as to Gevherriz. In it he described the issue at hand in detail, then wrote, "A doctor will be brought into the harem in complete secrecy. Inform His Highness of this, and make every effort to assist us loyally in our cause."

They informed our master of the plans, and when he gave his assent, they set about getting everything ready.

Once again it was Nakşifend Kalfa who took the lead in making the preparations. In order to complete all the necessary arrangements both inside and outside the palace, she pretended to be ill and asked to be sent outside for convalescence. As I related above, after Sultan Hamid's permission was requested and obtained, she went straight to the tray bearer Hüseyin Ağa's house and settled in there, getting right to work. First of all the Grand Master of the Masonic lodge, the dragoman at the British Embassy, Hüsnü Bey, and a British doctor who spoke no Turkish met together in secret as a kind of committee. They interviewed Nakşifend, asking her all sorts of questions about what condition our master was in, what he was eating and drinking, how he went to bed, and how he got up. They had Nakşifend Kalfa sign her name beneath the answers she gave. Then they boldly set about their task.

First they used the lure of money to obtain the cooperation of the imam of the Kılıç Ali Pasha Mosque and the caretaker of the mosque's water conduits. They inspected the water pipes running from the storage tank behind the mosque's ablution reservoir over to Çırağan, and ascertained that a person could indeed make his way through the pipes, even standing up in places. The water in this stretch flowed through iron pipes.

The interested parties within the harem were kept informed of these arrangements in part by the tray bearer Hüseyin Ağa and in part by the notes wrapped around the rocks tossed into the garden. At length clear instructions arrived to this effect: "On such-and-such a night, a British physician by the name of Donny will enter the palace by means of the water pipes.[45] Wait for him at the entrance to the water storage tank, and ask him for the password. The doctor will give you the password, "Edward."[46] Admit him and take him immediately up to His Highness and introduce him. Once he's met

45 Spelled "Doni" in the Turkish original, so that "Donny" is a guess as to the surname of this British physician, whom research has failed to identify.
46 The name of the Prince of Wales, whom the concubine states had shown an interest in determining whether Prince Murad, whom the Prince of Wales had met at Murad's visit to England in 1867, was indeed insane.

His Highness, the doctor will explain to him his task and the circumstances surrounding it."

On the arranged night, the water-pipe caretaker led Dr. Donny into the pipes, each with a lantern in hand. After a great deal of difficulty, at times slithering along on their stomachs or crawling on their hands and knees, they arrived at the palace's water storage tank, to be met by Gevherriz and one of the Imperial Kalfas. To Gevherriz Kalfa's demand for the password, the doctor responded, "Edward." In her proficient French, Gevherriz invited the doctor in while the water-pipe caretaker returned the way he had come.

Without any of the kalfas seeing him, the doctor was taken straight to our master's apartments and introduced to him. In complete control of his mental faculties, our master welcomed him in correct French, "Doctor, you have exhibited extreme courage and devotion. I extend my deepest thanks both to you and to those whose humane thoughtfulness has sent you here." He then showed the doctor, who was deeply touched by these perfectly cogent and courteous words, to the room prepared especially for him adjoining the Prince's bedroom.

This doctor stayed a full week, with only Gevherriz looking after his needs. He examined our master several times a day, having him calculate some arithmetic or play the piano for long periods. At times he took meals with him, and several nights he even sat at our master's bedside, observing him for hours on end as he slept. After it all he announced, "If you are in the least bit ill, I shall tear up my medical diploma and deny that there is any such thing as knowledge and science."

At the end of the week the doctor left as he had come, guided out by the water-pipe caretaker.

I should like to know who this doctor was. Was Donny his real name? Was he the physician at the British Embassy in Istanbul? Or was he sent from England through some special means arranged by the British heir, Prince Edward? This no one knows.

However, there is one additional point of interest. The day after the doctor came to the palace, the afternoon call to prayer began from the minaret of a nearby mosque as the doctor was conversing with Gevherriz. The doctor stopped speaking and turned to look at the muezzin reciting the call. Noting the miserable clothing that the muezzin was wearing, the doctor muttered "The poor wretch" as he turned to Gevherriz and said, "What a strange custom. You mean to say that in your country poor persons beg by shouting out from some high place, is that it?" Of course Gevherriz gave an appropriate answer and explanation, but from this one can deduce that the doctor was new to Istanbul and most probably had been sent on a special mission from England by the heir to the British throne.[47]

No one ever breathed a word about the Dr. Donny episode, and somehow or other Yıldız never did find out about it. No doubt it emboldened our master's sympathizers in the city, though, because some six weeks later another figure was smuggled into the palace, this time in a veil from head to toe. I didn't see him, but from the people who did see him I heard that this gentleman was a tremendously elegant and cultivated Turk of medium height, as thin as a rail, and with a small black beard.[48]

TWO BOLD ENDEAVORS

At first this person had come to the apartments of Prince Kemaleddin in the Fer'iye Palace adjoining us. Secret communications went back and forth between Prince Kemaleddin and our palace, with the result that one day this gentleman was dressed up in a veil and smuggled into our palace between two of Prince Kemaleddin's kalfas.

He stayed in our palace one night, with a bed provided him in our master's apartments. But the two of them stayed up all that night, writing page after page of what constituted the fundamentals of a plan of escape. The way we heard it, a British ship was to anchor off the palace, and on the same day, the group of men who were going to liberate our master would enter the palace on some pretext. They would wait until midnight, when the ship would signal by lamp and send over a boat, at which point the group in the palace would quietly bring our master down to the palace pier. They would win over one of the guards on duty there, or overpower him by force if necessary, get our master into the boat and out onto the British ship.

---

47 More likely this doctor was sent directly by the freemasons themselves, or else by supporters of Sultan Murad who were working secretly to restore him to the throne. [Ş]

48 This would be the late Şefkatî, one of the most ardent liberals of the era. [Ş]

Ali Şefkatî (1843–1896), liberal journalist known for his humorous and caustic writings, and member of the Proodos Masonic Lodge where he became devoted to his Masonic brother Prince Murad. Following the latter's deposal he participated in the underground committee led by Cleanthi Scalieri to restore Murad to the throne. With the 7 July 1878 police raid on the house where the committee was meeting, Şefkatî, Scalieri, and Nakşifend Kalfa fled abroad. Through the newspapers he published in London and Paris Ali Şefkatî furthered the opposition movement to Sultan Abdülhamid, until his death in Paris on 16 January 1896.

On quite the other hand, Uzunçarşılı (1944 "Kaçırmak," 590) identifies the veiled visitor as Stavrides, brother of the Ottoman-Greek dragoman at the British Embassy.

Murad (center) in happier times, while still Heir to the Throne circa 1870, flanked by his half-brothers Prince Reşad (left) and Prince Kemaleddin (right). All are wearing the stambuline coat. Photographer unknown.

Having spent the night in the palace engaged in these intense discussions, the next day the bearded gentleman departed as he had come, between two of Prince Kemaleddin's palace girls.

Damad Mahmud Pasha was one of our master's sympathizers.[49] He used to pay calls at Prince Kemaleddin's apartments as well, during which the Prince let him in on this business of arranging an escape for our master. He too was groomed as a member of the dynasty for a role in the planned operation.

But around that time something occurred that put Mahmud Pasha in Sultan Hamid's bad graces. In order to get himself out of this difficulty he went to Sultan Hamid and told him about the planned operation. "Instead of bothering with me you'd better deal with your real enemies," he said. "They're about to free the ex-Sultan and really make things hot for you."

Sultan Hamid did not believe that anyone would really be so bold. He launched a covert investigation into the matter, but the plotters had acted with such discretion that he could not turn up even the slightest clue despite the effective means at his disposal. So he summoned Mahmud Pasha back to the palace and interrogated him further. "Seeing as you yourself brought this matter to my attention," he said, "you shall resolve it by personally surrendering these brazen scoundrels into my custody. If you demonstrate your loyalty to me in this way I shall be assured of your devotion and will see to it that you are rewarded in whatever way you desire."

Damad Mahmud Pasha set right to work, in secret. First he transferred seven or eight armed guards from Yıldız to the gates of our palace and gave them their instructions. Then, through his frequent calls on the suite of Prince Kemaleddin he came to learn when the smuggling operation was to take place.

The guards assigned to the gates of our palace were crafty. They kept their eyes wide open while they greeted those who passed in and out of the gates as if they were old friends—which encouraged the perpetrators still further.

One day a carriage pulled up to the palace gate. Four veiled ladies got out, including one of the palace women in Prince Kemaleddin's service. This

---

49 The author does not clarify which of the two imperial brothers-in-law named Mahmud Pasha she means, but evidence points to the husband of Princess Cemile. True, in reality this man was not "one of our master's sympathizers," as our author describes him—in fact, he had played a leading role in bringing Abdülhamid to the throne—but quite likely he presented himself as a friend of Murad's, which would account for the trust Prince Kemaleddin placed in him, and for the charge of hypocrisy that our concubine tells us (in the upcoming paragraphs) the older palace kalfas leveled at him.

woman approached the guards and said, "We've come to pay a call on the Lady Mother." The guards replied, "Of course; please step this way into this room while we announce your arrival," and escorted the four veiled figures to the small room adjoining the main gate. All at once the guards burst into the room and pointed their weapons at the ladies. "Open your veils and let's have a look at your faces," they shouted. The veiled figures tried to escape through the door but all four were apprehended, bound up tightly, and sent straight over to Dolmabahçe Palace. There Damad Mahmud Pasha himself interrogated them and then hurried up to Abdülhamid to inform him of what had happened. To this the Sultan replied, "Well done, Brother-in-law. I now have complete confidence in your loyalty."

I do not know whether this is true or if it's a fabrication. If the latter, may those who invented it reap the consequences of their sin. Some of the old kalfas who talked about this incident had nothing good to say about Mahmud Pasha. In fact they'd accuse him of double-dealing, even claiming, "Our master had no intention of trying to escape. And anyway by nature he wasn't up to such violent activities. But Damad Mahmud Pasha has done what he has done. He was scheming all right, concocting this whole episode just to look good for Abdülhamid."

The arrest of those men at the palace gate triggered the following repercussions:[50]

1. From that day forward all communication between the palace and the outside world was completely severed. Access to the palace was severely restricted for all except those on official duty.

2. An investigative commission was dispatched to the palace, with quite a few people subjected to intense interrogation.

3. We heard that Nakşifend Kalfa had fled to Greece, and not alone. When she was sent out from the palace on the pretext of being ill, she received permission from the Lady Mother to take with her the beautiful young girl Naciye, thereby dragging her into this mess as well. This girl had been assigned to her as a novice for training.

---

50 Here Şakir in a footnote gives the names of those arrested, but both he and Filizten have confused the episode of the would-be veiled intruders—which occurred in December 1876—with the Cleanthi Scalieri conspiracy, which ended in July 1878 (Uzunçarşılı 1944 "Kaçırmak," 592–595). Thus the three repercussions that Filizten is about to mention, including the flight of the kalfa Nakşifend to Greece, actually occurred some eighteen months later than the "Veiled Intruders" episode she has just described.

And so, isn't it obvious? Everything was turning out against us. Our Prince's supporters thought they would help him, but instead they ended up hurting him. Everything that happened only served to tighten the noose around the palace. Matters finally got so bad that an order went out to the officials posted at the palace, warning them, "On no account will you have any personal contact with the former Sultan, nor will you exchange so much as one word with any of the kalfas." Things continued in this way until the Ali Suavi incident.[51]

Much has been written about this incident, so I will not say anything about the events that transpired outside the palace. I shall confine myself to relating how this frightful incident played itself out within the harem, hoping thereby to assist in exposing the truth about a number of points that heretofore have been distorted.

As to how the event was organized outside the palace, I have no idea. But I do know that I do not encounter the names of the real authors of the event among the books and articles describing the incident. Let me begin by saying that the real organizers of the incident were not just any so-and-so's, but in fact Prince Kemaleddin himself, joined by Prince Süleyman, Princess Seniha, Princess Fatma, and Damad Mahmud Pasha, the father of Prince Sabaheddin.[52] Proof of this lies in the important revelation confided in us by Prince Kemaleddin's consort, the mother of Princess Münire.[53] "The day before the incident took place," she said, "the Prince [Kemaleddin] was overcome with anxiety and alarm. Of course I noticed his most unusual agitation, and I asked what was bothering him so. At first I couldn't get him to tell me, but finally I absolutely insisted on knowing, so at last the Prince swore me to secrecy and said, 'Tomorrow we're going to put Brother back on the throne.' The next day that bloody incident happened, without achieving the slightest measure of success. This failure upset the Prince terribly. That day and night he wept bitter tears. He couldn't stop weeping."

After he revealed this to her, let me tell you, the plan was kept completely secret; not even our master was made aware of what was afoot. However, this much did happen, that some of our harem eunuchs had girded their strapped,

---

51 On 20 May 1878, the prolific author, journalist, and teacher Ali Suavi led some 250 refugees from the recent Russo-Ottoman War in an assault on Çırağan Palace with the presumed objective of restoring Murad to the throne. As Ali Suavi was killed in the unsuccessful attack, his motives and methods remain largely conjectural.
52 Mahmud Celâleddin Pasha, husband of Princess Seniha.
53 Fatma Sezadil, 1856?–1943, only consort of Prince Kemaleddin and mother of his one child, Princess Münire.

silver-worked ceremonial swords about their waists, and when the refugees stormed the palace these eunuchs led them in. I wonder if they knew that something was going to happen and were ready for it. Or did they put on their swords just at the moment the refugees flooded the palace, out of hope that something good was about to happen—is this how they were ensnared in that grisly event? I cannot answer either question, because the bodies of those harem eunuchs, who cast themselves into that reckless operation before it turned bloody, were swept away without a trace. They were buried in the same pit as the refugees and there they disappeared from this earth.

As for how the incident began, I shall never forget; it was a Monday, and terribly hot. We had gotten up early, washed our master's clothing, and hung it out to dry in the garden. Toward noontime, the customary hour for the midday meal at the palace, our master's luncheon was sent to his apartments on the upper floor. We ourselves had just sat down to lunch when we heard a commotion on the seaward side of the palace. A few of the girls wondered what it was so they went to the windows to investigate. "Some workmen have gone the wrong way," they said. "They've come off a barge into the palace garden."[54] But as they were speaking these words, the uproar suddenly increased. We heard the girls at the window crying out in agitation, "Oh, no . . . the workmen are fighting with the guards!"

At that point guns began to go off. One of the girls screamed, "They're killing people!" That's when pandemonium began to break out. From everywhere we heard people shouting, "The palace is under attack!" while the men we had thought were workers were running hither and yon, shouting to one another in some unintelligible language.

We all dropped our forks and spoons but had no idea what to do. Frightened, we gathered round the senior kalfas. The Lady Mother had thrown a chair scarf over her head; we could hear her shouts echoing down the halls, "Quickly, bolt the doors! Protect my son!"

Prince Salâheddin's apartments were on the ground floor. One could hear the attackers there in his apartments, as they had crawled in through the windows. At the same time some men appeared at the foot of the grand staircase in the central hallway on the ground floor. A man was running up the stairs in front of them, shouting in agitation, "Ladies, don't be alarmed!

54 At that time a large wall was under construction behind the palace, along the road. Quite a few refugees from Rumelia were working on this site, so that when the palace girls saw men wearing the same clothing, they assumed they were the workers on the construction project. [Ş]

Don't be frightened! We will do you no harm! And where is our Prince? Where is our Prince, Sultan Murad? We have come to rescue him!"

Meanwhile the clamor on the ground floor increased dramatically. A group of men with disheveled turbans draped about their heads and sashes about their waists, in baggy breeches, and grasping weapons, filled the hall at the foot of the stairs. They were shouting, "Long live Sultan Murad!" which mixed with the wailing of the frightened palace staff to turn the palace into complete bedlam. The place was a swarming beehive.

Some of our harem eunuchs had put on their swords over their uniforms and were walking around in the midst of that mob scene. We heard cries of "Make way, make way!" and Prince Salâheddin came in through the path that the harem eunuchs cleared for him. He was pale as a ghost. As he passed us he murmured, "Don't be alarmed, girls," and went straight to our master's apartments. Since the incident began our master had frozen in place, like a stone, but when he saw his son he said, "My dear Prince—what is happening to us?" Prince Salâheddin answered him with agitation and alarm in his voice, "They're asking for Your Majesty. They've come to offer you their allegiance."

This short exchange followed:

"Who are these people?"

"I don't know, Sir. They're all dressed like refugees."

"But men like that wouldn't think of coming here and offering allegiance. Don't they have a leader?"

"One or two of them seem reasonably perceptive. In fact they sent me to see you."

"Let me speak with these men."

Prince Salâheddin hurried out and summoned with his hand the men waiting at the foot of the stairs. These men had given their reassurances to the palace staff there. In the meanwhile our master had slowly come out of his apartments with the Lady Mother at his side and stood facing them. As soon as the men saw our master they ran over to him and threw themselves at his feet, then got up and gathered all around him. Our master spoke in a loud voice. We heard the following exchange:

"What have you done with my brother?"

"Sire, nothing's been done with him yet. First we've come to swear allegiance to Your Majesty, then we're going to depose him."

In the meanwhile the clamor downstairs was steadily increasing as the throng of refugees advanced in a frightening mass toward the grand salon. The men surrounding our master ushered him toward the salon, at which the Lady Mother called out, "Where are you taking my son?" A man with a thin beard, who had grasped our master by his right arm, answered her, "Princess, do not be alarmed. We're going to offer our allegiance here, then take him out to the battleship *Mesudiye* anchored offshore and fire the guns to announce his accession."

The Lady Mother objected, "No, do not take my son out of the palace. In no way do I give permission for this. Something will happen to him in all the uproar." But the two men who had taken our master by his arms were not listening to her, and were nearly dragging him away.

At that moment we noticed a large man standing in front of the doorway to the stairs leading to the middle floor. His uniform bore the epaulets of a pasha. He was leaning on the cudgel in his hand and almost seemed to be waiting in ambush. Later we learned this was Hacı Hasan Pasha, the Beşiktaş police prefect.[55] Hasan Pasha was standing there almost inconspicuously, with an armed policeman behind him, and stayed that way until our master passed by him, not budging from his spot. But as soon as our master had passed, suddenly he whirled around and the cudgel was in the air as he began thrashing the man with the scraggly black beard at our master's right arm. He beat the back of the man's head so hard that the man dropped face down onto the floor before he could even utter a sound.

Our master let out a cry and stepped back, leaving the man at his left exposed. This man crouched down as though he were about to lunge at

55 Hasan Pasha was not at that time the Beşiktaş police prefect. He had recently returned wounded from the front [in the war with Russia], and at the time of the Ali Suavi incident was sitting with friends in front of the café in Beşiktaş across from the clock tower. First they heard the din coming from the direction of Çırağan Palace, then some men came running from that direction yelling, "Refugee workers are attacking Çırağan Palace." At this, Hasan Pasha hurried to the palace, where at the gates he found only a gatekeeper by the name of Zeybek Mehmed. He then saw an armed policeman and ordered him to follow him, while he demanded of the gatekeeper what was going on inside. Paralyzed with fear, Zeybek Mehmed answered him, "Go on in and you'll see what's happening." Since he had no weapon with him, Hasan Pasha took the gatekeeper's cudgel and went inside, accompanied only by that single policeman, and told the gatekeeper, "Run to the police station and tell them what's happening. Tell them to bring troops." With that he went into the palace. [Ş]

Hasan Pasha (?–1905), police official and security chief of the Beşiktaş district of Istanbul, which included Yıldız and Çırağan Palaces within its boundaries, was fiercely loyal to Sultan Abdülhamid. Illiterate, he signed his name with the numbers 7 and 8 (in Ottoman VΛ), which gave rise to his nickname, "7-8 Hasan Pasha."

Although Ziya Şakir states in this note that Hasan Pasha was not the prefect of police of Beşiktaş at the time of the Ali Suavi Incident, other evidence, including his own reports, indicate that he did indeed occupy the post at the time. Uzunçarşılı 1944 "Ali," 82n1.

Hasan Pasha, but Hasan Pasha's cudgel came down on him like a bolt of lightning and he, too, collapsed on the floor. The man tried to get up but a second blow of the stick split open his head.[56]

Our master stood there by himself, leaning against the wall out of fright. The refugees fell upon Hasan Pasha with their large knives, and Hasan Pasha shouted to the policeman, "Shoot them!" But the policeman just froze in fright, so Hasan Pasha grabbed the policeman's shotgun and started to shoot at the refugees himself, driving some of them back with the repeating fire of the gun.[57]

At this point some of the more courageous palace girls ran over to our master and surrounded him, putting themselves right in the midst of the refugees. Rifles started going off—the troops had arrived. Singly and in pairs, the refugees began dropping to the floor or running here and there, shouting frightfully. Others fell upon the soldiers, trying to wrest the weapons from their hands. A jumble of men, all fighting with one other, surged up to where our master was standing, and one man armed with a bayoneted rifle pushed his way between the girls and lunged at our master. But the young kalfa by the name of Ruşen, the Lady Mother's pantrywoman, threw her strong and burly body at this man and knocked him to the floor on his back, then showed great courage by wrenching the rifle from his hands during a scuffle that slashed our master's tall bootleg. Afterwards, rather than turn the rifle over to the government authorities, Ruşen Kalfa hung the rifle on the wall of her room and there it stayed until the day she died.

Everything descended into anarchy after that. A hail of bullets flew over our heads there in that narrow space. It was horrible. The Lady Mother was swaying her head and moaning "My son, my son . . . girls, for God's sake get my son out of here." Hasan Pasha stopped fighting with the refugees when the troops arrived, and hurried over to our master. The girls started to tug our master away. They led him off and finally hid him in the place called the Stone Room, which was the small treasury vault in the palace where valuable things were stored. The two kalfas Nazcemal and Dilber Sima went inside the Stone Room with our master and bolted the iron door behind them.

This entire incident lasted no longer than fifteen or twenty minutes, after which the whole place fell silent. Some of the refugees were lying on the floor, others had hidden themselves here and there. But the quiet was short-lived;

---

56 The first man killed by the blow of the cudgel was Ali Suavi; the second man killed in the same manner was an army deserter by the name of Nişli Salih. [Ş]

57 At that time the police were using Winchester double-barreled shotguns, which fired sixteen shells. [Ş]

in fact it proved to be only the first act. After some minutes we could hear the sound of trumpets from outside, signaling another assault on the palace by troops. The trumpets and the military assault threw us into a state of panic. For the second time people began shouting and screaming on all sides.

The Lady Mother had hidden herself between two doors in the privy opposite the Stone Room. Hasan Pasha and others in the Long Hall between the harem and the men's quarters were shouting, "Do not be alarmed—the army troops are here," in order to calm the anxiety that had overwhelmed us for the second time.

That's when the second stage of the attack began. The army troops spread out all over, searching every nook and cranny for men who had hidden themselves. The refugees had fled to all parts of the palace, even into the girls' rooms in the harem, while some were so frightened they had thrown themselves into the Bosphorus. The army troops fired at them as well, blotching the surface of the sea with patches of blood. Those caught inside fell victim to bayonets and rifle butts. Still others behaved intelligently, throwing themselves at the feet of the girls and the kalfas and pleading, "For the love of God, hide us." Some of the more courageous kalfas hid them for days (I'll speak more of them shortly).

At length, things settled down. A group of pashas showed up from Yıldız, among them Sultan Hamid's brother-in-law Hüseyin Pasha,[58] the Senior Chamberlain Nâfiz Pasha, the commander of the Imperial Corps of Music Necib Pasha, and Kâzım Pasha, brother of Sultan Hamid's Senior Consort Nazikeda Kadınefendi, as well as a number of pashas known to the kalfas. The pashas gave orders to gather up the corpses lying about the halls and corridors in pools of blood, carry them out into the courtyard, and search them thoroughly.

We watched the searching from our windows, and were amazed, because most of them turned out not to be refugees at all. They were wearing all sorts of unexpected things like silk-cotton blend shirts such as men in the city wear, a refugee's gathered knee breeches pulled over clean underclothing, and multicolored, heavy overblouses. The delegation of pashas lingered most of all over one corpse in particular, examining it in great detail, for it seems that on his European-style shirt underneath the refugee's overblouse, as well as along the band of his underclothing, also in European style, they discovered a monogram composed of the initials "A. S." in Latin letters.

---

58 As Abdülhamid did not have a brother-in-law of this name, most likely the reference is to Hüseyin Hüsnü Pasha (d. 1899), husband of his first cousin Princess Seniye.

To be sure, even we had noticed this man right in the opening moments of the incident, for he had been one of the first to enter the palace. As I described earlier, he and one or two companions had first come to the foot of the stairs to the middle floor and waited there for our master in the long corridor between the doorways separating the harem and the men's quarters. When our master appeared he spoke to him, took him by the arm and tried to pull him into the grand salon, but at that moment he was knocked to the floor by the blow from Hasan Pasha's cudgel. None of us realized at that point that this man was not a refugee; later we learned that apparently he was Ali Suavi.

Once the corpses had been carried off, the time had come to bring our master out of the Stone Room.

The Lady Mother reappeared after the soldiers and pashas arrived, this time seized by another concern. "Are they going to think we had something to do with those refugees attacking the palace?" she worried, "And so maybe they'll do something to my son?" She sent word to the Stone Room that they were not to allow our master out all at once.

The pashas were searching for our master but couldn't find him. They asked the kalfas but only got the answer, "We don't know." Finally, Hasan Pasha, who had been busy elsewhere, came by and told them, "My good fellows, don't worry, I saw kalfas putting him into this room," pointing out the Stone Room. The pashas knocked on the door, but not a sound came out. At length they put a ladder up to the windows along the rear, climbed up and looked inside. "They're in here," they called out.

Again the pashas knocked on the door. They pleaded with him to open the door, reassuring him there was nothing more to fear, but still they couldn't get him to open it. Finally they decided to break the door down and brought in shovels and axes and iron crowbars. That's when the Lady Mother and some old kalfas intervened. "For mercy's sake, don't do it," they pleaded. "You know something bad once happened to him from fright. He's probably frightened now, and something might happen to him. Leave it to us, we'll get the door open. You stand off to the side—don't let him see there are a lot of people here."

The Lady Mother went up to the door and tried to reassure him: "Son, it's I. Have them open the door now. There's nothing to be afraid of any more." With that, the iron bolts inside the door drew back and the door opened a bit to reveal first the withered old visage of Nazcemal Kalfa. The door opened slowly and the kalfas helped our master out of the room by the arms. No doubt from fear, our master looked completely overwhelmed, much as he had during his first illness. His face was as sallow as a lemon, his eyes darted about fearfully. When he saw the pashas, he froze on the spot and leaned against the door. Nafiz Pasha and Necib Pasha performed a floor *temenna*, then slowly approached him and reassured him with gentle words: "We're very glad that is over, Sir. Please don't worry about anything. There's nothing to be concerned about now. Do please come into the grand salon." They took him by the arms and helped him toward the room.

At that moment the sound of a bugle blared through the palace and made all of us jump with fright. Our master looked ready to bolt, but the bugle was sounding the call to present arms. All the soldiers had lined up at attention. Our master passed through the soldiers standing there at attention and entered the grand salon, where the equerries and stewards gathered round him and assured him that he was no longer in any danger.

Even though the danger had passed, everyone was still on edge. Once he entered the grand salon our master sat down, looked around, and asked, "Where is the Prince?" Prince Salâheddin was nearby and went over to his father when he asked for him, consoling his father with the appropriate words.

Obviously Sultan Hamid could no longer risk leaving our master in Çırağan Palace. Before long a few aides-de-camp arrived from Yıldız with a number of enclosed carriages. They announced Sultan Hamid's command: "His Majesty is most grieved by the incident that has occurred, and is concerned that some ruthless adventurers may again try to perpetrate such an abominable deed. He has commanded that his imperial brother reside in the Chalet Villa along with such members of his harem entourage as he desires."[59]

The Lady Mother and the consorts had all been so terribly frightened that nobody objected to the Sultan's command. They put our master into one carriage, the Lady Mother and the consorts climbed into the other carriages, and the procession passed over the bridge that connects Çırağan Palace to Yıldız Palace. Soldiers lined the entire route, bayonets at the ready. Not enough carriages had been sent, so a good many of the palace personnel were left to follow the slowly moving carriages on foot.

And that's how we came to the Chalet Villa. We went in, completely drained. What with the sheer terror and uproar we had lived through that day, our exhaustion left us in a state of utter collapse.

---

59 Murad and his entourage were actually confined in the Malta Pavilion. The Chalet Villa was not built until 1880. Uzunçarşılı 1946 "Tedâvîsine," 320n6.

We stayed in the Chalet Villa precisely fifteen days. The building was completely surrounded by guards and troops armed with bayoneted rifles. Several times each day Sultan Hamid sent men over to convey his greetings to our master and to inquire whether he had any requests. We assumed he himself would come over one day to pay a call and ask for details about the incident, but he never did. He obtained the information he wanted just by sending over men who asked very brief questions.

Our return to Çırağan was somber. The girls came running to the door to greet us, all in tears. The first words our master spoke in the central hall of the harem were, "Kalfas, are all of you here? Is any one of you missing?" All the young and old kalfas answered together, "We're all here, no one is missing." "Oh, I'm glad," he said. "I was afraid they were going to remove some of you from the palace." With that he went straight to his apartments.[60]

That night every room in the harem was awash with joy. We were all making the rounds from room to room, filling each other in on what had happened while we were apart. According to the kalfas who had stayed at Çırağan, two days earlier a British warship had anchored off the palace and turned its guns toward Yıldız. The captain said, "Either you send Sultan Murad back to Çırağan right away or I'll bombard Yıldız Palace." This had frightened Sultan Hamid so much that he sent our master back to Çırağan.[61]

What intrigued us the most, those of us who had just returned from the Chalet Villa, was the story of the men hidden away in various places by the palace attendants after the grisly incident that had taken place. According to the rumors making the rounds, our girls had been incredibly daring. They had shown themselves to be heroes by secluding several men who survived the incident and then getting them out of the palace.

As one example, two young city boys, dressed as refugees, had dashed into Prince Salâheddin's apartments when the army troops showed up and that ghastly struggle began. There they ran into the Prince's senior kalfa, Tirendaz. They threw themselves at her feet and begged her to save them. Tirendaz, a completely fearless and courageous woman, maintained her

---

60 Upon his return from the Malta Pavilion, Murad and his mother took up residence in the Harem Building on the grounds of Çırağan—immediately south of the palace, separated from it by a garden—and not in the main building itself, where the ex-monarch and his mother had first been settled immediately after his deposal. It was in this Harem Building, today the Beşiktaş Girls School, that Murad lived out the remainder of his life. Akbayar 1998, 75.

61 Nothing of the kind transpired. No doubt the arrival of the warship coincided with Sultan Murad's return to Çırağan merely by chance. [Ş]

composure.[62] She simply said, "Follow me" and locked them both in the soap pantry.

After a while the commotion died down and everything became still again—except that a relentless search had begun. They were turning over everything, even going through wardrobes, and the kalfa realized it was dangerous to leave those two youths where they were. She took them out of there and up to the steam bath above the Prince's apartments, hid them in the stokehold, and piled logs in front of them. When the searchers reached the steam bath and the stokehold, they saw the logs piled up like that and thought nothing of it, so they left.

Afterwards, however, the palace came under such rigorous and constant guard that there was no way they could sneak those two lads out. The kalfa Şemsi Felek began to get nervous: "What if those men start a fire and burn down the palace with us in it?" she said. "I'm going to tell someone." But Tirendaz Kalfa and a couple of other kalfas who were in on the secret stopped her in her tracks. "If you pull a rotten stunt like that," they threatened, "we'll take care of you all right."

Tirendaz said that a little while after she hid them in the stokehold, she crept up to the door of the stokehold and put her ear to it, just out of curiosity as to what they were saying. She heard one of the young men utter, "Last night my mother came into my room and there I was in that really soft bed, under the quilt, and she pulled the blankets over me so that I wouldn't be cold. Now look where I am tonight, stuck in the corner of a stokehold."[63] This story she retold to her companions, weeping as she came up to them.

They brought the two young men out of the stokehold once the searches had come to an end. For ten days they hid them in a more comfortable place, then one night in the wee hours just before dawn they sneaked them out through the water pipes leading through the hill behind Çırağan to Kılıç Ali.

An iron cordon truly tightened around the palace after the Ali Suavi incident. Double guards were posted along both the land and the sea approaches to the palace. The outer gates were entirely closed off, leaving only a side gate that was placed under the surveillance of Albanian armed sentries dis-

---

62 This was the kalfa who saw to it that Prince Salâheddin escaped to the cruiser *Mesudiye* at the height of the fracas. [Ş]

63 The passage related here by the *gözde* is important as it constitutes the most compelling evidence that the perpetrators of the attack on Çırağan Palace were not entirely refugees but rather included as well some intellectuals among the young people of the city. [Ş]

patched from Yıldız. The number of persons passing in and out of this gate was restricted.

All told, of the male staff in service at the palace hardly anyone remained. Even some of our master's longtime Privy Staff who had voluntarily remained in his service were removed from the palace. The immense building came to resemble an old mill in which the water had dried up and the customers gone elsewhere. No one could enter the palace aside from people on official business from Yıldız or physicians dispatched with an imperial warrant in hand. Harem eunuchs who had to go into town on important and unavoidable business, and even gardeners, found themselves trailed closely by civil police, gendarmes, and palace spies.

After some time they even reduced the number of doctors sent to look after us, with the task entrusted exclusively to Rıza Pasha. But he was young, and before long rumors about him began to circulate among the kalfas, which led the Lady Mother to request Sultan Hamid to assign a new doctor. With that the sovereign stopped sending Rıza Pasha and instead reappointed our former physician Rifat Pasha. Rifat Pasha was a most conscientious and good-hearted man. He treated all of us with diligence and responsibility, both our master and ourselves, and at the same time displayed the utmost propriety towards the youngest of the kalfas.

One day he took Prince Salâheddin aside and said to him, "Your Highness, I'm an old man. Something may happen to me, or perhaps His Majesty will see fit to send someone else in my place. Not every physician will treat you with the same concern and compassion as have I. Your father especially needs to be looked after carefully, but not everyone is trustworthy. This is why I propose that you let me teach you a bit about medicine. One day you may profit from it if you find yourself in a serious situation."

Prince Salâheddin gladly accepted his proposal. The two of them decided to say that Prince Salâheddin was suffering from some illness. Rifat Pasha then began to come to the palace frequently, first treating whoever might really be sick before shutting himself up in a room with Prince Salâheddin and working with him. Rifat Pasha would dictate the important things to Prince Salâheddin, who wrote them down and then sat and memorized them at night. The Prince's study of medicine in this way proved to be quite useful, for the day came when he even treated our master himself.

Some two years passed in this way, and then Resan Hanım, one of our master's *ikbals*, gave birth to Princess Fatma. This brought about a change in daily life at the palace, which otherwise was the same from one day to the next.

Once Resan Hanım began her labor pains, word was sent to Yıldız requesting a midwife. Sultan Hamid dispatched Hayriye Hanım, who bore the title, "Midwife to the Imperial House." Hayriye Hanım was devoted to our master and held him in deep respect, so she was delighted to be sent to the palace and see him again. When she arrived she beseeched both the Lady Mother and our master's kalfas, "Please let me see our dear boy, if only for a moment." Now, since the Ali Suavi incident our master had been instructed many times that no one other than his harem people should come face to face with him. In fact the personnel in the male quarters of the palace had received orders to this effect on any number of occasions. For this reason our master was reluctant to receive the midwife Hayriye Hanım.

But at length the means was found to resolve the dilemma, as it was decided to grant the midwife permission to see our master on the pretext that she would congratulate him on the birth of his child, as was the custom. Resan Hanım gave birth to the Princess after some eight or ten hours of labor. The midwife wrapped the tiny Princess in swaddling clothes and took her to our master's apartments where the two of them were admitted to his presence. There she joyfully presented the Princess to him and expressed her delight at seeing him. Our master was equally delighted to see the midwife and they exchanged all kinds of pleasantries, but then he warned her, "Don't tell anyone outside the palace that you spoke with me, or they'll make things unpleasant for you."

The following conversation also passed between our master and the midwife:

"I haven't seen my sister Princess Fatma for years and haven't heard a thing about her health. How is she, I wonder, do you know?"

"I haven't seen her for quite some time, Sir, but I understand that she is in excellent health, I'm glad to say."

"I'm so very fond of her. Indeed, I do believe I'm going to name this tiny princess Fatma, in her honor. She'd be pleased, if she heard about it. Perhaps you might find some way to let her know, if at all possible?"

"There's no need to try to find a way, Sir—I shall go myself and tell her personally."

"But how will you find a way into her villa? Isn't it forbidden?"

"Indeed it is, Sir, it's quite a crime. But since you wish it, Sir, I shall get into that villa, come what may."

Our master tried to talk the midwife out of it, but she had set her mind on going and was not to be dissuaded. "In fact," she said, "I'll find some pretext to go tomorrow or the day after. So the next time I come to see Her

Highness the tiny little Princess, I'll even bring our master a message in response."

Our master wanted to shower the midwife with all kinds of gifts and favors, but she wouldn't accept them. "Before I came down here, His Majesty summoned me and gave me a strict order, 'Do not accept anything from my brother,'" she said. "So please forgive me, I couldn't accept so much as a needle."

Her work finished, the midwife departed. Three or four days later she came back in order to look after the little Princess, but this time she could not meet with our master personally so she had the message relayed to him that she had visited in person with Princess Fatma, who sent her greetings and her best regards to him. The most noteworthy part of all this was the midwife's story of the ruse she devised to gain entry to Princess Fatma's villa. Here is how the vivacious and clever midwife described it.

The day after she returned home from the palace after attending to the birth of Princess Fatma, she had one of her servants' old overgarments torn into tatters, and had patches sewn onto it here and there, so that it truly looked like the overgarment a beggar woman would wear. She set straight off for Baltalimanı in this tattered old rag with a thick and faded veil about her face. There she started to wander about, begging bread or money here and there so as not to attract the attention of detectives thereabouts. When darkness fell she slowly started to approach the doorway of the villa's harem.

The detectives and guards began to shoo her away, but by pleading, "Please Sirs, let me have some coins—let me have something hot to eat," she got them to take pity on her. Nothing about a beggar woman aroused their suspicions, so they let her go on up to the door. She knocked, and the harem eunuch who opened the door gave her some coins, but then she said, "Oh no, my good Sir, I'm not the kind of beggar to be put off with a few coins! I want to receive alms from the Senior Eunuch personally and say a prayer for him so that God will bless your Princess and Pasha. Now go tell the Senior Eunuch!"

This amused the eunuch, who went and informed the Senior Eunuch. There is a custom in the palaces that if someone wants to say a prayer for princesses or princes or imperial sons-in-law, or to swear an oath in their presence, they must be allowed to do so. The Senior Eunuch was furious at this beggar woman who had summoned him to the doorway, but there was no way he could not come. He made his way grumbling, "Woman, what do you mean making me come to the door, old as I am? Here's some money— now off with you," and pulled a silver coin from his pocket. "There—now be on your way."

As the midwife bowed to kiss the hem of his robe, she whispered quickly, "I come from Çırağan." Astounded, the Senior Eunuch then began to bark orders. "This poor woman, she can barely stand on her two feet she's so hungry! Eunuchs, take this woman inside and give her plenty to eat! One of you run in and announce she's here. Bring some old robes from the kalfas!"

The eunuchs wasted no time ushering the midwife in and finding her a place to sit, serving her plenty to eat and drink. The midwife turned her back to the eunuchs, as if she were embarrassed for them to see her, and pretended to eat.

Meanwhile the Senior Eunuch hurried in to inform Princess Fatma, who grasped the situation immediately. "Most certainly she's from my brother. He must be sending me news about something important. Bring her to me, but don't let anyone get wind of it."

With that the Senior Eunuch returned to the midwife and announced, "Woman, eat quickly. The kalfas have taken pity on you and want to give you some things." He led her inside. No sooner had she entered the central hall of the harem than she threw off the veil from her face and tossed aside the tattered scarf. Needless to say the Senior Eunuch and the kalfas all recognized her. They stood there astounded and exclaimed, "My God, it's the midwife! What is this disguise?" and gathered round her.

Princess Fatma was delighted to see her and placed herself entirely in her confidence. That night they kept her there, talking till dawn. The midwife told many things about Çırağan Palace, including the news that our master had named his new daughter Fatma. Princess Fatma had been under the impression that our master was still ill and in her grief had not allowed the curtains in her rooms to be drawn completely back. But when she heard he had completely returned to good health she cried, "Thank God I've received good news about my brother. Until this moment the world has been a prison for me, but now I'm happy again. Girls, throw back those curtains!" She showered gifts and favors upon the midwife and asked her to convey to our master her greetings, her love, and her delight.

As dawn was breaking they arranged matters at the doorway and somehow got the phony beggar out of the villa. Everything reached the ears of our master, who of course was tremendously pleased and sent his greetings and thanks to the midwife for the courage and loyalty she had shown.

Yet despite all precautions, nothing was being kept secret. In due time Sultan Hamid was definitely learning of these undercover communications established by Çırağan Palace. For this reason the measures designed to imprison us were increasing day by day. The water conduits were completely walled in, with the result that a portion of the hitherto ample water supply into the palace was cut off. At the same time some of the windows and balcony doors facing the Bosphorus were sealed so they wouldn't open. Not so much as a bird could be made to fly over Çırağan Palace from the landward side, while on the seaward side all the caiques, boats, and steamships kept a wide berth as they passed.

THE TERRIBLE END OF VANLI MEHMED

Mehmed Ağa, who bore the title "Palace Administrator," inflicted every possible act of tyranny upon us.

One day while he was walking through the garden between two apartments, his eye fell upon a scrap of paper. He decided this must be a letter someone had tossed over the wall from the street. Exposed to the rain and sun as it had been, nothing was legible on the paper except for the signature, "Hasan." Mehmed Ağa immediately questioned each of the eunuchs and tray bearers, showing them the paper, but of course all of them said they didn't know whose it was and that it had nothing to do with them.

At length one of the tray bearers by the name of Hasan perhaps smiled or acted suspiciously in some way, but whatever he did, he attracted the attention of Mehmed Ağa, who grabbed him by the collar and started to beat him and shout, "This is your letter, isn't it? Come on, let's have it—what were you writing? And to whom?" He broke nearly every bone in the poor man's body but wasn't satisfied with that and hung the poor wretch upside down by his ankles. The harem eunuchs told us this, which reduced us all to tears.

As time went on Mehmed Ağa became impossible, practically behaving like an independent monarch in the palace. He would beat, break, slash, and cut, but no one dared say anything out of fear of the Senior Equerry Cevher Ağa.

It was the custom that at set times the palace tray bearers brought in the meal trays as far as the stone threshold of the harem, accompanied by the harem eunuchs. Mehmed Ağa forbade even this. "Meal trays will be left at the middle door," he said. "The girls can fetch them from there." And so henceforth the tray bearers left the meal trays there, with the girls picking them up once the servants had gone. But when the girls picked up the food Mehmed Ağa was sure to be there, perpetrating all kinds of vile and disgraceful acts.

This situation insulted the dignity and pride of us all. At length we complained to the Lady Mother. "We will not fetch this food and we will not eat it," we said. "We'd rather starve to death than fetch food and eat it under these conditions." The Lady Mother immediately sent for Cevher Ağa and explained the situation. Permission was granted for the tray bearers to bring the meal trays inside as far as the door of the harem, on condition that they not catch a glimpse of our master.

One day they were bringing the meal trays inside, with the tray bearers lined up one behind the other. Mehmed Ağa was in the lead. The harem eunuchs were preceding them, calling out, "By your leave, by your leave." At just that moment our master was coming back into the palace from the inner garden. Suddenly the tray bearers stood face to face with our master. They had no idea what to do. Some of the poor men took such fright that they looked ready to heave the great trays off their heads and flee in a panic. Just then Mehmed Ağa's evil and arrogant voice rang out, "About face, turn to your rear." The encounter annoyed our master greatly, and he sprinted inside.

After the meal trays were finally delivered to the harem and taken away again, Mehmed Ağa assembled all the tray bearers and warned them, "If any of you tell anyone that you saw Prince Murad, I will have you all banished to the deserts of Fezzan. But I won't just banish you, that's not enough. I'll see that you starve on the way, and writhe under the lash of the whip."

On another day, a gooseherd was driving a flock of geese down the street behind the palace. Something startled the geese and they took to the air, some of them flying over the wall and landing in the palace garden. Once they spotted the great pool there they jumped in and started fluttering their wings and paddling merrily about. When Mehmed Ağa saw this he rushed out to the street, baton in hand, and beat the daylights out of the poor goose-herd. Then he bound up the poor wretch's hands behind his back and hus-tled him off to the Beşiktaş police station, muttering, "This rogue sent his geese into the garden on purpose! What's he after, I'd like to know? We'll have the police get it out of him."

Would this be the end of the incident? No. Mehmed Ağa went inside, picked out a long stick, jumped in amongst those geese fluttering their wings so gaily, and set about bludgeoning them all to death. And was that all? No, there's more. First he searched under the geese's wings and between their feathers, but he didn't stop there, he had those poor birds' bellies split open one by one, inspected each to see if there were some note in their stomachs or throats, and then finally had them all tossed into the sea.

We suffered everything imaginable from this man. As we heard later on, things even reached the point that he stole and then sold off the preserved meats and jams and other foods that traditionally were sent to each of us in jars on the Festival of Offerings.

Now I shall tell you of a most strange episode. If you like you can laugh and shrug it off, or if you prefer, you can attribute it to the intervention of a spiritual power.

Those of us in palace service had opened our hands and prayed to God, beseeching Him to bring something down upon this blackguard so he would wallow in his own troubles and leave us alone. Not much later, a fly flew into this scoundrel's ear. Well, he completely forgot about us as he sought out doctor after doctor outside the palace, not even coming near the palace for days on end. Then one day the harem eunuchs brought us good news. It seems not one of those doctors could get the fly out of his ear. Things were so bad he was hurling himself about, banging his head against the walls. After some days of this an artery broke in his brain and he died a terrible death.

Now, no one should rejoice at someone's death, but I cannot fib: the day we heard of that man's death we were celebrating in our rooms as if there were a wedding or a holiday.

The man who replaced him was harmless and treated us justly, but then thanks to Cevher Ağa, Beşir Ağa was appointed to the post. Beşir Ağa had come to the palace a short time after the Ali Suavi incident. At first he served as Senior Eunuch, a post without much authority, but when he was appointed Palace Administrator his attitude changed—so much so that we almost rued the loss of Mehmed Ağa. He gave us no respite, upbraiding us mercilessly at the slightest opportunity.

One day, one of the younger girls was looking through the peephole in the door when her eye met that of Beşir Ağa. This blew up into a huge incident, with all kinds of explanations explored and truly preposterous reasons for it put forth. Even Sultan Hamid's suspicions were finally aroused based on the absurd fabrication that Prince Murad was trying to escape and this little girl was sent to observe whether anyone was in the anteroom.

And so for some days the palace again underwent a veritable siege of oppression and cross-questioning. A few days after this the doorways and halls rang with the voices of the harem eunuchs calling, "By your leave! By your leave!" A number of craftsmen and workmen followed the eunuchs in, carrying on their backs huge doors each made of a solid piece of iron. These craftsmen started to work right away, under close watch, installing these iron doors behind the gilt doors on both the sea and the shore sides of the palace.

Our master grew anxious and fearful when he heard the noise, but once the situation was explained to him he calmed down. After the job was finished and the workmen had gone, our master told his Third Consort, Filistan Kadınefendi,[64] to go and see what they had done. She could barely keep herself from breaking into tears when she saw the great iron doors, but so as not to upset our master she made light of the situation. "The old doors were falling apart," she said, "so they put in new doors because the old ones probably wouldn't have held up if there were another assault." But our master wasn't satisfied with that so he himself went with Filistan Kadınefendi to have a look at the doors. He inspected both of them, then gave out a bittersweet laugh. "Well, Filistan, it's not quite the way you said. They're practically burying us alive."

These doors upset our master greatly. We all knew they were the work of Beşir Ağa, and after that day our hatred of him knew no bounds. We cursed him so much with the words "May God blind this scoundrel" that the phrase became a ritual formula for us.

Now you will smile yet again, but strangely enough God seemed to have heard our prayers, for before long the man developed glaucoma and couldn't see a thing. But he was a devious one, and he tried to hide his condition from everyone. For example, when the kalfas needed things from the bazaar they would write down what they wanted on a piece of paper that customarily went to Beşir Ağa, with a man sent out to the bazaar to make the purchases after he had approved them. But finally the time came when Beşir Ağa could no longer read what was written on the paper, and so the eunuchs, who like us had also lived in dread of his evil ways, began to have a little fun with him. One day Cafer Ağa, the youngest of the eunuchs, danced the çifte telli[65] right in front of him, swaying and undulating his hips. If Beşir Ağa's eyes had seen that, poor Cafer Ağa would have been banished to Medina straightaway!

But Beşir Ağa's woes didn't stop there. He began to behave as though he had lost his mind, so much so that finally they locked him in a room. They say he went so entirely mad that his arms and legs turned bloody because he constantly bit them, until one day they found him dead in that room.

The time has come for me to discuss an important issue. Quite a few articles and books have been written since the proclamation of the Constitution and especially since the deposal of Sultan Hamid.[66] Bundles, sackfuls, even

64 Since Filizten never attained the rank of Third Consort with its corresponding title of *Kadınefendi*, and since the text here refers to Filizten in the third person, here Şakir is clearly quoting one of Filizten's surviving colleagues from Murad's harem. Throughout the text Filizten herself acknowledges the lady Şayan as Third Consort.
65 A evocative dance usually performed by women.
66 In 1908 and 1909 respectively.

boatloads and trainloads of writings have appeared on subjects such as "The Secrets of Yıldız Palace" and "Sultan Hamid's Servants." Now, because I am limiting myself to a certain topic here, I shall neither digress from my topic nor exceed my bounds by either criticizing or endorsing these writings, but I would like to mention one painful truth that concerned all of us, me in particular.

Like someone who memorizes the Quran, I have committed to memory a few lines that appear in these writings. I'll relate them to you here, from memory, altering not so much as a period or a comma. Please listen: "It seems that as a token of personal respect for Sultan Murad, a few young kalfas were placed in a villa. While on the surface of it they were Sultan Murad's kalfas, in truth they served the pleasure of Hacı Hasan Pasha and indeed, it was he who deflowered them."

Had these lines appeared in some worthless little book, or in the columns of a newspaper destined to be torn up and thrown away within a few days' time, I would see no need to dwell on this subject. Unfortunately, however, these lines appeared in a monumental work of three volumes concerning the early years of Sultan Hamid's reign and his personal and political life—a work that future historians might consult as a source in their research. Therein lie the danger and the distress that affect me personally.

Written as it was in the midst of a revolution's turmoil, this book renders considerable service to the cause of constitutional liberty in that it exposes the vileness and corruption of the period of despotism[67] and reveals to the people the inner workings of the palace and the men who served there. However, such a work should adhere unswervingly to the path of truth and refrain from slandering innocent people.

While reading these reminiscences, most likely you have realized that our master was not alone during the time of his confinement in Çırağan Palace. Some eighty people shared the surroundings of the former ruler under the harem roof, including his mother, his four consorts, his son, his daughters, his *ikbals*, his *gözdes*, his Imperial Kalfas, and his other senior and junior kalfas. Our ranks included young and lovely, even beautiful, girls, but not a single one of them ever had her honor threatened or her good name stained in the slightest way.

We came to Çırağan Palace pure at heart, and for twenty-eight years we bowed our heads to the bitter destiny decreed for us, bearing it with deep-seated patience and resignation. Throughout these years we remained con-

67 Meaning the reign of Sultan Abdülhamid, 1876–1909.

scious of our duty to serve our master, as is incumbent upon a life in slavery. Apart from him we touched no one, to no individual did we show the hem of our skirts. Having passed through our ordeal lasting twenty-eight years, we exited the palace still pure at heart, free to enjoy the blessings of liberty.

Let us take care not to slander the deceased, who can no longer defend themselves. We only laid eyes on this man named Hacı Hasan Pasha once, and that was during the Ali Suavi incident. After that event Hacı Hasan Pasha never once set foot inside our palace, even though he was charged with security for the palace. In fact he never so much as passed by our windows.

Throughout our twenty-eight years in Çırağan, I cannot recall even the smallest incident of philandering, much less an attack upon a woman's honor. However, I do recall one scene that occurred during the Ali Suavi episode, a scene that we mimicked for years afterward and made us laugh.

It happened just a few minutes after the episode, when the palace was in complete uproar and we were still in a daze. Many of the kalfas were rather immodestly dressed since we were suffering a heat wave on that May day. At that moment, into the harem apartments strode Mehmed Pasha, Sultan Hamid's chief aide-de-camp, just down from Yıldız Palace. The poor man got quite a start when he saw us in that state. There he stood in the middle of the hall, frozen like a statue, leaning on his sword, rolling his eyes from side to side, and twisting his mustache as he looked us over. Although he was right in our midst, right there with us, no one other than a few of the more observant kalfas spotted him in his comical state. At any rate this scene lasted not more than a minute or two.

For years afterward, the kalfas who saw him would mimic him standing there, which triggered our innocent laughter through all those years. Yet really, if truth be told Mehmed Pasha could be forgiven for his actions. In the presence of so many beauties selected from the most ravishing of girls, no hot-blooded young man-about-town could have done otherwise.

HOW DID WE SPEND OUR DAYS?

If I had kept a diary of our twenty-eight years in Çırağan Palace, every day would have resembled the next, for each day of our life passed in absolutely the same manner. Yet every few years something important happened that provided a measure of variety in our otherwise unvarying lives. Even the most trifling event gave us plenty to talk about for days on end.

The best part of the whole business was the peace and quiet that suddenly descended upon us after the tumult and uproar of our previous lives.

Our master's deposal from the throne also put a sudden end to the human ambitions that we harbored at our court. Peace and mildness blanketed us all. Disaster gathered us together like one animate mass in the same spot. All the gossiping and rivalry, all the effort and bother expended on trying to win our master's favor so as to secure a position, simply evaporated into thin air. Everyone behaved more sympathetically, more sincerely, more gently toward one another. Everyone—the senior and junior kalfas, the hazinedars, the *gözdes*, the *ikbals*, the consorts—truly went to great extremes to avoid offending each other.

There is one sorrow that stalks the palaces with its secretly burning flame, and that is jealousy. Every young girl who steps across the palace threshold is caught up in this business as soon as she has pulled herself together a bit and gotten to know her surroundings. She tries to imitate the hazinedars, *gözdes*, and *ikbals* in the way they dress and the way they conduct themselves—trying to understand how they attracted their master's attention—because every girl who is in any way attractive and feels herself capable of achieving it, has as her goal to become a hazinedar, *gözde*, or *ikbal*. Naturally enough, the competitive feelings thus aroused of course create an atmosphere of jealousy in the palaces.

And so our master's withdrawal into seclusion, and in particular the unknown future that lay before him, put an end to these rivalries and extinguished the pointless jealousy and backbiting.

To be sure, our master's conduct contributed significantly to this. By nature and spiritual disposition our master made a practice of treating everyone well. Quite clearly he held no preference for one person over another. He never gave his ladies any cause to complain since he dispensed his fondness equally to everyone, as though he were giving each concubine exactly the same blue bead.

Once we completed our twenty-eight years of confinement in Çırağan and finally tasted freedom, I heard all kinds of stories of things that supposedly happened in our palace—stories that astonished me! I can assure you that most of these stories originated in the imagination of Sultan Hamid's officious spies or of persons who sought to somehow exploit the situation in the palace.

As these tales would have it, after she was confined in Çırağan Palace the Lady Mother hatched scheme after scheme to place her son back on the throne, entirely consumed by her constant state of suspense and ambition. But in order to reach such a judgment, one must first know the lady. To be sure, one cannot deny that the Lady Mother harbored the desire and the ambition to rule, but this lady's character did not lend itself to the arcane intrigues attributed to her. This much-favored and esteemed consort of Sultan Mecid was a gracious and charming lady of medium height, slightly plump, with black eyes and black eyebrows. When all was quiet she was most gentle, but when things were in an uproar she would change on the spot, pulling no punches to defend what she saw as her legitimate rights and position. She wasn't especially brilliant; in fact she was so simple as to be incapable of cunning. But she was easily influenced, which is why a woman as intriguing and deceitful as Nakşifend Kalfa, who could fool the devil himself into putting his sandals on backwards, was able to drag the Lady Mother into a number of intrigues that she launched on behalf of our master, both while he was Heir and after his confinement in Çırağan.

The great weakness of the Lady Mother Şevkefza was the deep devotion she nurtured toward her son. If she had had to sacrifice her life in order to restore the throne to her son, whom she loved madly, she would not for a moment have shrunk from doing so. But she lacked the ability to cook up plans for such an event and bring them to fruition. That is why an all-enveloping stillness descended over the palace once Nakşifend Kalfa had been banished and the Ali Suavi incident was over. From the Lady Mother on down, everyone realized there was nothing for it but to resign themselves to their fate.

Some time later, a couple of girls were sent down from Yıldız Palace on some pretext, for the purpose of extending the fingers of control into every last corner of the harem. How remarkable, then, that not only were they unable to carry out their assigned task to betray us; quite the contrary, after joining our company they soon ended up fellow sufferers with us.

More than anything, Yıldız wanted to find out whether we were in secret contact with the outside world, even though the cordon of security cinched around Çırağan Palace made such an eventuality completely unimaginable.

At this point one might pose the questions, What were the thoughts and inclinations of the ex-Sultan at this point, and Did he harbor the desire and the goal to regain the throne for himself? But of course, to read undivulged thoughts requires the miraculous intercession of a saint, so I cannot say definitively what was percolating in the mind of our master. I do know that our master was always talking about fortune and fate, and that he considered himself a most unlucky man. Time and again he would say things like, "I have no luck. Such is my fate. God has decreed that my younger brother should rule even while I am still alive." From these words one could conclude that our master had abandoned all hope of recovering the throne.

And so each passing day in Çırağan Palace threw water on the flames of ambition in each heart, and veiled every room in the palace with the silence of a convent of reclusive dervishes.

In the beginning all of us lived grouped together in the great palace. The Lady Mother's apartments were on the middle floor and our master occupied the suite of rooms opposite hers. At first the harem girls occupied the rooms on the lower floors, but the dampness there overcame them and gave most of them rheumatism. After that the girls received permission to move into rooms and salons on the top floor, with the kalfas and the girls occupying these rooms and salons in groups of five or six each. Such living conditions were not in accordance with palace custom, to be sure, but our circumstances had reduced us to the point of having to sacrifice quite a few customs.

One of our master's unchanging rituals was to visit his mother every morning to kiss her hand. He would rise from his bed, wash, dress, and eat a light breakfast, then go straight to the Lady Mother's apartments. As soon as they saw him coming the kalfas would inform the Lady Mother, who greeted him at her door and escorted him in, uttering soothing things such as, "Welcome, my son, do come in, you're most welcome." Often mother and son would talk at great length, deciding what things to do in the daily life of the palace. At times these morning visits might even go on until lunchtime, when our master would lunch in his apartments, either alone or perhaps with one or two of his consorts. This unvarying ritual of our master's continued until the death of the Lady Mother.

The Lady Mother remained in solid good health despite her advanced years, until the year 1889 when the swelling on her neck suddenly began to grow and sent her to her bed. Her illness lasted some three months, with periods of intense fever. Dr. Rifat Pasha made every effort to bring her illness under control, but despite all treatment he was not able to save her.

Her lips murmuring over and over again, "My son, my poor Murad, you couldn't have the one thing you hoped for," the former Princess Mother uttered cries of pain that would break one's heart, until finally she closed her eyes for all eternity on life in this world.

His mother's death plunged our master into despair. For days he wouldn't eat and for many nights he could not sleep, so that all of us truly began to fear that his old illness would return.

After the Lady Mother's death our master focused all his love and attention on his children. Prince Salâheddin became his companion in grief, and the two of them passed long hours together reminiscing about bygone days as well as speculating on the future. For some time father and son took an interest in the *Mesnevi*,[68] spending hours reciting verses from that work and taking great pleasure in doing so. Our master also devoted a good deal of attention to the Princesses. All in all he loved his children very much indeed. At the time of our confinement in Çırağan Palace, Prince Salâheddin was some fourteen or fifteen years of age, Princess Hadice around six, and Princess Fehime had just turned two.

Since he loved children so much, most likely our master would have liked many sons and daughters. But remarkably enough, during the reign of Sultan Aziz princes were forbidden to sire more than one child, as it was claimed that the House of Osman was proliferating excessively.[69] Sultan Aziz's mother, Pertevniyal, was behind this. In fact when the lady Şayan—later our master's Third Consort—became pregnant, the Princess Mother Pertevniyal sent over her palace midwife to abort the child. But our master went to Sultan Aziz and begged him, pleaded with him, so that he was able to gain permission for the child to be born outside the palace and raised in secret.[70] At length, when her contractions began the lady Şayan was taken to the home of Dr. Emin Pasha, where Princess Hadice was born. Seven days later the baby was smuggled into the Heir's apartments. There she was raised within a storage space in the room of one of the kalfas, hidden from everyone. Only when our master ascended the throne was Princess Hadice brought out to see the world.[71]

Quite a few children came into this world in Çırağan Palace during the years of gilded imprisonment.

68 The monumental work of didactic mysticism, composed in 26,000 rhymed couplets in Persian by the great mystic Mevlânâ Celâleddin Rumi in the thirteenth century.
69 If Sultan Abdülaziz did restrict princes to one child each (we do know that he was the first monarch in some 260 years to allow princes to have children at all), either he was lax in enforcing the decree or he abandoned it as the years went by, for both his nephews Murad and Abdülhamid sired more than one child during the latter years of Abdülaziz's reign. The issue awaits research.
70 The same conditions under which Sultan Aziz's eldest son, Yusuf İzzedin, had come into the world in 1857. Yıldırım 2006, 40–47.
71 The daughter of Dr. Emin Pasha later declared that both her mother and Şayan Kadın related to her a slightly different version of the episode. When the midwife arrived to abort the child, Prince Murad obtained permission from Sultan Abdülaziz for this child to be aborted (not born) outside the villa. The pregnant lady Şayan was taken to the home of Dr. Emin Pasha for the abortion, but at Prince Murad's request the doctor prepared a harmless concoction for her and sent her back to the Prince's villa, while reporting to the palace that he had administered treatment to induce abortion. Princess Hadice was born in Prince Murad's villa in Kurbağalıdere and indeed the baby was brought up concealed in the villa until Prince Murad ascended the throne. Only after the overthrow of Abdülhamid in 1909 could the lady Şayan convey her thanks, and render assistance, to the doctor's family for the risk he had taken thirty years earlier for her sake. Uzunçarşılı 1944 "Doktor," 334–335.

Murad's granddaughters (left to right): the Princesses Âdile, Rukiye, Behiye, and Atiye. In the center is his great-grandson Prince Vasıb. Circa 1907, after their release from confinement in Çırağan Palace. Photographer unknown.

The lady Resan gave birth to Princess Fatma in the year 1879, and subsequently to Princess Aliye.

Then in turn Prince Salâheddin became the father of several children. In September 1881 His Highness's *gözde* Naziknaz gave birth to Princess Behiye, then in July 1883 this same lady gave birth to Prince Nihad, and in February 1887 she gave birth to Princess Âdile.[72] That year too the *gözde* Gülter gave birth to Princess Safiye, while in 1892 the lady Tevhide gave birth to Princess Emine.[73] In 1895 Prince Fuad was born to the lady Jâlefer. In October 1903, Prince Nihad's son Ali Vasıb came into the world.

Another princess was also born to Prince Salâheddin but she lived only four days. Nonetheless this child's death resulted in quite a major incident in the palace. When she was born, news of her birth was sent to Sultan Hamid as was the custom, and then when she died only four days later once again news was sent to the sovereign along with the request for permission to bury

---

72 Osmanoğlu 1999 lists Princess Âdile's mother as the concubine Tevhide Zatıgül, not Naziknaz.

73 Both these Princesses died young. As to their mothers, the *gözde* Gülter died in 1893, while Tevhide Zatıgül died in 1896.

her with proper ceremonial, in accordance with convention. Yet no response to the request came back from Yıldız, so that the corpse remained in the palace. Again the request was sent to Sultan Hamid. Finally this answer arrived: "Upon my word, what need is there to bury such a tiny infant with grand ceremonial outside the palace? Let the child be buried without fuss somewhere in the palace garden."

Here was a noteworthy answer. Clearly Sultan Hamid did not want the inhabitants of Çırağan Palace to come into contact with the outside world by means of a funeral. But what an inhumane response, to have a child buried right where the parents could see the grave, and so rekindle their heartache each time the mother and father passed by.

A still more tragic event followed this sorrowful episode. Of all the events during our years in Çırağan Palace, this one left the most indelible trace on our hearts.

The death of the little Princess had upset almost all of us terribly, none more so than her father, Prince Salâheddin. But a bottomless wound punctured the heart of her mother, Dilârû.

Dilârû had been one of the slave girls presented by Damad Mahmud Celâleddin Pasha. She was intelligent, sweet, and most of all, acutely sensitive of heart. She possessed a beautiful voice that was so moving, as smooth as the strings of a violin. When she started to sing, no one could fail to be stirred. It was these good qualities that led Prince Salâheddin to select her as one of his *gözdes*. He came to love her deeply, and I can even say that the first pure and true love the Prince enjoyed in life was with Dilârû. He sipped the delicious wine of this love from her hands, drop by drop. Dilârû, too, loved her master with the purest, most immaculate, and most sincere of hearts. She had set her heart on him not with the natural affection a purchased slave or a concubine feels for her master, but with the inspiration of love.

Dilârû also loved children. When she learned she was pregnant, her heart filled with a love beyond bounds and she would say, "This child will be the greatest reward for my pure love." And so Dilârû's heart overflowed with love when the little Princess was born, only to suffer the most painful torment life can inflict when her baby died four days later. The agonizing blow nearly crushed her. But this exceptional woman possessed an entirely unique soul, a nature quite different from everyone else's. So as not to upset and torment the master she loved so dearly, she swallowed her pain and exhibited a truly exceptional calm. At least outwardly she appeared thus, but in her heart a dreadful fire had begun slowly to consume her, a fire that locked her young and vibrant body in the cruel grasp of tuberculosis.

Quite soon the disease began to leave its mark as Dilârû grew ever sadder and more morose. Sorrow overcame Prince Salâheddin, seeing his beloved this way. He withdrew off by himself and wept for hours on end. Word was sent to Yıldız and a few physicians were brought in, but the doctors who examined Dilârû could offer nothing except to prescribe out of sympathy for her that she needed a change of air.

But just how could a change of air be possible? Given the attitude at Yıldız, how on earth would they consent to grant a Prince's concubine confined in Çırağan permission to leave the palace and mix among the people? Nonetheless an attempt was made, petitioning Sultan Hamid to grant permission, under any conditions, to send Dilârû away from that damp palace for a change of air.

At first Sultan Hamid responded with silence to these two requests, one following the other, but then after a while instructions came down that the patient was to be taken up to Yıldız. This news only worsened Dilârû's state of mind, because to part from her deeply loved Salâheddin meant for her nothing less than a spiritual death. The Prince felt the same, but he overcame his feelings and made the effort to encourage his devoted and adoring beloved to be brave.

The date was set when Dilârû was to go to Yıldız. On the preceding day, Dilârû made the rounds of all the kalfas' rooms, taking her leave and wishing each of them well. That evening she dressed herself from head to toe in black and went to our master's apartments to take her leave from him.

The long-skirted black outfit suited her slender and elegant figure well. The poor woman was terribly sad. Even our master was quite taken aback when he saw her in that state and he just stared into her face for a few moments without saying anything until he softly asked her, his voice trembling with emotion, "Why are you dressed in black, my dear child?"

Dilârû bent her head down so as not to show our master the tears welling in her eyes. She managed to answer, "How could I not dress in black, Sir? I have to leave both you and my master." Perhaps she wanted to say more, but since her last words caught in her throat, she could only lower her head completely and say nothing. Our master said some words to console her and revealed his great sensitivity and compassion as he said, "I think dinner must be ready. Come, my dear child, let's dine together."

Now, illness was something heartily disliked in the palaces. Everyone feared even the slightest illness and tried to guard themselves against it. In fact every member of the Ottoman dynasty, whether great or small, was terribly frightened of illness and behaved extremely cautiously around sick people. Knowing this, we were astounded that our master invited Dilârû to dine with him in his apartments that evening.

During supper our master was most solicitous and gentle, and not in the least reserved, so that the entire mealtime passed with the most tender and consoling of words.

After the meal our master said, "Dilârû, now you are leaving us, but God willing soon you will be back with us, restored to full health. But now, just as a memento of this evening, sing a song for us." With that the Senior Musician, Dürrünab, sat at the piano, while Dilârû stood and leaned against it. Dürrünab began with a short improvisation, after which Dilârû began to sing:

> Doctor, why have you taken my pulse
> As you did, at my hand?
>
> Is this how you diagnose
> The wound in the heart?
>
> Pull out the dagger,
> Inflict no more pain onto my wound.
>
> Is this how you diagnose . . .

Dilârû's voice had risen into a lament, but here she suddenly broke off, her heartbreaking sobs accompanying the chords that continued to sound from the piano. Our master rose and went over to her, so stricken in her grief. "Don't be sad, my child," he said, stroking her hair, "you're breaking all our hearts. God willing, you'll go in peace and come back to us in all good health." Then he turned to us and ordered us to take her away and see she got some rest.

That evening the sounds of fitful sobbing could be heard from nearly every room. The next morning, the same sounds accompanied poor Dilârû to the carriage with the drawn curtains that had pulled up to the carriage block outside the harem door.

As we heard it afterwards, Abdülhamid settled Dilârû in a lovely and airy room in one of the villas on the grounds of Yıldız and sent her an exquisite chest filled with gold coins. He saw to her treatment by sending for famous doctors from the city, such as Horasancıyan, alongside the palace doctors. Yet none of them could alter the sad fate that had overtaken the unfortunate

Dilârû. After four months in the Palace of the Star,[74] one day this broken-hearted young woman came to her end, just like a star that grows dim and disappears from the heavens.

Dilârû's death left its wound in all our hearts, as her sensitive nature had touched every one of us. But Prince Salâheddin fell into such despair that he could not eat or drink or sleep for days on end. He only wept bitterly. Nothing could distract him from his grief.

With the passing of the years our heartache eased, but then another sorrow inflicted itself upon us. Princess Aliye had come down with a slight cold, but after the cold passed she could not recover her health. Slowly she began to weaken, even though no trace of her illness remained. Our master was terribly worried about her, since he loved his children very much, so word was sent to Yıldız and doctors were brought in. They set about with much concern to treat the Princess, who must have been around age fourteen or fifteen.[75]

The doctors did not divulge their prognosis, but two days later Cevher Ağa came in and announced to the Senior Consort, "The doctors have found that the Princess's lungs are a bit weak and they feel she needs a change of air. It's really an insignificant indisposition but nonetheless His Majesty is concerned and thinks it fitting for Her Highness the Princess to come to Yıldız for a change of air. He has arranged separate rooms for her there, where she will be taken either today or tomorrow."

This news upset our master quite a bit as he did not want to be parted from his daughter. Still he knew he had to bow to the will of fate, considering the gravity of the situation. With a good deal of pain in his heart, he sent Princess Aliye up to Yıldız Palace.

The day the Princess left, the palace truly went into mourning. For days on end no one smiled, while for weeks no one saw our master as he did not come out of his rooms. News of her situation flowed from Yıldız and we heard that the Princess's treatment received the highest importance. But the reports contained nothing that gave us hope for recovery. As it was, not long afterward we received the terrible news that there was no longer any need to describe her condition. This bitter turn spread salt on the gaping wounds in our hearts.

But still we are human beings, so that although all these events left their deep mark upon us, with the passing of the days our lives returned to their

74 The meaning of *Yıldız*.
75 She was actually twenty-three.

usual routine. In truth nothing that happened changed anything at all in the daily life in the palace. Everything moved on as it always did, just like a silent mass of water flowing down a canal. And everyone seemed at peace with his or her lot.

Most likely you, too, have pondered the question that has been asked of me time and again since our release from that dreary existence: did the kalfas ever have naughty adventures?

If I were to answer this question with a definite *no*, you wouldn't believe me. Perhaps you would even respond with something such as, "Since humans are made of flesh and bone mixed in with a bit of feeling and fantasy, would they choose to forego the pleasures and delights of this world? Not all of the kalfas, but probably some of them gave into some light temptation? They must have devised a number of misadventures, insofar as possible given the circumstances."

Yes, all right, your conclusion may be correct. There are all kinds of people under the sun. In a brood numbering some eighty women, ranging in age from thirteen or fourteen to sixty-five or seventy, quite probably some will be chaste, in command of their will-power, and so devout that one could use their skirts as a prayer rug, while others will be profuse in their feelings and spirit, wanton, debauched, and a slave to passion and pleasure. But what could these girls do inside those four walls? Within the confines of the harem apartments at Çırağan Palace, first and foremost only four persons could be called "men."[76] One was our Prince, the owner and master of every woman there. He had selected his *gözdes* in sufficient number from among the women present, although probably others tried to catch his eye here and there.

As for the other three men, one was Prince Salâheddin. But he nurtured only the deepest respect for his father, and so we heard no talk about his embarking on an adventure with any kalfa outside the boundaries of his own entourage. Or to speak more correctly, let me add a limitation: no such thing was ever perceived.

The remaining two males included Prince Salâheddin's older son, Prince Nihad, and his younger son, Prince Osman Fuad. Prince Nihad was born in 1883 while Prince Osman Fuad came into the world twelve years later. For a good number of years they could be considered but children. Prince Nihad attained young adulthood only toward the end of our years in Çırağan. He did become a father at the age of nineteen, just one year before our ordeal in

76 I.e., not a eunuch.

Çırağan Palace came to an end.[77] If during those last years someone did try to seduce these two Princes, the one just entering manhood and the other one still a child, then the sin rests with them.

Now and again the older and more sedate kalfas would get together and enjoy a good laugh by saying about some of the young kalfas, "So-and-so Kalfa was meandering down Peach Street again." In the latter years they had come up with this phrase "Peach Street" to refer to secluded corridors, in allusion to the girls who lingered in them just a little too long in the hope of crossing paths with Prince Nihad.

Otherwise it was simply outside the realm of possibility for a kalfa to have an adventure with men such as guards, gardeners, and the like. If any of the men associated with Çırağan Palace displayed any measure of attraction toward the kalfas, even toward those who did not exercise self-control, they would have forfeited their lives. Throughout all those twenty-eight years, we neither saw nor heard mention of any man so brave.

I mentioned it while discussing Hasan Pasha, the police prefect at Beşiktaş, and I will state it again here: throughout all those long years, our lives passed in the dreariest state of isolation and renunciation. No blemish ever stained our reputations; none even came close to doing so.

And now let us come to the princesses.

At the time of our confinement in Çırağan Palace, Princess Hadice was some seven or eight years old.[78] By the time she was ten, she was already a happy, laughing, joyful girl. Now, every child loves a story, wouldn't one say? Well, she loved stories more than any child ever did. She would even make up her own endings to stories while listening to them, and she'd tell us her ideas about them, proving both that she possessed a vivid imagination and that she was quite advanced for her age.

As she grew older her sentiments quickly became more apparent. She took up novels as soon as she learned to read. Once we had settled in Çırağan Palace she would surreptitiously pick out the novels from among our master's books, now and then staying up all night reading them. Most of these novels were the works of French authors, since she had been taught French by Gevherriz Kalfa as well as by our master. After she read them she would tell us what they were about, and as she was relating them to us we noticed she was particularly drawn to the complications of love. So it became apparent

---

77 Prince Nihad's eighteen-year-old concubine Safiru gave birth to their son Prince Vasıb on 13 October 1903.

78 Princess Hadice was born in May 1870, making her six years of age by Western reckoning but in her seventh year by Ottoman reckoning.

Prince Salâheddin flanked by his sons Prince Nihad (left) and Prince Fuad (right),
circa 1906. Photographer unknown.

*Murad's daughter Princess Fehime in court dress with decorations
and train, circa 1900. Photographer unknown.*

that Princess Hadice was a bit too romantic by nature and that most likely passion fired her soul.

If opportunity had presented itself, would this romantic and passionate Princess have embarked upon an amorous adventure? This I do not know, nor can I venture to say anything in this regard, but I do well remember that as years passed and Princess Hadice matured into a fully grown woman, she quite openly longed for a husband. She thought nothing of bemoaning her situation, saying such things as, "Time is passing me by, and my sister (Princess Fehime) as well! What good does it do us to sit around here like this? Are we to become nothing but two old housekeepers here in this palace?" If you take into consideration her personality and her style of life, Princess Hadice was not altogether unjustified in her complaint.

Speaking of her younger sister Princess Fehime, she was about one and a half or two years old when we moved into Çırağan Palace. However, in no way did this Princess resemble her older sister. First of all, she was not nearly as intelligent, lively, and fun-loving as Princess Hadice. Hers was a rather too simple personality and she thought herself terribly important. For example, although she was not particularly pretty she fancied herself so and wanted everyone else to think so too. Above all she loved to be praised. Unlike Princess Hadice she did not advance quickly and she showed little inclination to read books despite the fact that she could read and write both Turkish and French. Instead she spent most of her time gazing into the mirror.

Princess Fatma, who was born during the third year of our confinement in Çırağan, for her part resembled neither of those two Princesses. From childhood on there was nothing abnormal about her. She was calm, dignified, serious-minded, polite, and gentle. She spent an important part of her time in playing the piano and reading books in French.

At length, Princess Hadice's complaints came to our master's attention, thanks to her mother and the older kalfas. At first our master threw his hands up at her not unreasonable complaint. "What can I do, stuck inside these four walls?" he said. "Where am I to find husbands for them?" But then he put some thought into it and changed his mind, talking it over with the Senior Consort and telling her, "Send for Cevher Ağa and explain the situation to him. Have him go to my brother and speak with him. We'll see what comes of it then."

And so Cevher Ağa was summoned. When he arrived the appropriate things were explained to him. Two or three days later this response came back from Sultan Hamid: "My compliments to my brother. His daughters are my children as well; I consider it my duty to find husbands for them. But there is one condition, that once they leave the palace they may not return."

This response weighed heavily upon our master, who then sent in reply, "My brother knows how devoted I am to my children. Is it not cruel to separate me from them forever? Very well, let me bear the pain for the sake of my children's happiness, but what about their mothers? I cannot imagine how those poor ladies could bear the deprivation of living without their daughters."

But Abdülhamid would not budge from his decision.

With that, the Princesses were asked what they wished to do. Both preferred to leave Çırağan Palace and get married. Abdülhamid had the two Princesses brought up to Yıldız. He ordered one of the villas at Ortaköy to be completely renovated and another new villa to be built. He had them completely furnished, then ordered photographs taken of them and sent the photographs to our master.

Although he still grieved at the sacrifice he had to make in order to see his daughters married, our master was absolutely delighted at the splendid villas built for his daughters. "I think my brother is getting over his fears," he said. "He's changing his mind in our favor. Since he's done so much to provide for my daughters today, no doubt in the future he'll allow us to see one another."

The search began to find husbands for the Princesses, but because of the situation with Sultan Murad, no one was aspiring to such a dangerous alliance, and so for a long time no husbands could be found for them. Finally Sultan Hamid realized that he personally would have to select husbands for them. As we heard it, he truly treated them as generously as he did his own daughters and spent a good deal of money on their weddings. And yet, as fate would have it, Princess Hadice's married life lasted no more than a year and a half before it ended in a tragedy that contributed to our master's death.

But let us leave the story of that tragedy for a later moment and return now to recounting life in the palace.

When we finally achieved our freedom, everyone asked me this question: "Twenty-eight years . . . how on earth did you pass the time within those four walls?" I always gave this answer, with an air of deep resignation: "By always doing the same things, like a clock that never goes wrong." In saying "the same things," I meant that we always performed the same tasks every day. Everyone had learned his or her job so very well, had adopted it so thoroughly, that we all carried out our duties like a well-run machine and had no need to remind or prod anyone. Since there were a lot of us, we usually finished our chores quite quickly.

The most enjoyable chore was laundry day. The general washing of cloth-ing, not including our master's clothing, we called *beylik çamaşır* [Gentle-men's Laundry]. The Gentlemen's Laundry was washed every two weeks, gathered together from every entourage by girls known as *beylikçis*. Great samovars were set up in the imperial kitchen, while seven large basins were placed on the floor, three girls sitting round each one. Laundry from the first basin was passed to the second, and so forth, so that all the laundry eventu-ally passed through seven basins. Here was truly a sight to behold, all these young and fresh beauties washing the laundry, rubbing the clothes in the white suds and chattering away amid sweet peals of laughter.

It was not customary to light fires in the samovars, inside the room; instead, coals were heated in the kitchen of the *Mabeyin* and brought in by the harem eunuchs. The girl in charge of the samovars, the Samovar Kalfa, was selected from the strongest of the girls because it was no easy task to fill seven basins with water. While the girls were washing the laundry, the older kalfas would walk about and inspect the laundry to be certain it was clean. It was their task too to hang up the laundry and take it down, essentially because they did not want to send the young girls out into the harem garden where the laundry was up drying. The very young girls, though, never left the older kalfas' side, so while the older kalfas were hanging up the laundry, they would hand them the clothespins. Once the laundry had been dried and taken in, it was handed over to the High Hazinedars who saw to it that the bed sheets and so on went through the laundry presses, that the cloth-ing was ironed, and that each entourage's laundry returned to its proper destination.

Our master's laundry was subject to a special procedure for washing. First of all I will say that our master was extremely neat and fastidious.[79] He changed his clothing nearly every day. In particular he wished to have his bed linen changed quite often. He did not use the covered quilt (i.e., the tra-ditional Turkish quilt), but instead thick blankets were wrapped in large, bil-lowy linen sheets. The sheets were then spread over the bed absolutely evenly, with their embroidered edges made to hang down both sides.

These sets of bed linen and quilts were set out to air every morning, sprin-kled with rose water and other petal extracts, then ironed on the laundry press to be flat as a board. Throughout the whole operation extreme care was

---

79 Sultan Mecid was also extremely neat and fastidious. Gentlemen he admitted into his pres-ence were sternly warned not to touch his feet or the hem of his robes with their hands, if they were required to kiss his feet. In this respect his sons took after their father. [Ş]

exercised to keep the ends of the sheets from touching the floor, which is why two persons always worked together to take up the sheets and gather them in again. Extreme care was also taken in washing the bedding sets, which were changed every other day.

Our master's handkerchiefs and stockings were washed only by the hazinedars. They would not allow ordinary kalfas[80] to touch them, nor to put their hands into the basins for washing the Gentlemen's Laundry.

One of our most important tasks was to stand watch. Every night two hazinedars stood watch outside our master's doors. When going on duty the hazinedars dressed their best, all neat and tidy. They reported first to the Lady Mother in order to let her know they would be on duty; she inspected them rigorously and if anything was amiss in their appearance she had them set it right. She then warned them, "Keep your eyes and your ears open. Carry out whatever orders my son gives you, and be careful not to disturb him."

Those on duty stood their watch in the hall outside our master's apartments, awaiting any orders he might give. At the end of their watch they again reported back to the Lady Mother in order to tell her they were off duty and to inform her if anything noteworthy occurred on their watch. After the Lady Mother's death, the Senior Consort took over the task of supervising those on duty.

Although the duty hazinedars were nearly all selected from the tidiest, most agile, and most intelligent of the kalfas, more than others our master preferred the services of the hazinedars Dilber and Tarzınger.[81] These two sharp-witted hazinedars had learned the traits of our master's character down to the details. For example, our master often asked for the muslin cloth called *destimal* used for wiping hands. At such a request, other hazinedars would hurry down to the laundry mistress and bring one back, during which time of course several minutes would have elapsed. But those two hazinedars made sure to always carry clean *destimal*s with them and could present them to him as soon as he asked for them.

Our master would also grant permission for those on nighttime watch duty to sleep in the armchairs in the hall.

Our master, who always stayed up late, would tell one of the duty attendants which *gözde* he would spend the night with. They would go to the *gözde* and quietly inform her. Sometimes our master would undress, wash up, and change into his bedclothes, not wanting anyone with him that night,

---

80 I.e., kalfas not of hazinedar rank.
81 This would be Tarzınigâr. [Ş]

so he would tell the duty attendants, "Turn the door.[82] You too get some rest." The attendants would close the door and stretch out on the sofas in the hall.

Only if our master were ill would a hazinedar stay in his bedchamber, sitting quietly behind a folding screen as he slept.

Our master had some unusual habits. When he went to bed at night, he wouldn't lock the door to his bedchamber. No one other than he himself was allowed to lie on the bedstead where he slept, so the *gözdes* who accompanied him for a certain amount of time in the evening would be guests on the other bedstead that was always kept in his room.

Furthermore, he didn't like to sleep always in the same place. At times he would live in the large palace, but at other times he would move into the Senior Consort's apartments on the Istanbul side of the large palace.[83] Here too he would change rooms often, sleeping sometimes in a large bedchamber in the upper story of this building, while at other times he preferred to sleep in a small salon on the ground floor.

Sewing constituted another activity that we constantly engaged in during those twenty-eight years, apart from our regular, everyday duties. Our master didn't like the girls to be idle and wanted every kalfa definitely to be busy with something, particularly with learning a new way to be useful. This is why nearly every kalfa received more or less of an education, with some of those who were more drawn to reading and writing being quite well educated, even speaking foreign languages.

But if there was one thing nearly all of us knew, it was how to cut and sew cloth. Bolts of fabric would arrive from outside the palace whenever we requested them. Every kalfa made her own clothes, with the Senior Consort in particular so skilled that she could have been considered an expert seamstress. Several times she even made clothes for our master.

Many of our days were filled with music and dance, since music was perhaps the favorite pastime of all at the palace. Our master's love of music had infected nearly all of us. When the musical ensemble formed of Dürrünab, Tarzınevin, Lebiriz, and other kalfas started in to play with their piano, violin, and flute, our master would be sure to join in. He would order the chief of the dancers, Desteriz Kalfa, along with Teranedil and other kalfas, to perform a dance. No vulgar traditional Turkish songs would be sung, nor

---

82　This is how one said "close the door" in the palaces. [Ş]
83　This building stands below Çırağan Palace, the first white stucco building on the Istanbul [south] side. The harem gardens were located between the two buildings. [Ş]

any *köçek* dances performed.[84] We loved the traditional Turkish *zeybek* folk dance,[85] while practically every day we performed European dances such as the polka, quadrille, and waltz.

Our master spent a good deal of time at the piano. He composed a number of airs, which he then taught to the kalfa musicians. He even taught a few of the girls how to dance in the European fashion.

For some time after his mother passed away our master wouldn't touch the piano. Her death had affected him so deeply that whenever the Lady Mother was mentioned in conversation he would say, "I wish that Almighty God had not shown me my mother's death." For a while so many deaths occurred one after another in the palace that our master was nearly reduced to loathing life. The loss of so many of his loved ones, from causes that seemed insignificant yet ended in death, left his kindly heart completely broken.

One such loss was that of the Fourth Consort Meyliservet, the mother of Princess Fehime. She had just gotten over a fever but was still in a delicate state. One evening she gathered around her the kalfas of whom she was fond and had them read aloud to her the novel *Hasan the Sailor*[86] while she listened attentively. Princess Fehime was at the piano, softly practicing on the keys her lesson for the next day, when one of the kalfas—I believe it was Lebiriz—jumped up and shouted, "Eek! A mouse!" All the girls began screaming and running about, trying to escape, with Princess Fehime even clambering onto the piano in her fright.

The sudden screaming and scrambling took an immediate toll on the Fourth Consort. She fainted for some time, which culminated in a worsening of her illness. Indeed she took such a turn for the worse that she became unable to speak. After three days of this she made known that she wanted pen and paper. She wrote the following testament and showed it to our master: "I shall not recover from this illness. I entrust my daughter into your care." Toward dawn on the next morning, she passed away, sadly and quietly. This plunged our master into such a state of despair that in the last years of his life he never again took to music with anything near the same enthusiasm that he once had. Yet he never was displeased at our playing music and dancing. He would tell us, "I'm pleased when you all are having a good time," and never forbade us to engage in our simple and innocent pleasures.

---

84 *Köçek*, the boys who danced rather suggestively to music, most often in taverns.

85 A traditional folk dance of western Anatolia.

86 *Hasan Mellâh*, the popular novel of the adventures of an Ottoman sailor in the Mediterranean, authored by the journalist and novelist Ahmed Midhat (1844–1912) during his exile on Rhodes in 1873–1876.

THE LAST DAYS IN ÇIRAĞAN PALACE

And so the days, the months, the years slipped by in this manner. Every pass-ing day left either a deep mark or a light trace on our hearts and in our faces, depending upon how sensitive a nature each of us possessed. And yet, of course the one most afflicted by these twenty-eight years of gloom and suf-fering was our master.

His hair turned stark white, as had the scant beard that gave a shadowy pall to his face. He started to stoop over, even though he had kept up a fair measure of his strength and vitality. He began to speak more laboriously, as if his voice were encumbered with fatigue. Now and then he would cast a look around him, and when his gaze fell on us he would sigh deeply and say, "You poor things! Because of me you too are wasting away in this place," and one could see in his face the sadness in his heart.

It was true. We were wasting away in that place. The damp stone walls of that palace were draining us of the sweetest days of our youth, and there were days when we felt the pain of it in our hearts. Yet we forced ourselves to look cheerful so as not to upset our master, and—having endured the sor-rows of that gloomy prison for twenty-eight years—to make it seem to him that we would remain resolute during the time left to us, which naturally could not last a similar length of time.

And so, while out of respect and solicitude we were shielding our mas-ter from the howling winds, that love story of Princess Hadice reared its accursed head. It struck like lightning into the world of that hapless father whose entire life had passed in misfortune.

Exactly seventeen months had passed since Princess Hadice's marriage.[87] I shall never forget the day; it was a Thursday. Just as we were about to sit down to the noon meal, kalfas hurried in, beside themselves with this news: "Cevher Ağa came down from Yıldız with his face all twisted in a rage and demanded to see Prince Salâheddin! They called in the Senior Consort and the three of them shut themselves in the room and started talking all in a flurry and all upset!"

This news darkened our faces with the shadow of disquiet and filled us with a skulking sense of foreboding.

A while later the kalfas of Prince Salâheddin and of the Senior Consort

---

87 Princess Hadice had married Ali Vasıf Pasha on 12 September 1901, according to Alderson 1956, so that if the concubine has remembered her dates correctly, the episode described here occurred around February 1903. However, early 1904 seems more likely, since the world press reported on it then—for example, the *New York Times*, 25 May 1904, p. 5.

came over and informed us in lowered tones, "Something's happening—may God only let it turn out all right. Prince Salâheddin's in the room with them, shouting horribly." Now we were really panic-stricken and petrified.

Quite soon we learned what was behind this sequestered meeting. Cevher Ağa started things off by coming in and shutting himself in the room with Prince Salâheddin and the Senior Consort, telling them, "Look at the state I'm in—my whole body is trembling. I'm so appalled at what I have to tell you today that I don't know where to start. The honor and the good name of the imperial family have been blackened. Since yesterday evening Yıldız has been in an uproar, and last night we could barely restrain His Majesty.

"Sir, here is what I have to tell. Princess Hadice and Kemaleddin Pasha have been having an affair. They decided to have Princess Naime murdered so they could get married. Kemaleddin Pasha convinced the physician treating the Princess to do the job, and he injected her with poison."

Prince Salâheddin jumped up and began to shout, "This is a lie! This is slander! My sister is incapable of such a thing! These vile informers are trying to ruin us! They're using this slander to attack our honor!"

Cevher Ağa asked the Prince to sit down while he explained to him in complete detail the results of the investigations carried out all night long in Yıldız. The investigations showed that Princess Hadice had been conducting an affair for three months with Kemaleddin Pasha, the husband of Princess Naime—her neighbors in the adjoining villa. They had been using a ladder to scale the wall between the two villas at night, carrying out their affair there under the trees, among the flowers. Witnesses to all these things had divulged everything the night before. Search parties raided both villas and gathered up letters from the apartments of both Kemaleddin Pasha and Princess Hadice, and the chemicals used to poison Princess Naime were analyzed. In sum, the whole business was spelled out so very clearly that any attempt to deny or explain it away became patently impossible.

Having related all this, Cevher Ağa said, "And now I shall come to the point of my visit. His Majesty has sent me on a special mission. He commanded me, 'Go and tell my brother how I took in his child and embraced her as my own. I expended a good deal of money on her to make her happy. I gave her a villa, beautifully furnished. I arranged a marriage for her that would do her honor. I denied her nothing at all. Am I to be repaid for this by having her cast eyes at the husband of my daughter, and plotting an attempt on her life?

"'I know what I shall do with Kemaleddin Pasha. But what sort of punishment shall I arrange for Princess Hadice? This I am asking of my brother, as her father. Let him give me an answer.'"

Prince Salâheddin and the Senior Consort objected even more strenuously. "This is not possible! It is a fabrication and slander! If His Highness were to hear this, it would upset him terribly. On no account can we say anything like this to him. This matter must be fully investigated." Prince Salâheddin went even further. "Go and tell my uncle that if this matter is proven to be true, I shall personally kill my sister with my own hands," he promised. "I swear to this, as God is my witness."

Cevher Ağa departed, but pandemonium broke out in the palace. Quite a few of the kalfas and hazinedars defended Princess Hadice. "It serves Sultan Hamid right!" they fumed. "Here he gave his own grotesque daughters to handsome and hardy young men, but for our Princesses he couldn't find anything better than table servants! Did our darling Princess deserve a wretched husband like that?"

Princess Hadice was so beautiful, she could have been called "the star of the Princesses" of that day. And as we heard it, her husband was indeed a wretched thing. When husbands were to be found for the Princesses, one of her father's table servants was given the title "Ali Vasıf Pasha, Code Scribe" and presented to Princess Fehime, while another man of the same station and character was granted a rank as "Ali Galib Pasha," and bestowed upon his superior, Princess Hadice.[88] Given this, how could a beautiful, sensitive, fiery, and exuberant woman such as Princess Hadice remain oblivious when her eyes fell on a young, strapping, handsome lad such as Kemaleddin Pasha living right next door?

At any rate, whether rightly or wrongly, while feverish discussions in a circle of reasoned arguments were raging throughout the palace, our master still did not have the slightest idea that anything was wrong. The following morning our master asked for the newspaper as always—Prince Salâheddin subscribed to the paper, then passed it on to his father every morning—but Prince Salâheddin had seen the official notice printed in the newspaper that morning: "Due to effrontery resulting from various irregular circumstances, the Council of Ministers has taken the decision to strip Damad Kemaleddin Pasha of his rank, grant a separation to his wife the Princess, and banish him from the imperial capital." When he read that, the Prince ordered the kalfas not to give his father the newspaper that day and to tell him if he asked for it that the paper hadn't come. This was the answer the girls gave our master when he asked for the paper.

---

88 The names are reversed: Vasıf Pasha married Princess Hadice, Ali Galib Pasha married Princess Fehime.

In any event, the behavior since the previous day of the kalfas, hazinedars, and consorts had aroused our master's suspicions, so when he wasn't given the newspaper he became apprehensive. If not that day, then by the next sheer agitation would certainly overtake him, so after much consideration the decision was taken to tell him the news in a suitable fashion.

The Second Consort brought in the newspaper. Our master immediately looked through it quickly and there he came across the official announcement. In an agitated voice he called to the Consort, "My lady, here, read this!" pointing out the paragraph. As she read the announcement aloud our master listened intently. "How terribly strange," he said, "What could they mean by 'various irregular circumstances'? My daughters' villas are there. . . . hopefully nothing has happened? This must have something to do with us—that must be why you hid the paper from me. Now tell me, what has happened?" and with that he forced her to divulge what she knew.

Straightaway our master sent for Prince Salâheddin and the Senior Consort and questioned them. "If something like this happened," he demanded to know, "why did you try to hide it from me? Tell me exactly what Cevher Ağa said." Since there was no way to hide things from him anymore, they told him just what they had heard from Cevher Ağa. While listening to them our master was completely stunned, as though he had been struck by lightning. He categorically refused to believe his daughter could have mixed herself up in such a dangerous and sordid affair. "Dear God, these lies have struck into the pit of my soul," he said, revealing the depth of his anguish. "It is quite clear that by attacking my daughter they're trying to degrade me before the world. I really cannot bear this any longer."[89]

89 Semih Mümtaz, whose father, the Governor of Bursa, was charged with guarding Kemaleddin Pasha in his internal exile, mentions nothing whatsoever about a plot to poison Princess Naime, but rather claims that the affair between Princess Hadice and Kemaleddin Pasha consisted of the exchange of love letters tossed over the garden wall, heated love letters on the part of the impulsive Kemaleddin Pasha. He claims Princess Hadice had the Pasha's letters stolen and revealed to Sultan Abdülhamid on purpose, in revenge for the poor husband the Sultan had chosen for her, a motive intimated by our concubine (Mümtaz 1950, 344, 347).

The Western press reported only that the Sultan's son-in-law had been arrested and sent into exile as a result of the secret correspondence between him and the daughter of "the imprisoned" ex-Sultan Murad (*New York Times*, 25 May 1904, p. 5). Although Princess Hadice had to divorce her husband, and Kemaleddin Pasha was sent into internal exile, Abdülhamid later forgave the Princess and saw that she was invited again to Yıldız Palace (Şehsuvaroğlu 1956, 772).

THE DEATH OF SULTAN MURAD

From that day forward our master became subdued and pensive. He was no longer interested in eating or drinking and couldn't sleep at night, which left dark rings under his eyes. Many attempts were made to cheer him up but he paid no attention and did not reply. All of us grew quite concerned as we sensed that his heavy-heartedness and preoccupation would end in no good, and might even trigger a relapse into his notorious illness. We passed some four or five days in this state of agitation, and then what we feared came to pass.

One day our master was in the lavatory. Now, it was the custom that whenever he was in the lavatory we waited outside it, pacing slowly back and forth until he came out. I was pacing slowly near the door and talking with the Third Consort when suddenly I heard a painful groan. This frightened us and we ran over to the door and called in but our master gave no answer, he only continued moaning. We opened the door and went in to find our master sitting on the potty chair, which resembled a European-style toilet, and moaning terribly. All color had drained from his face and a look of dread had come over him. The Third Consort asked, "For mercy's sake, Sir, what has happened to you?" but our master could only respond in a weak voice, "Something in my bowels feels as though it's burst. I'm bleeding badly. Get me up and take me to bed."

We took him by his arms and put him into bed, then sent for Prince Salâheddin and told him what happened. Prince Salâheddin ran to the lavatory and examined the potty. The color drained from his face too when he saw that the chamber pot was half-filled with blood.

In bed our master fell into a half faint while blood continued to flow from his rectum. Prince Salâheddin ran out to the little pharmacy he kept in his apartments and brought back some medicines. His face distorted by the strain and distress he felt, he began to treat his father.

He treated him for several days, but the blood kept flowing. As his anxiety increased, the Prince told his father that he could not stop the blood and that they should send for a physician. At first our master refused to see a doctor, but finally he said, "You're right, my son. I see I shan't be freed of this affliction, and if something should happen to me they'll cause trouble for you and hold you responsible, so let them know what has happened and send for a doctor."

The Prince sent a note to Yıldız. Dr. Rıza Pasha came down at once. He examined our master carefully, inspecting the blood that we had collected in silver bowls, and gave him some medicines to stop the bleeding. Our master was in no pain or discomfort, but the medicines showed no effect whatsoever and the bleeding continued. The doctor ordered that our master must on no account drink anything hot, so cold meats and dishes, frozen sheep's trotters, and blocks of ice were sent down from Yıldız. We consistently fed our master this food and saw that he regularly sipped the ice, but still none of this had the slightest effect. The blood still flowed, and every day our master appeared that much paler.

After some days our master stopped eating and drinking altogether. We pleaded with him but still he wouldn't touch anything. "I'm not hungry," he would reply, "and don't try to force me because everything tastes bad."

One day the Senior Consort sent for me and handed me a tray of grapes on slivers of ice. "Filistan," she said, "you take these to our master. He wouldn't do anything to offend you. Maybe he'll eat something." I took the grapes in and offered them to him, asking him to eat some of them. He smiled and said, "Filistan, if I refuse you, you'll be terribly hurt. For your sake I'll eat a few of them." He ate some and then handed the tray back to me.

A veil of gloom descended over the palace. Nowhere was the sound of a human voice to be heard. We were worried on the one hand about what might happen to our master, while on the other hand we were pondering what destiny held in store for us.

The poor man lay there in his bed, every day more ashen but still without a cure for his suffering. Dr. Rıza Pasha declared that he had diabetes but the older kalfas said, "The doctor doesn't know. The illness our master has isn't diabetes. He can't bear the pain from that business with Princess Hadice. It's the shame of it that's struck him down."

The illness went on for thirty-eight days, when Dr. İbrahim Pasha came down with Cevher Ağa from Yıldız to examine our master.[90]

---

90 Here the concubine's memoir ends abruptly. Ziya Şakir follows the memoir with a description of Murad's death and funeral. Much as we may have wished to read Filizten's account of the harem's reaction to Murad's death and the subsequent dispersal of his entourage, if she dictated it to Şakir, in fact she could have told us nothing of the funeral itself since in Islamic custom women do not attend public burial ceremonies.

Şakir ends his biography of Murad V with this paragraph: "And so, in this manner on Tuesday, 30 August 1904, the crypt under the gloomy dome of the mausoleum at the New Mosque received the casket of Sultan Murad V, who had entered this world on 21 September 1840 and who had borne the imperial title but ninety-three days. With this sad conclusion the sixty-four years of his adventuresome life came to their end."

PART TWO

THE Princess Ayse

PRINCESS AYŞE, DAUGHTER OF SULTAN ABDÜLHAMİD II, WAS BORN AT her father's residence of Yıldız Palace on 31 October 1887.[1] She was the tenth child and sixth daughter born to her father, but the only child of her mother, the Circassian concubine Müşfika, who was later raised to the rank of Imperial Consort. At the overthrow of her father in 1909, the Princess followed her parents into exile at Salonica. The next year she returned to Istanbul, where she married and started a family, but later she divorced and subsequently remarried. At the expulsion of the imperial family in 1924 she left Turkey and resided in Paris. Her mother, on the other hand, chose to remain in Turkey, so that the two did not see one another for some twenty-eight years, until the Princess's return from exile in 1952. Princess Ayşe died 10 August 1960 at age seventy-two and was buried in the imperial mausoleum at the Yahya Efendi dervish convent, adjacent to Yıldız Palace. Her mother survived her by nearly one year.

Princess Ayşe wrote her memoir in Istanbul after her return from exile, completing it by 1955.[2] As Princess Ayşe tells us, for large portions of the memoir she relied on the memory of her mother, as the two lived together after the Princess's return to Turkey. The work originally appeared in serial format in the Turkish popular magazine *Hayat* in the late 1950s, followed by its publication as a book in Istanbul in 1960, shortly before the Princess's death. The fact that the memoir was written as a magazine serial accounts for its format: a series of short chapters on a variety of topics, generally but not necessarily arranged chronologically.

1 Per Osmanoğlu 1999, 46. Alderson 1956 gives 1 November. In her memoir the Princess herself provides only her year of birth, as does Uluçay 1992.
2 Osmanoğlu, Ayşe. *Babam Sultan Abdülhamid (Hâtıralarım)*. Originally published in 1960, this translation follows the third edition, published in Istanbul at Selçuk Press in 1994.

At its publication, the major attraction of the book lay in the Princess's recollections of her famous parent. Recognizing this, she titled her memoir *My Father, Sultan Abdülhamid*. In it she crafted a personal view of Abdülhamid the man and father, a kind of personal vindication to counteract what she saw as the distorted public image of the controversial ruler whose thirty-three-year reign ended in dethronement and vilification.

Born 21 September 1842, Prince Abdülhamid acceded to the throne at the deposal of his older brother Murad V on 30 August 1876. After a reign of nearly thirty-three years, he himself was deposed on 27 April 1909, sent into exile at Salonica until the imminent fall of that city to Greek troops in 1912, then confined to Beylerbeyi Palace in Istanbul until his death at age seventy-five on 10 February 1918.

At Abdülhamid's dethronement, his image among the educated classes at home and abroad was decidedly negative. To some among his subjects, he had usurped his brother's throne. To others, he had promised to support constitutional government but then dismissed Parliament and suspended the Constitution for thirty years. Wary by temperament and determined to eradicate challenges to his rule, he imposed strict press censorship, instituted a secret police force, and created a network of informers. In the Western press the Sultan was largely an object of mystery, or worse: "Abdul the Damned," the "Red Sultan" at whose bloodied hands his subjects—particularly his Armenian subjects—suffered.

But to the vast majority of the Ottoman Muslim population outside the ranks of reformers, the Sultan remained the vigilant monarch chosen by God to preserve the world's greatest Muslim empire against the efforts by infidels—both foreign powers and Ottoman Christian subjects—to undermine it. It was this view of Abdülhamid that began to emerge as the blunders of his successors brought the empire to disaster. In recent decades, Abdülhamid's skill in diplomacy, avoidance of war, sound fiscal policy, and furtherance of reforms in administration, infrastructure, and education have taken their place in scholarship alongside the criticisms of his reign.[3]

In the ongoing debate over Abdülhamid, his daughter's memoir plays a central role by contributing the human dimension to the political and economic portrait of the Sultan's reign. For our purposes, the excerpts of the memoir presented here provide insight into harem life from the view of a princess born into it. Unlike our concubine, Princess Ayşe's position enabled

---

3 By far the best biography of Abdülhamid is Georgeon 2003, in French. In English, Joan Haslip's *The Sultan* (1958) is still useful.

Prince Abdülhamid at twenty-four, during the imperial visit to Great Britain in 1867,
nine years before he ascended the throne. Photographer unknown.

Sultan Abdülhamid on the short drive from Yıldız Palace to the Hamidiye Mosque during a Royal Mosque Procession in 1908; one of the few surreptitious photographs of the monarch, who forbade his photograph to be taken officially. Photographer unknown.

her to describe the personalities of imperial family members outside her own entourage because she knew them, and to provide insight into a host of imperial ceremonies, from holidays to weddings, because she attended them.

Her rank afforded the Princess relative independence and a sense of entitlement that the other memoirists lack, because as long as her father reigned, under the palace entourage system she came under the authority of no one other than her parents. Nevertheless, her privileged position and the majestic ceremonies of state notwithstanding, the portrait Princess Ayşe creates of the Ottoman imperial harem is that of a beloved childhood home with devoted parents, the conventional panoply of siblings and relatives, and adored family retainers, each playing a role in the upbringing of a typical upper-class Ottoman girl who lived, however, in a highly untypical milieu.

THE 𝕸emoir

MY FATHER'S MOTHER

Whenever Papa spoke of his mother he would say, "My poor mother left this world at such a young age, but still I can picture her. I can never forget her. She loved me very much. When she took sick she used to have me sit opposite her and content herself with gazing into my face, for she couldn't bring herself to kiss me. May God rest her soul."

My grandmother, the lady Tîrimüjgân Kadınefendi, gave birth to two princes and one princess. Her first child was Princess Naime, who died of smallpox at the age of two and a half in March 1843. Papa was her second child, while her third was Prince Mehmed Âbid, who died in May 1848 around the age of one month. Papa named my sister Princess Naime and my brother Prince Mehmed Âbid after these siblings of his.

The Imperial Consort Tîrimüjgân was known among the long-serving kalfas at the palace for her refinement, her politeness, and her beauty. Those who knew her said she had hazel green eyes, quite long, light brown hair, white, translucent skin, and a slender figure, thin waist, and lovely hands and feet. The old Circassian kalfas at the palace—who came from the same region as she—said she belonged to the Shapsug clan, and Papa used to say about the Shapsug girls, "My mother's people."[4]

As with our own grandmother, so too did we know the other consorts of my grandfather Sultan Abdülmecid only through stories. Among them we saw only the lady Perestû Kadınefendi, who became Papa's adoptive mother;

4 The Circassian tribe of Shapsug/Shapsegh, Sunni Muslims, inhabited the Black Sea coastal regions of the northwestern Caucasus. Along with the Circassian peoples in general, most of the Shapsugs migrated to the Ottoman Empire when Russia expelled them in the early 1860s, following Russia's victory in the Caucasian war of independence.

the lady Serfiraz Hanımefendi, the mother of our uncle Prince Süleyman; and the lady Şayeste Hanımefendi, mother of our late aunt Princess Naile. These ladies lived to an advanced age.

All my grandfather's consorts were Circassian. Never was a Greek or Armenian woman known to have entered the palace harem, nor was any such thing ever even rumored. Despite this, my father's personal enemies claimed that his mother had been an Armenian woman by the name of Çandır. Naive people who knew nothing of life in the palace were taken in by this and set about fanning the flames of malice against my father. Yet those who knew the Ottoman palace in its final era, with all its practices, customs, and traditions, appreciate quite well that this is an impossibility and nothing but the product of sheer fantasy.

FATHER'S ADOPTIVE MOTHER

The lady Perestû Kadınefendi raised my father as her adoptive child, since his own mother died while he was but a boy. When he ascended the throne she took the title *Mehd-i Ulyâ-yı Saltanat-ı Seniyye* [Most High Mother of the Exalted Sultanate].

Even in her old age one could see that she had been strikingly beautiful in her youth. She was Circassian, as were all the ladies of my grandfather, and from the Ubykh clan.[5] She was a beautiful woman, possessing a petite and slender figure with translucent white skin, blue eyes, golden blonde hair, and truly lovely hands and feet. One could see how worthy she was of the rank of Princess Mother from her refined comportment as well as her dignity and charming disposition. This esteemed lady's luminous face, graciousness, delicate manner, and elegance inspired respect and affection in everyone's heart, so that all those living in the palace loved her deeply. Hers was a most melodious voice, though she spoke softly and infrequently.

Father believed that by their meddling in the affairs of state, the mothers of Sultan Aziz and Sultan Murad had contributed not at all positively to the state and the dynasty, so that on the day after he was called to the throne he kissed his adoptive mother's hand and said, "Not one day did you make me feel the loss of my own mother. As far as I am concerned you are no different from my own mother, and your rank is henceforth that of Princess Mother,

---

5   The Ubykh tribe of Circassians, horseback nomads of the northwestern Caucasus, was expelled by Russia in 1864, following the Caucasian War, most settling in the Ottoman Empire.

with all the rights and authority that position holds in the palace. But I particularly request that you absolutely refrain from interfering in the affairs
of state by taking it upon yourself to protect this or that person, or trying
to mediate on behalf of people hoping for a rank or a position." And indeed
Perestû Kadın remained true to Papa's wish and command until the day she
died. His consorts and his *ikbal*s, as well as his daughters who married and
established their own households in the city, always followed her example in
this matter.

On ceremonial occasions she would turn herself out in a dress of sumptuous fabric containing four flounces, with the Order of the Ottoman Dynasty,
the Order of Compassion, and the Order of Abdülmecid pinned on her
chest, atop her hennaed hair a calpac-shaped *hotoz* worked in the most exquisite lace-like embroidery, and wearing the emerald pin called the *Valide Tacı*
[Mother's Crown], which she flanked with the two emerald pins from the
same set.

She wore two of the four flounces in front and two at the side, with a sash
of the same material or else a shawl tied about her waist. On her feet she
slipped shoes of white chamois leather. She wore an exquisite ruby ring on
the little finger of her right hand, but nothing other than that. Over her dress
she wore a jacket embroidered in gilt thread; in the palace this kind of jacket
was known as a *salta*.

On informal occasions she wore a single-flounced long dress fashioned
of high-quality fabrics, over which she put on a *salta* jacket of the same color,
and on her head an embroidered *hotoz*. Despite her petite and slender form,
in this outfit she looked both grand and charming.

The internal matters of the palace were in her charge. But the Princess
Mother did not want to hurt anyone's feelings in the least, did not interfere
in matters, sought justice and equity, and because she was firmly religious
she passed a good deal of time in prayers. She possessed good, high moral
standards, which led her to help the poor and needy.

When we went to see her, we would enter her presence in the same way
we did the Sultan's, then take a seat in front of her. She would give us advice
and treat us kindly.

Perestû Kadınefendi had a house in Maçka that Sultan Aziz had presented to her at one time. Nowadays this villa is a school. Three days before
he became sultan, Papa went to this villa, and it was from there that he
proceeded to Topkapı Palace for the ceremony of homage at his accession.
Grandmother loved this house. Now and again she would want to go there,

but because Papa absolutely wanted his mother present in the palace he would withhold permission, sending word instead, "I beg that she not go."

Papa particularly wanted his adoptive mother to attend the Royal Mosque Procession every Friday. Sometimes after the ceremony Grandmother would secretly slip out to her villa, but when Papa learned of it immediately aides set off from the palace with a carriage and brought Grandmother back.

When Grandmother took ill she would want to go to her house, and sure enough one day without Papa's knowing it she went to her house and there she died. Papa was quite angry about this as well as terribly upset, but she had died, what could be done? Because of this death the palace was in mourning for quite a long period of time. All of us felt her loss. For one week the military band did not perform. And so, in this way our esteemed grandmother left our midst. The traditional service at which the Prophet's Nativity Poem is recited was held in her memory at the Shaziliya Dervish Convent and at the Hamidiye Mosque, and she was interred in the mausoleum she had constructed at Eyüp. When she died she was some eighty years of age.

Papa presented this villa of Grandmother's in Maçka along with all its furniture and household goods to Ahmed Rıza Bey, the speaker of Parliament.

I can't continue without recording here the story I heard about the marriage of Papa's adoptive mother, the Fourth Consort Perestû Kadınefendi, with my grandfather, Sultan Abdülmecid, because even though it has been embroidered into a bit of a fairy tale it still contains some historical truths.

It seems that Princess Esma, the daughter of Sultan Abdülhamid I and aunt of my grandfather Sultan Abdülmecid, lived in luxury in her magnificent villa in Istanbul, but still her life passed in sadness because she could not have the one thing she wished for most: a child. At length she decided to adopt a child, the daughter of one of the noble families of the Ubykh clan of Circassians, and after reaching satisfactory terms with the mother and father, she adopted this strikingly beautiful blonde toddler, one year of age. The child was particularly diminutive, delicate, and graceful, so she named her Perestû, the Persian word for the bird, swallow. Actually in Persian the word is *piristû*, but the palace custom was to alter the pronunciation of some words, so Perestû it was.

All the kalfas in Princess Esma's villa behaved toward this child as though she were a *hanımsultan*, the daughter of a princess, and indeed her disposition and her manners were so lovely that they became devoted to her. In the meantime Princess Esma carefully arranged the training and education of this little girl, whom she loved deeply.

In the days of his youth before he ascended the throne, my grandfather Sultan Abdülmecid used to pay calls on his aunt every so often, engaging in conversation. He continued these calls after he became sultan, and one spring day he had come to visit his aunt and was passing through the harem gardens when he saw Perestû, then fourteen years old. Suddenly here was this young girl in front of him, her long blonde hair falling about her shoulders, her eyes a turquoise blue. Surprised and astounded, Sultan Abdülmecid asked this fairy-like girl who she was, but the girl, who didn't recognize the Sultan, simply fled without answering him. The Padishah asked the kalfas he encountered who the girl might be, but when he couldn't get an answer he went to see his aunt. This girl had dazed him, and when Princess Esma noticed how completely dumbfounded he was she asked why. Sultan Mecid described the nymph-like girl. His aunt understood immediately what had happened but she merely replied, "It must have been one of the serving girls," and sent for all the girls to come before her. She was hoping that the Sultan might take a fancy to one of these beautiful girls and forget about Perestû. But when she saw that Sultan Mecid wouldn't look at them and seemed to become rather upset, she ordered the High Hazinedar, "Have Perestû serve my boy his coffee."

A bit later, in accordance with palace custom, in came the Mistress of the Coffee Service, flanked by the kalfas, among them Perestû, and with the tray and the coffee server suspended from its delicate chains. Perestû poured the coffee from the pot within the coffee server into the cup inside its holder decorated with enamel work and set with brilliants, then served it to the Sultan on a small golden tray. As custom dictated, she returned to the row of kalfas where she stood until the Sultan finished his coffee, then she took the cup in its holder from the Sultan's hand and they all left the room. That left aunt and nephew alone. Sultan Abdülmecid embraced his aunt and said that this girl was the nymph he had seen in the gardens. He asked his aunt to give her to him, but Princess Esma exclaimed, "My dear boy! This girl is my child; I've taken care of her since she was one year old so that I could marry her to an important personage, and with a proper wedding. I want to see her marriage feast—this I have promised to do!"[6]

To this the Sultan replied rather insistently, "Auntie dear, to whom could you give her who is more important than I? I'll marry her with a proper wedding, as you want it to be. I'm prepared to do whatever you wish."

6 The implication being that wedding feasts did not take place for kalfas who became imperial concubines.

Finally his aunt consented. Within the week the marriage ceremony was celebrated with all due tradition in Princess Esma's villa in the presence of the Sultan's ministers. One week after that, she was ushered into Princess Esma's silver-lined carriage in her pearl-trimmed red dress, tiara, and bridal veil, and sent off to the palace. In those days Sultan Abdülmecid still resided in Topkapı Palace, and he greeted his bride at the main entrance gate into the harem, wearing a splendid uniform with an aigrette plume atop his fez. He took her by the arm and escorted her into the Sovereign's Hall in the palace harem, having her take a seat in the nook that had been prepared for the bride. Grandfather's children were young then. Sultan Mahmud's daughters[7] and consorts came in and joined in the ceremony, as did the wives of important personages. Gold coins were scattered as Grandfather and his bride passed by, and the band, composed of forty ladies from Sultan Abdülmecid's harem, all dressed in men's costumes, played marches.[8] Sultan Mecid's other consorts attended as well, scattering coins. Until evening they passed the time listening to the ensemble playing traditional Ottoman music, after which sherbet was served, followed by a banquet. It was quite a splendid wedding celebration in the palace. That evening, according to custom, the couple entered the bridal chamber, where Princess Esma kissed the bride and groom on their foreheads and said a prayer on their behalf, then returned to her villa, giving praise to God that she had lived to see such a magnificent wedding feast for her little girl. As things turned out, both Grandfather and my great-aunt saw their wishes fulfilled.

Her manners as lovely as her form, the lady Perestû lived her life always without airs yet dignified, compassionate, and kind. She was pious and helped the needy. Although God did not give her children, as I mentioned above she became adoptive mother to my father and rose to the rank of Princess Mother.

I myself was fortunate enough to kiss my venerable grandmother's hand on many occasions and receive her blessing.

Nowadays she lies at rest in the private mausoleum she built during her lifetime in Eyüp. She even had the cloth covering over her catafalque pre-

---

7 Mahmud II was the father of Abdülmecid; hence these princesses were the half-sisters of Abdülmecid.

8 This band ensemble, composed of kalfas, played in the palace wearing uniforms of the Imperial Corps of Music and remained in existence until the end of Grandfather's reign. They took private lessons from Italian teachers, working in the Music Room in Dolmabahçe Palace. In those days Italian music was quite in vogue in the palace. [A]

pared. While she was having the mausoleum built Papa wanted to help her, but she declined his offer. "I myself shall build my home of eternal rest," she said. "Let the merit in it, or the fault in doing it, lie with me."

MEMORIES OF FATHER'S YOUTH

Our real grandmother, the lady Tîrimüjgân, adored her son, my father, with all the compassion and love of a mother. Having lost a daughter, the unfortunate mother devoted herself to her son, but when she realized that she was in the clutches of a merciless disease and would not live to see her beloved son married, she did everything she could to ensure his happiness. From his youngest days she gave him splendid gifts and prepared various household artifacts for him, anticipating as she did that he might one day ascend the throne. Both during his reign and afterwards, until the day he died, Papa would say of the golden coffee tray and saltcellar that he used, "Mementos of my mother." Somehow or other Ali Efendi, the Master of the Coffee Service, managed to bring this tray to Salonica.

During his mother's illness Papa would go every day to Beylerbeyi Palace to see her, then return to Dolmabahçe Palace. At these visits Tîrimüjgân Kadın would place a purse of quarter-pound coins and a purse of silver *kuruş* coins under the red velvet cushions spread out on the floor before her bedstead. "My Prince," she would say, "I wonder what you might find under those cushions?" When Papa found these coins he was delighted, as his unfortunate mother, who knew she could never have her fill of her son, tried to devise ways to amuse him, since she could lessen the sorrows in her heart only by seeing joy in her son's face. As her son returned to Dolmabahçe Palace she awaited the morrow, when she would see him again.

In those days each prince had in his retinue a dwarf, one of the white eunuchs. Papa had a dwarf by the name of İbrahim Efendi. He entertained my father but also kept vigilant watch over him. Every morning without fail Papa's poor mother would admonish the dwarf, "Take good care of my son, he is a trust placed into your hands." As the two of them arrived together at the palace they would hear on the palace quay the sing-song voice of the milk-pudding maker, Mehmed Ağa, in his white turban and apron, "Your servant Mehmed is here! The pudding-maker-maker-maker!" He would have the huge tray of pudding brought inside and portioned out to all the servants, while he himself consumed it with his siblings.

Papa had a beautiful pony in those days that he used to ride around the gardens at the palace, with İbrahim Efendi scampering along behind.

Things continued in this way until the day his mother died, but at last tragedy befell him. For a while they concealed his mother's death from him, but slowly Papa came to sense what had happened and felt to the bottom of his heart this first grief of his life, in the year 1852.

Sultan Abdülmecid summoned Papa to him and clasped him to his breast. "Don't cry, my son," he said as he kissed his eyes and cheeks and tried to console him. "We cannot oppose the commands of God. Now I am both mother and father to you." From this came the expression that Grandfather used for Papa, "my sensitive son."

Perhaps one month later, as Grandfather understood that Papa was too young to be able to manage his affairs himself and needed an adoptive mother so as not to be left unsupervised and unoccupied, he chose the Fourth Consort, Perestû Kadınefendi, who ranked as the most estimable of his consorts, and who was known in the palace for her piety, serious-mindedness, and experience. The fact that the lady Perestû had no children of her own also lay behind his choice.

One day Grandfather summoned Papa to his rooms where he sat him down and offered him a wide range of advice, then took him under his cape to the apartments of the Fourth Consort. As he entered he said, "Look, my lady, what a beautiful child I have brought you," and drew Papa out from under his cape. To Papa he declared, "From now on this is your mother. Now kiss her hand, my son," while to his consort he said, "After God, I entrust him to you," and also had her kiss her adoptive son. He admonished Papa to obey his new mother. The Imperial Consort took Papa in her arms and embraced him, and from that day forward she looked after him with all the affection of a real mother and raised him with great care. Papa always remained devoted to his adoptive mother with the love one gives a real mother, honoring her in every way for as long as she lived. When speaking of his adoptive mother he used to say, "If my mother hadn't died only she could have cared for me so well."

Somewhat earlier, in 1845, my aunt Princess Cemile's mother, the lady Düzdidil Hanımefendi, had died, leaving Princess Cemile motherless at the age of two. Grandfather took Princess Cemile to the lady Perestû and entrusted her into the lady's care, telling her, "Now see, I have also brought you a daughter." The two siblings grew up together in the same household and spent their childhoods with one another.

Among all her fellow consorts, our grandmother Tîrimüjgân felt closest to Perestû Kadınefendi and always held her in high regard. Of course she couldn't know that one day the beloved son over whom she fretted so would be entrusted to her cherished fellow consort as an adoptive child. What can one say, such is the hand of Providence.

PAPA'S OLD AND FAITHFUL SERVANTS

Quite a number of refugees came to Istanbul in the time of my grandfather, Sultan Abdülmecid.[9] These refugees, both men and women, showed up one Friday at a Royal Mosque Procession taking place at the Valide Mosque. Sultan Abdülmecid ordered the High Hazinedar to escort all the women to the Imperial Harem and offer them food, use of the baths, and a clean set of clothing. The widows among them as well as the women with no relatives were kept at the palace. They were distributed in groups of three or four among the households of the ladies of his harem, so that in this way they remained in the palace.

One of these women and her two daughters fell to the lot of the lady Tîrimüjgân. In line with palace tradition they received new names; the mother was called Nergisnihal, while the older daughter was called Nâmeksû and the younger daughter Gûşandil. The three of them received training in the household of the lady Tîrimüjgân, where they learned the ways and customs of the palace. Nergisnihal was placed in the service of Tîrimüjgân Kadınefendi's infant daughter Princess Naime (1840–1843), who was still alive at the time, serving until the child's death as her nurse. After the Princess's death, Tîrimüjgân Kadınefendi placed Nergisnihal in service to her son Prince Abdülhamid (that is, my father) because she was so pleased and satisfied with her. Before she passed away, Tîrimüjgân Kadınefendi imparted to Nergisnihal as her last wishes, "I entrust my son to you. Do not abandon him. So long as you live do not leave him. Sleep outside his door." And indeed this faithful and loyal dear woman lived up to the trust bequeathed her, sleeping outside Papa's door. She died when I was a child around age five or six, but in my mind's eye I can picture her clearly.

From Papa on down, all of us called this woman *Nine* [Granny]. Nergisnihal did not dress as the palace kalfas did, wearing instead a short dress with no flounce, draping a large cloak over it, with a shawl gathered around her waist, and on her head something in the shape of a fez tied up with an embroidered headkerchief. Everyone in the palace respected her, calling her "His Majesty's old Granny." While he was on the throne Papa arranged

9 Muslim refugees, predominantly Circassian, from the Black Sea region fleeing the Russians in the early 1840s.

marriages for her daughters to men outside the palace. Her sons-in-law and grandchildren are still alive today.

Other kalfas in the palace also knew our grandmother Tîrimüjgân Kadın. The first to come to mind is Şevkidil Kalfa, who came to the palace in Sultan Mahmud's day and rose to become Lady Steward. There were also a number of long-serving kalfas such as Hasbihal, Dilberniyaz, and Efser, and including the mother of the Beşiktaş police prefect Vasıf Pasha, Dilber Cenan Hanım, who had been Papa's nurse and died not that long ago. Whenever she visited the palace she would stay as a guest in the household of the lady Fatma Pesend, mother of our late sister Princess Hadice. Papa addressed her as "Nanny," and we would acknowledge her position by referring to her as "His Majesty's Nanny" and would give her presents. She would take a seat in Papa's presence and tell stories of his mother and of when he was young. One day she told him, "Dear Sire, one day you came up on my shoulder and you did something naughty. And did your mother scold me! 'Why are you teaching my boy such things!' she wanted to know. I certainly caught it that day!" Papa laughed out loud and presented her with an exquisite emerald ring.

We heard quite a few tales like these from the kalfas who were still in the palace from the days of Sultan Mecid and Sultan Aziz.

MY FATHER'S PERSONALITY AND HABITS

Papa's custom was to go to bed early and rise early. Before the sun rose he would go to the bath and bathe in the tub. He had a sofa installed just outside the bath where he could sit and get dressed, then take breakfast after performing his morning prayers. Then he made his way to the harem, going out from there into the selâmlık, took a seat at his desk, and sent for the Senior Secretary. Here he worked on official business until around 11:00. When the midday meal was ready he would return to the harem and sit down to luncheon with my mother, after which he would stretch out on the chaise longue in his bedroom and rest for fifteen or twenty minutes before rising to return to the selâmlık in order to resume work on whatever business awaited him there from the morning. During this afternoon work period he would receive the Senior Secretary or the Second Secretary as well as various ministers, up until evening.

When he was particularly tired or else if his work were light he would come into the harem and meet with any members of his family to whom he might wish to speak. Sometimes he would send for us and have us play the piano, etc., for him.

After dinner most evenings he took a stroll in the gardens with pashas and beys, and at times he would come into the harem or else work in his carpentry shop or in his library.

If he was inundated with work he stayed in the Palace Secretariat until midnight, but if his work was finished he retired to his bedroom directly after the night prayers.[10] Then he would send a hazinedar to my mother, giving her the order to come to him. Mother would go to Papa's apartments in her nightdress and there they would pass the night together. As an exception to the practice in other reigns, for twenty years of his reign he dined every evening with my mother and remained with her. His other ladies he received at a specified hour or time.

When Papa lay down to rest a quiet came over the palace. One did not hear laughing voices in the palace gardens, no one played the piano or gramophone, no one made any noise or commotion. Everyone hesitated to say anything lest they make a noise that could be heard in his apartments.

In front of the harem door the Second Hazinedar and two hazinedars in her retinue would sleep, while at the doorway into the selâmlık a eunuch guard, as well as the Senior Keeper of the Prayer Rug İzzet Efendi, and Mehmed Efendi, the Commandant of the Söğütlü Regiment, did the same.

At night in his bedroom he would have a book read out to him. A folding screen would be set up at the foot of his bed and the Master of the Robes İsmet Bey read a book aloud. Later Hajji Mahmud Efendi and the Enciphering Secretary Âsım Bey read as well. They read until Papa began to doze off, and then when they sensed that he was asleep they rose quietly and left the room. The Second Hazinedar locked the door behind them.

PAPA'S MEALTIMES AND COMPORTMENT AT TABLE, AND THE FOODS HE ATE

The Head Butler Osman Bey, followed by the Second Butler Hüseyin Efendi and the Third and Fourth Butlers, carrying the table service and cutlery that they had placed inside baskets, and the Senior Tray Bearer in his gold-embroidered jacket and baggy trousers, a large tray atop his head, all exited the Imperial Pantry and came to the stone court adjacent to the dining room. Here they placed the tray down atop a folding stand, then set the table. The two equerries on duty stood watch at the door. The plates and dishes were of porcelain edged in red and white gilding and marked with a monogram,

10 Performed one and one-half to two hours after sunset.

Abdülhamid's "Accession Daughter" Princess Naime, so called because she was born when he came to the throne, at around age seven in 1882. Photographer: Kargopoulo.

while the Baccarat water goblet service bore a monogram in red. Another set had the monogram in white. The saltcellar that had belonged to his mother Tîrimüjgân Kadınefendi was always placed in front of him, for he most definitely wanted it on his table.

The knife and fork services were of gold. It was customary in the palace for the midday meal to be served at eleven o'clock and the evening meal at five o'clock. Meals had been served at these times in the palace since days of old.

The Head Butler surrendered the tray to the old and faithful kalfa Sırrıcemal and then waited in the guardroom throughout the meal.

From the days before I was born through to the end of his reign, Papa took his meals with Mother. As soon as the meal was ready a hazinedar came and announced to Mother, "Our Master is requesting." Mother would go directly and take a seat at table with Papa. Sırrıcemal Kalfa brought in whichever dishes Papa had selected from the menu. The kalfa Feleksû, who belonged to the entourage of Sırrıcemal Kalfa, also waited in service.

After the meal the butlers came in again and cleared the table. The household staff and equerries in the guardroom would eat any leftover food.

PAPA'S RELATIONS WITH US, AND HIS CONCERN FOR OUR PROPER MANNERS

When his duties were light, Papa would summon whomever he wished from among his consorts and daughters and spend time in conversation with them. On no account did he want either his consorts or his daughters to interfere in official business. He paid special attention to the matter of our good manners and did not overlook our slightest infractions, nor did he permit overfamiliarity with him. When he saw or sensed that we had committed an infraction, he wouldn't say anything to us; instead he sent word to our mothers. We knew quite well how we should speak and behave in his presence.

He wished us to dress quite simply and didn't want us to deck ourselves out with trinkets. Our necklines might be open a bit but our arms were completely covered.

We wore light colors with our hair in a braid down our backs and ribbons in the same color as our dress. We put on neither perfume nor face powder, but since Papa used the eau de cologne Jean-Marie Farina, we used it too. Our older sisters used to pile their hair on top of their heads, following the fashion of those days.

Papa didn't want us to speak in a loud voice or with hand gestures. He made sure that we always comported ourselves quietly and gracefully. He wanted us to behave respectfully at all times toward our elders, our mothers, and our siblings, and saw to it that we kept to our proper place in order and did not slip in ahead of them. Impertinence he tolerated not one whit.

He never addressed anyone with the familiar form of the word "you" and even issued orders to his kalfas in a polite manner, using the formal form of "you" and saying things such as "would you be so kind as to bring . . ."[11] When addressing us he said either *kızım* [my daughter] or *Sultan* [Princess]. He behaved extremely respectfully toward his consorts, employing the phrase "Senior Consort" or "Senior *İkbal*," for example, when sending messages to them or summoning them.

He would meet with his sons, the princes, in the *selâmlık*, issuing the order that whichever of them he wished to see should come. He was more formal toward his older sons, and when in his presence they always wore the stambuline coat, never appearing before him in a common jacket. He received his favorite son, Prince Burhaneddin, and his younger sons more often than the other, older princes.

Admonishments he made to the princes would be conveyed through the equerries or the chamberlains.

Papa wanted his children to be exposed to music, and he purchased pianos and various musical instruments for us. He had us play the piano for him and would listen to us and correct our mistakes, also making sure we played at the correct tempo. "That's not how it goes, try it again," he would say.

PAPA'S AUNT, PRINCESS ÂDİLE

Daughter of Sultan Mahmud II and wife of the Grand Vizier and Imperial Son-in-law Mehmed Ali Pasha, Princess Âdile was a poetess and a scholarly, cultivated, and pious woman renowned for her benevolence, good works, and charity. She penned beautiful elegies to her husband when he died. Those in her service and in close relations with her always spoke with pleasure of her and her polite manners. After she died, the kalfas and eunuchs who came to the palace could not hold back their tears when they told us stories about their mistress and spoke of her goodness.

When she wanted to visit Papa she would send a message to let him know, upon which special preparations were made, and in this fashion she would come to the palace. Unlike the other princesses she wouldn't come by during

11 Turkish has a familiar and a formal form of the word *you*, as in French *tu* and *vous*. Typically a master would have addressed his slaves in the familiar form.

the holidays and so forth, or write petitions requesting something of the Sultan. Instead she made her wishes known through her Senior Eunuch, and her requests would be granted immediately. When Auntie Princess wanted to come by, Papa would wait for her in his private apartments and none other than the High Hazinedar along with ranking hazinedars and Lady Secretaries would go to receive her. While she was in his presence equerries and hazinedars waited in service. Her carriage would approach the Imperial Apartments, the Senior Equerry would take her arm to assist her out of the carriage, and when she entered through the doorway Papa and the Princess Mother were there to greet her. She would be conducted straightaway to the salon, where Papa devotedly and respectfully kissed his aunt's hand and had her take a seat on the large sofa while he sat in a chair facing her. Hazinedars brought in her coffee on a tray suspended within chains, and Papa took the cup from the tray and handed it to his aunt. Princess Âdile was in the habit of smoking the water pipe, so a bejeweled crystal narghile, prepared beforehand, would be brought into the room, whereupon Papa would rise and bring it over to his aunt, handing her the tube. As for us, we would come in and kiss her hand, and render her the same formal salutation that we made to the Padishah by performing a floor *temenna* to her; then we withdrew. She addressed Papa as *oğlum* [my son], to which Papa responded *Emredersiniz halacığım* [At your command, Auntie]. They would spend an hour or two in conversation, then she departed in her carriage just as she had come, Papa escorting her to the door.

From her face one could tell she had been beautiful in days gone by. Slender, of medium height, with chestnut brown hair, blue-hazel eyes, and a radiant complexion, she was a princess possessed of the bearing, conduct, and cultivation that proclaimed her innate nobility of character. She always dressed in a completely Turkish fashion: gown of heavy fabrics with four flounces, shoes of chamois leather, shawl tied as a sash around her waist, the so-called *salta* wide-sleeved jacket over this ensemble, on her head something like a fez wrapped in a silk headkerchief pinked along the edges, and onto which she had fastened exquisite brooches of emeralds and rubies in the shape of roses, a larger one in the center flanked by two smaller ones. Other than these she wore no jewels or decorations. The last time she visited us, she took a magnificent ruby ring off her finger and said as she put it on Papa's finger, "My grandfather Sultan Abdülhamid I gave this ring to my father Sultan Mahmud II as a remembrance. One day my father placed this ring on my finger and told me that it was a memento from his father. He said, 'Now I am giving it to you as a keepsake.' From that day to this, I have worn this ring on my finger. But now I sense that my journey to the hereafter is near, and so this ring, from which I could never bear to part, I am giving to you as a remembrance, my son!" Papa stood up right then, kissed his aunt's hand, and gave her his thanks for presenting him with this historic ring.

In fact that was the last time they saw each other, as well as the last time she came to the palace. As Papa was not in the habit of wearing rings he kept this keepsake of his aunt in a small golden purse and set it in the little glass cabinet that he always ordered placed in whichever room where he slept the night. This cabinet at the head of his bed contained quite a few family keepsakes that had belonged to his father, but at Papa's dethronement they all went missing.

PAPA'S SISTERS

I saw three of my father's sisters. The others I never met, I just heard about them through stories. In order of age, the aunts whom I saw were the princesses Cemile, Seniha, and Mediha. On ceremonial occasions Princess Cemile took precedence as she was the eldest, and always took her place at Papa's right. A large armchair was reserved for her on the right-hand side, where she took a seat. In processions she walked at the side of the Princess Mother, ahead of everyone else. She always wore brown-colored dresses and on her head a *hotoz* of the same color, fashioned of lace or tulle. She dressed in the Turkish style, with a long train fastened to her waist. Since the sumptuous fabrics she wore were always various shades of brown, this color served as something of a hallmark for her. She wore no jewels whatsoever. Despite this simplicity, her imperial bearing amply conveyed her rank of princess. Those in a position to know said that she looked just like my grandfather, Sultan Abdülmecid, and indeed from the photographs the eyes and features are the same. Everyone in the palace felt great respect and fondness for Princess Cemile, holding her in affectionate esteem. She spoke so graciously and intelligently, not laughing when it wasn't called for, and exhibiting toward everyone the appropriate conduct due him or her. In sum, she was the perfect princess. Princess Cemile was the wife of Mahmud Celâleddin Pasha, son of the Imperial Son-in-law Fethi Pasha.

Princess Seniha used to wear dresses of the most superb cloth, with her tiara on her head on formal occasions, and she also wore gowns with long trains in the European fashion spreading out behind her. She had a regal look about her. Her face was pretty. She had her hair cut like a man's and never let it grow out. In manner she was entirely unconstrained. Often

Sultan Abdülhamid's half-sister Princess Mediha in court dress with train, circa 1885, when she was around age thirty. Photographer unknown.

would she burst into laughter, and she spoke rapidly and in a deep voice. Princess Seniha was not particularly welcome at the palace because some of her gestures were a bit too indecorous. This Princess Seniha was the wife of Mahmud Celâleddin Pasha and mother to Prince Sabaheddin and Prince Lutfullah.[12]

Princess Mediha was fond of European ways. She dressed beautifully and with great dignity, appearing splendidly regal in her gowns with their long trains. She was petite with white skin and gorgeous black eyes, and she too resembled Sultan Abdülmecid. In manner she was gracious, attractive, and wonderfully kind. Everyone in the palace loved this princess. As did Princess Seniha, she too spoke laughingly, with an air of good humor in her voice. When these two sisters were together chatting with Papa, they would both laugh and try to amuse Papa and get him to smile as though they were in competition with one another. We would all watch in astonishment as they did this.

In 1879 Princess Mediha married Necib Pasha. They had a son, Prince Sami, who later became personal aide-de-camp to Papa and served in the Ertuğrul Regiment. As a member of the entourage of my brother Prince Abdülkadir, he participated in ceremonial occasions and at the Royal Mosque Processions each Friday, following on horseback behind Papa, and always came to the palace. After Necib Pasha died Princess Mediha married Ferid Pasha, but no children came of this marriage. Princess Mediha died 9 November 1928.

A BIOGRAPHY OF MY MOTHER

Mother is the daughter of the Abazian notable Ağır Mahmud Bey and Emine Hanım.[13] Mother's real name was Ayşe and she has a sister named Fatma one year younger than she, as well as a brother named Şahin Bey seven years older than she.

Mahmud Bey volunteered for service in the Ottoman-Russian War of 1877–1878, entrusting his wife and children to the care of Hüseyin Vasfi Pasha,

---

12 Princess Seniha's husband and her son Sabaheddin both fled the country due to their opposition to Abdülhamid's rule. More likely this fact accounts for why she was not particularly welcome at the palace.

13 The Abazian people of the northwestern Caucasus, inland from the Black Sea, fell under Russian rule in the eighteenth century. In the nineteenth century large numbers of Abazians, who were Sunni Muslims, migrated to Turkey, particularly after the 1862 Russian governmental edict that ordered their removal from their traditional homeland.

an army officer posted in the area. Hüseyin Vasfi Pasha's wife Bezminigâr Hanım was Mahmud Bey's cousin, hence a close relative, and moreover had been in service to the Princess Mother Pertevniyal before her marriage, so for these reasons the Pasha sent Mahmud Bey's family to live with his wife in Istanbul.

At the time Mother was three years old,[14] my aunt was two, and Şahin Bey ten. In those days the Princess Mother Pertevniyal was despondent over the death of her son Sultan Aziz. Her only pleasure and distraction lay in passing time by training young and lovely children, gathering them about her and finding consolation in the things they said and in their sweet behavior. The Princess Mother Pertevniyal had another habit: between dusk and the nighttime prayer she would prostrate herself in worship, weeping loudly as she cried out, "I forgive everything, only I seek justice for the blood of my son!" Afterwards in her room she would have the whole Quran recited and then have the children say "Amen."

Knowing these things, Bezminigâr Hanım decided to present Mother and my aunt, her two guests, to the Princess Mother. With difficulty she won over Mother's mother Emine Hanım; then she took the two girls round. The Princess Mother was enchanted by Mother's beautiful face, blue eyes, and blonde hair, and by the sweet aspect of my aunt's head of curls. "These children are for me," she declared. "I shall adopt them and raise them. Never shall I send them back. They are to stay here!" She ordered Nâvekyar Kalfa to look after Mother and Şevkidide Kalfa to look after my aunt, under the protection of her own High Hazinedar, Şemsicemal Kalfa. Their mother Emine Hanım and older brother Şahin Bey remained in the home of Bezminigâr Hanım, but when word arrived that Mahmud Bey had been killed in the war, despite all attempts to dissuade them they returned to the place from which they had come. After this nothing further was heard of them.

When years later the Princess Mother died, as custom dictated all the servants in her villa, headed by the High Hazinedar, were transferred to Dolmabahçe Palace. Mother grew into a young lady in Dolmabahçe Palace, and when she had entered her fourteenth year she was noticed by Papa, who in those days was in the habit of going to the harem after the ceremony of receiving felicitations on festival days. She was taken into Yıldız Palace straightaway.

---

14 Reckoning by the Islamic calendar. By the Gregorian calendar, the future lady Müşfika was around five.

When the Princess Mother Pertevniyal took in my mother and aunt she changed their names, as palace tradition had it, calling Mother Destizer and my aunt Destiper. As mentioned above, when Papa married Mother he changed her name, calling Mother Müşfika and also making Auntie a hazinedar with the name of Şükriye.

My aunt Şükriye Hanım, whom I loved dearly, grew up in Yıldız Palace as a hazinedar of Papa's until she reached the age of twenty-five, when she was given in marriage to Halid Pasha, the second son of Papa's Master of the Robes İsmet Bey. İsmet Bey's mother had been Papa's wet nurse.[15] Auntie's children are still alive today. Some five months before Papa's death, Auntie died of typhoid while I was in Switzerland. Papa was in Beylerbeyi Palace when he was informed of her death, and it was Papa who paid the expenses for her shroud and for laying out her corpse. She lies in the cemetery at Rumeli Hisarı. May God have mercy on her soul.

WHAT I HEARD IN LATER YEARS ABOUT MY BIRTH

Papa married Mother one year before I was born. Mother's marriage was performed by the Deputy of the Noble Sweeper, Seyid Esad Efendi, and witnessed by the Superintendent of Departures, Hajji Mahmud Efendi, by the imam of Kâğıthane, Ali Efendi, and by the Senior Equerry, Şerafeddin Ağa.

As his first gift to her, Papa presented Mother with an exquisite copy of the Holy Quran. When he gave her the Quran he said, "I want to give you a name. I will open this Quran purposefully and we will see what sort of name Almighty God will decree for you." When he opened the Quran his eyes fell on the word müşfikun [the compassionate ones] in verse 28 of the chapter "The Prophets."[16] "God willing, this will prove auspicious for me, and you will indeed be a compassionate lady," he said. He ordered her seal engraved, and gave her the title Müşfika Başikbal, the Senior İkbal Müşfika.

Truly Mother did prove to be a felicitous, exceedingly compassionate life's companion for Papa, as until the end of his days she shared in all the tragedies that befell him, and when Papa passed away in Beylerbeyi Palace she was holding him in her arms.

15 In Ottoman culture this created a bond between the two men, as exemplified in the term for their relationship, sütkardeşi, "milk brother."

16 By opening a book in this way one attributed divine inspiration, auspiciousness, and good fortune to whatever passage or word one encountered. This was known as tefe'ül [taking something as a good omen]. [ÖO]

Mother donated that Holy Quran to the pious foundation that maintained Papa's mausoleum and had her name inscribed in it. If it has been lost I will be terribly saddened.[17]

BEFORE AND AFTER MY BIRTH

As had been the case with Papa's other ladies, once Mother joined their ranks the apartments known as the Lesser Chancellery were then made ready. A household staff was delegated, with Dilesrar Kalfa appointed Mistress of the Household. She was well known in the palace because she had been in service since the latter days of the reign of Sultan Abdülmecid and had served Sultan Aziz.

The day that I came into the world, one year later, Papa was delighted and presented a brooch to Filürye Kalfa, who had brought him the good tidings, and 300 liras to Ebezade Kâmile Hanım, who had served as midwife at my birth. In addition a decoration was conferred upon Dr. Triandafilidis, the specialist in women's diseases of that era who had examined and treated Mother every week during her pregnancy. I was born a healthy child of three and one-half kilos.

Before I was born Papa announced, "If it's a girl I shall name her Ayşe, if it's a boy he shall be Musa." Two days after my birth he ordered his prayer rug spread out in Mother's room to face Mecca, recited the call to prayer, and repeated my name three times in my ear, then handed me to Dilesrar Kalfa as he told her, "I entrust my daughter to you."

Servants of the Palace Secretariat brought in from the treasury my gilded cradle as well as, according to the fashion of those days, embroidered blankets, towels, silver bowls, and a silvered tortoiseshell bowl that was part of the ancient traditions.[18] For this these servants received their customary gratuity. In the evening of the seventh day after my birth, Mother's Henna Night,[19] an orchestral ensemble composed of palace ladies, played music, sweets and fruit drinks were served, and coins were distributed.

My wet nurse, or as the palace expression had it my *sütnine* or "milk granny," Pervin Hanım, had been made ready in advance in the home of Hajji Mahmud Efendi and so was brought straightaway to the palace.

---

17 This Holy Quran is in the collections of the Museum of Turkish and Islamic Arts in Istanbul, artifact number 406. [ÖO]
18 Silver-covered tortoiseshell was given as a symbol of long life. [ÖO]
19 So-called because the new mother's fingers and toes were painted with henna.

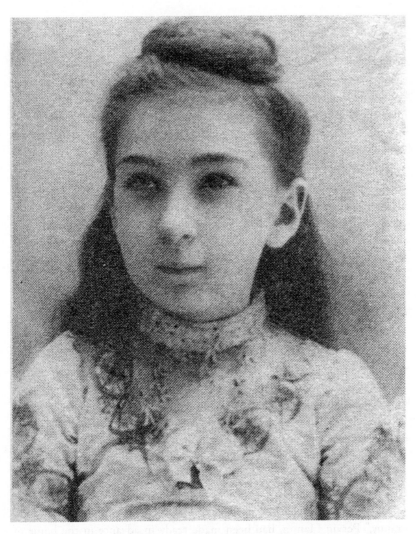

Princess Ayşe at age twelve, around 1899. Photographer unknown.

Papa had begun construction on the apartments known as the New Villa before I was born. This villa was built because the brick building dating to Sultan Abdülmecid's reign known as the Imperial Lodge was damp and injurious to Papa's health; moreover, his family was growing and quarters in the palace were noticeably cramped. The villa was truly gorgeous. Here I spent my infancy and the first years of my youth. Papa devoted a considerable amount of passion and care to its construction, so it was built in the loveliest and airiest spot on the Yıldız grounds, with the most splendid views. The architect was Vasilaki Efendi, with the interior appointments fabricated by the most skilled artisans of the imperial carpentry shop.

Once I was a bit older Papa's Third Equerry of the time, Said Ağa, was appointed my governor. One of my older sisters and my nurse took me to the door that led from the harem to the *selâmlık* and handed me over to my governor.

I used to ride about the gardens in my little carriage. Young eunuchs would bring along whatever things it was thought I might need—always in a silver-plated case—as well as a silver water bottle and my parasol. Every other day in the morning they took me to Papa to show me to him. Papa would caress and hug me.

When I reached age four or five, five little girls my age were brought in to entertain me. These little girls were well tended to and dressed neatly and prettily. I loved these small friends of mine. In the afternoons we would all play with my dolls in the toy room. My favorite toys were the dolls that made music. While we played my nurse Nilifelek Kalfa would always be sitting before the door, keeping an eye on us. If one of the girls did something naughty or said a bad word the kalfa would immediately pull her out of the game and punish her. When that happened I was terribly upset.

I LEARN TO READ

At length the time came for me to learn to read, so Mother let Papa know. A study room was then to be set aside in the Lesser Chancellery, where I had been born. In the mornings I was to go there with my sister Princess Şadiye, three months older than I, and we were to take lessons from one of the instructors assigned to us. Before we came over, the palace servants would place red velvet cushions and low reading desks in the large salon of the building. Our reed pens and our porcelain writing sets, with pen cases and sand sprinklers, were to be set out on the desks. Our instructors would be the privy secretary Hasib Efendi and the Private Enciphering Secretary

Kâmil Efendi. Hasib Efendi would give us lessons in the Holy Quran, Arabic, and Persian, while Kâmil Efendi was to teach us Turkish reading and writing, Ottoman grammar, arithmetic, history, and geography.

Our delight knew no bounds. Mother had prepared my school bag, a satchel of gorgeous purple velvet embroidered with silver, containing inside it, within exquisite gilded cases, an alphabet primer and gold pointers set with diamonds at the tip.[20] My school bag was purple because I loved that color.

The first Thursday of the month in which the Prophet was born (the month of Rebiülevvel) was chosen for us to go to our school and be handed over to our tutors in order to recite our first Noble *Besmele*. Everyone in the palace household was at the door of the harem wishing us good luck. *Allah zihin açıklığı versin*, they said [May God grant you clear thinking]. On the *selâmlık* side of the door the eunuchs and the old servants wished us the same thing.

Before I went to the school Mother sat me down and gave me a good deal of advice as well as quite a few examples of how we should obey our teachers and pay attention to them and work hard, and of how the respect owed a teacher exceeded that owed one's parents.

Our teachers were waiting for us. We greeted them respectfully. We sat down before our low writing desks and recited the Noble *Besmele*. We read a few letters of the alphabet. Our writing instructor had us write one or two letters. With that our lesson for the day was over, but we thought ourselves the most learned scholars in the world! We promised our teachers that we would work hard, then went straight off to Papa's apartments.

We knew well the customs by which one was to enter Papa's presence. This time Papa was in the large salon in the harem. Whenever we saw him he was busy with something, reading a document or meeting with someone, and this seemed natural to us. Mother was there as well. We told her that we wanted to relate that we had been to school and had read a lesson, and that we wished to kiss His Majesty's hand. Mother announced, "My dear Sire, the princesses have come. They have read their first lesson and would like to kiss Your Majesty's hand." When Papa said, "Have them enter," in we came, Princess Şadiye in front and I behind, each with our hands clasped together in front of us.[21] We performed a *temenna* and kissed his hand. Stroking our chins, he pulled us to him and kissed our foreheads. "So you had a lesson today, is that so?" he said.

20 The term *pointer* refers to the thin sticks made of a material such as bone, ivory, or silver, for the use of children who were beginning to read, in order to pick out one by one the individual letters of the words they were spelling out. [ÖÖ]
21 A mark of respect to one's superior.

"Hopefully you will work hard; let me see you doing so." We answered, "Yes, Sire, we worked hard." He smiled, "Very good. Bravo! That's how it should be." Mother motioned to us that we shouldn't stay, so we withdrew, performing another *temenna* while walking backwards before running out, delighted.

A YOUNGSTER'S SENTIMENTS

I loved my mother dearly, but I loved my father even more. She shared the love, respect, and veneration I felt toward Papa. Could I possibly have exhibited the same free and easy behavior toward Papa as I did toward Mother? Papa kissed and embraced me the same way as Mother did, calling me "my beautiful girl, my angel." These sweet words made me so happy. Yet in his presence I avoided committing the slightest infraction. Mother would admonish me to keep my hands clasped in front of me whenever I entered his presence and to respond *Efendimiz* [Sire] whenever he called me to him by saying "My daughter!" My father was the father of the nation, the Padishah. Everyone addressed him as *Efendimiz*—how could I have addressed him by anything else? As I grew older my feelings deepened, my love increased, but the truth remains that in every instance I remained aware of Papa's exalted position.

PIANO LESSONS BEGIN

The harem hazinedar Kevser Kalfa made sure I learned my lessons by heart, including my piano lessons. In those years the Second Hazinedar Zülfet Kalfa, who remained with Papa until the end of his days, played the piano beautifully. Guatelli Pasha used to come and give Zülfet lessons in the salon. One day I ran over to the salon and went in, going straight up to the piano. "Pasha," I declared, "I came to play the piano too." In his thickly accented Turkish he said, "Well then, my Princess, do play," as he lifted me onto his lap. With one finger I picked out the tune of Papa's march. My ears' sensitivity in picking out the keys and the sounds pleased the old Pasha greatly, and he sent Mother a message that I should start piano lessons immediately as he saw talent in me. Appointed as my teacher was the hazinedar Dürrüyekta, the student of François Lombardi, who had recently been hired as instructor to the Imperial Corps of Music and from whom I also took lessons once a week.[22]

---

22 The lady Dürrüyekta later became a consort of Prince Selim. She is buried in Tripoli in Lebanon. [ÖO]

Dürrüyekta was born in 1894—some seven years after Princess Ayşe—so at the time of the piano lessons could have been at most fourteen years of age.

He gave lessons in more modern music, whereas Guatelli Pasha was quite old-fashioned. In a short time I made progress, but I played by heart without paying the slightest attention or giving the least importance to the written notes. My teacher had transcribed for my level Papa's march as well as some pieces from the operas *La Traviata* and *Il Trovatore* and taught them to me. But he was quite exasperated at my not paying attention to the notes.

One day he had an audience with Papa and the decision was taken to have me perform. It was on an evening. With a proud swagger I picked up my music, of whose contents I was completely ignorant, and went to Papa's apartments. Mother announced, "My dear Sire, the Princess has come and would like to play the piano for Your Majesty." Delighted, I entered the room, kissed His Majesty's hand, and dashed over to the piano. Papa said, "Well then, my girl, play something and let's have a listen." I was pleased but a little bit nervous. My heart was pounding. I played the march well enough, then it was the turn of the other pieces I'd learned. For some reason the melodies had flown right out of my head. I couldn't find them at all. I looked at the notes but couldn't understand them. I died of embarrassment. In a gentle voice Mother said, "Do you see what's happened? Why didn't you listen when they told you to mind the notes? Do you understand now?"

Papa just looked at me without saying a thing. I couldn't bear it any longer and began to weep. I bent my head over the keys, sobbing. Papa must have taken pity on me because he said in his fine strong voice, "Get up, my girl, and come here." I did and he added, "Don't cry, my girl. It seems you were careless and didn't memorize the notes. That's why you can't play. From now on you'll work harder and learn the music, then you can come and play for me again." Mother, however, showed not the slightest pity. Words fail to describe how I slunk away, how ashamed I was. I can still feel it today. I ran home without looking anyone in the face, and wept. I was devastated.

But after that I was a careful and hard-working student.

OUR VISIT TO THE GRAND VIZIER CEVAD PASHA

Once we had grown up enough a carriage was placed at our disposal and we began to participate in the Friday Mosque Processions. As a mark of special favor on one such occasion, after the ceremony Papa sent my sister Princess Refia and me to pay a call on the Grand Vizier. In those days the mansion known as the Ferid Pasha Villa, nowadays occupied by a school, had been given to Cevad Pasha for his use.[23]

23 Cevad Pasha served as Grand Vizier from 4 September 1891 to 8 June 1895. [A]

My sister and I got into the carriage and the veteran palace eunuch Yaver Ağa took a seat across from us. We were taken to the villa. The Pasha had had carpets spread out before the door and was waiting for us at the outer gate, where he greeted us.

His wife the lady Nimet and his sister the lady Sare greeted us at the inner door. The Pasha was a tremendously jovial and lovable gentleman. He took me by his right arm, and my sister by his left arm, escorted us through the cordon of kalfas lined up on either side, and led us up the stairs. The kalfas were saluting us by bowing deeply.

We entered a salon where they had us sit on a large sofa in the middle of the room. The Pasha and everyone else remained standing, waiting for us to tell them to sit. We were still children, but familiar enough with ceremonial to say modestly, "I beg you, do take a seat."

They brought us coffee in the palace fashion, on a tray suspended from hanging chains, but we thanked them and did not drink it since we knew that children were not to drink coffee. Next they offered us sweets and fruit drinks, the Pasha himself rising and serving them to us, and this time we thanked them and accepted. They didn't know what to say to entertain us and get us to talk. Pretty young kalfas came in and danced while Nimet Hanım played the piano beautifully. They brought in all kinds of toys and set them down in front of us, but we just sat there like well-behaved little girls, not touching the toys, exchanging glances with one another so that neither of us would commit a faux pas. We just said thank you, and nothing else.

The Pasha presented each of us with a young kalfa. His brother Şakir Pasha came in and the Pasha introduced him to us. A buffet was prepared from which the Pasha himself served us all kinds of dishes. We stayed some two hours before departing with the same ceremonial, the Pasha helping us into the carriage and presenting Yaver Ağa with a ring set with a single stone.

Behind us, the Pasha followed in a carriage loaded with toys and proceeded to the Palace Secretariat to extend his thanks, while his wife and sister went to the harem in order to offer their thanks there.

MY VISIT WITH GAZİ OSMAN PASHA

One day Papa was about to set out on the Friday Mosque Procession. I was there too, about to go out into the Great Garden with the eunuchs. Papa's carriage had arrived and was standing outside the glass door, while Gazi Osman Pasha was waiting for Papa too as they were to ride in the carriage together. When Papa saw me there he said, "Come, my girl, let me show you to the Pasha," and he introduced me with, "Pasha, my daughter, Princess Ayşe." When he told me to kiss the Pasha's hand I started toward the Pasha, who smiled and bowed low but didn't extend his hand. That's when I saw up close the Pasha's glowing, cheerful face and blue eyes. He said to Papa, "God bless her, Sire," and offered up prayers.

Papa also showed me on a few occasions to our ambassador in Paris, Münir Pasha. I was present when he was sitting with Papa in the theater and in the garden. Now and then Papa would order dresses for us through Münir Pasha. I don't know how it was possible, but without anyone even taking our measurements these dresses from Paris fit us exactly.

I BEGIN TO WEAR THE VEIL

I began to wear the veil long before the usual time. I had just turned eleven years of age but was already grown, in fact had shot up in height, and had an imposing appearance. One Friday I had gone out to participate in the Royal Mosque Procession. I shall never forget that on that day I wore a pink dress. As Papa came out of the mosque he paused momentarily on the stairs and looked over at the carriages. It was not the custom to salute the Padishah from the harem carriages, so I was showing myself through the carriage window, smiling as I looked out.

As usual, Papa drove his own carriage back to the palace that day. That evening as he was sitting at dinner with Mother, he announced, "I saw my daughter in her carriage today. From a distance she looks much older than she is. Anyone who didn't know differently would think she was a grown-up young woman. Starting next week she will have to wear the veil. From here on she must not go out uncovered." Mother protested a bit, "But dear Sire, how could that be? She's so young." Nonetheless Papa answered her, "My lady, do you think people won't say, 'He's letting his grown daughter go about unveiled'? Sooner or later she's going to take the veil, isn't she? From now on she shall get used to covering herself."

My sister Princess Şadiye, some three or four months older than I, took the veil much later than I. But I was delighted that I'd be wearing the veil just like my older sisters did.

The next week my *ferace* was prepared. It too was pink, and embroidered in the front in gold thread down to the hem. The veil pins were made of pearls. That day I was so excited as I got dressed. All the older kalfas in the palace came round to offer their congratulations to Mother; "May this be auspicious and fortunate" was their wish. My governess, in whose care I had grown up, pinned my veil round my head. Kalfas lined both sides of the stairway from top to bottom. As I descended the stairs my governess tossed coins down toward the bottom. In this way I came to the carriage. My tutors offered their congratulations as they supported me by the arm. So now I was being treated like an adult princess. Mother presented gifts to the coachmen, the household staff, and my tutor.

This is how I took the veil.

By the time I turned fourteen I had grown so much that I began to wear dresses with trains at court ceremonies. The first time I wore a dress with a train was at the religious holidays. Once again coins were scattered about. When Papa saw me like that he commented, "Gracious me, you've grown and become quite lovely! This suits you well." I was thrilled to count myself among the ranks of adult princesses.

OTHER CHILDHOOD MEMORIES

In my childhood I loved animals. I had beautiful cats and dogs and even a parrot that always perched on my shoulder. Dr. İsmet Pasha had presented the parrot to Papa when I was still in the cradle, and Papa had given it to Mother. This parrot grew used to me when I was small, entertained me, and later on became almost like a friend. He used to walk all over the house in his hobbling fashion that was so sweet. He would rest his head on my knee and point to his head with his foot, which was the signal, "scratch me." When he was in his cage and wanted out he'd cry, *Ayşe Sultan, hayatım* [Princess Ayşe, my darling], and I would do his bidding and let him out. Papa loved this bird too and called him *Dadı Kalfa* [Nurse Kalfa]. I used to put him on top of the piano and play special tunes just for him. These he knew and he'd have some fun by spreading his wings and sticking out his head. When Papa was deposed I lost this beloved parrot, but later on I shall tell of how I got him back again.

Our favorite pastime was going for walks in the Yıldız gardens. After the Royal Mosque Processions on Fridays we would go round to the villas set about the great park that we in the palace called *kır* [the countryside]. There we'd pass the time together, one of us each week incurring the expense of bringing the cold dishes that we called "garden service." There we would enjoy ourselves until evening, strolling about and going round to the Tent Pavilion, the Malta Pavilion, the Head Gardener's Villa, the Persian Pavilion, and the Drill Hall Pavilion.

On these excursions we younger princesses would all get together. Our mothers came along and the old and young kalfas in our suites would also be

The gardens of Yıldız in snow, around 1890. Photographer unknown.

there with us. Sultan Murad's daughters would join in, as would the young daughters our age of Prince Salâheddin (son of Sultan Murad), after the death of their grandfather. Our married sisters came along as well. After enjoying ourselves in this way we returned to the palace in the evening. Now and then we went to Kâğıthane as well.

The Selâmlık Gardens by the harem contained all kinds of birds—peacocks, pheasants, different varieties of parrots, and doves. In the Great Pond, the Japanese ducks sent to Papa as a gift by the Emperor of Japan were gorgeous. Rare birds also sent by the Emperor were to be found on the island in the middle of the pond, and swans had been brought in from Switzerland.

All manner of falsehood has been told concerning the Great Pond in the Selâmlık Gardens at the palace. Papa had a small motorboat in this pond. When he would go out into the gardens with the harem he would get in this motorboat, taking his harem ladies and his daughters with him, and go over to the island where he would get out and sit in the Lesser Pavilion drinking coffee. Papa would also go out with his Privy Staff, sometimes accompanied by one or two pashas, sometimes by his brothers, sons, or adult princes. Now and then he would take his sisters and other visiting princesses for rides in the motorboat, himself at the wheel. On those occasions the Third Equerry Nadir Ağa would accompany him, acting almost like a sailor, helping to dock the boat and so forth.

When the Khedive came to the palace Papa walked about with him too, while the Khedive's mother and sisters strolled about with us. Kalfas also would stroll about the gardens and paddle around the pond in rowboats.

THE DEATH OF MY NURSE

The first sorrow of death and loss I experienced in my childhood happened on the day I lost my nurse. The anguish seared my small and innocent heart and left me weeping bitter tears. The image of my nurse Raksıdil Kalfa remained vivid for me, her voice always sounded in my ears, and the tears would fall again from my eyes. All the kalfas tried to divert me in order to help me over this grief and they would hand me over to my tutor to take me for walks in the garden.

My nurse died from tuberculosis. The doctors had forbidden her to spend even one minute in the company of her Princess, but I did not know that, I just wanted my nurse. They put me off by telling me, "She's ill but she's being taken care of; she'll get better and come back to you." I had grown quite used to her. When I was small she would put me to bed and sit at my bedside singing me lullabies in her high, gentle voice until I fell asleep. During the day she'd tell me wonderful stories and dress me with her limitless care, affection, and love. She did everything for me. I used to kiss her cheeks and call her benim cici dadıcığım [dear little Nursey], while she would call me bir taneciğim, melek sultanım [my one and only angel Princess].

When Nurse left my rooms to undergo treatment she sent a wrapped bundle with instructions to "give it to my Princess." She'd said for me to keep it as a remembrance of her. They brought it in. I opened it. The first thing inside was a picture of me. Next were mementos, each one of me; my first handwriting, the blouse and undergarments put on me the day I was born, the first spoon I ever used, my first pencil, a lock of my baby hair, my hair ribbon, and all kinds of other things from my life spilled out before me. I began to weep.

These mementos that she gave me I kept until recently. Like so many other things I finally lost them too. But the memory of my dear nurse lives forever in my heart. Even now in my mind's eye I can summon her tender gaze. Then I sigh from within and weep. I shall always remember her with veneration.

MY GOVERNESS

My governess Dilesrar Kalfa was one of the most esteemed and worthy of the veteran kalfas in the palace. The day that I was born Papa handed me to her. Papa used to call her *Büyük Kalfa* [Senior Kalfa], so everyone in the palace showed deference to her by calling her that.

My poor governess suffered a dreadful illness. All at once my strong, stalwart governess was ill and burning with fever. They said that a boil had appeared on her back. Once again I was in tears. Every doctor in the palace came to have a look at her, but none of them could make anything of it. The boil kept growing.

Finally the surgeon Emin Bey came to have a look at her and realized that it was a carbuncle. He told Papa, who ordered that Cemil Bey be summoned and shown her; Cemil Bey had just returned from Europe and was the son-in-law of the Şeyhülislâm Cemaleddin Efendi. When Cemil Bey saw her he announced that she must be treated immediately, that the treatment given her so far had only lost time, and that if even six more hours were to elapse he could not take responsibility for the consequences. Papa said he should intervene at once but if at all possible he should not anesthetize her because she was asthmatic. And indeed Cemil Bey accomplished this critical task without anesthetic, although since the Senior Kalfa had lost consciousness she felt nothing anyway. On the other hand, İşveriz Kalfa and my tutor Beşir Ağa were present in the room and both fainted as they couldn't bear to watch the operation, because the surgeon dug out a chunk of flesh underneath her right shoulder blade.

The operation took place late in the evening and ended successfully. When the doctors came round the next morning to visit the patient she had regained consciousness so she asked the doctors why they had come—and was stupefied at what they told her.

For three months Cemil Bey came by to treat the patient twice a week, and Emin Bey every day, so that in the end my governess recovered completely. As a reward for these services Papa bestowed a rank on Cemil Bey and gave him presents, while after her recovery my governess made him a gift of cufflinks set with brilliants. Papa similarly showed his appreciation to Emin Bey.

In later years I heard that some people wrote that my elderly governess was a concubine of Papa's. This has joined the ranks of the other lies and fabrications that have been put into print.

I went to Switzerland before Papa's death, leaving my governess in the villa. Before I returned she died at over eighty years of age. I always speak of her with tenderness. Her memory shall rest in my heart forever.

THE WEDDINGS OF PRINCESSES

The first weddings of princesses to take place during Papa's reign were those of his four sisters, the princesses Behice, Seniha, Mediha, and Naile. The marriages of these four sisters of his took place in the early years of his reign. Although Sultan Aziz had ordered their trousseaux, he was completely unable to arrange marriages for them.

Next, Papa arranged for the trousseaux and marriages of Sultan Aziz's three daughters, the princesses Saliha, Nâzıma, and Esma, as well as that of his own daughter Princess Zekiye.[24]

Subsequently he married off, in a single wedding, our sister Princess Naime, whom he called "my Accession Daughter."[25] Then he arranged for the marriages of Sultan Murad's daughters Princess Hadice and Princess Fehime as well as Sultan Aziz's youngest daughter, Princess Emine, after which he married off his own daughter Princess Naile, still later Sultan Murad's youngest daughter, Princess Fatma, and finally Princess Münire, the daughter of our uncle Prince Kemaleddin. These were the last marriages that Papa arranged.

And so, all in all the wedding ceremonies of fifteen princesses took place during Papa's reign.

The first wedding I saw was that of my sister Princess Naime. I was nine years old at the time. A beautiful mansion was built for my sister in Ortaköy next to the household of Princess Zekiye,[26] so that the two buildings used to be called "The Twin Mansions." My sister's trousseau was prepared and brought to the Lesser Chancellery, where the entire family went to look it over. A week before the wedding was to take place, the High Hazinedar went with her retinue to Sister's mansion and started the preparations. Papa invited the ministers and all the great men of state to the Imperial Chancellery, where he gave a banquet, and my sister and Kemaleddin Bey, second son of Gazi Osman Pasha, were married by the Şeyhülislâm. Just as wedding gifts had come from everywhere for Princess Naime, so too Papa

---

24 The weddings of the four princesses took place the same day, 20 April 1889.

25 Princess Naime was born 4 September 1876, five days after her father's accession to the throne.

26 Today's Ortaköy Convalescent Center was the mansion of Princess Zekiye, while that of Princess Naime is today the Lido. [A]

distributed various presents and gifts to the guests attending the ceremony. Gazi Osman Pasha sent Princess Naime a tiara, while Papa presented her new mother-in-law with the Order of Abdülmecid. No minister's wife had ever received this order. Gazi Osman Pasha's eldest son Nureddin Pasha was husband of our sister Princess Zekiye. Later on Kemaleddin Bey was made a pasha.

Before the wedding ceremony Papa summoned our sister and offered prayers and advice on her behalf. He kissed her on the forehead. We did not have the custom of wearing the bridal gown when departing, so our sister wore her everyday clothing to get into her carriage and go to her villa. As she left, sheep were sacrificed, with the meat distributed to the poor.

After this the palace carriages also set out, led by that of the Princess Mother, and we went to the home of the bride. The gates of the villa were opened and everyone went in. The place was thronged. In her gold-embroidered gown of white velvet, with a long train, tiara on her head, and her decorations on her chest, our sister Princess Zekiye was serving as hostess, conversing with the important guests, issuing orders. In this magnificent toilette, our eldest sister, who deserved to be called "kindliness personified," gathered us around her. I was sitting next to her, along with the Princesses Şadiye and Refia, and Nemika, the daughter of our eldest brother Prince Selim. The bride's gown was in the old style, with four very long flounces that extended to the floor, while from her shoulders she wore a fur that draped down over the flounces in the back. The fur was worked with pearls and gold embroidery. In the front, buttons set with brilliants extended from the bust down. Around her waist was a golden, jeweled belt fastened with a buckle. Her dress was white. Quite a few old-fashioned persons criticized the fact that her dress was white, because until that time all princesses had worn red at their weddings. But at Princess Naime's wish and insistence, hers was white.

At the side of our sister Princess Zekiye sat the daughter of the Khedive Ismail Pasha, Princess Fatma, all dressed in white, while quite a few grand *hanımefendi*s came and went.

The two consorts of Sultan Mecid sat at the side of the Princess Mother, as did our aunt Princess Cemile.[27]

At length they were to bring in the groom. Gazi Osman Pasha escorted his son as far as the doorway from the men's quarters, where he handed him

27 The two surviving concubines (*ikbals*) of Sultan Abdülmecid as of this wedding (1898) were the ladies Serfiraz (1837?–1905) and Şayeste (1838?–1912, foster mother of the future Sultan Mehmed VI Vahideddin).

Abdülhamid's half-sister Princess Naile, circa 1880. Princess Naile died of tuberculosis at age twenty-five, in 1882. Photographer unknown.

over to the Constable of the Maidens. The future son-in-law entered the harem amidst prayers and blessings, and made his way directly to the salon prepared for the occasion on the ground floor. Our sister was already seated there on a throne-like settee. He came up to her and asked her to rise. More than half an hour passed but still Sister did not rise.[28] Everyone was standing about waiting, and the groom was perspiring. All the harem eunuchs were waiting at the doorway, the Constable of the Maidens at their head. Finally the Princess Mother was informed, and she went to the doorway and said, "My dear girl, for my sake please rise. Don't hurt our son-in-law's feelings." With that our sister rose. From the ground floor we could hear cries of *Maşallah* [How marvelous], and the sound of the Hamidiye March being played.

At length the bride and groom appeared on the stairway. Words fail to describe how crowded it was, so that they could only make their way forward by small steps. As tradition demanded, her husband escorted the Princess on one arm and the Constable of the Maidens escorted her on the other arm. Six or seven harem eunuchs carried her train. Walking was quite troublesome and difficult because of the crowd but also due to the weight of her dress and tiara.

In this way they came to the bridal room. They passed before us. We small ones had climbed up on top of a table there, which was the only way we could see anything. The groom had his bride take a seat in the corner set aside for her. As he exited he smiled and put his hands in his pockets, then began tossing gold coins about. That set off a frenzy! Only with difficulty could the harem eunuchs clear a path for him, and out they went into the men's quarters.

Then the High Hazinedar called out, "From the Padishah!" and scattered gold coins that people scrambled after as well. Next, coins from the Princess Mother were also tossed about. After this the Senior Kalfas of our aunts and all the princesses began to scatter coins on the ground floor and in the garden, each calling out the name of her mistress. Since money was tossed to the musicians as well, the musical instruments couldn't be played—instead, strange sounds were emanating from them.

At last this noise and commotion came to an end and everyone could view one another in peace and quiet. We went to the room of the bride, where we kissed her hand and offered our felicitations. My sister was beautiful, petite

---

28 This is a palace custom. The bride does not rise for some time, as she waits for the groom to insist that she do so. [A]

as she was, so delicate, with her stunning hazel-green eyes, her long thin eyebrows, and white, translucent complexion. Her mouth and teeth were so lovely. Her eyebrows resembled Papa's; in fact in type she took after him as well. Her toilette showed her off perfectly. There she sat upon a throne specially fitted out for the occasion with silver embroidery. The entire room was hung in Hereke fabric embroidered in silver. She had us young ones sit next to her and talked with us while we gazed at her in complete awe.

The banquet was to begin. Trays for food were set up in the salons, anterooms, garden, and in the harem and the men's quarters. Butlers were scurrying about, with the spectators also offered food, and even just passersby took something to eat. Through it all the music was playing. The festivities continued until toward evening, when the guests and the wives of the ministers departed. At length we were left to ourselves. We were to take our leave after ushering the groom inside and after the groom had kissed the hand of the Princess Mother. Our aunts were present as well.

At the time of the nighttime prayer, once again Gazi Osman Pasha brought the groom as far as the doorway. The Constable of the Maidens then escorted him inside. Before he entered the room of his wife the Princess, the bridegroom first kissed the hands of the Princess Mother and the princesses. A prayer rug embroidered with golden thread was spread out, and as soon as the groom entered he straightaway performed his prayers. Meanwhile Sister was already standing there. Our aunts were peeking in through the doorway, laughing out loud and chattering away, while we too stood there watching every last thing.

Once all this ended, the Constable of the Maidens pulled the door of the room closed, then performed a floor *temenna* salutation to the Princesses as he prayed, "May God bless this marriage and bring good fortune to it." With that our aunts ordered their carriages, still laughing as they too offered their wishes for the marriage, and all of us took our leave at once and went to our homes.

So it was with the marriages of all the princesses. When two or more princesses were to be married on the same day, the Princess Mother was certain to be present as representative of the Padishah at the ritual seating of the bride in the corner. Seniority in age determined the order by which one went to the villas of the princesses who were getting married on such days. For example, at the second marriage ceremony to be held during Papa's reign, of the four princesses married that day we went first to Princess Saliha, then Princess Nâzıma, next Princess Zekiye, and finally to the youngest, Princess Esma. Among princesses, seniority by age always entered into account.

*Sultan Abdülaziz's daughter Princess Nâzıma as a young lady of
about ten, circa 1876. Photographer: Kargopoulo.*

THE VISITS OF THE GERMAN EMPEROR

I don't remember anything at all of the first visit of the German Emperor, in 1889, as I was two years old at the time. At his second visit, in 1899, our young-est sister Princess Refia presented a bouquet, while the Princess Mother, the lady Bidar, the princesses Seniha and Mediha, Sultan Murad's daughters the princesses Hadice and Fehime, and we sisters met with the Empress in the grand salon of the Imperial Lodge.[29] As the Empress came in from the Chalet Villa on Papa's arm, the harem eunuchs and equerries, in their gold-embroidered livery, lined up in two rows and paid her honors. Dressed in the Turkish fashion, the Lady Secretaries and the High Hazinedar stood at the outside door of the salon, while all the silver candlesticks, lamps, and chande-liers were lit, providing a magnificent ceremonial reception for the Empress. The Princess Mother and the princesses greeted the Empress at the doorway of the salon, with the daughter of Artin Pasha acting as interpreter.[30] After this ceremonial reception the Empress took a seat in the middle of the large sofa, with the Princess Mother taking a seat on her right and Papa on her left. All the princesses took their seats according to precedence.

At this reception the princesses wore white gowns in the European fash-ion, complete with their orders and decorations. The adult princesses also wore tiaras. The Princess Mother's gown and the outfits worn by the High Hazinedar and the Lady Secretaries attracted the Empress's attention, and she commented how much she liked them. She even sent for some of the Lady Secretaries and examined their clothing in detail.

Once when the Queen of Romania, Carmen Sylva, came to Istanbul, Papa showed her a traditional Turkish musical ensemble composed of female musi-cians. The Queen had told the Empress of this, so the Empress asked Papa whether she too might see this ensemble, but Papa replied, "The ensemble that the Queen saw doesn't exist anymore. All the girls were married off and sent out of the palace, and no new ensemble has been formed to take their place. I'm terribly sorry not to be able to fulfill your wish."

Familiar as he was with his sisters' habit of chattering away rapidly and guffawing, he had counseled and beseeched them to behave in a dignified fashion, but nonetheless the sisters fell back on their old habits. Papa felt com-pelled to tell the Empress, "Please forgive my sisters, they're a bit nervous."

---

29 The German sovereigns of the day being Wilhelm II and his consort Auguste Viktoria.
30 Yevkine Dadyan, daughter of Artin Dadyan Pasha (undersecretary in the Ministry of Foreign Affairs and prominent member of the Ottoman Armenian community), served as interpreter to the Imperial Harem due to her command of French.

The reception of the Empress lasted an hour and a half. She returned to the Chalet Villa in the same manner she had come, on Papa's arm.

At that time Sultan Murad's daughters were not yet married but were living at Yıldız Palace. Papa realized that if he introduced his own daughters to the Empress but didn't include them they would feel quite hurt, so he had them participate in the ceremony as well.

PALACE CUSTOMS

Just what was the "High Hazinedar" in the palace? The High Hazinedar, or First Hazinedar, functioned as a housemistress and ranked as the most influential personage in the palace after the princes, princesses, Imperial Consorts, and *ikbals*. She practically functioned as a female Grand Vizier of the Imperial Harem. On formal occasions the High Hazinedar wore the imperial seal suspended around her neck by a large golden cord, a prerogative of her office. The seal passed to her successor when she died. She was awarded the Order of Compassion, First Class. On some matters even the Princesses and Imperial Consorts would consult her. Her costume included long flounces and was in the traditional Turkish fashion. From the back of her *hotoz* was suspended a long, pleated double cord two fingerwidths broad, to which was attached a blonde fall of hair. It hung down below her waist. In olden days this was made of horsehair. She wore a short gold-brocaded *salta* jacket. Her retinue consisted of kalfas known as Imperial Kalfas, who were the longest-serving kalfas in the palace. Two or three Imperial Kalfas served as assistants and carried out the orders of the High Hazinedar. Nothing was done without her knowledge—everyone would consult her. Her responsibilities ranked commensurately with her duties and position. The High Hazinedar kept the keys to the harem storage vaults and to valuable objects. The number of staff in service in her office, together with the kalfas in her retinue, amounted to quite a large group of people.

Papa had four High Hazinedars during his reign. At the death of his first High Hazinedar, Dilberdide, Nakşıfelek Usta succeeded her, followed at her death by Şemsicemal Usta, who was succeeded in turn by Fetanfer Usta. This last High Hazinedar of his left the palace when Papa was deposed.

After the Senior Hazinedar, that is to say the High Hazinedar, came the Second, Third, Fourth, and Fifth Hazinedars. But one did not refer to them as *Usta*.[31] They wore the fall of hair and traditional Turkish costume

31 The title *Usta*, "mistress, superintendent," was reserved for the High Hazinedar, *Hazinedar Usta* in Turkish.

with long flounces, but without the jacket. The Second Hazinedar occupied a position superior to the others, and she was presented with the Order of Compassion, First Class.

The hazinedars were always in the Sultan's presence, rendering service. The Second Hazinedar conveyed the Sultan's salutations and commands. Her position rather resembled that of a field marshal, while the others perhaps corresponded to a divisional general and a brigadier general.

After them came the Hazinedar Kalfas. Papa's Hazinedar Kalfas totaled twenty in number. They served as apprentices to those senior to them in service, and when the latter died they were promoted a step. They maintained precedence according to seniority. As part of the entourage of the Third, Fourth, and Fifth Hazinedars, every day it was the duty of six of them to wait upon the Sultan. Their duties included waiting on call at the door of the sovereign's rooms, carrying out his personal orders. The hazinedars had their own separate apartments as well as separate meal trays. The entourage of each included one or two Imperial Kalfas, who rendered inside service.

The Lady Secretaries were chosen from among the more senior and sharp-witted palace kalfas who were well versed in the work and the organization of the palace. In order they were called the Senior Lady Secretary, Second Lady Secretary, Third Lady Secretary, and Fourth Lady Secretary. They wore robes with long flounces as well as a *salta* jacket, and attached a fall of hair to their costume. They carried a jeweled walking stick. These ladies served as superintendents of protocol and orderliness, looking after visitors as they entered and exited the palace, greeting them, overseeing everything, ensuring that nothing untoward happened. They were consulted first before anything could happen in the palace, and they always had to make the rounds. In addition their entourages included kalfas. Charged as they were with overseeing discipline in the palace, a great deal of responsibility rested upon their shoulders.

The Lady Steward always resided in Dolmabahçe Palace. She ranked as the senior in the palace, and her entourage included kalfas. Personal matters in the palace were her domain. She wore robes with long flounces and a fall of hair attached to her costume. The Lady Steward was awarded the Order of Compassion, First Class.

Next there were six ustas: the Mistress of the Laundry Service, the Chief Taster, the Hairdresser, the Mistress of Ablutions, the Mistress of the Pantry, and the Mistress of the Coffee Service. These ladies also wore the fall of hair and robes with long flounces. They were awarded decorations of the second class. The entourages of these ustas included kalfas bearing names corresponding to the tasks they had been assigned, for example: Coffee Service Kalfas, Pantry Service Kalfas, and Laundry Kalfas.

The entourage of the Mistress of the Laundry Service washed the Sultan's laundry, during which the Mistress was always on hand supervising them. The laundry was washed in a series of seven silver basins, in accordance with palace tradition, and the kalfas all wore white. The clean laundry was then placed in large baskets and hung up to dry in the garden on clotheslines reserved for the Sultan's laundry alone. The Laundry Kalfas would take down the laundry in the same way and iron it on large tables, then carry it to the apartments of the monarch and hand it over to the Third or Fourth Hazinedar. These kalfas always maintained their order of seniority, so that if a kalfa in a higher rank should die, those below her advanced one step in rank, finally reaching the rank of Mistress of the Laundry Service.

The Chief Taster looked after the table service. She also had kalfas under her. At her death the kalfa immediately below her assumed her place.

In the past, the Mistress of Ablutions looked after the ablution ewers when they were in use. But as this custom was later abandoned, only the name remained as the relic of an earlier age. In olden days the ablution ewer was presented in this way: one kalfa kneeled and placed a basin on one knee, another kalfa poured the water from the ewer, a third kalfa held the towel, while the youngest kalfa held the dish of soap. This was quite an ancient custom.

The Hairdresser in olden days oversaw the Sultan's shaving and hair-cutting instruments, but of that only the name remained.

The Mistress of the Pantry was in charge of the pantry supplies and trays.

The Mistress of the Coffee Service oversaw the coffee sets and the manner in which coffee was served. Coffee was served in a ceremonial fashion, throughout which the Mistress of the Coffee Service remained always in the fore, making certain that no mistake was made. When a Mistress of the Coffee Service died, the senior in that service took her place.

In order to initiate their right to a retirement pension, those among these ustas who wished to stop working because they had grown old, or those who were exceedingly senior in service, had to go to Topkapı Palace and remain there for at least one year. For Topkapı Palace was their seat. These kalfas would live in Topkapı Palace for one year at a minimum, then return to Dolmabahçe Palace, where they would cease working, receive their pension, and live comfortably.

At one time there used to be an infirmary in Topkapı Palace headed by a Mistress of Patients. Anyone in the palace who took sick was taken there for treatment. The attendants who cared for the sick were known as *nineler* [grandmothers]. In fact, in a cholera epidemic that broke out during the reign of Sultan Aziz, the sick were cared for there.

Upon the death of a prince, princess, or Imperial Consort, the laying out of the corpse and the wrapping in the winding sheet took place at Topkapı Palace. The cloths and sashes laid over them were there. Princes and princesses each received three sashes, and Imperial Consorts received two.[32]

Kalfas who took ill went to the homes of gentlemen of the Privy Staff for treatment, in what was called *tımara çıkmak* [to go out for care and attention]. Kalfas who died were also taken to the homes of gentlemen of the Privy Staff and conveyed from there for burial.

Each prince, princess, and Imperial Consort had his or her own separate kalfas. In charge of these kalfas were two or three senior Imperial Kalfas who supervised the education of the kalfas of the princes, princesses, and Imperial Consorts, and trained them. The Imperial Kalfas were the most esteemed kalfas in each household.

Each newly arrived kalfa was assigned a Junior Kalfa who taught her the ways and customs of the palace. For a period of time the new kalfa would work behind the scenes; then once she was trained she began to render service out in the open.

If two or more persons came to the palace at the same time, the first one to kiss the hem of the monarch was registered as senior.

Those who came to the palace quite young and grew up there were considered an exception, since they were like children of the house. They were given the right before anyone else to leave the palace to marry. If one of them wished to be set up in life, that is to say to leave the palace, on one of the religious holidays or the *Kandil* fetes she would write on a large sheet of paper, *Kulun istediği murad, ihsan efendimindir* [What the servant wishes is but a desire, it is my master's (or mistress's) to grant]. This she would sign at the bottom and leave in a conspicuous location, then shut herself in her room so as not to enter again into the presence of her master or mistress. When this occurred her master or mistress would prepare her trousseau, make her a gift of money, and send her to the home of one of the gentlemen of the Privy Staff. She was given in marriage once a suitable proposal was received. She would also receive an additional sum of compensation based upon her years of service as well as the degree of affection held toward her.

32 The coffin was traditionally covered with a cloth held in place by sashes.

When princesses married they also received their own High Hazinedar, secondary hazinedars, and Mistresses of the Coffee Service, Pantry, Ewer, and Laundry Service, as well as a Chief Taster. In other words, the same organization as in the Sultan's palace prevailed in the villas of the Princesses, albeit on a smaller scale of course. However this organization did not exist in the villas of the Princes; their kalfas did not bear these titles. Only if a prince became sultan did his kalfas receive titles.

When a new sultan ascended the throne, the kalfas, ustas, Lady Secretaries, and personnel of the previous court remained in place under the new sovereign. Only the High Hazinedar and the Second, Third, Fourth, and Fifth Hazinedars, as well as the kalfas of these hazinedars, would leave the palace; these did not continue in service to the new monarch. At the death of a prince, princess, or Imperial Consort, all his or her kalfas would come to the palace of the Sultan and be registered among the personnel there.

The Lady Steward in our day, Şevkidil Kalfa, was the last of the forty lovely kalfas sent as a gift to Sultan Mahmud by the Governor of Egypt, Muhammad Ali Pasha. This ninety-year-old lady, whom I saw in my youth, was in excellent health. Even at that age one could see that she had been dazzlingly beautiful.

Then, quite a few elderly kalfas remained from the days of Sultan Mecid and Sultan Aziz. All of them resided in the palace at their own wish, living out their lives in comfort.

One other custom still prevailed in the palace from days of old. Every night some fifteen or twenty kalfas would stand duty as sentries, under the supervision of one or two of the most senior kalfas in the palace. They would sit in the Imperial Lodge from the nighttime prayer to dawn, and make the rounds of all the apartments and gardens in groups of two or three, keeping watch. They were called *Nöbetçi Kalfalar* [Sentry Kalfas], while their supervisor was known as *Nöbetçibaşı* [Head of the Watch]. If some mishap or illness should occur during the night, they immediately informed the Senior Lady Secretary. A nighttime meal was brought to them. They ate to stay awake, and while some of them were making the rounds the others would sit and play games.

Games played in the palace included *Bekiz*, *Kös*, and *Sürme*. These three games were quite old, whereas backgammon, checkers, and dominos were new games. Card games never crossed the threshold of any palace. No one knew them. People said they were ill omened, and they were forbidden. Of those old games I once saw *Bekiz*, but despite my research I was unable to turn up anything on it. I have in my possession a game of Kös.[33] Sürme is the well-known game of Nine Pieces, quite common everywhere.[34]

There were other turns of duty too, known as "Kitchen Watch" and "Chamber Watch." Those posted to Kitchen Watch spent a week working with the service of food, going off duty when their watch came to an end. Those on Chamber Watch were posted for one week to the personal service of an Imperial Consort, princess, or prince, withdrawing once their watch duty expired. Others took their places as they went off duty, so that they worked for one week and then rested for fifteen or twenty days. Their Head of the Watch was always on hand supervising them. All of these activities functioned like clockwork.

Their free time they spent in the garden or sitting in their rooms.

There were three gates into the palace: the Kitchen Gate, the Departure Gate, and the Imperial Gate. Food provisions came in through the Kitchen Gate, and also all gentlemen of the Privy Staff used this entrance. Carriages entered through the Departure Gate, and princes, princesses, and important persons also entered and exited here. The Imperial Gate was for the exclusive use of the Sultan.

THE SULTAN'S EQUERRIES, AND THE CONSTABLE OF THE NOBLE ABODE OF FELICITY

These men constituted a separate organization. The Constable of the Noble Abode of Felicity[35] occupied an extremely important position. In the palace he was known as Kızlarağası [Constable of the Maidens], and was selected by the Sultan. He held the rank of minister of state and wore a jeweled order with a grand sash. His official uniform was that of a minister. On ceremonial occasions he came after the princes, the imperial sons-in-law, the field marshals, and the ministers of state. In days of old these men had a hand in matters of historical importance, but in Papa's time they did not insinuate themselves into anything outside their own purview. They had

---

33 The game known as spillikins, jackstraws, or pick-up-sticks, in which players attempt to remove one stick in a pile without disturbing the others. Research has failed to uncover further information, however, on the game of Bekiz.

34 Played in Europe since the Middle Ages, in England under the name Nine Men's Morris. The board consists of three concentric squares, connected by lines at right angles; beginning with nine pieces, each player seeks to capture his opponent's pieces.

35 The "Noble Abode of Felicity" being an elegant term for the imperial palace.

their own apartments and were considered the superintendents of the Imperial Harem.

Papa had four Constables of the Maidens. The first one, an extremely influential person, was Hafız Behram Ağa; the second was Şerefeddin Ağa; the third was Yaver Ağa; and the fourth was Abdülganî Ağa, who served in the post until Papa's dethronement.

The duties of the Constable of the Maidens included handing out the Noble Handkerchiefs during the Procession to the Holy Mantle; preceding the Noble Litter, staff in hand, into the harem during the ceremony of the Annual Gift Procession to Mecca; and participating in the escorting ceremonial of princesses at their weddings. In addition they were responsible for appointing and dismissing all the eunuchs.

Nine equerries rendered service in Papa's personal suite: the Senior Equerry and the Second, Third, and Fourth Equerries, with the remaining five known simply as *Musahip Ağalar* or Privy Equerries. In times past they wore livery embroidered with gilt thread. They wore a sword suspended from a silver-embroidered belt. These eunuchs were not like the other harem eunuchs, as they only waited in personal attendance upon the sovereign. The four ranking equerries were awarded orders with grand sashes, while the others were presented decorations corresponding to their rank. They lived in separate quarters and occupied exceedingly important positions in the palace.

The essential duty of these equerries was to stand watch at the doorway to Papa's apartments. By ringing the bell at the harem door they alerted the Duty Hazinedar that pashas and beys had come for an audience, or that incoming documents had arrived. She would inform Papa and then convey back to the equerry the order that she received in reply. Sometimes the equerries themselves would come into the Sultan's presence to submit the communication directly. Another duty of theirs was to transmit orders from Papa to the Imperial Consorts, princesses, and even to the princes, then to bring back the response. Equerries wore a black frock coat buttoned up in front all the way to the top.

When a sultan died, neither the Constable of the Abode of Felicity nor the equerries entered the service of the new monarch; instead they left the palace and lived as they wished. In this regard they were like the hazinedars. The Senior Equerry, Cevher Ağa, was hanged an innocent man, for although he was portrayed as a co-conspirator in the Incident of 31 March,[36]

---

36 The counterrevolution staged on 31 March 1909 (13 April in the Gregorian calendar) by opponents of the Constitutionalist Revolution that had occurred the previous year. The incident resulted in Abdülhamid's dethronement.

not a shred of evidence was submitted in proof. The unfortunate Senior Equerry was in fact sacrificed, the victim of an injustice. He had been presented as a gift to Papa by Arab Mehmed Pasha before Papa came to the throne, and since those days had served Papa faithfully. He was known in the palace as an honorable, conscientious official well versed in the customs and traditions of the palace.

The name of Papa's Second Equerry was also Cevher Ağa. He went to Salonica with Papa, but because he was ill he couldn't tolerate the difficult life there and returned to Istanbul with the princesses.

The Third Equerry, Nadir Ağa, was imprisoned at the time of the 31 March Incident, subjected to questioning, taken to Yıldız for days on end in this business of ransacking the safes as though searching for a treasure trove, and suffered greatly, but still managed to escape hanging thanks to his own ingenuity as well as the assistance of some of his friends, such as the Master of the Horse, Faik Pasha.

Nadir Ağa was in Papa's private service. He was exceptionally intelligent and diligent, and he understood Papa's temperament perfectly. As examples of his tasks, Nadir Ağa would go to the shops of Beyoğlu to make purchases, was put to use in matters regarding the household furnishings, and would be found working with the Master of the Horse in issues concerning the Imperial Stables. When for the first time an automobile was sent to Papa from Paris, no one in the palace knew how to drive it, but Nadir Ağa learned to drive it perfectly and used to ramble around the gardens in it. Again it was Nadir Ağa who navigated the motorized bicycle-boat in the Great Pond. He was tremendously quick-witted. Papa always made use of him in service because he had come to the palace at a young age and had mastered all its conventions.

The Fourth Equerry, Selim Ağa, was a rather simple court eunuch. Out of loyalty he went to Salonica, but he couldn't adjust to life there and returned to Istanbul with the princesses.

Of the remaining equerries, Nuri, Şöhreddin, and Cavid Ağas remained in Papa's service to his last days, both in Salonica and at Beylerbeyi, while Şahabeddin, Anber, and Tahsin Ağas remained in Istanbul.

THE ORGANIZATION OF THE CORPS OF EUNUCHS
OF THE IMPERIAL HAREM

These eunuchs wore livery with gilt embroidery on the collars and sleeves only. The belts at their waists were also embroidered in gilt thread, and

Abdülhamid's trusted eunuch equerry Nadir Ağa in court uniform, around 1907. Having saved his own life after the Sultan's dethrone- ment, Nadir Ağa left palace service and lived to an advanced age in Istanbul, where he died in 1961. Photographer unknown.

they wore swords of a design unique to them. This livery was a relic of times long past.

The most senior and elderly of these eunuchs lived in his apartments in Topkapı Palace and bore the title *Başkaplan Ağa* [Senior Tiger]. Below him came the *Hasırlı Ağas* [Eunuchs of the Matting]. These were the eunuchs who had exercised their right to be pensioned off, and could succeed to the post of Senior Tiger when he died. After them there followed the *Ortanca Ağalar* [Eunuchs of the Middle Rank], the Duty Attendant Eunuchs, and the *En Aşağı Ağalar* [Eunuchs of the Lowest Rank]. They could rise as high as a Senior Eunuch of the Middle Rank and were appointed in order of seniority to the retinues of princes and princesses as Senior Eunuch. Each year they would "rise to Middle Rank," which meant that they were promoted in seniority. When they reached this position they would send a turkey as a gift to the entourage to which they were attached in the palace. They used to play stick games amongst themselves, "go in the closet" in Topkapı Palace,[37] cook up *güveç* and consume it, and organize feasts amongst themselves.

Their duties included locking the doors to the Imperial Harem each evening and unlocking them in the morning, standing watch at the doors, keeping an eye on those who entered and left, accompanying people to their carriages, escorting doctors in and out, and not leaving alone anyone who had come from outside the palace. This they called *halvet tutmak* [to keep private company]. When entering they would call out *Destur!* [By your leave!].

While I was in Europe I read a book that claimed the harem eunuchs used to lash the girls with a whip. In our day no one ever saw or heard of such a thing. Quite the contrary, the harem eunuchs respected the ladies. Their basic task in our day was to serve as a conduit between the harem and the *selâmlık*.

The palace contained a good number of eunuchs who had arrived at a tender age and had grown up there. They rendered faithful service to their masters and remained devoted to them.

In general the harem eunuchs would wear a black frock coat buttoned up to the top. They never, ever walked about with bare chests.[38] The standard of behavior in the Corps of Eunuchs was quite strict, so that if one of them committed an infraction, the senior eunuchs would reprimand him.

37 *Musandıraya çıkmak*, the unusual custom whereby a palace eunuch would hole himself up in a storage room, disappearing for perhaps twenty-four hours of undisturbed seclusion. When he came out he sent a turkey with a blue ribbon around its neck to each of the ladies in whose service he worked. Ok 1997, 56.

38 A reference to orientalist depictions of scantily dressed black harem eunuchs.

THE ROYAL MOSQUE PROCESSIONS

The Friday Mosque Processions took place in the Hamidiye Mosque. Previously Papa went to the Sinan Pasha Mosque and to the dervish convent at Yıldız.

The Master of the Robes laid out the clothing and decorations that he customarily wore. For the Royal Mosque Procession the undress uniform was worn. In the palace there was a man called Kambara Efendi the Frenchman, who before the Mosque Procession would bring an astronomical instrument and set it up outside Papa's apartments, known as the Lesser Pavilion. The light from the sun would make this device fire off like a cannon, to which all the clocks were set accordingly.

Papa placed great emphasis on departing on time for the Mosque Procession. The harem carriages would depart half an hour before Papa entered his carriage. The Princess Mother and the High Hazinedar were required to attend every Friday Mosque Procession, while the princesses and the Imperial Consorts could attend if they wished. From outside the palace the married princesses and the wives of ministers of state would come as well. The mother of the Khedive attended every other week without fail.

It was a firm rule that the princes and their sons attend the Procession, since they were required to lead their regiments in saluting the Sultan. When Papa was riding out to the mosque, Prince Burhaneddin, like his brothers, took his place at the head of his regiment, but on the way back Papa had him sit with him in his carriage.

When the harem carriages arrived at the courtyard of the mosque their horses were detached and they were lined up according to precedence. The carriage of the Princess Mother was always at the head, with that of the High Hazinedar last.

As Papa's equipage exited the imperial gate the band struck up the imperial march, trumpets sounded the salute, and the soldiers shouted their hurrahs. As the salutes and the march rang out for the second or third time, Papa would arrive at the doorway to the mosque. The Grand Vizier did not take part in the Royal Mosque Processions; rather, the Şeyhülislâm greeted the Sultan at the mosque door. Once he entered, the worship service began. Hajjis come from abroad and Muslims from Yemen and Arabia would unroll rush mats in the mosque courtyard and perform their prayers along with the Sultan. Toward the end of the worship service the soldiers were granted leave. Each regiment marched past to the music of its own band.

The processions on the anniversary of the birth of the Prophet took the

*Royal Mosque Procession at the Hamidiye Mosque just outside Yıldız Palace, around 1895.
The Sultan's carriage stands before the portico on the left; he will ascend the private stairs
to the imperial loge within the mosque. At far left the harem ladies' carriages, their horses
unhitched, form a line. Photographer unknown.*

same form as those of the Royal Mosque Processions, only more troops took part and dress uniform was worn. The traditional poem on the birth of the Prophet was chanted at the mosque, then sweets and fruit drinks were distributed to the troops. Palace servants carrying silver trays also brought sweets and fruit drinks to the harem carriages, and gifts of money were distributed.

At the Friday Mosque Processions Halim Efendi, the "Departure Director of the Imperial Harem," took part. We young princesses would send the Departure Director to the mosque in order to ask permission for us to go to Kâğıthane or other places we wished to visit. Halim Efendi would go through the equerries to make our wishes known to the Sultan and so obtain permission. We would set off together with whomever had attended the Mosque Procession that day. Since the daughters of Sultan Murad and Prince Salâheddin usually attended the Procession, we would all be together.

In the palace the great garden at Yıldız was called *kır* [the countryside]. We would go around to the Tent, Malta, and Head Gardener Pavilions there.

Since these weren't considered to be outside the palace we didn't have to ask permission to go there.

When we went out on such excursions we would order what we called "garden service," which consisted of cold dishes such as yogurt, halvah, salad, and fruit. Until evening we young princesses would run about, play, and pass the time in the company of the young kalfas who accompanied us. Those of our mothers who had attended the Mosque Procession that day would not separately ask for permission to go out but simply came with us and so profited from the occasion. We came back from these excursions before the harem doors of the palace were locked. By tradition the palace harem doors were locked at 7:00 in the evening and unlocked at 7:00 in the morning, a task that fell to whichever equerry was on duty.

After the Mosque Processions the Pasha Mother (the mother of the Khedive) would proceed to the Chalet Villa, where the kalfas of the High Hazinedar waited upon her respectfully, and where she passed the time in the company of one of the Princesses. If any wives of the ministers of state had attended the ceremony, they too were received with all due honors in the harem, and they took the evening meal in the palace. At 8:30 they made their way to the theater. Together with the princesses who had come from outside the palace, they were received by the Sultan in the Small Salon, entering their boxes when the performance was to begin.

Following the theater performance the carriages for whichever Princesses and Princes had come from outside the palace pulled up to the harem. There the guests entered the carriages. Two aides-de-camp were assigned to accompany each carriage on the journey to the guests' homes, where they left the visitors. None of them stayed in the palace overnight.

THE *KANDIL* NIGHTS IN THE PALACE

On *Kandil* nights the Prophet's Nativity Poem was chanted in the Lesser Chancellery. Cushions were set out for Papa as well as for the pashas and Privy Staff gentlemen who would be present at the ceremony. From morning on, quite a number of persons would come to the Imperial Chancellery to offer their felicitations, which of course were presented to the Sultan. Papa would invite some of these visitors to the chanting of the Nativity Poem. Before the chanting ceremony took place, Papa, standing, received certain visitors in the Little Salon, first of all the Minister of War, then whichever ministers of state had come, followed by the imperial sons-in-law, both pasha and bey, and the imperial princes. Next to enter were the Head Imam of the Hamidiye Mosque, who was to chant the Nativity Poem, and the sweet-voiced muezzins of the Imperial Corps of Music; they too offered their felicitations. Papa would then go in, sit on the cushion, knees crossed, and give the order "Take a seat" to the pashas and beys, whereupon everyone made his way to his place and sat down.

Gilded screens were set up opposite the door that led to the corridor of the Grand Salon, and those of us from the Imperial Harem, led by the Princess Mother, took our seats according to precedence on the cushions, as did the guests who had come from outside the palace. Our aunts would attend, as would the daughters of Sultan Aziz and Sultan Murad and other princesses as well.

During the chanting sugar candies were brought in on large silver trays carried by two butlers each. First the candies were offered to Papa, then they were circulated through the room and everyone took one each. Equerries brought them round to the harem side. Everyone partook of these heaps of various candies piled up to fit the size of each tray.

When the chanting of the Nativity Poem ended Papa would rise, at which point everyone also rose, again expressed their thanks, and took their leave. He engaged a few of them in conversation for a bit. Everyone present at the chanting received decorated baskets and boxes of sweets from the confectioner Hajji Bekir Efendi.

After the Nativity Poem ceremony Papa went to the grand salon in the harem where the Lady Secretaries oversaw protocol. We entered the salon in order of age and offered felicitations to our sovereign. The High Hazinedar was always the last to enter. Papa and his mother sat on a sofa. The Princesses and Imperial Consorts were shown to their seat, and we sat and engaged in conversation for a while as the equerries brought in silver trays of fruit drinks and mint lemonades, which we drank. When Papa rose we all immediately stood and exited the room, making our *temenna* salutes. He would keep his mother till last and they would engage in private conversation.

Papa always received his mother at the door, kissed her hand, and took her arm to escort her to the sofa where he would have her sit down. When leaving he conducted her to the door and again kissed her hand. When bidding his mother farewell he would say, "Good-bye, Mother dear," to which his mother would reply, "May you live long, my son."

He always inquired as to the High Hazinedar's health by asking, "How are you, Usta?"; then he would address some kind words to her. The elderly Usta would offer up prayers on his behalf. As Papa made his way to his own apartments the Second Hazinedar and all the other hazinedars lined up before the corridor by rank and offered their felicitations. With this the *Kandil* nights came to a close.

At the *Kandil* fete that celebrates the Prophet's birthday, a parade took place during the day, we went to the Hamidiye Mosque, and sweets and fruit drinks were distributed to the troops and to persons attending in carriages.

One special feature of the *Kandil* fete of Berat was the arrival at the palace and the departure of the Noble Litter. In the palace the *Darüssade ağası* [Constable of the Abode of Felicity]—the chief black eunuch—was called the *Kızlar Ağası* [Constable of the Maidens]. With the gold-worked ivory staff particular to his office in hand, the Constable of the Maidens took his place at the head of the hundreds of harem eunuchs in the palace following him, to carry in the Noble Litter amid cries of *Allahu ekber* [God is Most Great] and to the accompaniment of religious hymns, and set it down in the harem garden. All the Princesses, Imperial Consorts, and kalfas came to pay their respects to the Noble Litter. Each princess and Imperial Consort presented a gift of silver-embroidered cloths. Two elderly palace kalfas decorated the Noble Litter with these cloths. These two kalfas were experts at this task who had been doing it skillfully for years and had perfected it by teaching one another the technique.

Once the task of decorating the Noble Litter was complete, the Constable of the Maidens and the harem eunuchs took it away again in the same manner to the apartments of the Constable of the Abode of Felicity, where it remained overnight. The following day the Gift Procession was assembled. Each Imperial Consort and princess in the palace had a friend in Mecca[39] to whom she sent money and gifts inside leather sacks. In the same way money would be sent to quite a number of petitioners. These sacks were tied up with string, sealed with seals inscribed *May safety accompany the journey*, and presented to the Noble Litter by the Constable of the Maidens.

My friend in Mecca was Seyyid Şeybizade Abdülkadir Efendi. The following year the Senior Bearer of Good Tidings would be announced, and gifts and expressions of thanks would come to us from our friends. When I was young I was thrilled and delighted when these sacks of gifts arrived, for our friends would send beautiful prayer beads, carnelian rings, fragrant oils in lovely bottles, and coral rings. These rings had no value but I loved them.

The next day the Noble Litter and the gifts were to be surrendered to the Steward of the Gift Procession, and for this a procession took place on the

---

39 A religious personage in Mecca whose duties included offering prayers on behalf of these ladies of the imperial family.

hill at Yıldız. His Majesty went to the Chancellery where he and the pashas would watch from the windows, while we watched from our carriages. From the apartments of the Constable of the Maidens, the Noble Litter was now placed atop a towering, decorated camel, with the reins handed to the person who served as the Steward of the Gift Procession that year. Proceeding before the palace gate, the parade would pass in front of the Chancellery. At the head of the parade men known as *Hakkâm*,[40] all of them black, would beat drums, simulate fights with swords and shields, and demonstrate their skill in acrobatics. This was really something wonderful. A cannon was fired when the Noble Litter crossed the Bosphorus to Üsküdar.

THEATER IN THE PALACE

In olden days the *orta oyunu* performances[41] were much in favor in the palace. A good number of persons in the Imperial Corps of Music performed in these theatrical presentations, many of them holdovers from the days of Sultan Aziz. Among them I recall Neşet, Ali, and Hilmi. Hilmi Bey, father of the violinist Zeki Bey, was instructor of both Turkish music and the traditional comedy theater. Twice a week he would come by and rehearse in Turkish dance and music the ladies' orchestral and dance ensemble of my sister Princess Naime. In those days my aunts Princess Seniha and Princess Mediha and my sister Princess Zekiye also had performers of their own. Their leaders were Mahruhsar and Tîrimiyal, two kalfas who had been in service since the days of Sultan Aziz, and who taught them the dances *Köçek*, *Tavşan*, *Matrak*, and *Kalyonca*.[42] These dances had been performed in the palace for ages. The dancers' costumes were gorgeous, embroidered as they were in gilt thread, and with baggy trousers and stout jackets with slit sleeves. Now and then the sisters would bring their dancers to the palace and have them perform in the Imperial Lodge in the presence of the Sultan, with all of us sitting in rows, watching. Each dance had its own costume. In recent years they were disbanded so that nothing more remains of them.

After Abdürrezak Efendi was brought into the palace the traditional

---

40 Properly *akkâm*, the attendants who accompanied the Noble Litter caravan to Medina and Mecca.

41 "Theater in the center," the tremendously popular traditional comedy theater performed usually in open air, with musical accompaniment from a small orchestra, and male actors in all the roles, portraying familiar themes with stock characters.

42 "The Dancing Boy," "The Rabbit," "The Cudgel," and "Like a Galleon," four traditional dances accompanied by musicians.

Turkish entertainments regained some favor, but performances of them were generally restricted to the two religious festivals. All in all, since Papa didn't care much for traditional Turkish music and dance, he took to having European-style music and dance performed.

As I heard it in my youth, at one time Ahmed Midhat Efendi wrote a number of plays and choreographed some dances, then had them performed as operettas, with songs. Ali Bey used to take the women's roles. I still remember a few pieces I heard from the operettas of those days.

Papa put quite an effort into improving the orchestral component of the Imperial Corps of Music, which truly came to produce outstanding musicians.

An excellent orchestra of sixty members was established. In the beginning instruction was provided by Guatelli Pasha, who had served as an instructor since the days of Sultan Aziz. Later on a good number of instructors came, including my teacher, the Frenchman Lombardi. After them the Spaniard Aranda Efendi was created Instructor to the Imperial Corps of Music. He was raised to the rank of pasha because he trained my brother Prince Burhaneddin to become such an excellent pianist. He also taught other princes, including our cousin Prince İbrahim Tevfik and my brothers the princes Abdürrahim and Nureddin.

Whenever any sort of troupe of musicians came to Istanbul, the ambassadors would promptly send word to recommend them. In this way these troupes came to the palace, with quite a few musicians performing in the presence of the Sultan. They were awarded decorations. Papa took into his entourage a family that had come to Istanbul with an Italian troupe, enrolling them in the Imperial Corps of Music. The family consisted of a father, two sons and their wives, and a daughter and her husband. They were known as the Ciampi Family. Following them two other Italian musicians were added to the Imperial Corps of Music, to perform operas and operettas.

The works they performed most often included *La Traviata*, *Il Trovatore*, *The Masked Ball*, *The Barber of Seville*, *The Daughter of the Regiment*, *Fra Diavolo*, *La Mascotte*, and *La Belle Hélène*. These operas were called by different names when performed in the palace. *Traviata* became "Madame Camellia," *Trovatore* was "The Ironmonger," *Barber of Seville* was "The Barber," *Masked Ball* became "The Masked Opera," *Fra Diavolo* was "The Brigand," *Daughter of the Regiment* became "Soldier Girl," *La Belle Hélène* was "The Shepherdess," *Rigoletto* became "The King's Daughter," and *La Mascotte* was called simply *Maskot*. Papa loved *Rigoletto* and had it performed time and again.

In addition to the Italians there were also two Frenchmen by the names of Bertrand and Jean. Bertrand was a mime and juggler who every year with

Papa's permission would go to France, from where he would return having picked up a host of new tricks. It was he who introduced cinema to the palace. In those days cinemas were not as they are today. Large brushes were used to thoroughly wet the screen, and short films were shown that were quite dark and over in a minute. Nonetheless we enjoyed them because they were something completely new.

Jean was an animal trainer who worked with horses, donkeys, and dogs. He and Bertrand had them perform delightful tricks. In later years two Americans were also brought into the theater, comics who danced and played the accordion and mandolin splendidly.

The Emperor of Russia sent the musical company of his private theater, which Maksimov[43] brought to the palace. They sang lovely Russian songs. The famous Chaliapin numbered among their ranks, although in those days he was quite young. We marveled at the beauty of his voice. In later years he became the toast of Europe.

When important events such as these occurred, Papa invited the ministers of state to attend. He would sit with the Grand Vizier while the other ministers were parceled out among the boxes. We would sit on the harem side. The lattice grills around Papa's box and those of the ministers were removed, but those on the harem side remained. The ministers' sons attended as well.

The orchestra took their places on the ground floor to the left, while gentlemen of the Privy Staff, pashas, and beys took their seats on the ground floor opposite the stage. Sometimes when ambassadors were present the theatrical or musical performance was reserved for men, in which case the harem ladies would not attend. On such occasions all the lattice grills were removed. The ambassadors' wives would come as well and sit in their own boxes. Some of the pashas would be invited, and at times Papa invited his brothers or the sons of Sultan Aziz. Prince Salâheddin also attended, after the death of his father. Papa would have his own grown sons with him in his box, at which times we too would enter the box and kiss their hands. On unofficial occasions all the princes, including of course Papa's own sons, wore the stambuline coat. They always dressed in this fashion when in the presence of the Sultan. Whenever the Khedive's mother, wife, or daughters attended they would sit in their own box joined by our grandmother or the Senior Consort. When the wives of ministers came to the palace they would sit with the Princesses to watch the performance.

On days when the weather was particularly hot, as an exceptional treat a

---

43 Chief Dragoman of the Russian Embassy. [ÖO]

portable stage would be set up in the part of the harem garden that faced the Imperial Lodge, and light pieces such as the traditional Turkish improvised theater or comedies would be performed. We watched these comfortably from the windows of the palace.

RAMADAN IN THE PALACE

Ramadan celebrations in the palace were delightful. Preparations began a week in advance. The palace was scrubbed clean. From the imperial pantry great pitchers of sweet fruit syrups would come round to all the apartments, along with all kinds of foods for breaking the fast. On the first night of Ramadan gilt lattice screens were set up and prayer rugs spread out in the anterooms of all the apartments, and in would come the harem eunuchs along with an imam and two muezzins of beautiful voice. The worship service prayers were performed while hymns were sung. In the night[44] the doors were opened and the before-dawn meal trays were brought in, after which everyone stayed up until the cannon boomed. Once the cannon announced that the daylight fasting hours had begun, everyone went to bed. Toward midday a religious instructor came round to each apartment and delivered a sermon. When the cannon boomed at dusk, the fast was broken with water from the Noble Well of Zamzam, the fast-breaking trays of food were prepared, and we drank iced lemonades and sweet syrup drinks. There was one syrup drink special to the palace, made of jonquils—it was delicious. During Ramadan the palace harem became rather like a mosque, with everyone spending time in prayer.

Papa would go to the Palace Chancellery every day and attend the "Lesson of the Imperial Presence,"[45] then after breaking the fast in the evening he performed the prayers in the company of his sons, his brothers, other princes who came from outside the palace, the high officials of the Chancellery, and several ministers of state who had come for the breaking of the fast. During Ramadan neither regimental band music nor instrumental music was performed. The Senior Chamberlain would distribute the Ramadan gifts to those who had come to the Chancellery, while each evening in the square at Yıldız a regiment of troops broke the fast together and performed the prayer, after which the Master of the Privy Purse distributed Rama-

---

44 Shortly before dawn.
45 The lecture, in the form of question and answer, delivered by scholars in the presence of the monarch during Ramadan. [A]

dan gifts, and the men shouted "Long Live the Sultan!" three times, then marched off.

We began preparations for the Procession to the Holy Mantle some two or three days before it was to take place, which was on the 15th of Ramadan. On that day we rose early, put on our most beautiful court dresses with long trains, attached our decorations, added our jewels, and proceeded to Topkapı Palace. Grandmother rode in a state equipage whose coachmen wore gold-embroidered livery, like that of the Sultan's coachmen, while our coachmen wore the livery of the Imperial Stables. Led by Halim Efendi, the Superintendent of Departures, the grooms and harem eunuchs in their gilt-embroidered livery followed Grandmother's carriage as it headed the procession. In this fashion we departed Yıldız and made our way to Topkapı, where we were welcomed by the veteran kalfas there and by the veteran ustas who had come over from Dolmabahçe. We proceeded to the rooms set aside for each of us in the Topkapı harem. Invitations had been sent out previously to the married princesses, who lived outside the palace, and to the wives of the ministers of state, so all of them came round to pay us visits. We had also invited our personal acquaintances. Truly the palace filled to the brim and took on a holiday air.

In her magnificent toilette, Grandmother would take a seat on the settee in the room known as the Armchair Salon, where we would go to kiss her hand and all wait together for the visit to the Holy Mantle to begin. Two consorts of Sultan Mecid, the ladies Serfiraz and Şayeste, would also attend, sitting next to Grandmother. Usually the Pasha Mother took part in this ceremony as well. The Senior Equerry would enter and perform a *temenna* salutation before our Grandmother the Princess Mother, to inform her that the Chamber of the Holy Mantle was now open for the ladies to visit. The Princess Mother rose and proceeded to the Chamber of the Holy Mantle, followed by the two consorts of Sultan Abdülmecid, then in order of rank by our aunts, by the princesses, and by the Imperial Consorts. Each lady wore a white tulle veil over her head.

Everywhere smoldering incense burners filled the air with scent while from behind the curtain a sweet-voiced muezzin chanted verses of the Holy Quran. Each of our hearts brimmed with pious reverence as we advanced in order, taking slow steps and allowing our trains to brush along the floor, until we approached the Padishah, who stood before the throne. Before the Holy Mantle we rendered a floor *temenna*, then turning to the Sultan we rendered another *temenna* and received the Noble Cloth that he placed in our hands. We kissed it and placed it atop our heads. With that we withdrew backwards and stood in line, still in our order of rank. The Constable of the Abode of Felicity took out the Noble Cloths from the golden chest in front of the throne and placed them in front of the Sultan—a duty particular to his office.

In their uniforms, the young princes and the sons of the Sultan stood by the foot of the throne in order of rank.

After us it was the turn of the Pasha Mother and the wives of the Grand Vizier, the Şeyhülislâm, and the other ministers of state. The High Hazinedar also took part in this ceremony, as did the other senior kalfas in palace service as well as the wives of important members of the Privy Staff. When the ceremony reached its end the Senior Equerry came in and performed a floor *temenna*, after which we all filed out in the order in which we had entered, led by the Princess Mother.

Our carriages approached the doorway of the harem at Topkapı in order of precedence and in we'd climb, returning to Yıldız in the same way we had come. Drawn by horses and thus moving rather slowly, the carriages usually brought us back to the palace to the sounds of the cannon that announced the breaking of the fast for the day.

When I was young Papa made the trip by carriage, but in later years he sailed down on the yacht *Söğütlü* and so arrived before us.

The delicious dishes cooked by the Pages of the Inner Service at Topkapı would come to the palace. In earlier days Papa used to break the fast at Topkapı, but in later years he stopped doing so.

The parade on the Night of Power, which occurs on the night of 27 Ramadan, was something grand. Papa used to take Gazi Osman Pasha with him in his carriage, then after the Pasha's death the minister of War Rıza Pasha rode with him. As usual Prince Burhaneddin was always by his side as well.

We departed the palace before the prayer service, with the carriage of the Princess Mother once again in the lead, and stayed in our carriages as they lined up by rank in the courtyard of the Hamidiye Mosque. The married princesses and the wives of state ministers would come as well. The area from the Harem Gateway at the palace down to the mosque was illuminated. Two grooms in front of each harem carriage carried leather lanterns encased in silver, while fifteen footmen carrying these lanterns flanked the Sultan's equipage on each side. The pashas, the ministers—everyone was in dress uniform. More troops were present than at the Friday Royal Mosque Processions, and after the Sultan had entered the mosque all the troops received from the imperial kitchens delicious fruit drinks and large hot pita breads baked with melted cheese. Fireworks were shot off in Yıldız Square until the end of the prayer service. I used to love watching these fireworks when I was a child.

Just as at the Friday Mosque Processions, so too at the end of the prayer service the soldiers were granted leave and they marched back to their barracks to the music of their military bands. This spectacle was particularly marvelous at night.

As for us, we returned to the palace in the same way we had come.

THE FESTIVAL DAYS IN THE PALACE

Preparations for festival days[46] began a week before the event. Everyone had a new dress sewn but wouldn't let anyone else see it beforehand. Important preparations were under way in the guest apartments as well. Everyone rose with the cannon shot that announced the beginning of the holiday and made her way directly over to her mirror to begin her toilette. Because the worship service for the holiday was to take place at an early hour, the harem carriages set out in advance of the Sultan's carriage. Usually we went to the Sinan Pasha Mosque in Beşiktaş, where our carriages lined up in a row before the mosque. We wore all our orders and jewels, threw over us a *ferace* in the cut of a coat, and attached our *yaşmak*s made of exceedingly delicate tulle. Into our carriages we stepped as the harem eunuchs carried our long trains. Papa arrived at the mosque in his imperial equipage drawn by four horses, usually taking the Minister of War Rıza Pasha and my brother Prince Burhaneddin with him, both seated opposite him. Brigades of troops and military bands lined the entire route from the Yıldız gate to the mosque, with the pashas and the ministers of state in their gala uniforms. Papa proceeded to the mosque accompanied by the sounds of trumpet fanfares and marches playing in various locations.

The festival day worship service didn't last long. After it Papa made his way to Dolmabahçe Palace in the equipage drawn by four horses. There he passed through the Grand Gate, which was reserved for the use of the monarch alone. From there he proceeded to the Chancellery. After Papa's arrival the harem carriages entered the palace grounds through the Harem Gate. As we arrived at the harem our carriages pulled up to the horse-block, the carriage of the Princess Mother always in the lead. Two rows of harem

46 The grand reception ceremony at Dolmabahçe Palace that the Princess is about to describe occurred twice yearly, during the two great annual religious holidays: the Festival of Fastbreaking at the end of the month of Ramadan, and the Festival of Offerings two months later, 10 Zulhijja of the Islamic calendar.

eunuchs flanked the stairway of the palace. At the top of the stairs we were greeted first by the Lady Steward, then by all the ustas as well as the Senior Kalfas of the palace, each in her ceremonial dress. With the kalfas holding our trains, we made our exits to the rooms set aside for us, where we removed our *yaşmaks* and *feraces* and straightened our toilettes. After resting for a bit we made our way first to the apartments of the Princess Mother, where we offered our felicitations, kissed her hand, and received her blessing. Then we called on our older sisters and our elders, where we all exchanged felicitations. The wives of the ministers of state came in the order of their husbands' seniority, offering their felicitations to the Princess Mother and to us.

When the religious festival occurred in the winter months, how on earth we roamed about that vast palace in silk gowns, and rather décolleté at that, simply baffles me nowadays. To be sure, large silver braziers ablaze with flames were set out in all the salons and along both sides of the large antechambers, but obviously those vast anterooms and chambers could not be heated sufficiently by this method. I daresay we could stand the cold because we were young.

In their gold-embroidered jackets, wearing their hair down their backs, and clutching their jeweled walking sticks, the Lady Secretaries ambled about, ensuring the decorum and good order of the palace.

The equerries would inform the Senior Lady Secretary that the imperial reception had begun, whereupon she made her way to the Princess Mother, performed a floor *temenna* salutation, and announced, "The imperial reception is beginning, please come this way." With that the Princess Mother, in her magnificent toilette, led all the princesses, then the ministers' wives, through the grand salons and down the corridor of the Chancellery wing of the palace to the loges high above the Ceremonial Hall. There each took her seat upon the tall, cushioned divans set out for them there and watched the ceremony. Foreign ambassadors occupied the open loges along the other side of the Ceremonial Hall.

The imperial march was struck up and the Sultan entered, saluting the assembly as he took his seat upon the throne. Marshal Fuad Pasha held the sash of the throne.[47] Later on, Ömer Rüşdü Pasha held it.

Meanwhile the princes, the imperial sons-in-law, the Senior Secretary, and other gentlemen of the Privy Staff stood behind the throne. Led by the Grand Vizier, all the ministers of state and field marshals performed the

---

47 Court custom called for those offering obeisance to the Sultan at imperial receptions to kiss the sash held by an official next to the throne, in order to avoid touching the imperial person himself.

sash-kissing ceremony in order of rank. This brought the first ceremony to a conclusion. The Padishah then retired to a salon where he rested for a quarter of an hour. For the second ceremony the Padishah again entered as he saluted the assembled guests, then stood in front of the throne. Led by the Şeyhülislâm, the ulema approached the throne in groups. They wore robes of different types: the Şeyhülislâm in white, the others in green, red, or purple. The Şeyhülislâm stood before the throne and prayed while the Sultan listened with palms opened, then all together everyone drew their hands over their faces.[48]

Next the Christian patriarchs entered, each with his own entourage, and the Logothete Bey stepped forward to offer a prayer.[49] Last of all, the Grand Rabbi came forward with his entourage. Once again the imperial march resounded and the Sultan retired to the salon to rest. After another quarter-hour recess once again he entered the hall. This time the ceremony came to a conclusion with the reception of the lower-ranking pashas and officers and, last of all, the Privy Staff.

Throughout the entire ceremony the Imperial Corps of Music played marches without pause.

After the ceremony, trays of sweets were brought into the harem, and sweets were also sent by the Sultan to the homes of members of the imperial family, to cabinet ministers, and to high-ranking dignitaries.

We took lunch at Dolmabahçe Palace. By tradition the High Hazinedar came into the Sovereign's Hall in her magnificent costume and stood in the middle of the room, where she dipped her hands into the gold-embroidered apron cloth held up at the ends by two Assistant Kalfas and scattered coins in all directions. These coins were gathered up by the harem eunuchs, the children, and outside guests.

In olden days the Sultan would retire to the harem after the reception. He also used to take his lunch at Dolmabahçe Palace, but in later years he stopped doing so.

Once the Lady Secretaries announced that the Sultan had returned to Yıldız, the Princess Mother ordered the carriages brought round. Everyone made herself ready, and back to Yıldız we went in the order in which we had come. The Sultan returned to Yıldız in a Friday carriage drawn by two

---

48 Ritual motions of prayer in Islam.

49 In the Byzantine era the term *logothete* had been in use since the days of Emperor Justinian in the sense of "chief counselor" or "minister of foreign affairs." This is most likely the origin of *logofet*, which in the Ottoman era signified a kind of consul or representative of the Greek Orthodox Patriarchate in Istanbul to the Ottoman government. [ÖO]

horses. When he came into the Imperial Harem he received felicitations only from his own family, beginning with the Princess Mother, and from his hazinedars.

The band of the Second Division would gather on the lawn in front of the Lesser Pavilion and strike up the imperial anthem, followed by five airs before they marched off. Early the next morning, the Second Division band would return and strike up the imperial anthem, then play five airs. From then until five o'clock in the afternoon bands would come in from all the barracks and play five airs each. Toward evening they massed together to give the salute and receive their gifts. It was wonderful at five o'clock in the afternoon to hear them playing all together the air in salute to the Sultan. The Keeper of the Privy Purse dispensed their gifts. All of this we watched from the windows.

The three days' Festival of Ramadan and the four days' Festival of Offerings always passed in the following fashion. On the first day of the fete the ministers' wives who had come to Dolmabahçe Palace made their way up to Yıldız. In the evening the Sultan received them and they attended performances of traditional Turkish music and comedy theater. After the theater performances at night, aides-de-camp escorted them back to their homes. On the second day of the fete the adult princes came to the Palace Chancellery while the married princesses came to the harem. They were welcomed with all due courtesy and, in the evening, having been received by the Sultan, they attended a theater performance, after which aides-de-camp escorted them back to their homes. On the third day the wives of the gentlemen of the Privy Staff came to the harem.

The religious fetes were fatiguing but merry.

The Festival of Offerings differed in two respects. Two days before the festival began, the rams and sheep to be presented by the Sultan as gifts arrived at the palace in a procession. These were gifts for the princes and princesses as well as the cabinet ministers and high-ranking dignitaries. The arrival of the animals was truly splendid, as the Keeper of the Privy Purse led the animals past the windows from which the Sultan was viewing them. These rams were decorated with gilding, their fleeces painted in various colors and decked out with ribbons, while the attendants who led the animals by cordons fitted around the animals' necks wore decorated, gold-embroidered jackets with baggy green trousers and, atop their heads, a tasseled, gold-embroidered turban like a skullcap. This too was part of the tradition. In this fashion they passed through the palace garden. Watching this absolutely delighted us.

The second distinctive feature about the Festival of Offerings was as follows. When the sultan exited the mosque, before stepping into his carriage a great ram was made to lie down before the door. The sultan took the knife into his hand and passed it over the animal, then entered his carriage, after which the ram was sacrificed. This was another tradition. As for us, we sacrificed rams in addition to the ram sent us by the sultan, and also we sent sacrificial sheep to our friends, to those in our service, to the mosques, to dervish convents, to the police stations, and throughout the neighborhoods in which we lived.

On the anniversaries of his accession and of his birth, Papa would go quite early to the Grand Chancellery, where he received the congratulations of cabinet ministers, high-ranking dignitaries, field marshals, and foreign ambassadors, all of whom would call at the palace throughout the day. Only toward evening could he find the time to come to the harem and receive the congratulations of his own family and the other Princesses. In our beautiful toilette with long train and all our orders on our chests, each of us went to the Grand Salon to offer our felicitations to the Padishah. We would decorate the palace garden in front of our apartments with lamps and flags, hanging plaques inscribed *Long Live the Sultan* on the doors. We organized amusing divertissements amongst ourselves, invited one another to call, and gave dinner parties. All the kalfas in the palace wore their most beautiful outfits, and we enjoyed ourselves with music and merriment until the late hours.

When we were small, Papa would send us on excursions in the city so that we daughters could see something of the celebrations there. With our eunuch menservants we would set off in carriages for Stambul, see what there was to see, and come back. But after we'd grown into young ladies we too stayed in the palace with our elders, going up to the Grand Chancellery to view the celebrations and fireworks. From the Chintz Pavilion to the Chancellery, awnings had been erected so that the Imperial Harem could pass by. We would go to the upper floor of the Imperial Chancellery and look out from the sultan's private room in the center, afterwards returning to our own apartments.

NEW YEAR'S IN THE PALACE

The first of Muharrem was New Year's Day.[50] People came to the palace from everywhere in order to offer their felicitations. So too did the ministers of

---

50 Muharrem being the first month in the Muslim lunar calendar. Under Atatürk the Republic of Turkey switched to the Western calendar with its New Year's Day on 1 January.

The Grand Chancellery at Yıldız Palace, the first building inside the gates and so the most visible and most photographed Yıldız building of its day, but only one of nearly four dozen on the vast palace grounds. Photographer unknown.

state. In the apartments of the Senior Chamberlain, plates of gold quarter-lira pieces of twenty-seven[51] and silver quarter-pieces and *kuruş* coins were set out on a table. In an amount corresponding to their rank, position, and importance, all the visitors, and the gentlemen of the Privy Staff as well, would take of these coins—known as *muharremiyelik* [Muharrem money] or *yıl bereketi* [New Year's blessing]. In the harem too, quarter-lira pieces of twenty-seven and silver *kuruş* coins were distributed. We also gave some to those in our service.

New Year's Day had nothing else special about it. Among the ladies, wearing a new dress was thought to bring good luck, so one definitely put on something new.

On the tenth of Muharrem, *aşure* was cooked and would come to the palace and the various apartments in pitchers. It was sent round to all the members of the imperial family and distributed to the poor from cauldrons set up in the square of the courtyard of the Hamidiye Mosque. *Aşure* was also distributed to the troops in the palace parade grounds and sent round to all the barracks.

51 The Ottoman gold lira had equaled 100 silver *kuruş* coins, but due to the fall in silver prices, after 1879 one gold lira stabilized at 108 silver *kuruş*. This meant that the quarter-lira gold coin was worth 27 silver *kuruş* coins.

Just as *aşure* would go out from the palace to the dervish convents, so too would it come in from the dervish convents to the palace. Pashas and great families would send *aşure* to the palace in exquisite pitchers wrapped in tulle. The pitchers would be emptied, refilled with *aşure* cooked in the palace, and sent back. Such was the custom.

NEVRUZ

As *Nevruz* was the first day of spring, the preceding day the Imperial Pharmacy would prepare the red-colored sweet that was sprinkled with gold dust and known as *Nevruz Macunu* [*Nevruz* Paste]. In lovely bowls wrapped in tulle it was portioned out to the members of the imperial family as well as to ministers of state, ranking dignitaries, and the Privy Staff. It had the most delicious taste, and to eat it early of a morning on an empty stomach had the most restorative effect. It was served on silver trays alongside seven different foods whose names begin with the letter "s," namely *susam, süt, simit, su, salep, safran,* and *sarmısak* [sesame, milk, simit, water, salep, saffron, garlic]. A taste of each, it was believed, would benefit the health.

At *Nevruz* cloth-covered trays bearing exquisite porcelain plates and decorated boxes of *Nevruz* paste and Persian sweets arrived at the Palace Secretariat from the Persian Embassy and were presented as a gift to Papa. Over these *Nevruz* confections Papa's name was spelled out in small Persian gold coins that bore the portrait of the Shah of Iran. Papa would send these over to us or to whomever he wished.

PART THREE

THE
Teacher Safije

THE SCHOOLTEACHER SAFIYE ÜNÜVAR PENNED THE ONLY KNOWN MEM-
oir by an employee of the Ottoman harem.[1] Hers is the unique perspective
of an educated, inquisitive, perspicacious adult hired from outside the palace
to fill a specific job within the harem, schoolteacher to the monarch's grandchildren. As Safiye herself tells us, she was not only the first palace instructor
with a degree, but also the first to reside within the harem instead of coming
to the palace each day to teach.

Though living and working in the imperial palace, our schoolteacher
was never pretentious, nor did she tolerate pretensions in others within
the harem. Instead, over her nine years' residence in the palace, this educated woman engaged her trained mind to observe the manner in which the
women of the harem coexisted with one another. The author does not tell
her reader whether she based her memoir on notes she recorded at the time,
but evidence supports the conclusion that she did, at least to a large degree:
she mentions at one point that she took notes about palace traditions related
to her; she records a formidable level of detail normally forgotten over an
interval of forty-five years, including, in more than one episode, the exact
time of her meetings with other palace residents; and her text is interspersed
with documents and messages she saved from her palace days and which she
reproduces as photographs or transcriptions in her book.

Always the teacher, then, Safiye fashioned her memoir as an educational
text to inform her reader of the structure and customs of the imperial harem.
Beyond this, her manifest concern, when interacting with harem residents,
for tact and strategy—neither of which featured prominently in the preceding two memoirs—reveals the critical importance of both in a large house-

---

1   *Saray Hatıralarım* [My Palace Memories]. Istanbul: Cağaloğlu, 1964.

Sultan Mehmed V Reşad shortly after his accession to the throne in 1909, having survived thirty-three years of restrictions at the hands of his older half-brother, Sultan Abdülhamid. Photographer unknown.

hold of numerous entourages. Even more, her observant eye for details of human interest, for characteristics of personality that lay beyond façade or title, add color and depth to our knowledge of palace inhabitants for whom we might otherwise know only name and rank, if that.

The monarch in whose palace she served, Sultan Reşad (officially Sultan Mehmed V), a younger half-brother of Murad V and Abdülhamid II, came to the throne at age sixty-four following the latter's dethronement in 1909. Reşad was pigeon-toed, inclined to stoop, and rotund, qualities that combined with his slow speech and mannerisms to leave the impression that he was simpleminded, even stupid. He was neither. He read widely, wrote poetry, actively managed his farm, and took pleasure in practicing and studying Sufism. He was courteous and kind. It was these personal qualities that suited Sultan Reşad for his role as the first constitutional monarch in Ottoman history, a role he quickly accepted and studiously followed in order to provide government leaders no cause to dethrone him, the fate that had befallen his brothers and uncle.

Disasters marked his reign. In 1911 Italy seized the Ottoman province of Libya, followed immediately by the Balkan Wars, in which the empire lost nearly all its possessions in Europe. In 1914 the government led the Ottoman Empire into World War One on the side of Germany, initiating four years of struggle and ultimate catastrophe for the Turkish army and people. It is during these wartime years that the schoolteacher Safiye enters the palace, yet, as she relates, the struggles raging throughout the empire had only a tangential impact on the traditional life of the palace.

THE *Memoir*

My palace service began with the pleasant duty of serving as teacher to the princesses.

My uncle, İsmail Hakkı Efendi, the Senior Imam to Sultan Reşad, was on duty at the palace each Tuesday, and also led the Sultan in prayers during the Royal Mosque Procession on Fridays. This meant that an imperial carriage appeared at our door two days each week. Still today I can vaguely recall my uncle stepping into the carriages dressed in the official robes he wore on Fridays.

Around that time my aunt passed away. The Sultan himself sought to console my uncle by graciously presenting him with Gülnisar, one of the ladies who had been in service at the imperial palace, to be his wife. At first we behaved rather coolly and sharply toward this palace lady, who arrived at our house forty-one days after the death of my aunt,[2] but later on we became close friends. She was an exceedingly refined, high-minded, and pious lady. After that, palace ladies visited our home in the Sultan Ahmed District quite frequently.

In writing this memoir I must begin with my acceptance into palace service, which I feel is important not because it concerns me personally but rather because of the light it throws on certain characteristics peculiar to the palace.

As I shall always recall, the date was 22 March 1915.[3] That night I had had a dream in our house on Şeref Street, and I told my older sister about it. She thought it worthy of note and told me to relate it to our uncle. When I went

2 The period of mourning in Ottoman culture extended for forty days.
3 An unresolved discrepancy, as the author subsequently states she entered the palace on the following Saturday but gives *that* date as 22 May.

to see him in his room, my late uncle was reading the Holy Quran. I hesitated, as in those days we did not disturb our elders by constantly coming and going in their presence. But he himself asked me if there were something I needed, and I told him that my sister wanted me to relate my dream to him. He set down his Quran and said, "Well, tell me about it, my dear."

And so I did. Here was the dream: I was in the *selâmlık*, the room in the house set aside in olden days for the male guests of the head of the household. When I raised my eyes to the sky there was the most glorious moonlight. The room sparkled brilliantly as the moon slowly began to set. When the moonlight reached the level of our door, I was dumbfounded, for the moon had turned into Sultan Reşad. When I looked into the skies, the moon was again there, but Sultan Reşad still stood at our door. Our cook, Azime, opened the door for him, and the Padishah came directly to my room. I rushed to kiss his hand and the hem of his cloak. He sat down on the sofa while I sat on the chair that he indicated to his right. He said some things to me, with his right hand patting me on my shoulder. I did not understand what he said, and he rose to leave. When I awoke I tried hard to figure what he had said to me, but I could not piece it together.

After he listened to my dream, Uncle tore a sheet from the calendar on the wall and kissed it. He then went back to his reading, which of course meant I was to leave the room at that point.

I have mentioned that Uncle was on duty at the palace on Tuesdays, so he went to the palace as his presence was required that day. The Sultan received him and said to him, "Imam Efendi, I wanted to arrange for religious lessons to be given the kalfas in the palace and I raised the matter with the Chief Physician, Hayri Pasha. He brought in a woman and the lessons began, but as I heard it, while she had her pupils read from the Holy Quran she herself sat in a chair and smoked a cigarette. I didn't care for this at all. I paid her six months' salary, ordered her paid the money due for her board, and dismissed her from the post. Now I need to get the job done. If you were to take on the task and find someone to serve as instructor, I should be most grateful. She would teach the princesses Dürriye, Rukiye, Hayriye, and Lutfiye, as well as the princes Nazım and Fevzi. Their mothers wish for this as well." (All were the children of his son Prince Ziyaeddin.)

When my uncle heard this imperial command his eyes filled with tears. The Padishah could not help but notice and asked what had brought this on. Uncle related my dream and told how I had graduated from the Teachers' College and was preparing for my examinations this year to enter the mathematics department of the Dârülfünun.[4] The Sultan replied, "Then I herewith offer her the post of teacher."

Unexpected good fortune had indeed smiled on me since my dream. At supper that evening my uncle kept looking at me and smiling, then he said exactly these words to me: "I have good news for you, my dear. The Good Lord has seen fit to confer upon you the honor of serving as instructor to the princesses in the Imperial Palace. I'm conveying to you the command given me today by His Imperial Majesty. May God see that righteousness guides your work."

I was dumbfounded at this sudden news. My fork fell from my hand, my head swam, and something stuck in my throat. I felt as though I'd swallowed my tongue.

Two wondrous sensations brewing in my soul collided with one another to produce this effect on me. We knew nothing about life inside the palaces; now, indescribable excitement gripped my heart at the sudden news that I was to become part of this important but mysterious way of life that had glittered so appealingly in my mind. The palaces, and life within them, spread out before me in my imagination. The palace gates that closed behind those who entered robbed them of their dreams in their former life, but in compensation for this grief they might also usher in the fantastic paradise of the Thousand and One Nights. I was scared and overjoyed at the same time, and trembling in wariness of this future that seemed so alluring, but also frightening to one unfamiliar with it. "But what about the Dârülfünun?" I wondered aloud. "I've dreamed of attending it—wouldn't this ruin my chances?" I wanted to finish my education. Graduation Day had figured in many a sweet daydream.

The sudden sound of Uncle's voice woke me from this jumbled daze.

"My dear girl," he said, "until now no one with a degree has ever entered service in the Imperial Palace. The men took lessons from private tutors in the selâmlık, the ladies from kalfas who were trained in the palace, and in recent years the princesses have been taught by itinerant instructors who lived outside the palace. You, however, will live in the Imperial Harem. You'll witness life in the palace first-hand. I'm sure you must be quite pleased at this news." I said nothing and just lowered my head, while he continued as though to back up what he had said and perhaps to try to convince me further.

4 Predecessor of the University of Istanbul, the Dârülfünun ("Abode of Sciences") opened in August 1900.

"There are so many women teachers in Istanbul—I ask you, which one of them has been honored in this way? In any event, I've already given my promise to His Majesty. You're going to the palace on Saturday."

With that he turned to my older sister and in an authoritative tone instructed her, "You will make all the arrangements. If something is needed, you may ask the lady who came from the harem," and gestured to the palace lady.

My sister's answer, said to smooth over the situation, is still ringing in my ears. "Don't pay her any mind, she's just stunned by it all. After all, who else has been honored with such a post? May God grant His Majesty and you yourself long life!" she said, offering up thanks and a prayer both at once. With that, Uncle rose from the table, immensely gratified and reassured at her response.

After quite a struggle with myself, at length I decided I would go to the palace. Only, how does one go to live in a palace? What must one take along? In our household only the palace lady would have any idea, so we set about gathering the things she advised and instructed me to bring. In truth, not so many things were needed, indeed as I recall everything all together amounted to three changes of undergarments; four dresses, two with long flounces and two with short flounces; toilette articles; six pairs of stockings; and three pairs of shoes, one for summer, one for winter, and one for formal occasions. In fact the palace lady told me there was not even any need to take these things, as they would provide everything for me there. But my sister had it in mind to send me off with enough things to fill an enormous travel bag.

I spent three days completely on tenterhooks. Nighttime brought no sleep. A strange kind of jitteriness took hold of me as I pondered the new life upon which I was so soon to embark. It was as though I were about to pass from one world into an entirely different one. And so it was, for the palace truly constituted a world of its own. It is no small matter to enter into a way of life completely unknown to the public at large, and needless to say, it was impossible to surmise beforehand what sorts of adventures awaited in life in a palace, which plays itself out, as it does, behind thick and solid walls.

At last, Saturday, the 22nd of May 1915, arrived. At 10:30 in the morning an elegant palace carriage was waiting in front of our door. I was trembling with apprehension, as if this carriage were carting me off to uncharted horizons. My sister could read the fear and sorrow in my face and was fluttering around, not sure what to say, encouraging and consoling me in a low murmur, "Put your trust in God, Sister. If he wills it, all will turn out well."

We'd always cast envious eyes at the occupants of such a carriage, and now I was about to step into one myself. With an unexpectedly agile hop, the Master of the Coffee Service, Ahmed Efendi, leapt down from his seat next to the driver and opened the door. I settled into the coupé, which was fitted out with the dark satin I had always admired, while a servant took my bag. Inside the carriage I rather froze up, sensing nothing, then kissed the hands of my weeping sister and of the palace lady, whose lips were trembling with emotion. We took our leave of one another. As the carriage crossed over the bridge[5] I noticed two ladies lifting their veils and eyeing me with envy, which made me smile. At length we turned up the road leading from Beşiktaş to Yıldız Palace.

IN YILDIZ PALACE

As we arrived at the palace and passed through the outer gate, footmen saluted the carriage by bowing deeply in a mark of great respect. A goodly number of eunuchs awaited me at the doorway into the harem. The Master of the Coffee Service Ahmed Efendi, who had accompanied the carriage, handed me over to Seyfeddin Ağa, the eunuch on duty, and said, "Take the lady teacher to the rooms of the High Hazinedar."

The eunuch took me into the harem, where young palace girls, each more beautiful than the other, greeted me. Later on I was to learn that these were the kalfas assigned the duty of welcoming guests. We climbed the stairs to the upper floor and entered a salon entirely fitted out with Hereke fabric and tastefully furnished. There I removed my covering shawl. Through the open doorway I could see inquisitive heads peeking in—inspecting people in this way being a palace custom. Apparently these were the palace girls who had been informed beforehand that the new teacher was coming. They were bending over whispering things about me in each other's ears, of which I was able to overhear: "Oh, how young, isn't she, Sister?" with the latter word pronounced *kaaşım* as it always was in the palace, instead of the proper *kardeşim*. And they were justified in the comment, because until then all the female teachers appointed to the palace had been elderly ladies, so no doubt they assumed that the new teacher would be the same. As it was, however, I was but a young girl who had just received her diploma from the Teacher's College. They were doing their best to show me the utmost respect and courtesy, and soon they brought me coffee in a cup encased within a delicate holder.

5 The Galata Bridge across the Golden Horn, connecting Stambul with the northern districts of the city, where Dolmabahçe and Yıldız Palaces are located.

After perhaps a quarter hour they left the room and the Head Kalfa came in. After the High Hazinedar this Head Kalfa commanded the most respect in the palace, and all the ladies in service at court called her *kaafam*, the palace pronunciation of the word *kalfam* [my kalfa]. She was wearing a dress with a long flounce at the back and a *hotoz* on her head, fastened on the left side by a pin set with brilliants—all in all a tall, dignified, refined palace lady. This was Rişkidil Hanım.

I rose. "Oh, please don't get up," she said by way of greeting, then continued, "If you've rested sufficiently, I shall take you to the High Hazinedar."

This was certainly a deeply moving experience for me, to meet these important palace personages whose names I had heard for so long but whose faces I had never seen. Together we climbed the stairs to the upper floors of the same apartments, passed down an elegant and attractive corridor, entered a salon, and then passed into one of the rooms opening into it.

She was in her sixties and wearing a long dress that reached all the way to her ankles, with the short jacket known as *salta* around her shoulders. Simply put, I was in the presence of a most exquisite gentlewoman standing before me. Rişkidil Kalfa introduced me. The High Hazinedar took two steps toward me and said in a kindly voice, "My dear girl, His Imperial Majesty has appointed you as teacher to the princesses and, until they are old enough to go to school, to two of our princes. He has also commanded that you are to give religious lessons to kalfas who desire them, at times that are convenient to you. I certainly wish you much success in working accordingly, so that you will earn His Majesty's favor."

She paused for a moment before continuing, "Your predecessor committed some acts of disrespect while having the Holy Quran read aloud, and for this reason her duties were terminated. You, however, are a daughter of the ulema, and so you appreciate these matters even better than we do. May Almighty God grant you success in your work." With that she turned to Rişkidil Kalfa and said, "My dear kalfa, take the lady teacher to the rooms set aside for her." Both of us then rendered *temenna* salutations to the High Hazinedar as we withdrew.

Remarkably enough, it was only then that I was able to breathe easily.

We crossed over into the apartments adjoining those of the High Hazinedar and then ascended a broad marble staircase. Our feet sank into plush carpets. As we passed through a glass door, another elderly kalfa wearing a long, trailing dress received us.

During our walk Rişkidil Kalfa informed me of several things. "The name of your kalfa is Piyalerû. She was the kalfa in charge of the household of His

Majesty's Third Consort, the lady Dürrüaden. As this lady stated in her will, at her death Piyalerû became Head Kalfa to her son, Prince Necmeddin. But as Prince Necmeddin recently passed away, out of respect for his memory the kalfa has been retained in service in his apartments at Dolmabahçe and Yıldız Palaces. May God spare all of us the grief that she suffered at his death.

"She is a highly respected lady," she continued, "with five persons in her charge: three girls by the names of Şevkidil, Nigaristan, and Ispantayyar; a harem eunuch by the name of Said Ağa; and the Tray Servant, the eunuch Halil Ağa. All were previously in the service of Prince Necmeddin. I do hope you will like all of them. And she will look after your every need."

"Ma'am, you must be tired," Piyalerû said to me. "Let me show you your room." She led me to the adjoining room, which was a lovely room, beautifully decorated. Here were the four walls within which I was henceforth to live. Something about them truly pleased me. Who knows, perhaps it was just the human tendency to accept whatever circumstances fate brings our way.

For the rest of that day until evening, the palace ladies paid calls to bid me welcome, *beyan-ı hoş amedi*[6] in the palace terminology they used. Lovely, well-mannered, and sociable ladies numbered among them. They constantly mentioned various palace customs and so began the task of enlightening me. Seeing such well-bred and refined young women, I could understand why pashas and beys preferred palace-trained ladies in marriage, and I thought them perfectly justified in doing so.

The next day was Sunday and once again palace ladies ebbed and flowed through my room all day long, speaking in their charming if grammatically incorrect Circassian way. Now too I learned that a young kalfa by the name of Hüsnüaver was to be taken into palace service and would wait on me.

MY DUTIES, AND MY FIRST STUDENTS

Ünsiyar Hanım was one of the consorts of Sultan Reşad's eldest son Prince Ziyaeddin and mother of the princesses Dürriye and Rukiye as well as Prince Nazım. On Monday I was informed that Ünsiyar Hanım would be coming to see me, so I made myself ready and waited for her. At eleven o'clock she arrived, a slightly plump woman of medium height, more elegant and prettier than the ladies I had seen so far, with small, slanting eyes and full, fleshy lips. She had come along with her mother, Firdevs Hanım.

---

6 "Declaration of welcome," a Persian phrase in the Ottoman language that only the upper classes would have employed.

Ünsiyar Hanım began the conversation. "I am very glad to meet you. Until now Their Highnesses (that is how she referred to her children) have been taking lessons in the Holy Quran from a scholar by the name of Mustafa Efendi, but I asked His Majesty for a female teacher in possession of her diploma. May God grant him long life—he immediately accepted my request and graciously brought you to us."

I thanked her. She continued, "I am certain that your instruction will conform to that in the schools. If you need anything, please let me know." I wrote up and handed her a list of articles I would need, including school desks that sat two students each, a blackboard, a desk for myself, and some other things. "Don't worry," she said. "Everything will be procured immediately. I do just have these requests of you: once inside the classroom, there are no more princes and princesses. You are free to behave toward them as you see fit. The other instructor's engagement in the position will be terminated; we are giving the position to you. And His Majesty has ordered that their study of the Holy Quran should be concluded first, after which their school lessons may begin. Please do carry things out in this way." With that they stood up and took their leave.

The royal children's mother was a charming lady and left a good impression. While awaiting the class materials ordered for the princesses, I took down the names of palace kalfas who wished to take lessons. The number of my students was increasing! They would be able to pursue the courses they desired, but for now they would study the Holy Quran, religion, reading, spelling, arithmetic, mathematics, and physical education. My students gradually increased in number, and here I shall record my students' names, insofar as I can remember them: Ispantayyar, Ferhamet, Suzidil, Lem'an, Neşe Resan, Neşeriz, Lâlerû, Çeşmidilber, Çeşmiferah, Melâhat, Nevzad (subsequently a consort of Sultan Vahideddin), Nesrin Şadırû, Nigâr, Milnigâr, Nigâristan, Bezminigâr, Zülfitab, Mihrimah, Mihriban, Pesend, Ferzan, Virdirevan, Zermisal, Nüzhet, Dilşikâr, Feriha, İrfanter, Nazikeda, Hüsnüaver, Kemalifer, Resan, Rayidil, Dilgüzar. All of them were good girls who valued their lessons and worked diligently.

VISITING THE CONSORTS OF SULTAN REŞAD

While the schoolroom was being prepared I decided to pay my respects to the ladies—that is, the Imperial Consorts—of Sultan Reşad resident in Yıldız Palace. When I broached the subject to my kalfa she replied, "Yes!

You must visit the consorts, the princesses, and the ladies in the entourages of the princes."

A VISIT TO THE SENIOR CONSORT, THE LADY KÂMURES

One must not pay a first call in the evening, and so it was on a Friday afternoon that I put on my dress with long flounces. Having obtained permission beforehand to pay a call, I passed in company with my kalfa through the lovely gardens of the palace, laid out as they were with orderly rows of flowers, and entered the apartments of the *Baş Kadınefendi* [Senior Consort], as the monarch's highest-ranking consort is called. Kâmures Kadınefendi[7] was the mother of the Sultan's oldest son, Prince Ziyaeddin.

There the two palace women charged with receiving visitors, one young and the other elderly, led us to the Guest Salon, where we greeted the Senior Consort's kalfa, Azmireftar. One is not ushered directly into the presence of the Senior Consort; one converses first with her Senior Kalfa over coffee, then the Senior Kalfa escorts one to the rooms inhabited by the Senior Consort, on the second floor. There the Senior Consort received us. Quite clearly she had once been beautiful, and she still retained something of her looks. I was pleased at the sight of myself in the mirror, wearing my dress with the long flounce behind and on my head the *hotoz*, which I had previously received permission to wear. I'd become quite the palace lady! Although I tried to bow low in order to render the *temenna* salutation, as I had been instructed to do, the Senior Consort reached out to stop me. "No, please, no need to do so," she said, indicating it was enough for me to greet her simply. I stepped back a bit and waited, whereupon the Senior Consort gestured toward the chair and said, "Please sit down."

I knew that at social calls such as this it was the custom for guests to be seated not in a chair but rather on cushions on the floor. I realized that her offering me the chair stemmed from the belief that one exhibited a mark of respect toward teachers. My kalfa sat on the cushions.

The Senior Consort asked when my students (the princes and the princesses) would begin their lessons, to which I answered appropriately. She then inquired what orders the Padishah had given for their instruction and

---

7   The spelling *Kâmures* probably reflected pronunciation. Strictly following the rules of Persian grammar, the name should be *Kâmres* (in its Persian original the name means "bringer of pleasure"). The lady Kâmures was grandmother of the author's prospective pupils.

I told her of his orders to complete their study of the Holy Quran before starting their regular school program. "If they learn their religious lessons at a young age," she said, "then they won't forget them, nor will they have put off acquiring this most important knowledge of our religion by the time their lessons have increased in number. May God grant that your students profit from all you have to teach them," she continued. "It has been a pleasure to make your acquaintance." Then she spoke a bit about palace matters with Piyalerû Kalfa, who was sitting next to me. When their conversation reached an end we received permission to withdraw.

A VISIT TO THE SECOND CONSORT, THE LADY MİHRENGİZ

The Second Consort, the lady Mihrengiz, and her son Prince Ömer Hilmi were at their summer residence,[8] so we were unable to make their acquaintance until winter, when they returned to Dolmabahçe Palace.

Once they had returned from their summer villa, I went to Piyalerû Kalfa's room to ask her opinion about calling on them. I saw her performing her prayers, so I waited until she had finished. When I asked her whether I should pay them a visit, she dispatched her assistant, Şevkidil Kalfa, to the household of the Second Consort and asked for an audience. Not ten minutes later Şevkidil Kalfa returned with the news that we were to be received the following day at 3:00.

So once again I found myself having to prepare for an audience, and also struck with a bit of nervousness over it all since I had never met this Imperial Consort or the Prince. The next day my kalfa and I went together at the appointed time to their apartments, where we were taken first to the room of the household kalfa, as occurred on our visits to the other households, but then without our having to wait at all we were ushered straightaway into the presence of the Imperial Consort.

Now, except for the Fourth Consort, the others were quite heavyset, so I cannot refrain from saying that I never expected to meet someone so slim. Later on I heard that she had been suffering from illness for the past few years. I didn't like thinking such pointless thoughts, and anyway my official duties soon enough roused me out of them. I found this gracious and kindly lady and the Prince standing to receive me. Even now as I write these lines, I cannot

---

8 In 1910 Prince Ömer Hilmi came into possession of the villa built by the Egyptian khedive Ismail Pasha in the 1870s in the hills above Üsküdar, on the Asian shore of the Bosphorus in Istanbul. While the harem section of the wooden villa burned down in 1921, the *selâmlık* still stands.

Sultan Reşad's consort the lady Mihrengiz, mother of his son
Prince Ömer Hilmi, around 1910 when she was approximately
forty years of age. Photographer unknown.

forget my gratitude at this mark of esteem and respect they displayed toward me, and which I did not in the least deserve. The Imperial Consort then took a seat on a sofa while her son sat in an armchair, and they politely requested me to take a seat in a chair as Piyalerû Kalfa sat onto a high cushion at my side. After inquiries as to everyone's health, they asked questions about the lessons we were studying, which of course I answered appropriately.

A VISIT TO THE THIRD CONSORT, THE LADY NAZPERVER

The lady Nazperver was raised to the rank of Third Consort upon the death of the lady Dürrüaden. The same day of our visit to the Imperial Lodge, my kalfa and I went over to the apartments assigned to this consort. She was plump, as were the other consorts, and tall. Although at first impression she did not appear particularly learned, she did have a refined and kindly air about her that made a good impression. There was something rather sad about her, the cause of which I learned later. It seems that having no children weighed heavily upon her, despite the fact that the Sultan treated her most kindly and graciously, and so she lived out her life in this rather downhearted fashion. She asked me to visit her often and showed me much kindness.

A VISIT TO THE FOURTH CONSORT, THE LADY DİLFİRİB

From there we paid a visit on the lady Dilfirib, whose apartments were quite nearby. I'd been curious about her because the previous evening I'd been told that she was young and well educated. Without causing us to wait at all, she ushered us into the salon where she lived and returned my greeting most sincerely.

"For the first time, a female teacher with a diploma has come to the palace!" she exclaimed. "If you visit me often, we shall read history together. I love history." We chatted about all sorts of things. She said the palace people liked my uncle because he led the nighttime service prayer during Ramadan in a way that was tremendously mindful of the rules of proper and courteous behavior, and he did not prolong it.[9] She had heard that Uncle had married the lady Gülnisar and she added, "As everyone knows, we have a lot of elderly

9 As one fasts during the daylight hours of Ramadan, the congregation would appreciate an imam who did not draw out the prayers said before one could break the fast at dusk. This is particularly true when Ramadan falls during the long and hot days of summer, as it did in the years when the author was in palace service.

kalfas here and they can't stay on their feet for long when they've been fasting. Your uncle understands how it is with older people."

The young Imperial Consort and I chatted over less formal matters. I went often to her apartments. After Sultan Reşad's death she remained in the palace for a while, then moved to her villa in Erenköy. She passed away in 1952.

VISITS TO THE SULTAN'S DAUGHTERS-IN-LAW

I wanted to pay a call on Sultan Reşad's senior daughter-in-law, Ünsiyar Hanım, consort of Prince Ziyaeddin. She was the mother of two princesses and one prince, the princesses Dürriye and Rukiye and Prince Nazım.

The grounds of Yıldız Palace contain numerous small villas. The lady Ünsiyar lived with her retinue in one of them, a six-roomed villa. I was no sooner inside the door than I met Ünsiyar Hanım, a most unaffected lady, well educated, and smiling. In later years she died in Alexandria.

At this visit I was also to meet my students. I remember the occasion as if it happened today. Lemonade was served, then after a bit Princess Dürriye, Princess Rukiye, and Prince Nazım came into the room. I rose to my feet and Ünsiyar said to her children, "Kiss your teacher's hand. Who knows what things she will teach you? Then you will teach the same things to me, won't you, my brave ones?" She used the term *arslanım* [my lion], the customary word for close family to use when addressing princes and princesses.

From there we went together into the room where we were to hold our lessons. They told me there would even be a plaque inscribed "Classroom" placed on the door. For some time the royal children, their mother, and I conversed, then the children asked permission of their mother to show me the gardens. We went out into the grounds, whose orderly and lovely flowerbeds pleased me so much. It seemed almost a garden in paradise as we strolled through the brownish-green shade of the trees. We climbed aboard the small steamboat in the large pond there and made a couple of tours in it. Experiencing such things as these had begun to make me feel quite contented. One of the harem eunuchs on duty accompanied us. For a while we sat down on one of the benches and rested.

The apartments where the Sultan resided were known as *Hünkâr Dairesi*, the Imperial Lodge. Its windows overlook these gardens, and completely unbeknownst to me at one point the Padishah was watching us. Apparently he asked the Third Hazinedar who the woman was accompanying the prince and princesses.

As I heard it later from the hazinedar Peyveste, the following exchange took place between the Senior Consort and the monarch: "Sire, this woman teacher is quite young, how will she get her students to mind her? Our grandchildren will make her do as they please." To this the monarch replied, "Her years are few but her intelligence is vast."

That day the lady Ünsiyar kept me over for luncheon with the prince and princesses. They were well-behaved children who took pleasure in being with their teacher and liked to stay close to me.

I took breakfast and supper in my room but ate lunch with the prince and princesses.

The Second Consort of Sultan Reşad's eldest son Prince Ziyaeddin was the lady Perizad. She was the mother of two princesses, Hayriye and Lutfiye. I wanted to visit them that same day, and when I went to their apartments I found two blonde little ones, each so pretty, there with their mother. Like the previous two sisters, these little girls were also quite interested in me. We sat down and conversed for a long while. Their mother had the children kiss my hand.

"Hopefully you will give lessons to these two as well, once we move into Dolmabahçe Palace," she said. Known in the palace for her good nature and discretion, years later the lady Perizad was to pass away in the French Hospital in Alexandria and was buried there in the mausoleum of Prince Omar Tusun Pasha.

The Third Consort of Prince Ziyaeddin, the lady Melekseyran, was the mother of Prince Fevzi. She lived in one of the villas located in the same area of the grounds. Now, when I told my kalfa about the places I had seen and the calls I had paid, she was quite pleased, but when I mentioned that I hoped to visit this third lady as well, for a reason I couldn't fathom at the time she said, "Maybe it would be good if you postponed this visit . . ."

When I persisted in the idea, mentioning that I didn't wish to appear rude and certainly wanted to have the pleasure of making her acquaintance, my kalfa didn't object, so in the afternoon of the following day I went to pay a call on the lady Melekseyran. She was young and pretty but her education had been somewhat spotty. When during the course of our conversation I mentioned that I could give her lessons as well, her face lit up with pleasure and she said she needed lessons in writing and spelling.

After we finished our coffee she wanted to show me her little prince. We went to the room of the young Prince Fevzi, who was playing with the numerous toys on the floor in company with his nurse and a young kalfa. His mother said, "Hopefully when he's older he'll take lessons from you."

When I returned to my room I related how things went to my kalfa, who was looking anxiously into my face. From the expression in her eyes I could see her relax.

A COMMAND OF THE PADISHAH TO MY STUDENTS, TRANSMITTED THROUGH ME

It was the third day after my arrival at the palace. A kalfa came by to tell me that the High Hazinedar wished to see me. For some reason, summonses like these made me nervous, but in the course of my short residence I had begun to get used to them too. I went to the High Hazinedar's rooms and she greeted me graciously. We drank coffee and exchanged pleasantries about our health, after which the High Hazinedar stood up, so I did as well. She was to communicate to me a wish of the Padishah, and it was the custom to stand while delivering an imperial command. This was the command:

Whosoever does not say prayers or keep the fast, I forbid partaking of my bread and salt.[10] The lady teacher will inform her students of this, my command.

The Padishah was a religious man who never failed to pray the five times each day and to live his life strictly in accordance with religious injunctions. To the High Hazinedar I straightaway responded, "I would like to state that His Majesty can rest assured that I will carry out his imperial order." But the thought lurked in the back of my mind that if I were to carry out this order immediately it was possible that the palace inhabitants who were coming to me for lessons would have to end their studies. This in turn could lead to all sorts of gossip about how I had failed them. There would be talk about how my students stopped coming to me because they didn't like me, or for some other unknown reasons. Here was a dangerous situation for someone in my position, and I had to think of a solution.

Gently I began to counsel my students. I tried to explain to them that however imperative it is to learn one's arithmetic in order to know the cost of items purchased, if one really desires comfortable circumstances in this life and in the world to come one has to respect the tenets of the religion. Gradually my students began to warm to me, as I strove to be as kindly and gra-

---

10 Islam requires prayer at five specified times each day and fasting during the daylight hours of the month of Ramadan.

cious toward them as possible. This technique truly worked, as I noted my students' faithfully coming to classes and working diligently.

After perhaps a month and a half had passed, I hung this sign on the door of the classroom:

Whosoever does not say prayers or keep the fast
May not enter the classroom[11]

When my young students read the sign they immediately returned to their apartments and told their kalfas about it. Of course the kalfas replied that I was simply communicating God's command, and that they were compelled to respect this counsel. One by one they came to me and said, "We promise ... we won't neglect our religious duties," requesting me to accept them still in the classroom. I asked their kalfas to write me each a note confirming their compliance, requesting those who could not write to come to me personally to give their assurances on the matter. In this way the imperial command was carried out.

Talk of this matter spread through the entire palace, even reaching the ears of the Sultan. Apparently he smiled and brought up the matter with my uncle one Tuesday when he was on duty. "Hopefully their mothers and fathers are seeing to their children's religious education," the Sultan said. "But still I too am responsible for them, please God. I thank you also." That evening when Uncle came home he said to my aunt the palace lady, "May God be pleased with Safiye—because of her I received the blessing of the Caliph himself."[12]

I was truly delighted to have attracted the Padishah's notice in this way. Some days later the Senior Equerry Enver Ağa arrived bearing the gift of an inscription, the work of a noted calligrapher. This was followed by a glass case designed to hold the Holy Quran.

WE BEGIN WITH LESSONS ON THE HOLY QURAN

I shall not forget the date on which I began lessons with Prince Nazım and the princesses Dürriye and Rukiye, the children of Prince Ziyaeddin and the lady Ünsiyar: it was 24 May 1915.

11 The author's hanging of this sign was timed to coincide with the beginning of Ramadan, with its requirement to fast during daylight hours. In 1915, the year the author began palace service, Ramadan began on 2 July.
12 The Ottoman monarch was not only sultan but also caliph of Islam, in the eyes of Sunni Muslims.

Sultan Reşad's grandchildren (left to right) Princess Dürriye, Prince Nazım, and Princess Rukiye, the children of Prince Ziyaeddin and the lady Ünsiyar, in 1915, the year they began instruction with the schoolteacher Safiye. Photographer unknown.

When I was told that the classroom was ready, I hurried over to see it and was amazed and delighted at what I saw. It was the sharp mind of Ünsiyar Hanım that had come up with such neat order. There were two rows of desks painted white, with the pupils' chair seats and backs upholstered in red velvet, and facing them a table prepared for me, covered in green broadcloth and laid out with a writing set, ruler, rubber eraser, and so forth. To the side a polished blackboard gleamed, simply perfect right down to the eraser and chalk, while a bench and two chairs completed the furnishings of the room. Everything had been provided, including the sign reading "Classroom" hung over the door. All in all, I was presented with the perfect little school.

That afternoon the royal children came to the classroom with their mother. We all took our places and I asked them first how far they had read in the Holy Quran. The elder princess had read to the *Yâ Sîn* sura, while the younger had read to the fourth *cüz*.[13] I quizzed them on some points to determine the extent of their knowledge and concluded that we could proceed from the point where they had left off. The tiny little Prince Nazım, however, would have to start again from the beginning.

The princesses were wearing headscarves of Bursa silk, as indeed everything in the palace of Sultan Reşad was made of either Bursa or Hereke cloth[14] since the Sultan was known not to care for foreign products but rather to prefer native ones. After a while the little Prince noticed that his sisters had their heads covered, so he too wanted to have his head covered, whereupon his mother immediately ordered the tiny Prince's fez brought. When he put on his fez I could see the eyes of his nurse Suzidil Kalfa moisten with delight.

The lessons continued over the next three months, so that on 19 August 1915 the two Princesses completed their study of the Holy Quran.

THE RECITATION CEREMONY

I had an idea: it might be a good idea to have a "Recitation Ceremony."[15] I broached the thought to their mother, who thought it would be a great success and was pleased at the idea. And so we set about organizing the Recitation Ceremony.

13 *Yâ Sîn*, the thirty-sixth chapter of the Quran; *cüz*, literally "part," a one-thirtieth section of the Quran.

14 Both of these Turkish cities being known for their silk products.

15 *Hatim merasimi*, a ceremony to mark a complete recitation of the Quran, but here meaning to mark the completion of her students' study of the Quran.

I taught the Princesses two verses: Princess Dürriye memorized the prose composition entitled "The Flag," while Princess Rukiye memorized the poem by İbrahim Alâeddin also entitled "The Flag." Ünsiyar Hanım sent for Sabit Bey, the Master of the Robes, and ordered a flag to be made of red satin with the borders trimmed in golden fringe. While the Princesses and I were engaged in preparing the program for the ceremony, their mother saw to the refreshments that would be offered. Fruit drinks and lemonades were to be served in ice-cooled glasses, while the guests would be presented with candies in elegant boxes appropriate to the rank of the guest.

We had quite a number of guests, headed by the princesses' father Prince Ziyaeddin, then their uncle Prince Ömer Hilmi, other young princes, the Imperial Consorts, Princess Rukiye and Princess Âdile, who by chance happened to be visiting the palace that day,[16] the ladies of the princes, ustas who held important positions in the palace, the Senior Kalfas, the High Hazinedar, the Lady Steward, and other palace residents. To tell the truth practically everyone in the palace was invited.

The day of the ceremony arrived, and the large central hall in the building we called the Lesser Chancellery was divided in half by means of gilded latticework screens to form one part reserved for the men and the other reserved for the women. In the middle of the men's section a low reading table was set up and covered with a cloth worked in gilt thread. Two cushions embroidered in gilt thread were set down for the princesses to sit upon, while facing them both round and oval cushions fashioned from velvet, satin, and other valuable cloths were placed out for the princes to sit upon. Here too the officials of the Palace Secretariat were to gather. Behind the latticework screens, gilded chairs and armchairs were arranged to form a front row, behind which cushions of various colors were lined up in rows to the back of the room. The Imperial Consorts and the princesses took their places in front, followed by the invited palace residents toward the rear. Escorted by a harem eunuch, the princes took their seats, as did the gentlemen of the Palace Secretariat.

Since no such ceremony had ever before taken place in the palace, everyone was clearly quite curious. At last the two princesses came in. Each was wearing a dress embroidered in gilt thread and a headscarf made of Bursa silk underneath an exquisite diadem. The princesses were pretty to begin with, but in these outfits one could easily think them veritable angels. When the princesses came in, the Secretariat officials stood up and in return the

16 Granddaughters of Sultan Murad V and second cousins of the young princesses.

princesses rendered them a salutation. The sight of this aroused a tender emotion in everyone present, and brought tears to my eyes.

The princesses took their places on the cushions. When the Senior Imam motioned for him to do so, their previous instructor, Mustafa Efendi, teacher to the princes, came forward and took a seat on the cushion facing them. First Princess Dürriye, then Princess Rukiye, recited three times the İhlas, the Muavvizeteyn, and the Fatiha chapters of the Holy Quran.[17] Everyone in the audience then pronounced the formula Allahu ekber [God is Great]. The teacher offered up the Concluding Prayer,[18] whereupon the refreshments were served.

At this moment the equerry Ramiz Ağa came in carrying the satin flag, which he offered to Princess Dürriye. The Princess took the flag and began to recite the prose composition.

Even though the piece was somewhat long everyone listened attentively and applauded Princess Dürriye warmly and sincerely. Quite a few of the men of the Palace Secretariat—my uncle among them—had tears in their eyes.

Next came Princess Rukiye to recite the poem by İbrahim Alâeddin, "The Flag."[19]

They applauded the tiny princess just as heartily. Then their father and uncle and the Secretariat officials each congratulated the princesses, bringing the ceremony to a close.

When the princesses came in behind the latticed screens, they kissed the hands of the Imperial Consorts, the invited princesses, and their mother, then received various precious gifts including jewels, which they put on. Both the princesses and I were delighted that everything had turned out so well.

FOUR DAYS' HOLIDAY AND EXCURSIONS

After the ceremony commemorating our completion of the study of the Holy Quran, the children were granted four days' holiday in accordance with the wishes of Ünsiyar Hanım. Escorted by a harem eunuch, each afternoon we

17 The İhlas [Sincerity (of Religion)] sura, the 112th chapter of the Quran, affirms God's unity and is followed by the Muavvizeteyn or Suras of Refuge—the last two chapters of the Quran—which invoke God's protection; the Fatiha or opening chapter beseeches divine guidance. The four chapters are the briefest of the Quran and recited on numerous occasions.
18 The prayer pronounced after a recitation from the Quran.
19 İbrahim Alâeddin Gövsa (1889–1949), poet, author, and educator, known among his many works in particular for his children's verses.

all set off together from the palace on excursions to wherever we desired, in the carriage coupé outfitted with blue satin. This had been placed at the disposal of Princess Dürriye. We went to the Ihlamur Lodge, Kâğıthane, and the farmstead in Balmumcu.

Whenever I went outside the palace I wore the *yaşmak* and *ferace*, but on the evening of the second day the Sultan sent his Senior Equerry, Enver Ağa, to tell me that while it was necessary for me to wear the *yaşmak* and *ferace* on ceremonial occasions and when viewing the Royal Mosque Procession on Fridays, on other days I could wear just the *çarşaf*.[20] Nevertheless, as I heard it the Sultan did not particularly approve of frequent excursions outside the palace. In particular he rather frowned upon people connected to his family going about outside the palace in a way that attracted attention.

THE CEREMONY FOR THE RECITATION FROM THE HOLY QURAN BY THE PRINCESSES HAYRİYE AND LUTFİYE

Although I had become increasingly busy at Dolmabahçe Palace, nevertheless I set about organizing a program at which the princesses Hayriye and Lutfiye would recite from the Holy Quran. Along with the two princesses, a girl in their entourage by the name of Nesrin would also recite from the Holy Book.

Now and again the princesses' mother, the lady Perizad, would stop by the classroom in order to urge her children on in their work, and there she stated that she wished them to move on to other lessons as soon as possible. At last the happy day we had all been anticipating arrived.

The large central hall between the apartments of the Senior Consort and Prince Ziyaeddin were prepared in the same way as I related for the earlier Recitation Ceremony for the princesses Dürriye and Rukiye. The scent of aloe wood from the golden censers transformed the atmosphere in this magnificent salon.

The princesses and Nesrin took their seats. As each of them recited chapters in turn, they inspired calls of *Allahu ekber* from the rows of guests. At the conclusion, the instructor to the princes, Mustafa Efendi, recited the prayer that follows the repetition of the Quran. The guests were then offered fruit drinks. In their exquisite dresses embroidered with gilt thread and with the diadems atop their heads, each princess looked a veritable angel.

At length this religious portion of the ceremony came to an end and the girls stood up in order to recite the composition. So, too, did the audience

20 The *yaşmak* and *ferace* were fancier and more stylish than the *çarşaf*. See glossary.

stand while listening to them. For the occasion we had incorporated Sultan Reşad's poem on the Battle of the Dardanelles into a piece of prose.[21] As they recited, my uncle, the monarch's imam, was in tears.

Then, the plight of the little girl Nesrin as she recited the verse *Ah Vatan* [O My Homeland] truly touched everyone deeply, since she herself was but an orphan with no family. From behind the latticed screen the Third Consort was weeping openly. Who knows, most probably the remembrance of her own homeland had moved this great lady to such copious tears at that moment.

And so with this the ceremony came to an end. As they left the salon the princes and officials of the Palace Secretariat congratulated the princesses repeatedly.

With that the princesses came round to the section of the room occupied by the ladies of the Imperial Harem. There they kissed the hands of the Imperial Consorts and the consorts of the princes, each of whom congratulated the princesses as they presented them with a piece of jewelry. After receiving the congratulations of the other guests present they left the salon. At last all three of us now had this important ceremony behind us.

One hour later they recited the composition in the presence of Sultan Reşad, who was greatly moved and offered his congratulations along with exquisite gifts. He then turned to the little Nesrin and declared his wish to hear the poem that had brought the Third Consort to tears.

O MY HOMELAND

A fatherless child was I, the sandy desert my home,
Our possessions but camel and tent,
Nowhere could we settle, wilderness we traveled.
Poor we were, but happy, yet at length good fortune
Decreed one evening an orphan's happiness overmuch.
Abducted, to a palace was I sold,
From one world into another hurled.
On all sides splendid riches, light, grandeur,
And in that land of grandeur I live still.
Once an elfin orphan, a grand princess I became,
Yet at night, in the palace, alone,
I summon the beautiful desert and weep for my homeland.

21 The short verse composed by Sultan Reşad on the occasion of the Ottoman victory at the Dardanelles (Gallipoli) over the British and French, in 1915, was entitled simply *Manzume-i Hümayun* [Imperial Verse]. İsen and Bilkan 1997, 251.

Sultan Reşad was greatly pleased. Both the princesses and Nesrin received the presents they deserved.

THE ELDERLY HIGH HAZİNEDAR ALSO TAKES LESSONS IN THE HOLY QURAN

The Senior Kalfa was one of my favorite ladies in the palace.[22] I admired her so very much. Now and then she would come to pay a call on me, and on one such occasion she told me that the High Hazinedar wanted to see me. I went that very day to see her. We sat for a while, and after some friendly conversation she said to me, "My dear teacher, I would like to recite in your presence the *Yâ Sîn*, *Tabareke*, and *Âmme* chapters from the Holy Quran.[23] If you have any time to listen to me, I would be most grateful. You see, I'm afraid that I'm making errors in reading them and so committing a sin." Of course I readily agreed.

She was a most respected lady. I worked with her in her rooms for two months. In my mind's eye I shall always picture her perfectly modest reading of the Holy Quran as she sat at the low reading table, her head covered in an ironed shawl.

Now and again Sultan Reşad would say, "Now see, I've brought in quite a lady teacher, please God. Anyone can profit from her learning." The High Hazinedar used to repeat these words of his all the time. Even though I was young enough to be her granddaughter, she was not embarrassed to take lessons from me.

THE ROYAL PUPILS INCREASE IN NUMBER

On Saturday, 18 September 1915, we moved from Yıldız Palace down to Dolmabahçe Palace where, for me, a whole new world would begin. A room was prepared for me in the apartments of Sultan Reşad's recently deceased son, Prince Necmeddin, and there I settled in. The side windows of this room overlooked the Bosphorus and it was decorated in excellent taste. But for some reason, despite all the magnificence of Dolmabahçe Palace I loved Yıldız more.

After an interval of two days to rest and settle in, we started back to work.

---

22 The author must be referring to the Senior Kalfa of the apartments in which she was residing, as each entourage in the palace had its own Senior Kalfa, appointed by the Sultan, as the author will explain later in her memoir.

23 Quran 36, 67, and 78 respectively.

Some five days had gone by when I received an invitation from the lady Peri-zad, Prince Ziyaeddin's Second Consort. When I went to pay her a call she said, "I've received permission from the Sultan for my daughters Princess Hayriye and Princess Lutfiye to begin their studies. His Majesty has ordered that they should first complete their studies of the Holy Quran and then begin their other lessons. If there is anything you may need, let me know." I wrote down the things I would require and handed the list to her.

Henceforth I was to teach four princesses and one prince. Except for Fri-days, then, every day in the morning I gave lessons to palace residents in my rooms, then in the afternoon I had to go round to the princesses' apartments. This not only wasted a good deal of time but was also quite fatiguing. Surely it would be propitious in every way to combine them. But I wanted to go about this cautiously.

When I told my kalfa what I was thinking she said, "Be careful now, don't try to do that. It would backfire on you." I learned that the ladies Ünsiyar and Perizad were on bad terms with one another. Thanks to my good-hearted kalfa's forewarning and my own caution, I had managed to avoid a nasty tan-gle. And so each afternoon I taught lessons by going first to the apartments of the lady Ünsiyar, then to those of the lady Perizad.

Throughout history one can see that rivalry amounting almost to enmity exists between siblings who share the same father but have different mothers. I, however, tried to eliminate this tendency to split apart and worked instead to foster a spirit of commonality. As it turned out, a chance opportunity was to lend me a helping hand in doing so.

That wonderful Recitation Ceremony for the princesses Dürriye and Rukiye had made quite an impression in the palace, as everyone was talking about it. This made the lady Ünsiyar proud as a peacock. One day as I was meeting with her to go over some issues about her children's course of study, I noticed that this well-educated and sensitive mother was listening quite closely and attentively to the points I was making, so I broached the subject in this way: "You know that in the public schools," I said, "children from dif-ferent families attend class together, in the same place. Teaching class in this way provides tremendous benefits in terms of inspiring the children. They benefit from receiving the appreciation they need to overcome carelessness or laziness, and they benefit from the encouragement to achieve a good grade. So, what would you think if we were to bring all the children together into one classroom?"

Ünsiyar Hanım was an intelligent and reasonable woman. "Very well," she replied, "do as you think best."

I was ready to jump for joy, as here was a great feather in my cap. Now I had to think in whose apartments to hold the class in order to guarantee the success of this venture. True, Ünsiyar Hanım had said she would be content wherever the class was held, but once again I benefited from talking the issue over with my kalfa. The good-hearted woman advised me to discuss the proposal in a meeting with the lady Perizad, but not to mention my plan to anyone before meeting with her.

Some days went by before I visited Perizad Hanım after class. I had heard that Perizad Hanım was a stubborn woman, but in my opinion she seemed one of the most refined and kindly ladies in the palace, liked by everyone for her patience, forbearance, and good character. Still I would need to mind how I phrased things.

During our meeting I gave my views on public school education and social life. I stated that the princesses were working at an appropriate level, paying careful attention to their work on the Holy Quran, and that before long we would be able to hold a Recitation Ceremony. She was quite pleased and listened most attentively to all my thoughts on the schoolroom and on how her children were performing in class. My heart was pounding! At last she said, "You're right. Do as you see fit; we have complete confidence in you."

Now I was walking on air. Here certainly was quite a victory, convincing both sides. Everyone in the palace was amazed at this success of mine.

Soon afterwards I began having my pupils attend class together and they were quite happy with the arrangement. Let their mothers despise one another as much as they wanted—that did not concern me here. It was enough for the children to like one another, that was all we needed. As a result of this episode I set about my work with increased enthusiasm and maximum energy.

The Sultan heard about this episode and was pleased by it, while the High Hazinedar herself came to my room to congratulate me on it.

Some days later a palace resident brought me word that the High Hazinedar wanted to see me. That sent me into worry and doubt that someone had spread a rumor about me. Heaven knows this was possible in such a congested palace. But the High Hazinedar simply said to me, "His Majesty has commanded that henceforth you will go home once every other week."

Since coming into palace service I'd received permission to go outside the palace once a week. One week on Thursdays following the afternoon prayer I would go to my great-uncle's house near Yıldız Palace, the second week I went to my eldest sister's house in the Nuruosmaniye District, and the third week I went to my little sister's home near the offices of the Şeyhülislâm.[24] And so, whereas it may seem that limiting my excursions outside the palace to once every other week would weigh heavily upon me, it really wasn't that way at all. Sometimes I wouldn't leave the palace for a whole month. To tell the truth, at first it was quite fun to go visiting my relatives in the various quarters of the city in a palace carriage, but once I grew accustomed to palace life I started to go out less and less frequently. Now and then I would go out for a ride with the princesses Dürriye and Rukiye on Fridays and we would visit my sisters, albeit always with the princesses' permission.

PRINCE ZİYAEDDİN ASKS TO TAKE ALGEBRA LESSONS

While Prince Ziyaeddin was attending medical school he used to bring his notebooks to me and I would copy them out cleanly.

A command I received after we had later moved into Dolmabahçe Palace quite surprised me: Prince Ziyaeddin, then studying at the Imperial Medical School, wanted to take algebra lessons from me. I gladly accepted, though with a bit of self-doubt, and began to give him lessons in his apartments.

Now, in the palace there was no such thing as a secret. On the day that Sultan Reşad was informed of these lessons the Fourth Consort happened to be with him and he turned to her and said, "You see, my lady, some time ago when you commented how young she is I said 'Her years are few but her intelligence is vast.' Now look, she is even giving lessons to Ziyaeddin." And so by this the Sultan was pleased.

PALACE PEOPLE VERSUS CITY FOLK

In palace parlance the expression *şehirliler* [city folk] was used for people who resided in the city and were not connected to the palace. But the palace needed to be brought in touch with the common people. This is the reason I took the princesses on excursions into town now and again. My goal was to introduce the palace just a bit to the world outside it.

My older sister's daughter was the same age as Princess Dürriye and attended the Bezmiâlem Valide Sultan Secondary School for Girls. The Princess took such a liking to my niece that they spent months together during school holidays, first at the palace and then later at the villa of Prince Ziyaeddin in the İbrahim Pasha Meadows in Haydarpasha.

---

24 Near the Süleymaniye Mosque, in Stambul; today the site of the offices of the Mufti of Istanbul.

I didn't like it at all when palace folk talked derogatorily about city folk as though they were a different race. One night I was a guest in the room of one of those palace people who had taken to the idea that they were always superior to city folk. No doubt thinking she was paying me a compliment, she said, "Upon my word, my dear Teacher, you don't seem like a city person at all! You really seem just like one of us!"

This remark was enough to set me off. I readily decided the time had come to put a stop to this kind of talk, so I responded, "My dear Kalfa, who are the city people, and who are you? Don't you belong to the people of this nation? This you need to know, that if there were no city people, there wouldn't be a palace. So let's drop this notion of being separate and apart." Then I added, "One can have a people without a dynasty, but can one have a dynasty without a people?"

The kalfa's face blanched. She was elderly and I didn't want to hurt her feelings any more than that, but for years afterward she was irritated with me.[25]

MY AUDIENCE WITH SULTAN REŞAD

Although quite a bit of time had passed since I entered palace service, I had not yet been received in audience by the Sultan. One day five samples of Hereke fabric in different colors, wrapped in a cloth bundle, arrived from the High Hazinedar. From three of them my kalfa ordered gowns to be made by the lady tailor who came to the palace and took my measurements.

The order was for three costly gowns with long flounces, decorated with lace and tulle. The lady dressmaker sewed the dresses and brought them to me within a week.

Around that same time the kalfa gave me the good news that on the following day I was to be presented in audience to the Sultan. I can't describe

25 Years later, when the imperial family was exiled after the proclamation of the republic, the municipal authorities granted permission for dependents of the imperial family to live for a while at Dolmabahçe Palace in what was known as the New Building. On some simple pretext I went to visit these elderly kalfas. As coincidence would have it, didn't I encounter this lady on the way up the steps? She bent over, whispered softly in my ear, "You were right; a nation can survive without a dynasty," and wanted me not to hold it over them that I had been right. As it was, I had gone there in hope of providing them a bit of consolation in the wretched plight that had befallen them. But she had reminded me of this painful episode from the past.

And now they still did not know where they would go. Subsequently they told me that my visit had truly been a good deed in God's eyes. Later on, those who had homes went to them, some left the country, and others placed themselves in the public care by entering the Darülaceze municipal poorhouse. [Ü]

how I felt at that moment! But trepidation also seized me: how should I prepare myself? That same day my kalfa and I together rehearsed how one conducted herself in an audience with the monarch, and I learned such things as
how to respond to the pleasantries that would be exchanged.

The next day I dressed myself with the assistance of my serving girl, who
had fashioned a *hotoz* in a color that complemented the tailor-made dress.
The *hotoz* is a kind of headgear that is a bit higher in front, lower in back, and
made of fine silk fabric in a color that complements the color of the dress.
One could wear jewels on the *hotoz*, if one wished.

My kalfa explained to me that I could wear the first of these three new
gowns when going to audience with the Sultan, the second when attending
the ceremony of the Sultan's felicitations on the high holidays, and the third
when paying calls on the Imperial Consorts. All three gowns were long and
had flounces. At other times I was free to wear dresses with a shorter skirt.

I placed the *hotoz* on my head and when I caught a glimpse of myself in the
mirror I could hardly recognize the figure staring back. Dress certainly does
change the person!

My kalfa and I made our way down the long and magnificent corridors of
the palace to the apartments of the monarch. The hazinedars on duty greeted
my kalfa and me when we arrived at the Imperial Apartments. In front of the
doors of the room occupied by the Sultan we saw the Third Hazinedar, this
powerful woman I have mentioned earlier. From the smiling welcome she
gave us I understood that she was aware of my summons to an audience.

Even though my kalfa was elderly she always stayed a few steps behind
me and would stand aside so that I could precede her. On a number of occasions I had asked her not to do that, but she told me that she did so out of
respect for the knowledge possessed by the person who was giving them lessons. This time as well, just before entering into the Padishah's presence my
kalfa stood behind me, but taking her arm and pleading with her, I made her
go in front of me. The Third Hazinedar opened the door and in went first
the kalfa, then I, and there we found Sultan Reşad standing by the windows,
looking out to sea. He turned around but I could not bring myself to look
into his face. When one encounters a person whom one has built up in imagination to mythical proportions, one simply begins to tremble all over. I was
ready to die from sheer excitement.

The Third Hazinedar Kalfa said, "Sire, the lady teacher and your kalfa
Piyalerû," whereupon Sultan Reşad took a step toward us. My kalfa instantly
dropped to her knees and I began to do the same thing in imitation of her
when I heard the Sultan's voice, "No, no, please don't, you are a daughter of

the ulema, and I am a dervish,"[26] demonstrating his courtesy and solicitude. "I thoroughly enjoyed the flag verses you taught the princesses for their Recitation Ceremony," he continued. "For days I had them on my mind. I should like everyone to love and respect our flag. I love it myself. May God will that your students continue to profit from your example and inspiration."

"God willing, Your Majesty," I replied, "I shall endeavor to impart my insignificant knowledge while in imperial service. May Almighty God grant Your Majesty long life." I then added a prayer in the style and language used in those days.

I performed another floor *temenna* and then withdrew slightly, as the Sultan turned to Piyalerû at my side and asked about her health. She thanked him for inquiring. Addressing us both, he said, "Do rest for a bit," and with that the audience was over.

As this episode made its way around the palace my stature rose another peg. Afterwards I learned that the Sultan always stood to receive teachers out of respect for their knowledge, no matter what degree of knowledge they possessed.

When afterwards I paid evening calls on the various residents of the palace, regardless of where they ranked on the hierarchical scale, I would note and commit to memory information on palace customs and traditions and on how one comported oneself in the monarch's presence. I confess that I profited greatly in this effort from the Imperial Consorts, the High Hazinedar, and the consorts of the princes. In particular I must mention my debt to the Fourth Consort for so many things.

SULTAN REŞAD'S CHARACTER

Sultan Reşad was conservative and disliked displays of show. As one example, during the war he forbade palace amusements and musical performances that had been the custom in the palace for ages. On the other hand he did not want the old ways in the palace to be neglected, so for example he did not abolish such longstanding traditions as the *diş kirası* [Tooth Hire], which were the gifts distributed after a meal, the *iftar davetleri* [invitations sent out to the meal that breaks the fast each evening during Ramadan], and the *Nevruziye* [sweets offered as gifts at the *Nevruz* celebrations]. He wanted everyone to take care that the old traditions were not undermined in any way.

---

26 Sultan Reşad was a practicing dervish of the Mevlevi order.

The episode I shall relate next will suffice, I believe, to demonstrate yet again the benevolence and kindness of the Padishah.

When one of the palace residents desired to move out into the city in order to get married, she would write a note addressed to the prince or princess whom she served, including the phrase *çırağ buyurulmalarına müsaadeleri* [his (or her) permission to depart from palace service]. Petitions of this type addressed to the Sultan were called *Çırağ kâğıdı* [Departure Notes].

Sultan Reşad never refused any of these requests expressed by the palace residents; on the contrary he received them graciously and granted them all. He even paid the living expenses incurred by the woman for as long as she lived, and supplied her whatever assistance was necessary in the home where she came to reside, so that she would not be a burden. "This country has provided for me for sixty-six years," he would say as he dispensed his largesse to them, "and now these young women are leaving service to start families, raising sons and daughters for the country."

Sultan Reşad was a poet and also a religious man. Not once did anyone see him neglect to perform his daily prayers, for he was devoted to his religion in a way that befitted one who bore the title "Caliph on Earth." He commanded everyone in his entourage to perform their daily prayers and if he heard that someone was not performing them, an appropriate person was sent to advise them as to proper behavior. He did not like to dismiss or replace persons who were seasoned in his service. He made certain that all of these persons were religiously minded, and as it was, his entourage contained not a single person who failed to perform the daily prayers.

He treated with great consideration the elderly veteran kalfas who remained in the palace from the reigns of the monarchs preceding him. He would even summon them in turns to his presence so as to inquire of their health and learn if they might be in need of anything.

One such kalfa, Nervet Usta, remained in the palace from the days of Sultan Abdülaziz.[27] He sent for her often and enjoyed conversing with her. She was a highly educated elderly lady who knew the Persian language well and also gave lessons at this time to Prince Abdülmecid. In later years she was to die in the Darülaceze poorhouse.

The Sultan frequently stated that nothing must prevent a person of any age from taking religious lessons if he or she wished to do so, because of the traditional saying attributed to the Prophet that "one should acquire

27 As Abdülaziz's reign ended in 1876, at the time the author knew her this kalfa had served in the palace some forty years at least.

knowledge from the cradle to the grave." Without any doubt the Sultan's devotion, attachment, and reverence for the religion could not fail to influence everyone in the palace, so that I witnessed a deep connection to the religion among all the palace residents. Indeed the grandmother of the lady Melekseyran, consort of the Sultan's eldest son Prince Ziyaeddin, was only vaguely familiar with the Holy Quran, so she mentioned to me that she would like to expand her knowledge of it. Of course I told her I was only too happy to assist her, for certainly I couldn't refuse such a request even though with my busy schedule it would not be easy to find time to attend to an elderly woman.

In my mind's eye I can still see this venerable lady kneeling with all humility before the low table to read the Holy Quran. Her example seemed almost to incite the younger palace women to action, for thereafter the requests for instruction multiplied. Despite all my fatigue I objected not at all, for this was a duty I carried out gladly.

By the time she completed reading the Holy Quran, this elderly lady had twice changed the prescription of her glasses for stronger ones, which quite moved the Sultan when he was informed of it. "I myself shall arrange a celebration for this worthy lady when she completes her reading," he told the High Hazinedar as he gave the requisite orders. "I should like to have quite an elaborate event. Convey my greetings to the lady teacher and tell her this."

The lady still had two sections to complete when Sultan Reşad died, so unfortunately the poor grandmother never did receive this honor.

Sultan Reşad approved of knowledgeable and prudent people. One such person for whom he harbored the greatest respect was Leman Hanım, one of the consorts of the Heir to the Throne, Prince Yusuf İzzeddin. Leman Hanım resided as a guest for four months in Dolmabahçe Palace as she sought from the Sultan the distribution of the estate of the late Heir after the latter's death.[28] She remained in the palace for this long period of time in order to defend her children's rightful inheritance so they would lose out on nothing they were entitled to. Her attentiveness on behalf of her fatherless children reached proverbial proportions, and I remember the Sultan saying, "She is the supreme champion of her children. Women such as she should serve as an example to others. Many times have I told her so. Whenever I saw Leman Hanım I would witness her bringing happiness to the poor and the weak for the well-being of my people and of her children."

28 Prince Yusuf İzzeddin died by his own hand on 1 February 1916.

شهزاده عمرحلمى افندى

Le Prince Eumer Hilmi effendi.

Sultan Reşad's youngest son Prince Ömer Hilmi in a patriotic postcard around 1914. His
bristly mustache reflects German influence at the Ottoman court. Photographer unknown.

THE IMPERIAL CONSORTS, DAUGHTERS-IN-LAW,
PRINCES, AND PRINCESSES

Consorts of the monarch were addressed with the title *Kadınefendi* [Her Ladyship]. Each resided in her own apartments. The sultans of olden days had seven ladies in their harem, four consorts and three with the rank of *ikbal*,[29] but in my day Sultan Reşad had but four ladies, as follows:

Senior Consort: Kâmures Kadınefendi
Second Consort: Mihrengiz Kadınefendi
Third Consort: Nazperver Kadınefendi
Fourth Consort: Dilfirib Kadınefendi

Upon the death of an Imperial Consort, each Imperial Consort who ranked below her advanced one step in rank.

When it was necessary for an Imperial Consort to go from the Imperial Harem into the monarch's apartments, one of the hazinedar kalfas would come in to deliver the invitation to her with a lantern in hand (this lantern custom was abolished when electricity was installed in the palace). In the palace the Imperial Consort would don a coat in summer or a fur in winter and remove it when she entered the monarch's apartments, handing it to the kalfa who escorted her.

The consorts could not sit in the monarch's presence unless they received his permission. Always they used formal language when speaking and formal comportment in their behavior. The consorts of Sultan Reşad were exceedingly refined, religious, and devoted to orderliness. Most were well versed in music and enjoyed studying history. Until the end of her life Sultan Reşad's Senior Consort occupied herself with reading history, so that whenever I visited her she would always bring up the subject of Ottoman history.

There were quite a number of interesting palace customs. For example, mothers of princes referred to their sons by the phrase *Efendi Hazretleri* [His Highness]. When their sons came to visit them, mothers of princes always received them standing, and they addressed them by the term *arslanım* [my lion].

When as a measure of respect the palace residents would try to kiss the skirts of the Imperial Consorts, the Consorts would respond politely with *etme* [please don't]. When departing from the apartments of an Imperial

29 While the author is correct that the number of consorts a Sultan might have was legally limited to four, the number of concubines—in the rank of *ikbal* or *gözde*—was unlimited.

Consort, a guest would take leave of the kalfa who escorted her out by saying *hak-i pâye yüz süreriz* [my respects to you].[30] To this the kalfa would respond *olsun efendim* [very well, Madam], which had the meaning of "My best wishes to you."

When an Imperial Consort wished to visit one of her fellow consorts, she sent a kalfa as a kind of ambassador to ask her "permission." One never saw the consorts on familiar terms with one another.

Young or old, princes would kiss the hand of an Imperial Consort, who in turn would embrace them sincerely and affectionately, kissing the young princes on their foreheads.

Each Imperial Consort had her own table servants, harem eunuchs, a number of servant girls, and *baltacıs* [footmen, literally "halberdiers"], the term given to general servants. The supervisors of the servant girls were called Senior Kalfas and were the kalfas in charge of each entourage. Their authority was supreme. Anyone who wished to visit an Imperial Consort would apply to her entourage kalfa. This constituted a kind of protocol in the palace, so that anyone wishing to see me—except for my students—would apply to my kalfa Piyalerû, for only through her was it possible to meet with me.

To sit in the presence of an Imperial Consort before she had granted permission to do so constituted a breach of etiquette. One had to remain standing until she gave permission to take a seat. Former palace women who had departed the Imperial Harem for the city in order to become the wives of beys and pashas would visit the palace on official occasions, and sat on the cushions shown them. These cushions were about as high as a chair.[31] For the most part they were upholstered in velvet or satin, although in later days linen-covered cushions began to be produced.

The Imperial Consorts approved of people who upheld palace traditions. When they went out of the palace into the city, elaborate ceremonial was the rule, and they would bring their Senior Kalfa with them, as well as others according to turn of duty. Without fail a harem eunuch would escort them, seating himself next to the coachman but never exchanging a single word with him. The harem eunuchs were charged with carrying out their duties to the letter. On their excursions the ladies would usually drive to Gülhane Park, Liberty Monument Hill, Kâğıthane, the Balmumcu estate and environs, and occasionally to Eyüp Sultan. Now and again they would visit the

---

30 Literally "We lower our face to the dust underfoot."
31 The English furniture term *ottoman* derives from these tall, firm cushions in Ottoman households.

tombs of Sultan Mehmed the Conqueror and Sultan Ahmed. When visiting tombs they would leave generous tips for the caretakers.

The carriages of the Imperial Consorts proceeded according to rank, and on no account could one pass another.

The respect that the lower ranks in the palace afforded to those in high positions was rendered with such perfect politeness and deference that it could serve as a sterling example and object of imitation. In this I can say that without exception, all palace residents were persons of supreme refinement.

All the Imperial Consorts had a number of poor persons for whose welfare they considered themselves charged. They would even have dresses made for girls who were to be wed, and would present them with one or two of their own dresses whose magnificence I could spend hours describing. It was also their custom to distribute money in containers.

During my years in the palace I never saw the consorts of Prince Ziyaeddin—the ladies Perniyan, Ünsiyar, Perizad, and Melekseyran—wear a dress more than three times. Instead they would remove them from their wardrobes and present them to needy women. In short, both the Imperial Consorts and the consorts of the princes were constantly making gifts, commensurate with their rank, to those of lesser station than they.

The entourages of the Imperial Consorts included numerous serving women. They worked in two crews, alternatively on duty from Thursday to Thursday. Two of them were assigned duties as pantrywomen, two as table servants, and two in personal service. They were not permitted the slightest negligence in carrying out their duties.

The table servants brought in the trays of food and set them down as near as possible to the dining room. One of them would serve the food while the other would set and clear the forks, spoons, and plates. When guests were present more servants would assist at meals.

These servants operated in a strictly regulated environment in which the pantrywoman prepared the table and her assistant, known as *acemi* [novice], washed the dishes. In the palace they used the term *kapkacak* [pots and pans] for dirty dishes. While the Imperial Consort was taking her meals, without fail one of the higher-ranking attendants stood duty at table.

The same mealtime customs prevailed for the princes and their consorts.

A highly ritualized formula governed the change of duty crews, whereby each crew surrendered the cleanly washed sets of dishes and cutlery, all pieces accounted for, to its sister crew coming on duty.

Whereas in earlier days the sons of the House of Osman were referred to by the title *çelebi* [Prince], in later years they were called *şehzade*, which carries the meaning of "son of the shah or emperor." Also in use were the terms of address *Efendi* [Sir] and *Hazretleri* [His Highness]. Newborns would be nursed by a wet nurse brought in from outside for the purpose. These wet-nurses came to wield significant influence in the palace. A prince's serving women fell under the supervision of his nurse, most of whom were knowledgeable and refined women.

The princes held great respect for their nurses and wet nurses, on no occasion acting against their advice. Apart from these nurses no one could take the princes into their laps or kiss them. Once they began to walk a kalfa would constantly follow behind them. As they grew older the princes would take lessons from private teachers in the *selâmlık* as well as from instructors called *lâla* [tutor], most of whom were selected from elderly and certainly refined and knowledgeable personages.

THE PRINCESSES

The daughters of a sultan or prince were called *Sultan* and addressed in a number of ways: *Sultan Efendi Hazretleri* [Your Highness Madam Princess], *Sultan Efendi* [Madam Princess], *Arslancığım* [My little lioness], or *Efendiciğim* [My little mistress]. But when the princess was not present, one added her name before the title, for example one would say *Zekiye Sultan, Dürriye Sultan*.

Their mothers supervised the princesses, who were provided a wet nurse, various serving women, eunuchs, and their own dining trays and table servants, just as were the princes. The apartments where they resided were known by their mother's name, for example *Perizad Hanım Dairesi* [the lady Perizad's Apartments]. They called their mother *Valide* [Mother], their paternal grandmother—an Imperial Consort—*Cici anne* [Granny], and their maternal grandmother *Büyük anne* [Grandmother]. In addition to their visits on ceremonial occasions and holy days, once a week they visited their Granny [*Cici anne*] and kissed her hand. In turn the Imperial Consort would embrace her granddaughter and kiss her on the forehead.

The Imperial Consorts taught the princesses from a young age to show compassion to the poor. Their mothers and nurses would usually tell them religious and moral stories. As they grew older they did not remain indifferent to those in need and never failed to accord respect to those older than they, no matter the person's rank.

They possessed a superior aptitude for music and could play the lute and violin even without taking lessons. They enjoyed entertainments. Evenings they would spend in their apartments busy with handwork or with music. Now and then they would play games with kalfas of their own age. *Papaz Kaçırmak* [Kidnap a Priest] numbered among their favorite card games.

All in all, then, they did nothing to excess. They rarely went into the city, but if they did go out they returned to the palace before the sunset call to prayer. Such were the Sultan's orders.

THE CONSORTS OF A PRINCE

In the palace the consorts of princes were called by the title *Hanım* [Lady].[32] These women were brought into the palace at a young age and provided special training and education. In order to become the consort of a prince a girl had to be pretty.

Some of the consorts learned foreign languages, while music occupied a place of importance in their lives, with most of them able to play the lute or violin. The mother of the late Princess Behiye became an accomplished calligrapher, so much so that when the Sultan happened to notice a work of hers one day he showed it to one of the calligraphers of that time, who admired it greatly. This lady hoped to arrange for lessons in calligraphy through Sabit Bey, Sultan Reşad's Master of the Robes, and aspired to become one of the great calligraphers of the day, but since court tradition proved an obstacle to her goals she had to remain content with having earned the monarch's admiration for her work.

These ladies addressed their princely husbands by the term *Efendi Hazretleri* [Your Highness]. No matter how often one addressed the ladies when inside the palace with the term *Hanım*, once outside the palace one addressed them as *Hanımefendi Hazretleri* [Your Ladyship]. If the adult princes had several consorts, the first was addressed as *Baş Hanım* [Senior Consort], while the others were addressed by their names.

THE DAUGHTERS AND SONS OF A PRINCESS

Children whose mother was a princess but whose father was not a member of the imperial family were addressed as *Hanımsultan* [Lady Princess] if female, and *Beyzade* [Noble Son] if male. Both *hanımsultans* and *beyzades* were considered members of the imperial family. Their children were addressed as *Hanımefendi* [My Lady] and *Beyefendi* [Sir].

---

32 This title followed the proper name, thus *Perizad Hanım*, "the Lady Perizad."

THE HAZİNEDAR USTAS AND HAZİNEDAR KALFAS

I should like to discuss for a bit the palace residents known as kalfas, and their various ranks. Perhaps these might be omitted from our discussion, but as mentioned earlier my intent is to write about everything that I witnessed.

To begin with, let me state that the women in the palace belonged to diverse ethnic groups. These ethnicities our history has recorded. If there is one thing I came to understand, it is that because these women came into the palace at a tender age they lived out their entire lives within a closed and restricted space. They were honorable and cordial. All whom I met were Circassian, most having been brought from villages, and deeply devoted to whomever they served, whether padishah, prince, or princess.

The serving women in the palace were divided into different strata or ranks, as follows.

1. *Hünkâr kalfaları* [Kalfas of the Monarch]
2. *Hazinedar Usta* [High Hazinedar]
3. *Kâhya Kadın* [Lady Steward]
4. *İbriktar Usta* [Mistress of the Ewer Service]
5. *Kilerci Usta* [Mistress of the Pantry]
6. *Çeşniyar Usta* (also known as *Çeşnigir Usta*) [Chief Taster]
7. *Çamaşırcı Usta* [Mistress of the Laundry Service]
8. *Kahveci Usta* [Mistress of the Coffee Service]
9. *Kutucu Usta* [Chief Box-Maker]

Each of these kalfas supervised her own retinue, which is why I find it advantageous to discuss them in summary by group. The sole desire of these hazinedars was to please their master or mistress. In earlier times the hazinedars wore their hair in four plaits atop their head as a symbol of their position, but in my day, in the reign of Sultan Reşad, they wore the headdresses known as *hotoz*, made of various colors that complemented the dress they were wearing.

In the palace a good deal of importance was placed on seniority by age. Thus kalfas who came into palace service at an advanced age would take precedence, on formal occasions, over younger women who had entered service before them and otherwise outranked them in terms of years of service. At other times too, the younger women would mind their good manners and treat their elders with respect.

The *Azad Kâğıdı* [Certificate of Freedom] was a handwritten note presented to serving women and slaves testifying that they had been granted their freedom. In olden days if a serving woman or a slave died before being freed, he or she was buried with this Certificate of Freedom, called *ıtık* [manumission], placed atop the breast inside the shroud. This I heard from the Fourth Hazinedar, Dirahşan Kalfa.

SOME PALACE EXPRESSIONS

Fem	abbreviation of *Efendim* [Sir or Ma'am]
Payzen [vagabond]	someone who was going barefoot
Yataklık [bedstead]	used instead of the more common *karyola*
Şehirli [city dweller]	someone who lives outside the palace
Hane [dwelling; compartment]	drawer (in a chest); coffer
Sükker [sugar; sweet]	*Ekmek kadayıfı* [dessert made of bread dough marinated in syrup]
Destimal [handkerchief]	towel, hand towel
Üsküre [a kind of tinned bowl]	bowl
Musandıra [cupboard, closet]	attic
Karşım	abbreviation of *Kardeşim* [My friend, my sister; a term of address]
Küçüfam	abbreviation of *Küçük Kalfam* [My dear kalfa; a term of address]
Uzun Yol [the long road]	W.C.

Novice girls would say *Küçüfam* when addressing the kalfas who had entered palace service before them and were assigned to train the newly arrived girls.

DUTIES OF THE LADY STEWARD AND OTHER USTAS

In hierarchy the Lady Steward ranked just below the Imperial Consorts.

The Mistress of the Laundry Service looked after the laundry and bedclothes.

The Chief Taster had charge over the tableware. In olden days this attendant would taste portions of the food served to a sultan or prince before he partook of it, in order to determine whether it had been poisoned.

The Mistress of the Ewer Service was the title given to the superintendent in charge of the ewer and bowl sets. These articles had their own superintendent because in the days before city water was supplied there were so many sets of water ewers and bowls throughout the palace, made of gold, silver, and copper.

The Mistress of the Coffee Service looked after the coffee service sets. Various serving women assisted the Mistress of the Coffee Service in order to care for the delicate jeweled gold and silver cups—splendid, unique items—in the villas of the princes and princesses as well as in the imperial palace.

The Chief Box-Maker oversaw the articles for the bath and toilette, and other similar objects.

The Mistress of the Pantry had charge over pantry supplies and the dishware sets for serving fruit.

When received in audience by the Sultan and on formal occasions, the Lady Steward and the Senior and Second Lady Secretaries donned jackets of velvet or silk, embroidered along the edging with gilt thread and known in palace argot as *salta*. The Sultan received these ladies in audience in recognition of their senior positions, a mark of imperial esteem of which they were proud.

These elderly ladies whose duties I have just mentioned really had no more involvement with the work; all that remained was their rank. Sultan Reşad treated these worthy doyennes with great respect. Each oversaw her own retinue and had her own personal harem eunuchs in service to her. They taught proper behavior and palace customs to the young girls, some of whom subsequently waited in service upon the princes or princesses and indeed could even rise to become the consort of a prince if her star were shining upon her.

When their mother sent the princesses Dürriye and Rukiye to call on these ustas on the high holidays and at *Kandil* festivals in order to offer felicitations, I went along and always received many a prayer of blessing from them.

THE KALFAS OF THE MONARCH

The women in personal service to the monarch were called hazinedars. Sultan Reşad had seventeen hazinedars, four of whom were always on duty at any given time throughout the day and night. Their superintendent possessed the rank of High Hazinedar, and only she would sit in the sovereign's presence. Usually just the Second and Third Hazinedars waited in service upon the Sultan, the others assisting only when called. When the Second Hazinedar, Şayanıdil Kalfa, took ill toward the end of Sultan Reşad's reign, the Fifth Hazinedar was brought in to serve in her stead.

All in all the hazinedars were knowledgeable and cultivated persons who dressed simply and elegantly. These high-ranking hazinedars all oversaw retinues of their own. They resided in rooms on the ground floor of Dolmabahçe Palace.

I mentioned that Sultan Reşad had seventeen hazinedars. Here, insofar as I recall, are the names of some of them:

High Hazinedar: Nermidil Kalfa
Second Hazinedar: Şayanıdil Kalfa
Third Hazinedar: Pirveste Kalfa
Fourth Hazinedar: Devrefşan Kalfa
Fifth Hazinedar: Dildöz Kalfa
Sixth Hazinedar: Nevfer Kalfa, sister of Sabit Bey, the Sultan's Master
    of the Robes
Seventh Hazinedar: Resendil Kalfa

The other ustas and kalfas pertained to the Sultan but worked in general service. Each had her own retinue that varied in size according to her rank.

The High Hazinedar whom I knew in Sultan Reşad's palace truly merited respect, and the kindness she displayed toward the kalfas in her retinue was indeed something to behold. She had been awarded decorations and possessed her own jewelry, while numerous serving women waited upon her. One did not sit in her presence unless she gave permission to do so. To be sure, her salon contained superb cushions to suit each rank, and when she perceived that the time had come for her guest to sit, one of the kalfas would immediately bring a cushion forward.

On formal occasions she assumed command over all the kalfas. The High Hazinedar received her own separate income as well as separate apartments, retinue, and her own sacrificial sheep on the holy Festival of Offerings each year. In olden times she used to receive each spring a gift of Nevruziye [sweets on the first day of the Persian new year, 21 March]. On formal occasions and festival days in particular she wore the salta, the jacket embroidered with gilt thread.

Selected by the Sultan from among the kalfas in the palace, the other hazinedars resided in his household. In the household where I resided, the kalfa by the name of Nigâristan, who had been in service to the late Prince Necmeddin, had been promoted to the position of hazinedar upon the Sultan's order. If memory serves me correctly she was the Sixteenth Hazinedar.

Upon the death of a monarch, his elderly serving women and eunuchs were cared for in Topkapı Palace as a mark of respect for their seniority and service. In later years, as I mentioned previously, a building was erected opposite the harem wing of Dolmabahçe Palace for the purpose of providing a home for these elderly kalfas. In the palace this building was known as *Yeni Bina* [the New Building].

THE SENIOR AND SECOND LADY SECRETARIES

The name of the Senior Lady Secretary was Nazmelek. As Mistress of Ceremonial in the harem she carried a staff of office fashioned entirely of gold. When Sultan Reşad ascended the throne and presented her with the staff, he said to her, "You will need this one day." And indeed she did, for in later years the lady sold the staff in order to buy herself a house, recalling her master with tears in her eyes as she did so.[33]

On formal occasions these Lady Secretaries would don a *salta*. The Senior Lady Secretary in particular presented a most intriguing sight as she received guests, golden staff in hand, glasses on her nose.

DUTIES OF THE SENIOR KALFAS IN THE PALACE

A Senior Kalfa was a kind of female administrator appointed by the sovereign to every household in the palace. This kalfa was responsible for the proper functioning and orderliness of the household, which is to say she was responsible for everything. They were well versed in the principles of good management. The princes and princesses treated this lady with respect, addressing her as *kafam*, the palace term for *kalfam* [my kalfa].

Below the Senior Kalfas in the palace ranked the position of Junior Kalfa, a kind of assistant female administrator who assisted each Senior Kalfa in her work. These second-ranking kalfas trained the incoming novice girls in the techniques of comportment and service. These new girls addressed them as *Küçük Kafam* [my Junior Kalfa], obeyed them, and served both the Junior and the Senior Kalfas as though they were rendering service to their masters. They would take lessons in the religion insofar as possible and would learn to read and write a bit. As I have mentioned in my earlier writings, their Junior Kalfas used to bring these young palace girls to me and introduce them. It

33 As I have stated elsewhere, after the imperial family left the country these elderly ladies remained for a while in Dolmabahçe Palace. After some time, those who owned a house or who had relatives left the palace, while those who had no family were sent to the Darül-aceze municipal poorhouse. [Ü]

was considered bad manners for them to go about in the palace in rumpled or tattered clothing, barefoot, or even in short stockings, as well as to sneeze or blow one's nose noisily.

If by chance they encountered their elders in a corridor or in the large central halls they would stop and wait for them to pass, or if they were attending to some pressing duty they would not pass by them without saying *Destur* [By your leave], that is, without asking their permission to do so. They used special words in their speech, for example:

Princess	*Sultaefendi*, instead of *Sultan Efendi*
Kalfa	*Kafam*, instead of *Kalfam* [my kalfa]
Oil lamp of the old style	*püsüz*, instead of *kandil*
Bowl	*üsküre*, instead of *kâse*
Waistcloth worn in the bath	*futa*, instead of *peştemal*
Head cloth worn in the bath	*kurnatıkaç* [wash basin stopper]
Imperial Consort	*Kanefendi*, instead of *Kadınefendi*
Junior Kalfa	*Küçüfam*, instead of *Küçük Kalfam*
"Vulgar; unseemly," said when angry at someone	*süyütsüz*[34]
Said to close friends	*A kız!* [my dear girl!]

When they wanted to send a gift to a friend they would fill a large laundry basket with whatever things they were sending and tie a white wrapping cloth around it, then cut a piece of paper into the shape of a heart and write the destination address on it. This piece of paper they called *isimlik* [name tag].

To wear a woolen jacket in the palace was considered vulgar. Instead they wore flannel undergarments. I never saw any Circassian serving woman appear before her master or mistress wearing a woolen jacket, as they paid strict attention to palace customs. In their own rooms they could wear whatever they chose.

Each Senior Kalfa had her own particular meal tray, with her meal table set by the novice girls. These kalfas might take their meals with other kalfas of their own rank if they wished, but this was not mandatory. Even if their masters were not of the same rank, their meal service was the same. The girls who waited on them each served on duty for one week, with other girls serving on duty every other week.

Some of what I have written about the kalfas I learned from Pinahraz,

---

34 Research has failed to reveal the literal meaning of this palace term.

nurse to Prince Ziyaeddin. Adopted daughter of the lady Bimisal (sister of the lady Gülcemal, Fourth Consort to Sultan Abdülmecid), this lady had been presented at her own request to the Prince when he was born, along with a golden bowl and ewer.

NEW GIRLS IN PALACE SERVICE

The girls who had recently arrived in the palace were called *acemi* [novice].[35] Since most of them were fresh out of the village they were not allowed into the presence of their master or mistress until they had learned palace procedures and standards of proper comportment from their superintendents. For this training they were placed in the service of a Senior Kalfa.

These Circassian girls were delicate, sensitive, and intelligent creatures. The village girls could not know Turkish, of course, but their quickness of mind allowed them to master it within a short time. Generally speaking they also picked up the palace customs quite rapidly. A few of their predecessors who had been in the palace for some time would intimidate the novices by saying, "Girls untrained in palace ways can't learn how to behave all at once. This is a school that will teach you to behave properly."

The Sultan would choose a name for them as soon as they arrived in the palace. Their name was written on a piece of paper and pinned to their chest for the first days after their arrival in order to help everyone learn and remember it.

Of course this custom prevailed in the days of Sultan Hamid as well. One day a bevy of new serving girls was ushered into Sultan Hamid's presence. One of them had tiny eyes, so he named her Çeşmiferah [Wide Eyes], and such her name remained. Years later this lady rose to the middle-ranking position of Kalfa in the Service of Guests. Çeşmiferah Kalfa was gifted in music and played the lute brilliantly in addition to having mastered *usul*.[36] She played in the Ladies' Orchestra in the palace in Sultan Hamid's day, and I myself took lute lessons from her. At the same time she was a talented calligrapher whose works adorned the walls of quite a few rooms in the palace. On top of all this she knew Ottoman history better than almost any of the palace residents.

35 Newly arrived harem eunuchs were also called *acemi*. [Ü]
36 The rhythmic patterns in traditional Ottoman music.

THE TRAY BEARERS IN THE PALACE

The classroom of the princesses Hayriye and Lutfiye directly faced the *Aş Kapısı* [Meal Gate] through which the tray bearers entered.[37] I used to enjoy watching these tray bearers marching past like a battalion, on their way through the door into the harem. One after another they would pass by, the duty eunuchs for each household at their side, balancing the meal trays atop their heads.

Here was something to behold: the army of tray bearers attached to the households of the Senior, Second, Third, and Fourth Consorts; of Prince Ziyaeddin and Prince Ömer Hilmi; of the princes' consorts, the ladies Ünsiyar, Perizad, Melekseyran, and Gülnev; of the Lady Steward at what was called the New Building, where the elderly kalfas resided; of the other ustas in service and of the High Hazinedar, all marching forth into the harem in divisions like a battalion, as I mentioned, then returning empty-handed, still escorted by the same eunuchs, and finally after a while striking forth yet again in order to fetch the trays. What a pity that I cannot remember how many trays they carried, although I counted them on numerous occasions.

THE VARIOUS RANKS OF EUNUCHS, AND THE CONSTABLE OF THE MAIDENS, THE EQUERRIES, AND THE HAREM EUNUCHS

The ranks among the eunuchs were as follows:

1. The *Kızlar Ağası* [Constable of the Maidens], also known as *Darüssaade Ağası* [Constable of the Abode of Felicity][38]
2. The *Baş Kapı Gulâm* [Chief Thrall of the Gate]
3. The *İkinci Gulâm* [Second Thrall]
4. *Ortanca* [Middle Rank], the equivalent of the rank of major
5. *Nöbet Kalfa* [Duty Attendant], who was in charge of the lower-ranking men

---

37 Although called a *Kapı* [gate], the space was actually a large room that served as a passage between the kitchens and the harem. The tray bearers brought the meal trays into this space, placed them on the tables, and departed, whereupon the table servants of the various harem entourages would enter and pick up the trays, carrying them on into the harem for distribution. Saz 1994, 105–106; Esemenli 2002, 215–216. As the author mentions shortly, the space also included a eunuch guardroom since it constituted a point of entry into the harem.

38 "Abode of Felicity" meaning the Imperial Palace.

The Constable of the Maidens, known also as the Constable of the Abode of Felicity, possessed the rank of minister of state, as we see from our history books. Petitions to him addressed him as *Devletlû, İnayetlû* [His Excellency, His Grace]. After the proclamation of the Constitution in 1908, Sultan Reşad issued an order abolishing the title *Devletlû*, leaving only *İnayetlû*. In olden days the Grand Vizier, the commander-in-chief of the armed forces, the gentlemen of the Palace Chancellery—all would pay calls on this constable. His duties included overseeing the affairs of the Imperial Harem and supervising the eunuchs in service there, and he possessed his own personal household, servants, tray for mealtimes, and tray bearers. The Sultan himself appointed the Constable of the Abode of Felicity.

As for the equerries, once again the Sultan appointed the Senior, Second, and Third Equerries. In order of rotation the equerries occupied quarters close to the apartments of the monarch.

I heard from these men themselves that Sultan Hamid had twelve equerries, Sultan Reşad six, and Sultan Vahideddin four. They would enter the Imperial Harem only when they were required to wait upon the monarch himself. They had special duty rooms for their use between the harem and the *selâmlık*, and at night they would sleep in rotation. If the Sultan wished to send his felicitations or to inquire after someone's health, these equerries would carry out the task, and when the Sultan invited a member of the imperial family into the harem, they would enter escorted by these equerries.

THE HAREM EUNUCHS

These eunuchs were brought to the palace from far-flung places by various means. Those who were young when they arrived were assigned a tutor outside the palace and a male kalfa inside the palace, both of whom saw to the education and training of these eunuchs. They took lessons from private teachers, with religious instruction the primary component, but they also studied other subjects if they displayed the aptitude for them. Trained musicians and men of letters came from their ranks. Tahsin Ağa, who lived in Göztepe and passed away only recently, greatly expanded the extent of our knowledge. I myself took lessons from him.[39]

39 Later known as Tahsin Nejad Bey, after the proclamation of the republic this well-educated eunuch of Ethiopian origin taught literature for some thirty years at the Erenköy Girls' School in Istanbul. Ok 1997, 75–76.

Long years ago I was invited to luncheon by the lady Nevcivan, mother of Prince Seyfeddin, who lived near the racetrack in Haydarpasha.[40] She had also invited Tahsin Efendi that day, and when she began to introduce him to me I said, "Ma'am, he is my teacher," and I went over to him and kissed his hand.

I saw Ramiz Ağa, one of Sultan Reşad's equerries, in the palace of King Fuad in Egypt. He played the violin beautifully, and when King Fuad happened to hear of it he sent him his felicitations.

When one of the eunuchs was promoted to the rank of *ortanca*, it was the custom for him to invite the others to a celebratory fete.

When a new eunuch was brought into the palace he was ushered first into the presence of the Constable of the Maidens, then taken round to the rooms of the tutor and the Chief Thrall of the Gate. Afterwards he was entered into the register of eunuchs and placed into the care of one of the elderly eunuchs, whose hand he was given to kiss. Until the end of his days, he referred to this older eunuch as *lâlâm* [my tutor].

When the eunuchs entered the harem they would call out *Destur!* [By your leave!] so that no one would be in the vicinity when they came in.

DUTIES OF THE GATE SENTRIES

The duties of the gate sentries included escorting into and out of the harem those who disposed of the trash, the stokers of the baths, those who looked after the quilts, the tray bearers who entered the harem at midday and in the evening, and the duty physician when his services were needed. They also were responsible for seeing that firewood was brought into the harem. These duties were also called *halvet nöbeti* [Seclusion Duty].[41]

FOOTMEN

The footmen of the palace were called *baltacı* [halberdier]. By means of the harem eunuchs they saw to it that necessary tasks were carried out. These men were divided into two divisions: those in service at Dolmabahçe Palace were called *zülüflü hademe* [footmen with tresses], while those at Topkapı Palace were known as *saray baltacısı* [palace halberdiers].

---

40 Members of the Egyptian royal family. The lady Nevcivan (1857–1940), wife of Prince Ibrahim Fehmi Pasha, was mother to Prince Ahmad Seyfeddin Ibrahim (1881–1937).

41 In reference to the seclusion of the harem.

Until the very end, footmen wore a special collar of blue fabric over the collar of their frock coat.

VISITS TO THE PALACE AND THE RECEPTION OF GUESTS

First of all, visitors were required to wear the *yaşmak*, the *ferace*, and a long dress that reached to the floor in front and extended perhaps three-quarters of a meter or one meter in back. Such, at least, was the outfit usually worn at high holidays. Generally speaking a dress had to extend to the floor in both front and back. The novice girls would take the *yaşmak* and *ferace* of an arriving guest, iron them, and fold them inside the wrapper known as an *üstüfe*. When the guest was ready to depart, the same girl would bring the wrapped bundle and assist the lady in putting on her veil and coat.

The enclosed carriage known as *kupa* [coupé] would be dispatched from the palace to call for visitors of consequence.

NEW YEAR'S DAY FELICITATIONS IN THE PALACE

On the 28th of Zilhicce[42] my kalfa came to my room, opened the door to my mirrored wardrobe, and selected one long-flounced, formal gown and one dress for informal occasions. She handed them to the girl she had brought along and told her to iron them, then said to me, "Ma'am, the day after tomorrow is the first of Muharrem, and as you know you will have to be presented to His Majesty for the New Year felicitations. Will you go with the princesses, or with me?"

"However you see fit," I instantly replied, to which the kalfa responded, "In that case ask the princesses' mother. We'll do as she suggests."

In that this estimable woman was possessed of good breeding, and well grounded in the customs of the palace, everything she did or thought always ended well, so that very afternoon I went to ask the lady Ünsiyar her opinion. And didn't she answer, "We'll go together. I've already asked His Imperial Majesty for permission for you to do so." I truly cannot find the words to convey my joy at that moment, for to pay a call on this high-minded and virtuous sovereign was an opportunity I would not miss for anything.

Two days later the Sultan received me along with the lady Ünsiyar and the princesses Dürriye and Rukiye. We each received red satin purses contain-

---

42 Zilhicce is the last month in the Muslim calendar, followed by the (soon to be mentioned) month of Muharrem, the first month of the year. If, as is likely, the author is referring to her first year in palace service, this 28 Zilhicce corresponded to 6 November 1915.

ing ten gold coins apiece for the princesses and five for me, presents for the
1st of Muharrem. When the Third Hazinedar presented the purses to each
princess she said *Arslancığım berekettir* [Blessings, my little lioness]. After
leaving the Padishah's presence we paid calls in order of rank on the Imperial
Consorts to offer our New Year's felicitations. The following day, the 2nd of
Muharrem, my kalfa joined us as we paid calls on the High Hazinedar, the
Lady Steward, and other high-ranking ustas.

During my service in the palace I never carried money with me, I gave it
to Piyalerû Kalfa to carry. When she counted up the gold coins that day, we
had received forty gold liras.[43]

In sum, New Year's Day was celebrated most splendidly in the Imperial
Harem.

THE CELEBRATION OF THE BIRTHDAY OF THE PROPHET

Sultan Reşad ordered a lattice screen installed in one of the salons of the
State Apartments wing of Dolmabahçe Palace so that the Imperial Harem
could also join in the celebrations. A raised platform was erected in the
middle of the room—just as in a mosque—for the chanter of the Nativity
Poem.[44] The Senior Imam and Sabit Bey, the Senior Keeper of the Sultan's
Prayer Rug, helped the chanter up the three steps to the platform. Three persons chanted the poem, each taking turns, as muezzins occupied the space
below the platform. Flanked by the Heir to the Throne and the princes sitting on cushions, the Padishah sat on a low divan during this ceremony as
he listened with respect to the recitation of the Glorious Quran. The ministers of state were invited to this religious ceremony, but their attendance was
not compulsory. White-gloved Pages of the Inner Service offered rose water
from bejeweled rosewater flasks to the Sultan first, then to the others, after
which they served the same persons fruit drinks in decorative glasses along
with three cones of sugar. Behind their lattice screens, the Imperial Harem
was served the same refreshments. In this part of the salon, that is to say the
part occupied by the harem, the electric lights were not lit, so that no one in
the men's section of the room could see anything here.

43 A very great sum indeed, remembering that the average worker in Istanbul at the time
earned approximately forty liras in a *year*.
44 The poem *Mevlûd-i Şerif* (The Noble Nativity) composed in Turkish by Süleyman Çelebi
in the fifteenth century, describing the birth, life, and death of the Prophet Muhammad,
traditionally recited on the anniversary of his birth, the 12th of Rebiülevvel in the Islamic
calendar. The first such anniversary during the author's palace service occurred on 18
January 1916.

At the conclusion of this religious ceremony the Padishah conversed for a bit with the Senior Imam before retiring to the harem. The Senior Keeper of the Sultan's Prayer Rug distributed the appropriate royal gifts due the chanter of the Nativity Poem and the muezzins.

THE ANNUAL GIFT CARAVAN TO MECCA AND MEDINA

Among the truly remarkable memories of my palace days are the preparations of the *Mahmil-i Şerif* [Noble Litter], the annual dispatch of gifts from the Sultan to the holy cities of Mecca and Medina. Great ceremonial accompanied this event, known also as the *Sürre Alayı* [Caravan of Gifts].

The "Kaaba Covering" that was to be dispatched to the Kaaba in Mecca was a remarkable piece of craftsmanship worth viewing both for the manner in which the Noble Litter was prepared, and for the preparations undertaken to transport it.

On the 14th of Shaban,[45] a large table covered with a rich cloth was set up in the Imperial Harem in front of the window that looked into the apartments in which the Sultan was present. Then the Constable of the Maidens, the Senior Imam, the Steward of the Gift Caravan, some of the officials from the Palace Secretariat, and the eunuchs who were held in highest esteem brought in the Noble Litter and placed it on this table as they pronounced the formula *Allahu ekber* [God is Great]. In this way the Noble Litter was presented to the Imperial Harem.

Once the men had left, the First and Second Lady Secretaries came in, took seats near the Noble Litter, and began to recite the Holy Quran. While the Holy Quran was being recited, young palace girls came in. Their heads covered in silken headscarves, they made their way up the three steps and began to cover the Noble Litter with the silver cloth sections known as *üstüfe*. They used specially made needles with silver heads to sew the edges of the cloths together, and while they were working they constantly recited the formula *Allahu ekber*. The cloth sections had each been sent as a gift from the Padishah, the Heir to the Throne, various princes and princesses, the Princess Mother, and the Pasha Mother. First His Majesty's cloth was placed on top, then the other cloths were wrapped in turn around the Noble Litter. The Sultan watched all these proceedings with pleasure and great interest from his chair beyond the window. When one of the hazinedars invited me to do so, I too stepped forward and sewed a few threads with the needle.

---

45 One of the religious festival nights in the annual calendar, corresponding to 27 June 1915 in the first year of the author's residence in the palace.

This ceremony went on until evening. That night the Noble Litter remained in the harem as palace women stood guard around it until morning, when the same small procession that had brought it into the harem the previous day came back and took the Noble Litter away, all the while pronouncing the formula *Allahu ekber*. Thus each year on the 15th of Shaban the Senior Imam, in the capacity of representative of the Padishah, recited the formula *Allahu ekber* as the Noble Litter was placed atop the lead camel, while the gifts were loaded atop the second camel. In this way the procession started off from the palace.

A second ceremony took place at the pier in Beşiktaş, performed by a group of officials under the direction of the Minister of Pious Foundations. People came from great distances to view this ceremony, filling the streets. The roar of 101 cannon shots announced to the entire population of the city that the caravan had departed for Üsküdar across the Bosphorus, where the same ceremony took place when it arrived. The procession wound its way through the streets of Üsküdar until it reached the Pasha Gate. At that point the cloths placed atop it earlier were removed to the accompaniment once again of the formula *Allahu ekber*, placed inside a chest, and transported to Topkapı Palace by the official who represented the Imperial Treasury.

RAMADAN AND THE PROCESSION TO THE NOBLE MANTLE

Quite a few special customs were observed in the palace during the month of Ramadan. For example between the first and the tenth of the month sermons took place quite frequently. Called *Huzur Dersleri* [Lessons in the Imperial Presence], these sermons were attended by the Sultan and the princes, as well as ministers of state and officials of the Palace Secretariat who so desired, while women of the Imperial Harem listened from behind screens.

Evenings at the palace during Ramadan were wonderful. During the day all was quiet because everyone was fasting, but once the fast was broken the palace residents would stream out of all the apartments in groups, gathering behind the latticework screens set up in the large central hall of the *Mabeyin*. The imam and muezzins would come to the Imperial Harem for the evening prayer. Altogether some sixty to seventy people would assemble there.

On some Ramadan evenings the palace kalfas would make up a musical ensemble and perform entertainments. Merriment reigned in the palace until the meal just before dawn, when at twelve o'clock at night[46] the tray

---

46 In Ottoman reckoning the day began at sundown, so "twelve o'clock at night" occurred just before sunrise.

bearers brought in the meal and their calls of *Destur!* [By your leave!] put an end to the festivities.

We were still in Yıldız Palace for the first Ramadan after I came into palace service.[47] Every night I accepted a different invitation, as the Imperial Consorts, the princesses and their mothers, the High Hazinedar, and other high-ranking ustas would invite me to join them for the breaking of the fast. The night prayers performed together after breaking the fast were truly a sight to behold, for satin prayer rugs embroidered with gilt thread were spread out, one for each person present, with coffee served during the preparations. As each guest departed she was presented with a decorated container filled to overflowing with the "Tooth Hire," the gifts presented to guests after a meal in Ramadan. With the exception of the kalfas on duty, everyone in the palace attended the Ramadan evening prayer services, making their way in flocks to the Lesser Chancellery.

The palace women would ask one another who the imam on duty was for that evening, and if it were the First Imam (i.e., the Senior Imam) on duty they were quite happy and would hurry over to the evening prayers. Finally at some point I learned the reason for this: the Senior Imam chose short chapters of the Quran to recite during worship and tried not to stretch out the prayer service too long. On the other hand, the Second Imam decidedly prolonged the services by reading out long chapters, so that quite a few of the palace women preferred to perform their prayers in their own apartments.

Between the end of the evening prayer services and the morning meal served just before dawn, the palace turned into a veritable festival, with each household organizing a different amusement. I too was invited to most of these festivities, in which the merry palace women organized dances and sought to pass the time in fun.

In these gatherings as in the other general social occasions in the palace, what struck one most was the importance accorded to polite behavior. This was *saray terbiyesi* [palace manners]—a kind of social intercourse in which superiors treated their inferiors with kindness while inferiors regarded their superiors with respect and affection, and it was something truly different. For example, if I came across a student of mine in the palace corridors, no matter what her age might be she stopped out of respect and waited until I had passed before she continued on her way. I witnessed countless examples of this respectful behavior and others like it.

On the fifteenth of Ramadan the Sultan would proceed in state to

47 The month of Ramadan that year lasted from 13 July through 11 August 1915.

Topkapı Palace in order to undertake a ceremonial visit to the Noble Mantle of the Prophet. The Imperial Consorts, adult princesses, princes, ministers of state, and the gentlemen of the Palace Secretariat along with some of their consorts would also attend. As a rule the ladies wore the *yaşmak* when participating in this state occasion.

During the visit to the Noble Mantle, *hâfızes* of pleasing voice chanted the Holy Quran while incense burners dispensed delightful scents throughout the rooms. The Padishah took up his position beside a rather high table upon which rested the Noble Mantle, wrapped inside a cloth. Then all present filed past Sultan Reşad one at a time, in order of rank, beginning with the Heir to the Throne, followed by the princes, the great men of the ulema, the ministers of state, the gentlemen of the Palace Secretariat, and the gentlemen of the imperial court.

After this the ladies filed past the monarch, beginning with the Imperial Consorts, followed by the adult princesses, the consorts of the princes, the high-ranking ustas and kalfas of the palace, the wives of invited ministers of state, and the wives of some of the gentlemen of the Palace Secretariat.

As they passed him the monarch touched the blessed wrapped bundle on the table with a section of muslin cloth inscribed along its edges, then personally handed the section of muslin to each person. The section of cloth presented personally by the Sultan during the visit bore the following inscription:

> For the mantle of the Glory of the Prophets,
> The satin of the sky could not serve as mat underfoot[48]
> Prostrating oneself to kiss its skirts,
> Render supplication to the Intercessor for the Community.

This ceremony lasted for hours. At his last Procession to the Noble Mantle, the benevolent-faced monarch seemed to everyone present to be terribly fatigued, and indeed that blessed visit turned out to be his last, as he died in that same month of Ramadan.[49]

Both before and after the ceremony, each adult princess and Imperial Consort occupied a room set aside for her alone. How wondrous and evocative, to see these great ladies of the Ottoman imperial family amidst the his-

---

48 Reading this line of the verse as transliterated by Sultan Reşad's Senior Chamberlain in his memoirs (Uşaklıgil 1940–1942, 1:177): *Atlas-ı çarh olamaz payendaz.*

49 Sultan Reşad's last Procession to the Noble Mantle took place on 24 June 1918 (15 Ramadan 1336), nine days before his death on 3 July (24 Ramadan).

tory-laden chambers of Topkapı Palace. In their splendid gowns and jewels they seemed in competition with one another to present a spectacular sight.

At one point the lady Perizad—mother of the princesses Hayriye and Lutfiye—and I called at the room occupied by Princess Saliha, daughter of Sultan Abdülaziz. We rendered her our salutations. This was the first time the Princess had met me, so she asked the lady Perizad, who was at my side, "Is this the lady teacher?" The room was so crowded that proper introductions were out of the question, so when the lady Perizad answered simply, "Yes, Ma'am," I again rendered the Princess another salutation. She said, "One day I should like to hear those compositions about the flag that the princesses recited," to which the lady Perizad replied, "They will be happy to call on Your Highness whenever you desire." So once again that episode had found favor for me. With that we continued making our rounds to the other rooms to offer our salutations.

THE FESTIVAL DAY RECEPTION CEREMONY IN DOLMABAHÇE PALACE

On two occasions during my service in the palace I attended the Festival Day Reception Ceremony[50] at the invitation of the Senior Consort and the mother of my pupils, the princesses Dürriye and Rukiye. I do not know if my unworthy pen can describe such a magnificent historical spectacle, but my goal is to record, or to try to record, what I saw exactly as it happened.

INSTALLATION OF THE HISTORICAL THRONE IN THE PALACE

Upon the Sultan's order, this preeminent legacy from ages past arrived at Dolmabahçe Palace and the stone steps outside the State Apartments wing of the palace, having been transported from Topkapı Palace in an enclosed carriage escorted by eunuchs of the Imperial Harem, the Steward of the Treasury, the Senior Chamberlain, and an officer of the gendarmerie along with eight of his men. The Steward of the Treasury carried with him the key to the carriage door, which he opened in the presence of the gentlemen I mentioned. The throne had been disassembled into sections, which the eunuchs carried into the Ceremonial Hall and reassembled. Both the seat

---

50 This grandest of ceremonies in the annual calendar at the Ottoman court occurred twice yearly: during the Festival of Fastbreaking at the end of the month of Ramadan, and on the Festival of Offerings two months later, 10 Zulhijja of the Islamic calendar. Princess Ayşe previously described the ceremonies during Sultan Abdülhamid's reign.

*Princess Saliha as a young girl of eleven, in 1873, during the reign of her father,
Sultan Abdülaziz. Photographer: Abdullah Frères.*

*Dolmabahçe Palace again became the seat of the monarchy when Sultan Reşad ascended
the throne in 1909. To the left, the State Apartments wing, to the right, the private apartments
of the monarch and part of the Imperial Harem, and in the center, the vast Ceremonial Hall.
Photographer: Abdullah Frères.*

and the back of this throne had been covered in red velvet embroidered with
gilt thread, while further behind the throne and above it there was a crown
ornamented with gems. A golden sash hung down from both sides of the
throne, while before it lay an exquisite prayer rug. Everyone whom the Sultan commanded to approach him during the ceremony took hold of the sash,
located as it was at approximately chest level, and kissed it, for guests did not
kiss the Sultan's hand or the hem of his clothing.

After installing the throne, everyone departed except for the gendarmerie
officer and his men, who stood watch throughout the night until the Reception Ceremony began the next day.

I humbly submit that my goal is to describe the Festival Day Reception
Ceremony in the Imperial Harem, and if I succeed in doing so I should like
to add a description of the ceremony in the magnificent Ceremonial Hall.

IN THE IMPERIAL HAREM

Preparations for the Festival Day Reception Ceremony began long before the
ceremony itself, with the busy activity among the palace women in the vari-

ous households truly something to behold as they made ready the holiday gowns, the jewelry that would be worn, and the *hotoz* headdresses that would complement the gowns. And oh yes, along with everyone viewing each other in formal court dress, guests from outside the palace would be coming to this magnificent ceremony that occurred only twice a year. These included adult princesses, grandchildren of sultans, consorts of princes, Egyptian princesses, and wives and daughters of the ministers of state. All in all, everyone—myself included—was on pins and needles in anticipation of this fantastic ceremony that seemed like something out of the Thousand and One Nights.

A long corridor ran from the Ceremony Wing to the Ceremonial Hall, and just beyond this corridor lay a space with low latticed windows from where one could view the festivities. Sultan Reşad did not forbid the Imperial Harem to view the ceremony.

The Imperial Consorts led the procession to view the ceremony, followed by the princesses who were daughters or granddaughters of a sultan, the Egyptian princesses, the High Hazinedar, the Lady Steward, and additional worthy ustas and kalfas, as well as other invited guests. Each took her place behind the low window assigned to her. At the end of the ceremony they returned to the harem, where during the half-hour's period of rest the coffee attendants served coffee. Not just anyone can perform this duty; the coffee attendants in the monarch's household spent a good deal of time learning the technique.

The Mistress of the Coffee Service oversaw some forty serving women, perhaps more. This Mistress, or *Kahveci Usta*, as this supervisory kalfa was known, did not serve the coffee herself, but rather carried out the duty of remaining on her feet to supervise her entourage.

As a distinguishing mark of their position as Imperial Coffee Service Attendants, these palace serving girls wore on the chest decorations they had been awarded, while the monarch himself ordered the outfits made that they wore just on the festival holidays. One can readily imagine how magnificent they looked. This contingent of some forty girls, a veritable procession of fairies, astounded everyone with how they flew across a room on the tips of their toes, dashing about without crashing into one another.

For the high holidays, exquisite coffee sets were brought over from Topkapı Palace. The Mistress of the Coffee Service counted their contents both when they arrived and later when she turned them back in. These cups were decorated from top to bottom with gemstones. They were served in holders that corresponded to the rank of the guests; some guests received bejeweled cup holders, others received gold or silver ones.

The cups and cup holders served to foreigners were different. As was everyone else, foreigners too were offered coffee, lemonade, or fruit drinks, as they wished, but they didn't have to take anything. After they finished their coffee they left for home, that is to say, they did not take part in the Reception Ceremony in the Imperial Harem.

The period of rest lasted for half an hour; then the Senior Lady Secretary appeared with her golden staff of office in hand and her jacket embroidered in gilt thread.[51] With all this and the *hotoz* atop her head fastened by a pin set with brilliants, she made an entry that had everyone staring at her in astonishment. One heard her proclaim to the guests, "Mesdames, His Majesty has arrived; please follow me to the reception."

Her manner of walking and her polished comportment struck one immediately. In my mind's eye I can still see her gently and modestly enunciating, "Mesdames, His Majesty has arrived; please follow me to the reception."

First the wives of the Şeyhülislâm were presented to the Sultan, then the wives of all the ministers of state, with the Senior Lady Secretary announcing their husbands' titles as she presented them to the monarch. Each in turn, these ladies saluted the monarch by performing a floor *temenna*. Unmarried young ladies in the families of cabinet ministers were presented separately to the sovereign.

At the conclusion of this ceremony, His Majesty retired to the adjoining room, while the Senior and Second Lady Secretaries saw his guests off. The chief of the harem eunuchs was in charge of their carriages, which pulled up to the doorway of the harem in the order of their husbands' rank. After resting for a while the Sultan returned to the historical room known as the "Crimson Salon," whose walls were covered in fine cloth.

As I mentioned earlier, if the Sultan's mother were alive she would enter the salon at this point.[52] Otherwise the daughters of Sultan Aziz and Sultan Mecid would enter the room now, along with the granddaughters of Sultan Reşad. Hence I too came into the imperial presence at this point along with

---

51 I am told that the golden staff is a symbol of the rank of Secretary. [Ü]

52 I was told that this Imperial Consort (the Princess Mother) had been alive until recently. As I entered palace service a short while after this lady passed away, I was unable to see her personally. [Ü]

Since Sultan Reşad's own mother died in 1851 and his adoptive mother died in 1878, most likely the author is referring to the lady Şayeste, last surviving consort of Sultan Reşad's father, Sultan Abdülmecid. This lady died at age approximately seventy-four in 1912, three years before the author entered palace service. Sultan Reşad would have accorded her great respect both as a consort of his late father and as the adoptive mother of an imperial prince, his younger brother Prince Vahideddin.

my two students, the princesses Dürriye and Rukiye, and their mother. The princesses entered the room in order of age, first bowing down low to perform a floor *temenna*, then kissing the sash. The Sultan decreed the person in the harem who was to hold the sash.

Known as the *Baş Kadınefendi* or Senior Consort, the ranking consort of the Sultan entered his presence first and alone, an exquisite tiara adorning her head and resplendent in court dress and train worked entirely in gilt thread. Then the Second, Third, and Fourth Consorts each entered the royal presence separately, followed by the senior-ranking ustas of the harem, the High Hazinedar, the Lady Steward, other ustas, the Senior Kalfas, the attendants of the Sultan's coffee service, and the kalfas assigned to visitors. The Sultan inspected the dress of the coffee attendants and the visitors' kalfas particularly closely, and if he were satisfied with what he saw he complimented their supervisors.

In sum, these splendid scenes when everyone offered their congratulations to the Sultan on religious holidays, and the appearance of the palace residents within the magnificent salons and central halls of the palace, not only reminded one of the Thousand and One Nights but also stayed vivid in one's memory for weeks afterward.

I have written about the ceremony as it was during the reign of Sultan Reşad. The older kalfas used to tell me that things were even more magnificent and brilliant in the days of Sultan Hamid.

Let us return for a moment to the Ceremonial Hall. I shall do my best to describe what I saw from behind the windows where we sat.

I believe only a few people have seen this Ceremonial Hall. I must confess that over a period of twenty-two years in the Egyptian palaces of Abdin, Kubba, Ras el-Tin, and Montazah, I never saw a hall as vast as this.[53] One end of the room adjoined the sovereign's apartments; the other end led to a doorway and marble staircase. As one can tell from outside, the windows are quite tall, but the hall is so immense that the light streaming through these windows can't illuminate it all. Under the superb chandelier in the center of the hall the court's Senior Master of Ceremonial takes up position; behind and to his left the Second Master of Ceremonial; and still further behind and to his left, the Third, each standing attentively with clasped hands, awaiting

---

53 Abdin and Kubba palaces, royal palaces in Cairo; Ras el-Tin and Montazah palaces, summer residences of the Egyptian royal family in Alexandria. After the exile of the Ottoman imperial family in 1924, Safiye took up employment as a teacher with the Egyptian royal family.

the Sultan's orders. Four red runners made of velvet form in essence a plus sign across the floor.

As the Padishah enters the Ceremonial Hall, the band strikes up an air in salutation to him. After a time the Chief of the Descendants of the Prophet, who was appointed especially to recite the prayer, approaches him and the Sultan rises to his feet, whereupon everyone in the hall simultaneously opens his forearms in prayer.[54] At this moment the spiritual beauty in that magnificent chamber is something to behold. Everyone offers a short prayer to God for the welfare of the nation and the people. Once the cry of "Amen" rings out, this prayer leader withdraws by stepping backwards to exit the hall. After this, those whom His Majesty has decreed respectfully clasp the historical sash to their breasts and kiss it, having first bowed to the Sultan and rendered the *temenna*.

As for the order of procession during the ceremony, first the Şeyhülislâm performs the *temenna* and kisses the sash, then the Grand Vizier does so, followed by the Minister of War, with all of them retiring in the direction opposite that from which they approached the throne. Next the Heir to the Throne approaches, followed in order by the princes, the sons-in-law—each by seniority according to the age of his royal wife—then the cabinet ministers, administrators in the government, and high-ranking officials. After these gentlemen, esteemed members of the ulema approach the throne, their turbans and in particular their robes at the chest worked in gilt thread. As a token of respect for their knowledge, the Sultan stands to receive them, and they do not kiss the sash.

Next the leaders of the various religious communities come forward to pay their respects. From the headdress of the Greek Patriarch a full length of tulle cloth drapes down. Only when in the presence of the Sultan does he cast this cloth back to reveal the various orders adorning his chest. After him the other leaders approach the throne in turn. Since this ceremony is so long, after the religious community leaders have offered their felicitations the Sultan retires to a sitting room to rest.

At the monarch's return to the hall the band again strikes up the salute.

Now the monarch receives the felicitations of the courtiers and household personnel in his service. The aides-de-camp lead the way, followed by the gentlemen of the Palace Chancellery, the secretaries, harem eunuchs, officers of the Household Detachment, the musicians of the Imperial Corps of Music, the footmen, and the royal boatmen and oarsmen. Each of them

---

54 The prayer position of extending the forearms, palms upward and cupped.

kisses the gold-embroidered and tasseled sash, after which the Reception Ceremony at last comes to an end.

My description may well have missed some things, but as I mentioned, from where I was sitting this was all I could see and observe.

PRIVATE MUSICAL EVENINGS IN THE PALACE (WHEN I WOULD DISGUISE MYSELF)

On some evenings in the palace, musical performances would be held in a capacious central hall, or else in a large room more or less equivalent in size to it. The ensemble would be composed of young palace residents drawn from various households, some of them truly accomplished musicians.

If an audience member did not wish to be recognized, she would wrap herself completely in a large bedsheet so as to reveal only her shoes at one end and her eyes at the other. In this way no one knew who she was. Some of the kalfa musicians and dancers were students of mine, so I too preferred to cover myself in the same way so as not to place these good-mannered and respectful women in an awkward position.

Such concerts were always private.

In addition to these performances they would hold grand concerts, after first receiving permission to do so from the princes or princesses to whose households they were attached. Also with the permission of their masters or mistresses they would invite eunuchs who served in the harems of villas outside the palace. The consorts of princes would attend as well, wrapped in the sheet. First the performers would take their places, then coffee and lemonade would be served their guests, who occupied the sofas and armchairs placed in the section of the room set aside for them. When the dance portion began, the harem eunuchs joined in. All in all the festivities lasted until midnight.

COFFEE SERVICE IN THE PALACE

On formal occasions coffee was served in the manner I shall describe below. The kalfa in charge, known as the *Kahveci Usta* [Mistress of the Coffee Service], used a round coffee-service cloth, embroidered in the middle with gilt thread, pearls, and chenille, and fringed around the edges. Two serving women would bend over slightly and carefully pull part of the cloth taut from the sides, while the remaining large part of the cloth hung down loosely in front. They took one of the containers from the silver or golden tray they were holding and placed the cup inside it. Then the Mistress of the Coffee Service would pour the coffee into the cup from the lidded copper jug. This jug stayed warm inside a legged bowl containing hot sparking ashes; the bowl was suspended from silver or golden chains held by another of the coffee service girls. If the guest were particularly distinguished, the Coffee Mistress herself would serve the cup.

In all truth, the ability of these elegant and dignified Circassian girls to serve coffee with two fingers never failed to astonish everyone who witnessed it.

MEDICINES PREPARED IN THE PALACE

A number of special medicines were concocted in the Imperial Harem of the palace. In my day one of these medicines, called *Saray Kırmızı* [Palace Red], had the effect of making one perspire and also alleviating nervous ailments. Until recently some upper-class ladies in the city were still making this medicine. Indeed the lady Fatma, late wife of Sokollu Abdülkerim Pasha, would cook up this medicine with great devotion and dispense it as a gift to anyone who wished it.

This is a good moment to explain the expression *Nevruziye* [New Year's sweets]. At the start of the new year in the Persian calendar,[55] the chief physician in the palace would oversee the preparation of a kind of *macun* [sweetened taffy-like medicated paste], which was spooned out into exquisite bowls and wrapped in colored cloths of tulle. Tied up with ribbon, these bowls of *macun* were sent to the Padishah, the Heir to the Throne, the princes of the imperial family, and the Imperial Consorts, as well as to the gentlemen of the Palace Secretariat. In later years this custom was abandoned, but one still encounters these bowls adorning the glass display cases of great houses. They are to be seen inside the jeweled display cases in the magnificent salons of the palaces of Egypt.

ILLNESS IN THE PALACE

If someone in the harem fell ill, a servant would instantly be dispatched to knock at the harem door and inform the eunuch on duty in the room beyond the door. The physician on duty would then enter the harem in company with the eunuch. If the illness were serious the patient was dispatched

55 21 March in the Western calendar.

straightaway to the hospital, but if it was not so serious she was sent to the home in the city of one of her comrades in palace service, along with sufficient money and other things she would need. There she remained until completely restored to health. I believe this is the reason why epidemics never broke out in the palace.

When two palace women were conversing they would use the phrase *tımara çıktı* [she went out for care] when referring to an ill colleague who had gone out into the city in order to recuperate. After a period of time these women returned to the palace.

THE DEATH OF SULTAN REŞAD

Throughout the reign of Sultan Reşad we spent but two summers in Yıldız Palace. The other years we went to the villa of the Sultan's eldest son, Prince Ziyaeddin, in the İbrahim Pasha Meadows at Haydarpasha.

On the 15th of Ramadan in the year 1334[56] I accompanied the princesses Hayriye and Lutfiye and their mother the lady Perizad from Haydarpasha to Topkapı Palace for the ceremony of the Procession to the Noble Mantle. During the ceremony one could clearly see how tired the Sultan was. Afterwards he returned to Yıldız Palace while we made our way back to Haydarpasha. As I heard it later, from that night on the Sultan was overcome by weakness. The palace doctors were summoned and ordered him to rest, but the weakness only grew worse, reaching such a state by Wednesday, 3 July 1918, that on the orders of Prince Ziyaeddin the lady Perizad and I started at once for Yıldız. While en route neither of us could find the strength to speak even a single word. We arrived at the gates of Yıldız in the coupé that had been sent from the imperial carriage house and was waiting for us at the bridge.[57] The melancholy demeanor of the footmen struck us at once and plunged us into a pit of despair. We passed by the palace servants, who even at such a time devoted themselves entirely to their duties and allowed their respect for their master to slip not the slightest degree, and arrived at the doorway into the harem.

When, as always, the eunuchs on duty escorted us into the apartments of the Senior Consort, we understood the gravity of the situation from the faces of the kalfas assigned to visitors. We found ourselves unable to summon the courage to ask anyone even a single question. They suggested that

56 24 June 1918.
57 The bridge over the Golden Horn at Galata, where the ferry from Haydarpasha would have docked.

we rest a bit and served us coffee, then we stood up in preparation for entering the Sultan's apartments. One of the kalfas escorted us. In the monarch's household each of the Imperial Consorts occupied a room of her own, and we saw them there together with their retinues. We entered each room one at a time and paid each lady our respects.

Sometime later we encountered the Fourth Consort outside the room where Sultan Reşad lay in bed, and we greeted one another. As always, once again this venerable lady favored us with her great kindness. As she turned to me with tears in her eyes and sadness in her voice she said, "His Majesty holds you in such esteem. Please follow me."

Together we walked into the adjoining room, where she tore off a piece of fine muslin cloth from the section of it there in the room and handed it to me. She reminded me that I must perform an ablution, but I replied that in fact I had already performed an ablution when we entered the monarch's apartments after the noon prayers. I removed the *hotoz* from my head and tied on the headscarf in its place. Together we entered the chamber where the Sultan lay on a rather high bedstead in the middle of the room. He was breathing shallowly. Standing at the foot of the bedstead were his two sons, his elder son, Prince Ziyaeddin, on the right and his second son, Prince Ömer Hilmi, on the left, with the Constable of the Maidens standing behind them, all three reading the Holy Quran. When the Imperial Consort motioned to me to do so, I took a seat on a sofa at the head of the bedstead and began to read the Holy Quran.

My uncle İsmail Hakkı Efendi (the Senior Imam to His Imperial Majesty) was standing at the Sultan's right while the Sheikh of the Noble Dervish Convent of Yahya Efendi stood at his left, each reciting the Confession of Faith and the formula *Allahu ekber* [God is Great]. Sultan Reşad was repeating them in a slow, soft voice. I read twice the Ya Sîn chapter[58] from the Holy Quran handed me by the Imperial Consort, and while reading it a third time had just come to the verse "See, the inhabitants of Paradise today are busy in their rejoicing" when the Yahya Efendi Sheikh motioned for everyone in the room to leave. First Prince Ziyaeddin stepped out, followed by his brother, then the Constable of the Maidens and the Fourth Consort. I was last, and was about to go through the door when I turned to gaze once more upon the face of that blessed, honored gentleman. At that moment I heard the Yahya Efendi Sheikh pronounce the formula, "Surely we belong to

58 Chapter 36 of the Quran.

God, and to Him we return."[59] In this way it fell to my lot to see this angelic-natured monarch as he gave up his last breath to his God.

Of course the harem people waiting outside couldn't ask any questions of the princes or the Constable of the Maidens, not to mention the Imperial Consort, so as soon as they saw me come out of the room they gathered round me and started to ask a host of questions about their master. I just answered briefly, "He's resting a bit better," and made my way to the room occupied by the lady Perizad, whom I told what had happened. Not five minutes later the news spread that he had passed away, and the wailing and fainting that broke out in the harem at that moment was indeed something to behold. So many years have passed since then, but that heartbreaking scene remains vivid before me. Later I was told that the cries could be heard in Beşiktaş,[60] but I don't know how true that is.

I passed the night together with the Prince's consort in Yıldız Palace. We would not be able to stay in the sovereign's apartments so we returned to the apartments of the Senior Consort. The Tray Bearers brought in the evening meal but later took it all away again, untouched. No one could eat a thing.

Sometime after evening prayers that night, the lady Perizad gave me permission to go back to the Sultan's apartments, taking with me one of the palace girls. Weeping, there I gazed again upon the lifeless body of the Sultan, who but a few days earlier had been resting in this room. A latticed screen had been set up before the door, as the men inside watching over the corpse must not see the hazinedar passing outside the door. I was standing behind this latticed screen seeing so clearly in my mind the handkerchiefs with writing along the edges, which just the week before he was distributing with his own hands in the Chamber of the Noble Mantle. Just then from behind me I heard the voice of an equerry saying "Make way," and I turned around to see my uncle accompanying the equerry to the room. The eunuch had thought I was someone else and begged my pardon as I kissed Uncle's hand. Again I began to weep, and Uncle said, "He has saved himself; the Sultan has saved himself," by which he meant, "Weep for yourself."

When he went into the room we started back, but like everyone else we passed that historic night unable to sleep.

Around seven o'clock the next morning, Thursday, Sultan Reşad's corpse was removed from the harem on a bier draped with a shawl and carried

59 Quran 2:156. The formula is repeated at a death or when hearing of a death.
60 Perhaps a quarter of a kilometer downhill from Yıldız Palace.

through the palace gardens to the quay at Çırağan Palace, where it was placed aboard a steamer that transported it to Topkapı Palace. From there a magnificent funeral procession made its way down to the pier at Sirkeci, where the bier was carried aboard a steam vessel that transported it to Eyüp. The late Sultan Reşad was laid to rest in the mausoleum he had constructed during his lifetime.

As for us, we paid calls one at a time in the apartments of each Imperial Consort and of some of the elderly ustas, both in order to offer our condolences and to take our leave of them. At length we departed from the palace, with heavy hearts.

In those days adjunct members of the imperial house traveled in the side cabins aboard the Bosphorus ferries. We left at our cabin door the harem eunuch who was escorting us and made our way to the section for women, on the upper deck. All talk that day centered on Sultan Reşad and the new monarch, some of the women praising the deceased monarch and others saying all sorts of things about Sultan Vahideddin. We reached Haydarpasha having listened to these women, who in truth lacked any knowledge of the situation.

Afterwards we resumed instruction for Prince Ziyaeddin and his sons and daughters in his villa at İbrahim Pasha Meadows, visiting Yıldız and Dolmabahçe Palaces only on high holidays and official occasions. The classes continued through the proclamation of the republic and indeed until the members of the imperial family left the country.[61]

The villa at Haydarpasha contained thirty-three rooms and was divided into three households.[62] The first household on the right was that of Prince Ziyaeddin's Second Consort, the lady Perizad, and her daughters the princesses Hayriye and Lutfiye. The lady Ünsiyar and her daughters the princesses Dürriye and Rukiye and son Prince Nazım occupied the middle household. The Prince resided in the upper floors of the third household, while the Third Consort of the Prince, the lady Melekseyran, mother of Prince Fevzi, occupied the second floor of this household. After the Prince divorced this lady, her apartments were given to the lady Neşemend and her daughter

61 The Turkish National Assembly declared a republic on 29 October 1923; its law of 3 March 1924 required all members of the imperial family to leave the country immediately.
62 I.e., the villa included three distinct units, each of three stories, so that each wife and her children could occupy their own quarters.
   This wooden villa, built around 1870, consisted of two separate buildings, the selâmlık and the harem. The larger selâmlık villa housed the Anadolu Lycee before it was demolished in 1975, with apartment blocks taking its place, but as of 2006 the harem structure still stood.

Princess Mihrimah. The first floor of this household contained Prince Ziyaeddin's private reception salon as well as the dining room for the princesses I mentioned. The lower floor was where the serving women resided.

All the kalfas occupied the ground floor of the villa.

A COMMAND FROM SULTAN VAHIDEDDIN

Altogether the entourage of Prince Ziyaeddin and his consorts totaled thirty-six persons. Not one week had passed since the death of Sultan Reşad when an equerry arrived from the new monarch and had me convey an imperial command to the Prince. Although the matter was really quite an insignificant one, nonetheless it distressed Prince Ziyaeddin. He was still grieving the loss of his father and frequently in tears, so this command from the new monarch affected him deeply.

Sultan Vahideddin informed the Prince that if there were any women in his service who might be granted permission to leave, he would accept them at Yıldız Palace. When I conveyed this imperial decree to the Prince, he simply lowered his head in thought. As the saying goes, "It's not the bearer's fault if he brings bad news," but I was thinking that if they had assigned someone else to deliver this decree to him, I wouldn't be feeling so unsettled inside.[63]

The Prince raised his head and said to me, "Please ask the equerry to convey my respects to my uncle the Sultan. I shall be delighted to carry out his order." Then he added, "Assemble all the girls and tell them from me that if I am hungry, they are hungry, if I am sated they are sated. But despite this, my house cannot compete with a sultan's palace. Sultan Vahideddin will take into his palace any girls who desire to go there. I will not ask anyone to leave. If anyone wants to go, I shall not hold it against her. But those who stay will have a special place in my regard. Let me repeat: I shall never hold a grudge against those who wish to go."

With that I went back downstairs to the equerry waiting in the parlor and asked him to wait just a bit longer. I brought all the kalfas together and told them of Sultan Vahideddin's command. They listened with great attention to the Prince's orders. Among the women in his service, twelve

63 Custom directed that at the death of a monarch, the lower-ranked kalfas at his court vacated it, to be married off or settled elsewhere. This left the senior kalfas to transmit their knowledge to the kalfas of the new monarch. But Sultan Vahideddin had maintained only a small retinue of aging serving women in his villa at Çengelköy, so that when he acceded to the throne he thought it expedient to populate the vast palace by the novel tactic of gathering experienced serving women from the retinues of his relatives. Bardakçı 1998, 239–240.

*The future Sultan Vahideddin while still Heir to the Throne, around 1917,
the year he turned fifty-six. Photographer unknown.*

expressed the wish to go to Yıldız Palace. At that moment I, too, was overcome with sadness.

The Prince and his consorts presented the necessary gifts and compensations to those who were leaving.

Sultan Vahideddin certainly acted intelligently in this matter. Of course the number of women in his service as Heir to the Throne would in no way suffice for a sultan's palace, yet bringing in new girls from the outside and training them in the ways of the palace would take a great deal of time. These palace women who were now going to enter his service, however, were first-rate in every way.

Concerning the villa in Haydarpasha: when it was furnished during the reign of the late Sultan Reşad, a classroom was added in the household of the lady Perizad. My own room was on the third floor of this household, next to the rooms of the princesses Hayriye and Lutfiye.

Unfortunately this room gave rise to quite a few disputes. The Prince's Senior Consort, the lady Ünsiyar, was furious that my room was located in the household of the lady Perizad. She said to her fellow-wife, "I was the one who asked His Majesty for the lady teacher. Thanks to me all of you have benefited. And I have a room for her in my household."

I could tell that this dispute would not end well for me, so I had to think of a solution. I went straight off to the lady Perizad, and this intelligent and sensitive lady said to me, "You are free to choose as you wish, don't be upset. Stay in Sister's household (fellow-wives called each other "Sister"). However, I do not wish the princesses to hear of this issue. There should be no competition among siblings, and we must not set a bad example for them."

In this way we managed to overcome the problem. I moved into the household of the lady Ünsiyar, in the same suite of rooms as her elder daughter Princess Dürriye, until the Princess married. Later on, the lady Ünsiyar and her children went to live in Princess Naime's shoreside villa along the Bosphorus. I moved into the room that had been prepared for me previously. After one week's holiday we resumed lessons in accordance with the program. Since custom dictated that the Prince and their mothers be present during our exams, one had to be attentive.

Though living in separate households, now and again these three fellow-wives would chat together, play cards, and spend time together quite pleasantly, especially on long winter nights, as sisters do. Also from time to time the Prince would bring in a musical ensemble, which we would listen to from behind latticed screens.

All these ladies' children took their lessons together in the same class-room. How unfortunate that some disreputable girls in their entourages would repeat gossip and thus open a rift between these fellow-wives, who otherwise lived together as sisters. This sort of thing left its mark on my pupils at once. The order came down that the royal children were to take their lessons in their own households, which meant that I would have to teach each of them in their rooms.

Eventually I could hope for no means of bringing them together other than on one of the *Kandil* festivals or at a high holiday. While extending them my felicitations on those occasions, I would make peace between the mothers by bringing up religious anecdotes, and also I would bring my students together again in one place. Never did I reveal the reason for these changes to the children, however. One occasion I shall never forget. It was the Night of Ascent[64] and I went to pay a call on the youngest of the consorts. I offered her my felicitations on the holiday and expressed my wishes for her happiness and good health, then brought up the subject of God's commands. I counseled her on the beauty of virtuous behavior, on the merit in God's eyes that accrues when one reconciles on this night with those toward whom one harbors anger, and on the positive effect this would have on her children. She immediately agreed. Together we paid calls on the fellow-wives older than she and offered our felicitations.

I witnessed the result of this the very next day. As mentioned above, I would bring my students together in one place. Not once did I hear a negative word from these consorts. Everything I said received a positive response.

There were also young girls in service, of the same age as the princesses, who were taking lessons. They too participated in the general examinations at the end of the year, with prizes suited to their position distributed to the little girls who passed their exams. Some of these girls received greater prizes than the princesses who were in the same class, for Prince Ziyaeddin and his consorts the ladies Ünsiyar, Perizad, and Melekseyran all believed that when it came to this there was no such thing as a prince or princess. Whoever did well won the prize she deserved.

As with all the servants of God, Prince Ziyaeddin had his faults, but his virtues outnumbered them. He always kept up ties to the poorer classes and never refused them his assistance in any way, expending a part of his small income to help the needy people of Kadıköy and environs as well as Üskü-dar. He paid for the burial of indigent persons, financially assisted penniless

---

64 The anniversary of the night in which the Prophet Muhammad journeyed to heaven, 26 Receb in the Muslim calendar; one of the five *Kandil* festivals just mentioned.

girls who were to be married, and requested his consorts to help in providing them clothing and other items. At the beginning of each month he would distribute an allowance to the needy persons in the neighborhood, insofar as he was capable.

During the month of Ramadan a latticed screen was set up in the front gardens at the villa, just as at the palace, and an imam and two muezzins would lead the prayer service for all the residents of the villa, including the Prince. After the worship service their consorts rested for a bit behind the latticed screens. In inclement weather the Prince would order two rooms on the second floor of the villa made ready for the assemblage. For the Festival of Offerings, he wouldn't neglect to dispatch one or two sacrificial sheep to the needy people of the neighborhood as well as to the policemen at the nearby İbrahim Ağa Police Station.

AN AUDIENCE WITH SULTAN VAHIDEDDIN'S FOURTH
CONSORT, THE LADY NEVZAD

In earlier days this lady[65] had served in the entourage of my student princesses and had taken the same classes and training as they, but then she was one of the kalfas who went over to Sultan Vahideddin's palace. A short while later she entered the ranks of the Sultan's ladies.[66]

All kinds of stories exist about the lady Nevzad. When I mentioned to the lady Perizad that I wanted to go offer her my congratulations, she thought it over for a while. I knew that it was a somewhat delicate matter for me to pay a call on the esteemed consort of Sultan Vahideddin, but still I definitely wanted to go.[67] Finally the matter was submitted to Prince Ziyaeddin to decide, and forthwith I received his positive reply. When I made my way over

---

65 Although Sultan Vahideddin married this concubine on 1 November 1922, when she was nineteen and he sixty-one, the Sultan never gave her the title *Kadınefendi* ordinarily given an official consort of the monarch, although he could have done so, since he had only one official consort at the time. For this reason the author refers to the lady Nevzad by the title *Hanımefendi*, indicating her rank below that of *Kadınefendi*. Thus we are left with the somewhat anomalous situation in which the lady Nevzad numbered as the Sultan's fourth concubine but not as an official Imperial Consort. Bardakçı 1998, 240.

66 I.e., the Sultan selected this kalfa to become one of his concubines.

67 The delicateness stemmed from the unusual fact that this new imperial concubine had previously served as slave girl in the entourage of Prince Ziyaeddin, and was commandeered, as it were, by the new Sultan, as the author previously described. That act exacerbated the already frosty and resentful relations between the children of Sultan Reşad and the family of his successor, Sultan Vahideddin. Furthermore, Sultan Vahideddin was so smitten by his new concubine as to be causing gossip in the capital due to his refusal to leave the harem and so part from her company. Stitt 1948, 242.

to Yıldız Palace the next day, I was able to enter quite easily, thanks to the assistance of the gate guards and especially the harem eunuchs. As a precaution I said that I had come to visit Piyalerû Kalfa. The eunuch Said Ağa took me to her rooms—the same rooms we had lived in earlier, during the reign of Sultan Reşad—where the noble-hearted kalfa greeted me with tears of happiness and joy. We talked for a while, and then once we were quite relaxed I explained to her the purpose of my visit. For some reason she thought about it for a time, then she arrived at a decision and said, "Well, let's just send word," and dispatched the kalfa Ispantayyar in her entourage over to the lady's household.

I was a little doubtful about what might happen, but since I held the lady Nevzad in considerable regard for her virtuous qualities, I was thinking that her answer would probably be positive. Some time later we saw three persons coming into the palace gardens—apparently the lady had sent two of her serving women back with the kalfa. They came in and kissed my hand. "Her Ladyship is awaiting you. Please come this way, Ma'am."

This news delighted me. After all, as a classmate of the princesses she had received her first training from me. So I went along with the two women who had come for me, telling them that on my way out I must stop in again to see my kalfa. I was hurrying to see the lady, my student, who lived in a household adjacent to the apartments of the Sultan. Such is the wonder of life—in that beautiful Yıldız garden where I'd spent lovely days with my students the Princesses, now here I was escorted by two kalfas on my way to pay a call on my student, one of the ladies of the Sultan.

I nearly forgot to mention that while my kalfa and I were talking I asked her, "How should I greet my student, since she is now a lady of the Sultan?" for everyone knew that when entering the presence of a concubine of the Sultan, palace custom required that one render the *temenna*. "Carry out the formal greeting that's required of you," my kalfa answered. "We'll see what she'll do in your case. You'll have to adjust yourself depending on that."

When we reached Her Ladyship's villa we entered through the outer door and the lady greeted me in front of the inner, glass door. I started to offer my salutations to her in the customary fashion but she said, "No, please," kissed my hand and took my arm to lead me to the guest parlor upstairs on the second floor. As we went upstairs I knew my intuition had proven correct.

I found her as she had been, gracious and modest. We dined together. When toward evening the time came to take my leave, she made me promise to come back with all the princesses next time. Off I went back to the kalfa's household, pleased and proud. I can hardly describe how delighted the good-natured kalfa was that day.

I arrived at the pier for Kadıköy in the palace carriage Her Ladyship had ordered for me, and from there made my way back to the villa at Haydarpasha.

A VISIT TO THE LADY NEVZAD

After Sultan Vahideddin left the country, the Caliph Mecid moved Vahideddin's family into the royal villa at Ortaköy.[68] One day I went to this villa to pay a call on the lady Nevzad. Of course I knew I would be detained at the gate answering various questions, but I gave the necessary answers, as for me visiting Vahideddin's Fourth Consort, the lady Nevzad, was a matter of conscience. Anyway, I was able to get in. The fact that I had come to visit during these disastrous days for her cheered the unfortunate lady quite a bit, and she listened with amazement and appreciation to my story of how I managed to get in. We visited together for a few hours before I made my way back home.

Then a second visit became necessary. This was to the building at Dolmabahçe Palace that had been recently repaired and given over to palace ladies and women servants from the harems of former sultans as their place of residence.[69]

I took some oranges with me. When I arrived at the palace gate the officers asked me all sorts of questions. In fact one officer subjected me to quite an interrogation, demanding to know who I was and why I wanted to see these ladies. To him I replied simply, "I am their friend in foul weather. You can open this parcel and see what I've brought them as a gift. And please, here is my purse, do look through it. In fact if you wish you can keep it here and I'll pick it up when I leave."

A fair and kindly man, the officer thought for a moment and then said, "All right, you can go in. But don't stay more than two hours." I was happy and thanked him. Dear Lord, how thrilled the ladies were! These were women from the imperial harems of Sultan Aziz, Sultan Hamid, Sultan Reşad, and Sultan Vahideddin. In the days of Sultan Reşad I used to go to their rooms

---

68 Fearing for his safety after the abolition of the sultanate by the parliament meeting in Ankara, Sultan Vahideddin fled the country on 17 November 1922 with his son Prince Ertuğrul and a small number of palace officials, leaving his wives and other children. He was succeeded by his cousin—as caliph only—under the title Abdülmecid II.

69 The so-called "New Building" at Dolmabahçe Palace referred to earlier by the author.

many a night, listening for hours on end to their tales of the old traditions in the palace, some of which I wrote down. And so, however much they were glad to see me, I was just as delighted to see them. They offered up quite a few prayers on my behalf.

Later on, those who had money bought a house in the city and moved out. Unfortunately I heard that the others had been sent to the Darülaceze municipal poorhouse. The opportunity never arose afterwards to go and pay them a visit.

Conclusion

When considering the portrait of life in the imperial Ottoman harem that emerges from these memoirs, intriguingly enough we can conclude that the authors both corroborate and dispel the picture of harem life that flourished in the popular imagination then as now. For while in some aspects life in the harem differed wildly from that experienced by anyone not living in an Ottoman palace, in most ways the existence portrayed here varied little from that led by aristocratic European women of the day.

We have seen that the imperial harem did indeed keep its female residents in seclusion from the public at large, and from inclusion in male social life, in line with the cultural standards that governed the participation of upper-strata women in public life throughout the Muslim world. Foreign as these strictures may seem from our vantage point, apart from the custom of veiling they differed little from the practice of contemporaneous European nobility, which similarly restricted the manner and locations in which respectable ladies of rank might appear in public and function in public life.

In our authors' descriptions of the concubines and royal children, we have met with lives devoted to useful activity and the development of talents (in the Ottoman palace, frequently musical), as well as lives marked by indolence and scant education—traits that the Ottoman imperial family also shared with contemporaneous European aristocracy. We have encountered the riches bestowed on a prince's children, concubines, and high-level staff, in line with their rank, and the opulence of their surroundings—riches that every royal court employs to underscore its claim to stand at the pinnacle of society. And in contrast to popular depictions of the Ottoman harem as a place of cruelty and fear, we have seen portrayals of warm and nurturing love between parents and children. While our knowledge of relations between parents and children in the Ottoman palace over the centuries is scant, quite likely this warming of relations between parents and children there evolved at the same time it did among European aristocracy: primarily only over the course of the nineteenth century.[1]

Our authors have depicted slavery, both female and male, surviving into the third decade of the twentieth century, yet slavery that from all three accounts ostensibly avoided cruelty (at least once the slaves entered palace service), provided a means of manumission, and included paths for the talented to rise to positions of eminent authority and honor. The slavery depicted here furnished the recruits, who were then schooled at considerable length, once they entered palace service, in the operation and management of a large public institution whose essential purpose lay in housing the head of state and in producing and nurturing successors to him. In addition to these purposes, as Princess Ayşe corroborates, under Sultan Abdülhamid the palace also became the effective seat of government, with its male slaves employed toward political ends in addition to household domestic service. For this political involvement some of Abdülhamid's eunuchs later paid with their lives, wrongly so in the Princess's estimation.

The memoirs certainly lay to rest two popular fantasies of harem life. One is the widespread supposition in contemporaneous Europe and America, where miscegenation aroused titillation, fear, and condemnation, that the Ottoman sultan took to bed women of any race.[2] All three memoirs make clear that imperial concubines uniformly originated in the Caucasus.

The second popular fantasy is that of unbridled sexuality on the part of the Ottoman prince. Indeed only the concubine raises the subject of sex at all, and that because, as she says, she knows her audience is wondering. Far from dissolute abandon, we have seen that dictates of practical considerations decidedly limited the tally of concubines a prince might take, despite the fact that Ottoman court custom allowed the monarch (and after the 1850s, all princes) such freedom in theory. As a result in part of the practical limitations on the prince in choosing concubines, the number of children in the Ottoman imperial family remained within manageable limits. And so we see the harem system at work: ensuring the future of the dynasty, in the face of high infant mortality, through the use of multiple mothers to produce royal offspring, yet structured to avoid an excessive proliferation of these offspring, as too many rival claimants could undermine the unity of the empire. In producing heirs, the harem system sought a balance between extremes.

1   On women's roles and child rearing among the European aristocracy, see Lieven 1992, 134ff.
2   On this see Dodd [1903] 2004, xix–xxiii.

Given the Ottoman court's practice of concubinage, the centrality of the entourage system in the harem comes as no surprise. With each mother of imperial offspring naturally keeping an assiduous eye over the welfare of her children as well as her own position, the division of the palace into entourages served to preserve order by minimizing friction, ideally, among concubines. For the same reason we have seen in the memoirs the high importance attached to decorum and etiquette in the palace. Unlike European palaces, which generally housed one monogamous ruling couple and their monogamous descendants, the Ottoman palace accommodated numerous mothers, grandmothers, and great-grandmothers, along with their descendants. This mélange of extended families demanded a firm system to impose order through strict standards of behavior and clear rules of precedence that all obeyed unquestioningly. Rules and rank ensured order and mitigated rivalry, at least in the ideal. For the slave women, they also encouraged loyalty and good work by delineating the paths to promotion theoretically open to all in palace service.

Not surprisingly, one primary consequence of the Ottoman palace system with its emphasis on decorum was to create a sense of superiority among those who lived in it. All the authors comment on this consequence of palace life, with our schoolteacher attempting to mitigate it. Along with the sense of superiority, for the imperial family the system also ideally inculcated a sense of obligation to help those less fortunate, outside the palace; works of charity constituted a duty for members and adjuncts of the imperial house. For the women and eunuchs who served them, the system created a sense of group solidarity, an esprit-de-corps. One was proud to be *saraylı*, a "palace resident," even if one were a slave, for one was an elite slave, privileged, and pleased to distinguish oneself from the common folk outside the palace walls.

Far from painting a picture of titillation, then, all three authors depict overall a system of rules, traditions, and standards of behavior that tightly governed life and interpersonal relations in the harem. As a result, hierarchy, procedure, and decorum reigned within the palace. Regardless of one's position in the harem, one learned the rules, and one followed them. This is the theme that emerges from their writings, rather than the sumptuousness of the surroundings, the ease of life in the palace, or certainly, even so much as hinting at unbridled lust and abandonment to pleasure.

Glossary of Names

*Members of the Imperial Family
and Important Personages
Mentioned in the Text*

Note: *Double names are listed under the second name when the person is known by
that name; e.g., for Prince Mehmed Âbid, see Âbid, Prince Mehmed.*

ABDÜLAZİZ (AZİZ), SULTAN   Younger son of Sultan Mahmud II, Abdülaziz
was born 9 February 1830 and succeeded his older brother Abdülmecid on 25
June 1861. He ruled for some fifteen years until his overthrow on 30 May 1876,
shortly after which he died by his own hand, on 4 June 1876, age 46. He is buried
in his father's tomb in Istanbul.

ABDÜLHAMİD I, SULTAN   Son of Sultan Ahmed III by the lady Râbia Şermî,
he was born 20 March 1725 and came to the throne 21 January 1774, ruling fifteen
years until his death on 7 April 1789 at the age of 64. His mausoleum is located
near the New Mosque in Istanbul.

ABDÜLHAMİD II (HAMİD), PRINCE AND SULTAN   Son of Sultan Abdülmecid by the lady Tîrimüjgân, he was born 21 September 1842. After the death of
his mother in 1852, the lady Perestû raised him. Abdülhamid came to the throne
31 August 1876, ruling nearly thirty-three years until his deposal 27 April 1909.
Abdülhamid lived another nine years in exile, first in Salonica and then in Istanbul, dying at Beylerbeyi Palace in his former capital on 10 February 1918, age
75. He is buried beside his uncle Sultan Abdülaziz and his grandfather Sultan
Mahmud II in the latter's tomb in Istanbul.

ABDÜLKADİR, PRINCE   Son of Sultan Abdülhamid by the lady Bidar, hence full
younger brother of Princess Naime, he was born in Dolmabahçe Palace on 16
January 1878. In January 1944 he died in Sofia, Bulgaria, where he is buried.

ABDÜLMECİD I (MECİD), SULTAN   Son of Sultan Mahmud II by the lady
Bezmiâlem, he was born 25 April 1823 and succeeded his father at age 16 on 1 July
1839, continuing his reforms. Among his some forty-two children numbered the
future Sultans Murad V, Abdülhamid II, Mehmed V Reşad, and Mehmed VI

Vahideddin. Abdülmecid died 25 June 1861, age 38, and was buried in the tomb erected for him on the grounds of the Selimiye Mosque in Istanbul.

ABDÜLMECİD II, PRINCE AND CALIPH   Son of Sultan Abdülaziz by the lady Hayranıdil, he was born 29 May 1868. An accomplished artist, Prince Abdülmecid served as Heir to the Throne from the accession of his cousin Sultan Mehmed VI in 1918 until the latter's deposal in 1922, whereupon he succeeded to the position of caliph only on 18 November 1922, but was deposed on 3 March 1924 when the imperial family was exiled. Caliph Abdülmecid II died 23 August 1944 in Paris, age 76, and was buried in Medina.

ÂBİD, PRINCE MEHMED   Youngest son of Sultan Abdülhamid, by the lady Saliha Naciye, he was born 17 September 1905 in Yıldız Palace. In Tirana in 1936 the Prince married Princess Seniye of Albania, sister of King Zog; they divorced in 1948. Prince Âbid died in Beirut 8 December 1973, age 68, and was buried at the Selimiye Mosque in Damascus.

ÂDİLE, PRINCESS   (1) Daughter of Sultan Mahmud II by the lady Zernigâr, she was born 23 May 1826. In 1845, age 19, she married Mehmed Ali Pasha and bore five children, of whom only her daughter Princess Hayriye survived childhood. Well educated, Princess Âdile became a gifted poetess. She died 12 February 1899, age 72, and was buried in the tomb of her husband in the Eyüp district of Istanbul. (2) Granddaughter of Sultan Murad V through his son Prince Salâheddin by the lady Tevhide Zatıgül, she was born 7 February 1887 in Çırağan Palace and died in December 1973, age 86, in Paris, where she is buried.

AHMED MİDHAT   Journalist and newspaper editor as well as bureaucrat, teacher, and prolific author of stories, novels, and plays, who saw his role as educating the general public. His novels included *Hasan the Sailor*. Born in Istanbul in 1844, he died 28 December 1912.

AHMED RIZA BEY   Politician and political writer, he was born in Istanbul in 1858. After 1889 he resided in Paris, where he penned memoranda concerning the political situation in Turkey, becoming a leader of the Young Turk movement in Europe. Ahmed Rıza returned to Istanbul after the re-proclamation of the Constitution in 1908 and was elected Speaker of Parliament. His political career and writings continued until his death in 1930.

ALİYE, PRINCESS   The youngest daughter of Murad V by the lady Resan, who had also given birth to Princess Fatma, Aliye was born after her father's deposal, in 1880, and died unmarried in 1903, age 23. Her mother outlived her, dying in 1910.

AYŞE, PRINCESS HAMİDE   Daughter of Sultan Abdülhamid by the lady Müşfika, born 31 October 1887 in Yıldız Palace. She married twice, gave birth to three sons, and lived in France during the exile of the imperial family before resuming residence in 1952 in Istanbul, where she died 10 August 1960, age 72. She was buried in the Yahya Efendi Cemetery in Istanbul.

AZİZ, SULTAN   *See* Abdülaziz.

BEHİCE, PRINCESS   Daughter of Sultan Abdülmecid by the lady Nesrin, she was born 6 August 1848 in the old Çırağan Palace. Suffering from tuberculosis, she died 30 November 1876, age 28, two weeks after her wedding.

BEHİYE, PRINCESS   Daughter of Prince Salâheddin by the lady Naziknaz, she was born 20 September 1881 in Çırağan Palace. Princess Behiye died at age 66 on 5 March 1948 in Cairo, where she was buried.

BİDAR   Second Consort of Sultan Abdülhamid, she was born 5 May 1858 and had entered the harem of the then-Prince by 1875, age 17. In 1876 she gave birth to Princess Naime, followed in 1878 by Prince Abdülkadir. The lady Bidar died 13 January 1918, age 59, and was buried in the royal mausoleum of Yahya Efendi in Istanbul.

BURHANEDDİN, PRINCE MEHMED   (1) Fifth son of Sultan Abdülmecid, by the lady Nekhetseza (or possibly by the lady Neveser). Born in 1849, he died at age 27 on 3 November 1876. (2) Son of Sultan Abdülhamid by the lady Mezide Mestan, he was born 18 December 1885 in Yıldız Palace. Two sons by his harem lady Âliye Nazlıyar survived him at his death in his home in New York City on 29 May 1949, age 63, as did his American wife, the former Elsie Jackson, whom he married in 1930. He was buried at the Selimiye Mosque in Damascus.

CAPOLEONE, DR.   Italian physician, originally from Naples, who came to Istanbul probably in the late 1830s and obtained a post as physician to the Ottoman army, followed by appointment as personal physician to the imperial son-in-law Halil Pasha. From this post Dr. Capoleone secured appointment as one of the palace physicians under Sultan Abdülmecid, probably around 1850, where he made the acquaintance of the young Prince Murad. When the latter established his own entourage at the age of 17, he obtained Dr. Capoleone's appointment as his personal physician, a post the doctor retained after Murad ascended the throne in 1876.

CELÂLEDDİN PASHA   See Mahmud Celâleddin Pasha.

CEMİLE, PRINCESS   Daughter of Sultan Abdülmecid, she was born 17 August 1843. Her mother, the lady Düzdidil, died when the Princess was but two years of age, so she was raised by the Sultan's Fourth Consort, Perestû, who also raised Cemile's motherless half-brother Abdülhamid. In 1858 she married Mahmud Celâleddin Pasha. The couple ardently supported Abdülhamid's accession to the throne, until the new Sultan's mistrust of Mahmud Celâleddin Pasha led to the latter's exile to Arabia in 1881, where he was strangled in 1884. Princess Cemile withdrew from society for some twenty years, afterwards reconciling with her brother and paying calls again at the palace. Princess Cemile died 26 February 1915, age 71, and was buried at the mausoleum of her father in Istanbul.

CEVAD PASHA, AHMED   Grand Vizier under Sultan Abdülhamid, he was born in Damascus in 1851 and graduated from the military academy in 1871. Rising through the ranks, in 1891 Cevad Pasha was appointed Field Marshal and Grand

Vizier. When in 1895 he submitted a memorandum asking for broader powers rather than simply being expected to carry out the Sultan's orders, he was dismissed from office. He died 9 August 1900 in Istanbul, where he is buried. A prolific author, in particular of his multi-volume *Ottoman Military History*.

CEVHER AĞA   Senior Eunuch Equerry to Sultan Abdülhamid, he had been presented as a gift to the then-Prince around 1870–1876. He gained the Sultan's confidence, charged with overseeing ex-Sultan Murad and his entourage during their confinement in Çırağan Palace, and assigned the important task of deciding which informer reports to forward to the Sultan. After the monarch's deposal Cevher Ağa was condemned to death on the charge of preparing and inciting the 31 March Incident, and was hanged on 26 May 1909, triggering speculation that his hasty execution resulted from his knowledge that the coup leaders themselves had served as informers to Abdülhamid.

DİLFİRİB   Fourth Consort of Sultan Reşad. She was born circa 1890, making her close in age to the schoolteacher Safiye when the latter entered palace service. Dilfirib died in 1952, around the age of 62. She had no children.

DÜRRİYE, PRINCESS   Daughter of Prince Ziyaeddin by the lady Ünsiyar, hence full older sister of Princess Rukiye and Prince Nazım. Born 3 August 1905, she married her cousin Prince Cahid in January 1922 at the age of 16, but she died 15 July of that year in Istanbul and so left no children.

DÜRRÜADEN   Third Consort of Sultan Reşad, she was born 16 May 1860 and had entered the harem of then-Prince Reşad by 1876, giving birth two years later (age 18) to Prince Necmeddin. She died in 1909 at the age of 49.

DÜZDİDİL   Third Consort of Sultan Abdülmecid, she was born around 1825 and had entered the harem of the Sultan probably in the late 1830s, for in August 1843 at the age of approximately 18 she gave birth to her only child, Princess Cemile. Düzdidil died 18 August 1845, around age 20, and was buried in the Mausoleum of the Imperial Ladies at the New Mosque in Istanbul.

ELÂRU MEVHİBE   Consort of Sultan Murad. Born in the Caucasus 6 August 1835, she had joined Murad's entourage at least by January 1857 when she was 21. Despite the fact that she bore Murad no children, he named her his Senior Consort at his accession. She died in 1936 at the age of 101.

EMİNE, PRINCESS   Youngest daughter of Sultan Abdülaziz, by the lady Nesrin, she was born 24 August 1874 in Dolmabahçe Palace. As both her parents died in the summer of 1876, when she was not yet two years old, her older brother Prince Yusuf İzzeddin raised her in his household. She married Mehmed Şerif Pasha (Çavdaroğlu) in September 1901. Princess Emine died 30 January 1920 at the age of 45 and was buried in the mausoleum of Mahmud II in Istanbul.

ESMA, PRINCESS   (1) Daughter of Sultan Abdülhamid I, she was born 16 July 1778. At age 14, in 1792, she was married to Admiral of the Fleet Hüseyin Pasha, but after his death in 1803 she was never remarried, unusual for an Ottoman

Princess. She involved herself in the maneuvering to retain her full brother Mustafa IV on the throne, 1807–1808, but after his deposal she drew close to her half-brother, Mahmud II. Wealthy landowner and leader in the social life of preeminent Ottoman women of her day, Princess Esma died 4 June 1848, age 69, and was buried in the mausoleum of Mahmud II in Istanbul. (2) Daughter of Sultan Abdülaziz by the lady Gevherî, she was born 21 March 1873 and was married the same day in 1889 as her sisters Nâzıma and Saliha. She died giving birth to her fourth child, 7 May 1899, age 26, and was buried in the Mausoleum of the Imperial Ladies at the New Mosque in Istanbul.

FATMA, PRINCESS   (1) Second child and eldest daughter of Sultan Abdülmecid, by the lady Gülcemal, hence full sister of her younger siblings Princess Refia and Sultan Reşad. Born 1 November 1840. At the age of 13, in 1854, she married Ali Galib Pasha, after whose death by drowning in the Bosphorus in 1858 she married, six months later, Nuri Pasha. Her children died young. Following the dubious conviction and exile to Arabia of her second husband for complicity in the death of Sultan Abdülaziz, Princess Fatma withdrew to her shoreside villa until her death a short while later on 29 July 1884, age 43. She is buried in the Mausoleum of the Imperial Ladies at the New Mosque in Istanbul. (2) Daughter of Sultan Murad by the lady Resan, she was born 20 June 1879 in Çırağan Palace. Princess Fatma married Karacehennemzade Refik Bey 29 July 1907 and subsequently bore three children. She died 20 November 1932, age 53, in Sofia, Bulgaria, where she is buried.

FATMA PESEND   İkbal of Sultan Abdülhamid, she was born circa 1876 and had entered the harem of the Sultan by 1896. In 1897 she became the mother of Princess Hadice. A painter by avocation, Fatma Pesend was close to Abdülhamid and accompanied him into exile at Salonica for a time. She died in her villa at Vaniköy, Istanbul, 5 November 1924, age approximately 48, and is buried in the Karacaahmed Cemetery at Üsküdar, Istanbul.

FEHİME, PRINCESS   Daughter of Sultan Murad by his Fourth Consort, Meyliservet. Born 2 July 1875 in Dolmabahçe Palace, she married twice but bore no children. Princess Fehime died in poverty in Nice on 15 September 1929, age 54, and was buried at the Selimiye Mosque in Damascus.

FEVZİ, PRINCE ÖMER   Son of Prince Ziyaeddin by the lady Melekseyran, he was born 13 October 1912 in Yıldız Palace. Prince Fevzi took two wives but had no children. He died 24 April 1986 in Amman, Jordan, age 73, and was buried at the mausoleum of his grandfather Sultan Reşad, in Istanbul.

FİLİZTEN   Gözde of Sultan Murad. Born 1861–1862, she entered Murad's service in 1876 and died circa 1945 probably in Istanbul. She bore no children.

FUAD, PRINCE OSMAN   Younger son of Prince Salâheddin by the lady Jâlefer, he was born 24 February 1895 in Çırağan Palace. In 1920 he married the Egyptian princess Kerime but had no children and later separated. From 1954 until his death, Prince Fuad served as head of the imperial family. He died 19 May 1973 in Nice and was buried in the Bobigny Cemetery in Paris.

GEVHERRİZ   *Gözde* of Sultan Murad. Born circa 1862, she died circa 1940. She bore no children.

GUATELLI PASHA   Composer, conductor, and music teacher, the Italian Callisto Guatelli was born around 1820 and by 1848 was musical director at the Naum Theater in Istanbul. In 1856 Sultan Abdülmecid appointed him Director of the Imperial Corps of Music, a post he held, with one interruption of eight years, until his death in 1899. Raised to the rank of Pasha by Sultan Abdülaziz in 1875, Guatelli served as music instructor to several members of the imperial family, including Sultan Abdülhamid II.

GÜLCEMAL   Fourth Consort of Sultan Abdülmecid, she was born in 1826. In November 1840, age approximately 14, she gave birth to Princess Fatma, followed in January 1842 by Princess Refia and in November 1844 by Prince (later Sultan) Reşad. The lady Gülcemal died of tuberculosis 16 December 1851, age 25, and was buried in the Mausoleum of the Imperial Ladies at the New Mosque in Istanbul.

GÜLNEV   Consort of Prince Ömer Hilmi, she was born 21 February 1890 and had entered the harem of the Prince by October 1910, giving birth to two children. She died 31 December 1919, age 29.

HADİCE, PRINCESS   (1) Eldest daughter of Sultan Murad, by his Third Consort, Şayan. Born 4 May 1870 in Kurbağalıdere Villa in Istanbul. In 1901 she was married to Ali Vasıf Pasha, from whom she was divorced following her affair with Mehmed Kemaleddin Pasha. In 1909 she married Rauf Hayreddin. She bore three daughters. Princess Hadice died 12 March 1938 in Beirut, age 67, and was buried at the Selimiye Mosque in Damascus. Her mother outlived her by seven years. (2) Daughter of Sultan Abdülhamid by the lady Fatma Pesend, she was born 10 July 1897 in Yıldız Palace but died at the age of eight months.

HAMİD, PRINCE AND SULTAN   *See* Abdülhamid II.

HAYRİYE, PRINCESS   Granddaughter of Sultan Reşad through his son Prince Ziyaeddin and the lady Perizad. Born 16 February 1908 in Dolmabahçe Palace, Princess Hayriye did not marry. She died 5 March 1943 in Beirut, age 35, and was buried in the mausoleum of Khedive Tewfik in Cairo.

HÜSEYİN AVNİ PASHA   Born in 1820, graduated from the War College, and twice served as Grand Vizier under Sultan Abdülaziz. As Army Chief of Staff in May 1876, he played a lead role in the deposal of Abdülaziz and elevation of Prince Murad to the throne. In retribution, Abdülaziz's former adjutant Çerkes Hasan Bey assassinated him 16 June 1876. He is buried in the graveyard at the Süleymaniye Mosque in Istanbul.

İBRAHİM TEVFİK, PRINCE   Grandson of Sultan Abdülmecid through his son Prince Burhaneddin, he was born 23 September 1874. He died 31 December 1931 at age 57 in Nice, where he is buried.

İSMAİL HAKKI, SHEIKH   Senior imam to Sultan Reşad during the latter's reign, before which he had served as imam at the Aya Sofya Mosque. A Mevlevi dervish as was the Sultan, he was uncle to the schoolteacher Safiye Ünüvar. His dates of birth and death are unknown.

JÂLEFER   Concubine of Prince Salâheddin, she was born in the Caucasus 19 August 1872 and had entered the Prince's harem by 1891. In 1895 she gave birth to Prince Fuad. She died 7 April 1937 in Istanbul, age 64.

KÂMURES   Senior Consort of Sultan Reşad, she was born 5 March 1855 and had entered the harem of the then-Prince by 1872, becoming mother to Prince Ziyaeddin the following year at age 18. She died 30 April 1921 at age 66 and was buried in the mausoleum of Sultan Reşad in Istanbul.

KEMALEDDİN, PRINCE AHMED   Fourth son of Sultan Abdülmecid, by the lady Verdicenan. Born 3 December 1847, he became second in line to the throne when his half-brother Abdülhamid ascended the throne in 1876. He died 4 April 1905 at age 57, to be honored posthumously, after the 1908 revolution, for his liberal leanings.

LEMAN   Consort of Prince Yusuf İzzeddin, she was born 6 June 1888 and had entered the Prince's harem by 1904 when she was 16. She gave birth to his three children. She died 5 August 1953 at age 65 in her villa in Çamlıca, Istanbul, and is buried in the graveyard of Selâmi Efendi.

LUTFİYE, PRINCESS   Daughter of Prince Ziyaeddin by the lady Perizad, she was born 20 March 1910 in Dolmabahçe Palace and married Hasan Kemal, by whom she had three children. Princess Lutfiye died 11 June 1997 at age 87 in Riyadh, Saudi Arabia, and was buried in the tomb of her grandfather, Sultan Reşad, in Istanbul.

MAHMUD II, SULTAN   Son of Sultan Abdülhamid I by the lady Nakşidil, he was born 20 July 1785 and came to the throne 28 July 1808, ruling nearly thirty-one years and instigating vast reforms before his death on 1 July 1839. Father of some thirty-six children, of whom his son Abdülmecid succeeded him on the throne. Mahmud II is buried in the mausoleum constructed for him in Istanbul.

MAHMUD CELÂLEDDİN, PRINCE   Second son of Sultan Abdülaziz, by the lady Edadil, born 14 November 1862 and died 1 September 1888 at age 25, leaving no children.

MAHMUD CELÂLEDDİN PASHA   Two men of this name married daughters of Sultan Abdülmecid: (1) (c. 1836–1884). Son of Ottoman general and ambassador Ahmed Fethi Pasha, he married Princess Cemile in 1858. Theirs was a successful marriage. Shortly after his brother-in-law Prince Abdülhamid acceded to the throne—in which he played a leading role—this Mahmud Celâleddin Pasha fell afoul of Abdülhamid's suspicions of having a hand in the alleged murder of Sultan Abdülaziz. The Pasha was exiled to Taif, Arabia, where he was strangled in 1884. (2) (1853–1903). Son of an Admiral of the Fleet and Minister of War, in 1876 this Pasha married Princess Seniha. Increasingly hostile to his brother-in-law Sultan Abdülhamid, in 1899 he left his wife in Istanbul and fled to Europe with his sons, the princes Sabaheddin and Lutfullah, the three becoming the Sultan's fiercest critics among the opposition movement based in Europe. This Mahmud Celâleddin Pasha died in Brussels in 1903; his son Prince Sabaheddin brought his remains back to Istanbul for burial after Abdülhamid's overthrow in 1909.

MECİD, SULTAN   *See* Abdülmecid I, Sultan.

MEDİHA, PRINCESS   Daughter of Sultan Abdülmecid by the lady Gülustu, hence full sister of Sultan Mehmed VI Vahideddin, she was born 31 July 1856. She married twice, her second husband Ferid Pasha serving as Grand Vizier to her brother Sultan Vahideddin. At the exile of the imperial family she went to live in France. Princess Mediha died in Menton 9 November 1928, age 72, and is buried in Nice.

MELEKSEYRAN   Third Consort of Prince Ziyaeddin, she was born 23 September 1890 and had entered the harem of the Prince by 1911. The following year she gave birth to Prince Fevzi. Later divorced, she died in 1966 at the age of 76.

MEYLİSERVET   Fourth Consort of Sultan Murad. Born in the Caucasus 21 October 1854, she entered Murad's harem probably in the early 1870s, as in July 1875 she gave birth to Princess Fehime. She died in Çırağan Palace in 1891 at the age of 37.

MİHRENGİZ   Second Consort of Sultan Reşad, she was born 15 October 1869 and entered the harem of the then-Prince probably around 1884, as she gave birth to Prince Ömer Hilmi in March 1886, when she was 16. Her second child, Princess Refia, born in 1888, died the same year. The lady Mihrengiz died 12 December 1938 at age 69 in Alexandria, Egypt, where she was buried in the mausoleum of the Egyptian prince Omar Tusun. She outlived her son by three years.

MİHRİMAH, PRINCESS   Daughter of Prince Ziyaeddin by the lady Neşemend, she was born 11 November 1922 in the Prince's villa in Istanbul. She married Prince Naif of Jordan, son of King Abdullah I. Princess Mihrimah died in Amman, Jordan, 30 March 2000, age 77, and was buried in the mausoleum of her grandfather, Sultan Reşad, in Istanbul.

MONGERI, DR.   Physician who examined Sultan Murad during his illness; a neurologist who established a clinic for treatment of psychiatric and neurological disorders in Istanbul. Italian in origin, as was his colleague Dr. Capoleone.

MUHAMMAD ALI PASHA   Ottoman Governor of Egypt 1805–1848; challenged the authority of the Sultan and founded the dynasty that occupied the throne of Egypt until 1952.

MÜNİRE, PRINCESS   Daughter of Sultan Abdülmecid's son Prince Kemaleddin by the lady Fatma Sezadil, Princess Münire was born 17 May 1880 in Dolmabahçe Palace. On 10 January 1907 she married Mehmed Salih Pasha, who was condemned to death after the assassination of General Mahmud Şevket Pasha in 1913. Princess Münire died 7 October 1939, age 59, in Nice, where she is buried.

MURAD, PRINCE AND SULTAN   Eldest son of Sultan Abdülmecid, he was born to the lady Şevkefza 21 September 1840. He acceded to the throne 30 May 1876 as Murad V but was deposed 31 August 1876 due to a state of nervous collapse exacerbated by alcoholism. A talented musician, the deposed monarch was confined for 28 years in Çırağan Palace, where he died 29 August 1904 at age 63. He is buried in the Mausoleum of the Imperial Ladies at the New Mosque in Istanbul.

MÜŞFİKA   Imperial Consort to Sultan Abdülhamid II and mother of Princess Ayşe, she was born in the Caucasus around 1872 and entered the Sultan's harem in 1886. In November 1887, age approximately 15, she gave birth to her only child, Princess Ayşe. The lady Müşfika accompanied Abdülhamid into exile in 1909 and returned to Istanbul with him in 1912. As but an adjunct member of the imperial family she was not exiled in 1924 and so remained in Turkey. She died in Istanbul 16 July 1961, age approximately 89, having outlived her daughter by nearly one year, and was buried in the Yahya Efendi Cemetery.

NADİR AĞA   Eunuch Equerry to Sultan Abdülhamid, he was born around 1882 in the Ethiopian village of Limnu, castrated and enslaved at a young age. Taken to Arabia, he was sold at the slave market in Medina around 1893 and brought to Istanbul. Around 1904 he entered service at Yıldız Palace, attracting the Sultan's notice for his honesty and reliability, which led to his appointment as equerry. At Abdülhamid's overthrow he cooperated in surrendering informer reports and divulging locations of money, for which his life was spared. Afterwards Nadir Ağa established himself in the business of milk production in Göztepe, Istanbul. He died in 1961, age approximately 79.

NAİLE, PRINCESS   (1) Daughter of Sultan Abdülmecid, she was born 1 October 1856 and married Çerkes Mehmed Pasha in 1876, but died in January 1882 at age 25 and is buried in the Mausoleum of the Imperial Ladies at the New Mosque in Istanbul. (2) Daughter of Sultan Abdülhamid by the lady Dilpesend, she was born 9 January 1884 in Yıldız Palace. No children ensued from her 1904 marriage with Arif Hikmet Pasha. After the family's exile she lived in Beirut but returned to Istanbul after the revocation of the law of exile for princesses in 1952. She died 25 October 1957, age 73, in Istanbul, where she is buried in the mausoleum of Yahya Efendi.

NAİME, PRINCESS   (1) Daughter of Sultan Abdülmecid by the lady Tîrimüjgân and hence full elder sister of the future Sultan Abdülhamid, she was born 11 October 1840 but died as an infant in March 1843 of smallpox. (2) Daughter of Sultan Abdülhamid by the lady Bidar, she was born 4 September 1876 in Dolmabahçe Palace. In March 1898 she married Gazi Osman Pasha's son Kemaleddin Bey, from whom she was divorced in 1904 following his affair with her cousin Princess Hadice. In 1907 she married İşkodralı Celâleddin Pasha. At the exile of the imperial family the couple settled in Albania. Princess Naime died in 1945 at age 69 in Tirana, where she is buried.

NAZİKEDA   Senior Consort to Sultan Abdülhamid, she was born circa 1850 and sold into various elite households in Istanbul. Then-Prince Abdülhamid noticed her in the household of his sister Princess Cemile, who presented her to him circa 1867, and in 1868 she gave birth to Princess Ulviye. Nazikeda died 10 April 1895, age approximately 45, and was buried in the Mausoleum of the Imperial Ladies at the New Mosque in Istanbul.

NAZIM, PRINCE MEHMED   Son of Prince Ziyaeddin by the lady Ünsiyar. Born 22 December 1910 in Dolmabahçe Palace, he died 14 November 1984 at age 73 in Istanbul and was buried there in the tomb of his grandfather, Sultan Reşad.

NÂZIMA, PRINCESS   Daughter of Sultan Abdülaziz by the lady Hayrandil, she was born 26 February 1866 in Dolmabahçe Palace and married the same day in 1889 as her half-sisters Esma and Saliha. She died in 1947 at age 81 in Juniye, Lebanon, and was buried at the Selimiye Mosque in Damascus.

NAZPERVER   Third Consort of Sultan Reşad after the death in 1909 of the lady Dürrüaden. She was born approximately 1870 and died approximately 1930. She had no children.

NECMEDDİN, PRINCE MAHMUD   Second son of Sultan Reşad, by the lady Dürrüaden, he was born 23 June 1878 and died 27 June 1913 at age 35. He had no children.

NEMİKA, PRINCESS EMINE   Daughter of Prince Selim, thus granddaughter of Sultan Abdülhamid II, she was born 9 March 1888 in Yıldız Palace. She married Ali Kenan Esin and gave birth to two children. Princess Nemika died 6 September 1969 at age 81 in Istanbul, where she is buried in the Yahya Efendi Cemetery.

NEŞEMEND   Third Consort of Prince Ziyaeddin after his divorce from the lady Melekseyran, she was born in 1905 and entered the Prince's harem around 1920. In 1922 she gave birth to Princess Mihrimah. She died in 1934, at age 29, in Egypt, where she was buried at the city of Helwan.

NEVDÜR   Concubine of Sultan Murad, her vital dates are unknown. She bore no children.

NEVZAD (NİMET NEVZAD)   Fourth Consort of Sultan Vahideddin, she was born in Istanbul in 1902 and entered palace service around 1910, then entered Sultan Vahideddin's service around 1918, becoming his Fourth Consort in January 1921 at age 18. She joined the deposed Sultan in exile in San Remo, Italy. After his death she returned to Turkey, publishing her memoir in 1937 under the title *Yıldız'dan San Remo'ya* (From Yıldız to San Remo), and remarrying. She died in Istanbul in 1992.

NİHAD, PRINCE AHMED   Son of Prince Salâheddin by the lady Naziknaz, hence grandson of Sultan Murad V, Prince Nihad was born 5 July 1883 in Çırağan Palace. He had one son, Prince Vasıb. Prince Nihad died 4 June 1954 in Beirut, age 70, having served since 1944 as head of the imperial family. He was buried at the Selimiye Mosque in Damascus.

NUREDDİN, PRINCE AHMED   Son of Sultan Abdülhamid by the lady Behice and twin of Prince Mehmed Bedreddin, he was born 22 June 1901 in Yıldız Palace. Prince Nureddin died in December 1944 at age 43 in Paris, where he is buried in the Bobigny Muslim cemetery.

NURİ PASHA   Born in Istanbul around 1840, he was appointed to the Palace Chancellery of Sultan Abdülmecid, marrying the latter's 18-year-old widowed daughter Princess Fatma 24 March 1859. An active participant in the overthrow of Sultan Abdülaziz in 1876, Nuri Pasha was appointed Senior Chamberlain to the new Sultan Murad. At the dubious tribunal convened after Murad's deposal, Nuri Pasha was convicted of complicity in Abdülaziz's death, stripped of his rank, divorced from his wife, and sentenced to life imprisonment at Taif, Arabia, where he died in 1883.

OMAR TUSUN   Prince in the Egyptian royal family. Great-grandson of Muhammad Ali, founder of the Egyptian royal family, he was born in Alexandria 8 September 1872 and died there 26 January 1944.

ÖMER HİLMİ, PRINCE   Third son of Sultan Reşad, by the lady Mihrengiz, he was born in his father's villa in Ortaköy, Istanbul, on 2 March 1886. He died 6 April 1935 at age 49 in Alexandria, Egypt, and was buried there, with his remains later interred in the mausoleum of Khedive Tewfik in Cairo. His mother outlived him by three years.

ORHAN, PRINCE MEHMED   Son of Prince Abdülkadir by the lady Mihriban, hence grandson of Sultan Abdülhamid II, Prince Orhan was born 13 July 1909 in the villa of his aunt Princess Naime in Istanbul. From 1983 Prince Orhan served as head of the imperial house from his home in France until his death on 12 March 1994 in Nice, where he is buried.

OSMAN PASHA, GAZİ   Born in 1832, he graduated from the War College and rose through the ranks of the army. Following his famous defense of the Ottoman garrison at Plevna during the 1877–1878 war with Russia, he was granted the title *Gazi* or Warrior of the Faith, created a marshal of the Palace Chancellery, and retained at court as honored companion of Sultan Abdülhamid. Two of his sons married imperial princesses. Upon his death 5 April 1900, Gazi Osman Pasha was buried in the tomb built for him by Sultan Abdülhamid at the mosque of Mehmed the Conqueror in Istanbul.

PERESTÛ, PRINCESS MOTHER   Consort to Sultan Abdülmecid, she was born around 1830 and became adoptive mother to Abdülhamid when his birth mother died in 1852, although she was only some twelve years older than the ten-year-old Prince at the time. She rose to the rank of Princess Mother upon Abdülhamid's accession to the throne in 1876. Perestû died around age 74 in 1904 at her villa in the Maçka district of Istanbul and is buried in the mausoleum she constructed in the Eyüp district.

PERİZAD   Second Consort of Prince Ziyaeddin, she was born in 1889 and entered the harem of Prince Ziyaeddin by early 1907, around age 17. In 1908 she gave birth to Princess Hayriye, followed in 1910 by Princess Lutfiye. The lady Perizad died in Alexandria, Egypt, in 1934, at the age of 45.

PERNİYAN   Senior Consort of Prince Ziyaeddin, she was born 2 January 1880 and entered the Prince's harem by 1898, around age 18. In 1900 she gave birth to Princess Behiye. The lady Perniyan died in 1947 at age 67.

PERTEVNİYAL, PRINCESS MOTHER   Consort of Sultan Mahmud II, born circa 1810, mother of Sultan Abdülaziz and hence Princess Mother during his reign, 1861–1876. Renowned for her charitable gifts to Istanbul, including the elegant mosque she built in the Aksaray district, the Princess Mother Pertevniyal lived in seclusion following her son's death and died 5 February 1883, age approximately 73. She is buried in the mausoleum she had constructed at her mosque.

REFİA, PRINCESS   (1) Second daughter of Sultan Abdülmecid, by the lady Gül-cemal, hence full sister of Princess Fatma and Sultan Reşad. Born 7 February 1842, she married once but bore no children and died at age 37, on 4 January 1880, following a long illness and several operations. She is buried in the Mauso-leum of the Imperial Ladies at the New Mosque in Istanbul. (2) Daughter of Sul-tan Abdülhamid by the lady Sazkâr, she was born 15 June 1891 in Yıldız Palace. Through her marriage to Ali Fuad Eyub she gave birth to two daughters. Prin-cess Refia died in 1938 at age 47 in Beirut and is buried at the Selimiye Mosque in Damascus.

REFTARIDİL   Second Consort of Sultan Murad. Born in the Caucasus 5 June 1838, she entered Murad's entourage probably in the mid-1850s, giving birth to Prince Salâheddin in 1861. She died 3 March 1936 at age 98, having outlived her son by twenty-one years.

REMİŞNAZ   Gözde of Sultan Murad, her dates of birth and death are unknown. She bore no children.

REŞAD, PRINCE AND SULTAN MEHMED (SULTAN MEHMED V)   Third son of Sultan Abdülmecid, by the lady Gülcemal, he was born 3 November 1844. On 27 April 1909 at the age of 64, he ascended the throne upon the deposal of his older brother Abdülhamid II and reigned for nine years until his death on 3 July 1918 at age 73. Two sons survived him, the princes Ziyaeddin and Ömer Hilmi; his son Mahmud Necmeddin and his daughter Refia predeceased him. He was buried in the tomb he had constructed along the shores of the Golden Horn in the Eyüp district of Istanbul.

RESAN   İkbal of Sultan Murad. Born in the Caucasus 28 March 1860, she gave birth at age 19 to Princess Fatma, and at age 20 to Princess Aliye. The lady Resan died 31 March 1910, age 50.

RUKİYE, PRINCESS   Second daughter of Prince Ziyaeddin, by the lady Ünsiyar. Born 11 November 1906 in Dolmabahçe Palace, she married Sokolluzade Abdülbaki İhsan and gave birth to her daughter Emel Nuricihan in exile in 1925. She died 20 February 1927 at age 21 in Budapest, where she is buried at the tomb of the sixteenth-century Ottoman Sufi, Gül Baba.

SABAHEDDİN, PRINCE MEHMED   Born in 1877, the son of Princess Seniha and Mahmud Celâleddin Pasha, hence grandson of Sultan Abdülmecid. He died in 1948, age 71.

ŞADİYE, PRINCESS   Daughter of Sultan Abdülhamid by the lady Emsalinur, she was born 30 November 1886 in Yıldız Palace. In 1910 she married Fahir Bey and gave birth to a daughter. Settling in Paris after the exile of the imperial family, in the 1950s Princess Şadiye returned to Istanbul, where she died 20 November 1977, age 90, the last surviving child of Abdülhamid II. She was buried in the tomb of her great-grandfather Sultan Mahmud II.

SALÂHEDDİN, PRINCE MEHMED   Eldest child and only son of Sultan Murad V, by the lady Reftarıdil. Born 12 August 1861, Prince Salâheddin died 29 April 1915 at age 53 in Üsküdar, Istanbul, having outlived his father by a mere eleven years and leaving two sons and four daughters. He was buried in the Yahya Efendi Cemetery in Istanbul.

SALİHA, PRINCESS   Eldest daughter of Sultan Abdülaziz, by his Senior Consort Dürrinev, hence full younger sister of Prince Yusuf İzzeddin, she was born 11 August 1862 in Dolmabahçe Palace. She was engaged to a son of Khedive Ismail of Egypt, but the engagement was broken off after her father's deposal and in April 1889 she married Ahmed Zülküfil Pasha. Princess Saliha died in 1941 at age 79 in Cairo, where she is buried in the mausoleum of Khedive Tewfik.

SAMİ, PRINCE ABDURRAHMAN   Grandson of Sultan Abdülmecid through his daughter Princess Mediha, he was born in 1880 and served as aide-de-camp to his uncle Sultan Abdülhamid. Prince Sami died in 1961 at the age of 81.

ŞAYAN   Third Consort of Sultan Murad. Born in the Caucasus in 1853, she entered Murad's entourage probably in the mid-1860s. In May 1870 she gave birth to Princess Hadice. The lady Şayan died in 1945 at age 91, having outlived her daughter by seven years.

ŞAYESTE   Fifth İkbal to Sultan Abdülmecid, she was born circa 1838 and had entered the Sultan's harem by 1851. Her one child was stillborn, so that in 1861 she was given the motherless infant Prince Vahideddin to raise. Among the longest-living consorts of Abdülmecid, Şayeste died at age approximately 73 on 22 January 1912 and was buried in the royal mausoleum of Yahya Efendi in Istanbul.

SELİM, PRINCE MEHMED   Eldest son of Sultan Abdülhamid, by the lady Bedrifelek, he was born 18 February 1872 in Dolmabahçe Palace. He sired a son and a daughter during his father's reign. Prince Mehmed Selim died 5 May 1937 in Juniye, Lebanon, age 65, and was buried at the Selimiye Mosque in Damascus.

SENİHA, PRINCESS   Sixth daughter of Sultan Abdülmecid, by the lady Nalânıdil. Born 22 November 1852 in Çırağan Palace, on 4 December 1876 she married her cousin Asaf Mahmud Celâleddin Pasha. Her husband and two sons left the country due to their opposition to Sultan Abdülhamid's rule. At the exile of the imperial family in March 1924, Seniha was the oldest living Ottoman princess, age 71. She died 15 September 1931 at age 78 in Nice and was buried at the Selimiye Mosque in Damascus.

SENİYE, PRINCESS   Granddaughter of Mahmud II through his daughter Princess Atiye and Ahmed Fethi Pasha, she was born in 1843 but her mother died when she was seven years of age. She married Hüseyin Hüsnü Pasha. Princess Seniye died in 1910, age 67.

SERFİRAZ   Second *İkbal* to Sultan Abdülmecid, she was born circa 1837 and had entered the Sultan's harem by 1851, around age 14. Of her three children one survived, Prince Süleyman. The lady Serfiraz died 10 June 1905, age approximately 68, and was buried in the royal mausoleum of Yahya Efendi.

ŞEVKEFZA, LADY MOTHER, PRINCESS MOTHER   Consort of Sultan Abdülmecid and mother of Sultan Murad V. Of Circassian origin, she was born in December 1820 and entered Sultan Abdülmecid's harem probably in the summer of 1839, at age 18, immediately following his accession to the throne. In September 1840 she gave birth to Prince Murad, her only child, when she was 19 and the Sultan 17. The lady Şevkefza died in Çırağan Palace 17 September 1889, age 68, and was buried in the Mausoleum of the Imperial Ladies at the New Mosque in Istanbul.

SÜLEYMAN, PRINCE SELİM   Sixth son of Abdülmecid, by the lady Serfiraz, hence half-brother of the last four sultans. Born in 1861, two sons and a daughter survived him at his death in July 1909 at age 48.

SÜLEYMAN PASHA   Military officer and scholar of literature and the Turkish language, born in Istanbul in 1838, after 1873 Commandant of the War College, participant with Minister of War Hüseyin Avni Pasha in the overthrow of Sultan Abdülaziz. His defeat of the Russians at Shipka Pass in Bulgaria during the war of 1877–1878 earned him the sobriquet "Hero of Shipka," but his failure to prevent the Russian occupation of Edirne later in the war earned him banishment to Baghdad, where he died in 1892, age 54.

TÎRİMÜJGÂN   Consort to Sultan Abdülmecid and mother of Sultan Abdülhamid, she was born 16 August 1819 and had entered Abdülmecid's harem by the beginning of 1840, when she was 20 and he 16. She gave birth first to Princess Naime, who died young, then to Prince Abdülhamid, and thirdly to Prince Mehmed Âbid, who died shortly after birth in 1848. The lady Tîrimüjgân attained the rank of Second Consort but died 31 October 1852 at age 33, leaving her 10-year-old son, Prince Abdülhamid. She was buried in the Mausoleum of the Imperial Ladies at the New Mosque in Istanbul.

ÜNSİYAR   Consort of Prince Ziyaeddin, she was born in 1887 and had entered the harem of the Prince by 1903, when she was 16. Some two years later she gave birth to Princess Dürriye, in 1905, followed by Princess Rukiye in 1906 and Prince Nazım in 1910. She died in 1934 in Alexandria, Egypt, age 47.

VAHİDEDDİN, PRINCE AND SULTAN (MEHMED VAHİDEDDİN, SULTAN MEHMED VI) Son of Sultan Abdülmecid by the lady Gülistu, he was born 4 January 1861 in Dolmabahçe Palace. As both his parents died in the year of his birth, he was raised by his late father's *ikbal* the lady Şayeste. Vahideddin ascended the throne 3 July 1918 at age 57, reigning until the abolition of the sultanate on 1 November 1922. Although allowed to retain the title of Caliph, in the unfavorable situation towards him he chose to leave the country surreptitiously, 17 November 1922, whereupon he was deposed as Caliph. The ex-Sultan and Caliph died in exile in San Remo, Italy, at age 65 on 15 May 1926, and is buried in the graveyard at the Selimiye Mosque in Damascus.

VASIB, PRINCE ALİ Son of Prince Nihad by the lady Safiru, hence great-grandson of Sultan Murad V, Prince Vasıb was born 13 October 1903 in Çırağan Palace. He married his cousin Princess Emine Mukbile, granddaughter of Sultan Reşad. Prince Vasıb served as head of the imperial house from 1977 until his death on 9 December 1983 in Alexandria, Egypt.

YUSUF İZZEDDİN, PRINCE Eldest son of Sultan Abdülaziz by the lady Dürrinev, he was born 11 October 1857, his birth kept secret until his father ascended the throne in 1861. Prince Yusuf İzzeddin became Heir to the Throne upon the accession of his cousin Sultan Reşad on 27 April 1909. He died 1 February 1916 in his villa at Zincirlikuyu, Istanbul, age 58, having taken his own life after suffering from depression for a number of years.

ZATIGÜL, TEVHİDE Concubine of Prince Salâheddin. Born in the Caucasus 25 January 1864, the lady Zatıgül began palace service as a kalfa in the entourage of Murad V in or before 1876. Selected as a concubine for Murad's son Prince Salâheddin probably around 1881, she bore the Prince four daughters. The lady Zatıgül died in Çırağan Palace in 1896, age 32.

ZEKİYE, PRINCESS Eldest child of Sultan Abdülhamid to survive into adulthood, his daughter by the lady Bedrifelek, she was born 21 January 1872 in Dolmabahçe Palace and at age 17 in 1889 married Nureddin Pasha, son of Gazi Osman Pasha. After the exile of the imperial family Princess Zekiye settled in Pau, France, where she died in 1950 at age 78 and is buried.

ZİYAEDDİN, PRINCE MEHMED Eldest son of Sultan Reşad, by his Senior Consort Kâmures, Prince Ziyaeddin was born in Istanbul 26 August 1873. Through five ladies he fathered eight children. Prince Ziyaeddin died 30 January 1938 at age 64 in Alexandria, Egypt, where he was buried, his remains later transferred to the mausoleum of Khedive Tewfik in Cairo.

Glossary of Terms and Places

Note: Where a Turkish word or phrase has been translated, the original term appears in parentheses after the definition.

AĞA   Title of respect accorded mostly to eunuchs, following their name

AŞURE   Pudding made of chickpeas, hulled wheat, and dried fruit, traditionally served on the tenth of the month of Muharrem

AYA SOFYA   The great Byzantine church of Hagia Sophia, converted into a mosque at the Ottoman conquest of Istanbul

BALMUMCU   District of Istanbul above Yıldız Palace, literally "Beeswax seller"; site of imperial farmstead with lodge, assigned to Sultan Reşad before he ascended the throne

BALTALİMANI   Harbor on the European shore of the Bosphorus, nearly halfway between Istanbul and the Black Sea

BERAT   See *Kandil*

BEŞİKTAŞ   District of Istanbul along the European shore of the Bosphorus, location of Dolmabahçe, Çırağan, and Yıldız Palaces

BESMELE   The religious formula in Arabic *Bismillah ir-rahman ir-rahim*, "In the name of God the Compassionate, the Merciful," the standard invocation when commencing an activity

BEY   Title of respect accorded to men of some rank

BEYLERBEYİ   District of Istanbul along the Asian shore of the Bosphorus

BEYOĞLU   District of Istanbul slightly north of the Golden Horn, center of the city's mercantile and cultural life

ÇARŞAF   Outdoor overgarment for women, usually concealing the entire body and consisting of three parts: a veil over the face, an upper garment covering the head and upper torso including the arms, and a skirt from the waist to the feet

CEREMONIAL HALL   Vast room at Dolmabahçe Palace that separates the harem from the state apartments wing of the palace; site of the most important state receptions (*Muayede Salonu*)

CEREMONIAL WING   Hall and adjoining rooms at the west end of the harem quarters at Dolmabahçe Palace (*Merasim Dairesi*)

CHALET VILLA   One of the grandest villas constructed by Sultan Abdülhamid on the grounds of Yıldız Palace (*Şale Köşkü*)

CHINTZ PAVILION   Building on the grounds of Yıldız Palace used for receiving ambassadors and foreign diplomats; built during the reign of Sultan Abdülaziz (*Çit Kasrı*)

ÇIRAĞAN PALACE   "Palace of the Lamps," the imperial residence completed in 1871 along the Bosphorus a short distance north of Dolmabahçe Palace on the site of an older palace demolished for it

CONCUBINE   A lady in a prince's harem who had had sexual relations with her master; in a sultan's harem, one of the sultan's ladies who was not appointed to the position of consort but ranked as either *ikbal* or *gözde*

CONFESSION OF FAITH   The religious formula in Arabic, "There is no god but the one God, and Muhammad is the Prophet of God"

CONSORT   Highest-ranking concubine of a sultan, limited to four in number. The monarch may or may not have undergone marriage with a consort, as he wished. Below the four consorts ranked the concubines (*Kadın* or *Kadınefendi*)

CONSTABLE OF THE MAIDENS   Black eunuch charged with supervision of the harem (*Kızlar Ağası*)

DAMAD   "Son-in-law," title accorded to husbands of princesses

DARÜLACEZE   Poorhouse constructed by order of Sultan Abdülhamid II in 1895 in the Okmeydanı district of Istanbul, under the Ministry of the Interior, for indigent men and women, handicapped persons, and children; still in operation

DERVISH   Member of one of the mystical orders in Islam

DOLMABAHÇE PALACE   "Palace of the Filled Garden," completed in 1856, the European-style palace constructed on the site of a filled-in cove along the shores of the Bosphorus; designed to serve as the primary residence of the Sultans in place of centuries-old Topkapı Palace

DRAGOMAN   Official engaged in the translation section of an embassy in Istanbul; liaison between his embassy, or nationals of the embassy he represented, and the Ottoman government

EDIRNE GATE   One of the gates in the land walls of Stambul, at the northwestern edge of the old city south of the Golden Horn

EFENDİ   Title of great respect for men of considerable standing; also accorded to women usually in tandem with another title, e.g., *Sultan Efendi* for a princess

ENTOURAGE   The household of a sultan's or adult prince's concubine; also the household of an adult princess or the top-ranking harem staff. Each entourage— assigned its own apartments—consisted of a Senior Kalfa, Junior Kalfa, serving girls, and one or more eunuchs. Thus the Ottoman palace consisted of several entourages (*Daire*)

ERENKÖY   District on the Sea of Marmara shore southeast of Istanbul proper, noted for its summer villas

EYÜP   District of Istanbul along the Golden Horn where the tomb of the Prophet's Standard-bearer is located, hence imbued with particular spirituality

FATIHA   The opening chapter of the Quran, recited particularly for the dead

FERACE   Cloak worn by women when outside the home, typically accompanied by the *hotoz* on the head

FER'İYE PALACES   "Auxiliary palaces," the buildings erected in the later nineteenth century along the Bosphorus directly north of Çırağan Palace, to house concubines and members of the imperial family

FESTIVAL DAYS   The two great annual religious fetes, each lasting several days. The first in the Islamic calendar, the Festival of Fastbreaking or *Şeker Bayramı* [Sweetmeat Feast] in Turkish, follows the month-long fast during Ramadan. The second, the Festival of Offerings or *Kurban Bayramı*, is celebrated some two months later, on 10 Zulhijja and the three following days. Because the Muslim calendar is lunar, the festival days rotate through the seasons (*Bayram*)

FEZZAN   Notorious place of banishment in the Sahara Desert in central Libya

FLOOR TEMENNA   See *Temenna*

GALATA BRIDGE   Span across the Golden Horn where it empties into the Bosphorus, connecting the old city of Stambul with the districts north of it

GAZİ   Title granted to a hero or victor in a war against non-Muslims

GIFT PROCESSION   See *Noble Litter*

GOLDEN HORN   Arm of the Bosphorus that forms the northern shore of Stambul

GÖZDE   "Chosen One," lowest of the three ranks of concubine

GÖZTEPE   District of Istanbul on the Asian shore of the Bosphorus

GRAND VIZIER   Senior minister of state, equivalent to Prime Minister, appointed by the Sultan (*Sadrazam*)

GÜLHANE   Gardens just below the landward walls of Topkapı Palace

GÜVEÇ   Stew of vegetables and meat

HÂFIZ   One who has memorized the Quran

HAJJI   One who has performed the hajj or pilgrimage to Mecca

HAMİDİYE MARCH   Air that served as Ottoman national anthem during the reign of Abdülhamid II

HAMİDİYE MOSQUE   Mosque immediately outside Yıldız Palace, built in 1886 by Abdülhamid II, for whom it was named

HANIM   "Lady," a title of respect accorded women in general, and in particular a woman in senior service in the harem, e.g., a Senior Kalfa

HANIMEFENDİ   Title of respect for concubines lower in rank than the four Imperial Consorts, and for princesses of the Egyptian khedival house

HANIMSULTAN   Title of the daughter of a princess, i.e., granddaughter of a sultan or prince in the female line

HAYDARPASHA   District of Istanbul on the Asian side of the Bosphorus, southeast of Stambul

HAZİNEDAR   High-ranking female chamberlains (the term means "treasurer") charged with supervisory duties in the harem. Also known as *Usta*, they ranked above ordinary kalfas and included in their number the *Hünkâr Kalfaları*, Kalfas of the Monarch, in personal service to the sultan. Their head, the *Hazinedar Usta* or High Hazinedar, occupied the second-highest position in harem service, immediately below the Lady Steward

HEREKE   Town southeast of Istanbul noted for its production of fine silken carpets and cloth

HOTOZ   Headgear worn by upper-class women, higher in front and sloping to the back, usually fashioned of silk in a color complementary to the dress; worn indoors on formal occasions

İBRAHİM PASHA MEADOWS   In Haydarpasha, on the Asian shore southeast of Stambul

IHLAMUR LODGE   "Linden Tree Lodge," the small imperial pavilion constructed in the 1850s in what was then countryside in the hills west of the Bosphorus

İHLAS   The 112th chapter of the Quran, recited particularly for the dead

İKBAL   "Fortunate One," the middle of the three ranks of concubine

IMPERIAL KALFAS   The kalfas in personal service to the monarch (*Hünkâr Kalfaları*)

IMPERIAL LODGE   The building in which the monarch resided on the grounds of Yıldız Palace (*Hünkâr Sofası* or *Hünkâr Dairesi*)

INNER SERVICE   The private apartments of the sultan and harem (*Enderun*)

KAABA   The sanctuary at Mecca toward which one faces in prayer; the object of pilgrimage incumbent upon all capable of undertaking it

KADIKÖY   District of Istanbul at the northern end of the bridge over the Golden Horn where it meets the Bosphorus

KADIN   "Lady," title of respect for a harem lady of middle or upper rank

KADINEFENDİ   "Ladyship," title of great respect reserved for the four Imperial Consorts

KÂĞITHANE   Valley along the upper reaches of the Golden Horn, also called the Sweet Waters of Europe, since the seventeenth century the site of villas and pavilions of the imperial family and high-ranking notables

KALFA   General term for the women attendants and supervisors in service in the palace. Novice girls had to await promotion to the rank of kalfa. Officially slaves, depending on their rank these women could wield considerable authority and influence in their duties and were generally treated with much respect by lower-ranking attendants in the harem as well as by members of the imperial family

KANDİL   Term literally means "oil lamp," in the shape of a small glass bowl. The *Kandil* festivals are the five religious feasts during which mosque minarets are illuminated at night, namely the birthday of the Prophet, his conception, his night journey to heaven, the night of *Berat* (when God summons the living in order to grant forgiveness of their sins), and the Night of Power, the night upon which the Quran was first revealed

KHEDIVE   The ruler of Egypt, nominal vassal of the Ottoman sultan until World War One

KILIÇ ALİ DISTRICT   Neighborhood of the Kılıç Ali Pasha Mosque, along the European shore of the Bosphorus not far above the Golden Horn

KURBAĞALIDERE   District of Istanbul on the Asian shore along the Sea of Marmara; site of a villa occupied by Prince Murad before he ascended the throne

KURUŞ   Unit of currency; the lira consisted of 100 *kuruş* until undergoing fluctuations in the 1870s, stabilizing at 108 *kuruş* after 1879

LADY MOTHER   Title of the mother of a prince, becoming "Princess Mother" if her son acceded to the throne (*Valide Kadınefendi*)

LADY SECRETARY   High-ranking kalfa position of mistress of ceremonial, responsible for overseeing protocol in the palace harem (*Kâtibe*)

LADY STEWARD   Superintendent of the entire harem. In protocol she ranked immediately below the Imperial Consorts, who treated her with esteem; her assistant was the High Hazinedar. Alternatively known also as *Saray Ustası*, Mistress of the Palace. As emblems of her rank, she received from the Sultan the gilt-embroidered jacket known as *salta* and a silver-plated staff of office (*Kâhya Kadın*)

LESSER CHANCELLERY   Three-story art-nouveau structure at Yıldız Palace where the sultan maintained an office and that contained a library, reading room, and salons for the use of the monarch and court officials (*Küçük Mabeyin*)

LIBERTY MONUMENT   Stone memorial constructed 1909–1911 in Istanbul to honor those who died in suppressing the Counterrevolution of 1909 (*Âbide-i Hürriyet*)

MAÇKA   District of European Istanbul slightly north of Taksim Square

MABEYİN   Literally "in-between space," in an Ottoman palace or villa the area containing the public rooms accessible to official visitors (Secretariat, reception rooms, and ceremonial halls), as opposed to the harem, which contained the private apartments of the imperial household. At Yıldız Palace the *Mabeyin* consisted of a detached building while the harem comprised various detached or semi-detached buildings in the gardens. At Dolmabahçe Palace the *Mabeyin* consisted of one wing of the building, the harem another wing, the two separated by the Ceremonial Hall. In both palaces the monarch resided in the harem but usually passed his workday in the *Mabeyin*; thus the Palace Secretariat maintained its offices there

MACUN   Sweetened, taffy-like medicated paste usually prepared at the celebration of the New Year in the Persian calendar (21 March)

MEVLEVİ   Order of Sufis named for Mevlânâ Celâleddin Rumî, noted for its whirling ritual; among the most prevalent Sufi orders in Ottoman culture

MUEZZIN   Attendant charged with calling the faithful to prayer five times daily from the minaret of a mosque

NEVRUZ   New Year's Day in the Persian solar calendar, occurring on the first day of spring, 21 March by the Western calendar

NEW MOSQUE   Completed in 1663, the imperial mosque at the south end of Galata Bridge (*Yeni Cami*)

NIGHT OF POWER   Anniversary of the night when the Quran was first revealed, celebrated on 27 Ramadan (*Kadir Gecesi*)

NOBLE CLOTH   Or Noble Handkerchief, the section of cloth that the sultan touched to the Prophet's cloak at Topkapı Palace during the Procession to the Noble Mantle, handing each invitee one such section as a memento of the occasion (*Destimal-i Şerif*)

NOBLE LITTER   Annual dispatch of gifts from the sultan to the holy cities of Mecca and Medina (*Mahmil-i Şerif*)

NOBLE MANTLE   Cloak attributed to the Prophet Muhammad, presented to Sultan Selim I after the Ottoman conquest of Egypt in 1517, and preserved in the chamber built for it and other holy relics at Topkapı Palace (*Hırka-ı Şerif*)

NOBLE SWEEPER   Office of the high functionary at Istanbul charged with overseeing the cleanliness of the sacred places at Mecca and Medina (*Feraşet-i Şerife*)

NURUOSMANİYE   District of Istanbul surrounding the Nuruosmaniye Mosque, near the Grand Bazaar

ORDER OF ABDÜLMECİD   Established 18 September 1852 by Sultan Abdülmecid for presentation to Ottoman subjects as well as foreigners rendering service to the state (*Mecidî* or *Mecidiye Nişanı*)

ORDER OF COMPASSION   Established 17 December 1878 by Abdülhamid II for presentation to women who distinguished themselves by service in times of war or national disaster (*Şefkât Nişanı*)

ORDER OF THE OTTOMAN DYNASTY   Established 31 August 1893 by Abdülhamid II for members of the dynasty, foreign royalty, and men of state who performed extraordinary service (*Hanedan-ı Âl-i Osman Nişanı*)

ORTAKÖY   District of European Istanbul on the Bosphorus a short distance north of Dolmabahçe Palace

PADISHAH   Emperor; alternative Turkish title for the sultan

PAGES OF THE INNER SERVICE   Eunuch staff in service at the imperial palaces (*Enderunlular*)

PALACE POINT   Point of land at the northeastern tip of the peninsula of Stambul, where Topkapı Palace stands (*Saray burnu*)

PASHA MOTHER   Title of the mother of the Khedive of Egypt (*Valide Paşa*)

PRINCESS MOTHER   Title of the mother of the reigning sultan (*Valide Sultan*)

PRIVY STAFF   Male staff in personal service to the sultan as opposed to staff in service in the harem; included most notably the monarch's Senior Secretary, Master of the Robes, Master of the Stables, Master of the Coffee Service, and Tray Bearer (*Bendegân*)

PROCESSION TO THE NOBLE MANTLE   Annual ceremony on 15 Ramadan, in which the mantle of the Prophet was honored in the presence of the sultan, members of the imperial family, and high officials (*Hırka-ı Şerif Ziyareti*)

RAMADAN   Month in the Muslim calendar devoted to fasting during daylight hours

ROYAL MOSQUE PROCESSION   Ceremonial progress of the sultan to midday prayers at a mosque each Friday (*Selâmlık*)

RUMELİ HİSARI   Fortress constructed in 1452 on the European shore of the Bosphorus

RUMELIA   The European provinces of the Ottoman Empire

SALEP   Hot drink made of a kind of orchid root

SALTA   Short ladies' jacket embroidered with gilt thread; a symbol of high office in the harem

SELÂMLIK   (1) Rooms or wing in a palace or large house where males resided and visitors were received; (2) The Royal Mosque Procession that took place each Friday

SENIOR CONSORT   Highest-ranking consort of the monarch (*Baş Kadınefendi*)

SENIOR KALFA   Supervisory kalfa in each entourage in the palace, also known as Entourage Kalfa (*Daire Kalfası*); appointed by the sultan and charged with management oversight of her entourage, each Senior Kalfa reported to the High Hazinedar (*Büyük Kalfa*)

ŞEYHÜLİSLÂM   Chief Muslim religious dignitary of the empire, charged with oversight of canon law and of institutions relating to Islam

SHAZILIYA   Order of Sufis founded in North Africa in the twelfth century

SHEIKH   Head of an order of dervishes

SİMİT   Bagel-like rings topped with sesame

SİNAN PASHA MOSQUE   Sixteenth-century mosque in Beşiktaş, downhill from Yıldız Palace, commissioned by the admiral Sinan Pasha (d. 1554)

SİRKECİ   District at the Stambul end of Galata Bridge, where the Golden Horn meets the Bosphorus, downhill from Topkapı Palace

ŞİŞLİ   District of European Istanbul on the hills above the Bosphorus, not far from Yıldız Palace

SÖĞÜTLÜ   (1) Title of an army regiment established under Abdülhamid II; (2) Name of the imperial yacht launched in England in 1904. The word means "of Söğüt," the locale in northwestern Anatolia where the Ottoman dynasty originated

STAMBUL   Historic central district of Istanbul, comprising the peninsula between the Golden Horn, the Bosphorus, and the Sea of Marmara

STAMBULINE   Long, slitted frock coat with closed collar, worn in Turkey from the 1840s to the 1910s

SULTAN AHMED DISTRICT   Neighborhood of the Sultan Ahmed Mosque in Stambul

SUPERINTENDENT OF DEPARTURES   Functionary responsible for excursions of the sultan and imperial family from the palace (*Gidiş Müdürü*)

TARABYA   Village on the European shore of the Bosphorus some twenty kilometers north of Stambul

TEMENNA   Salutation whereby one bowed (to a degree corresponding to the rank of the person saluted) and touched the right hand to the chest, then the lips, then the forehead; the "floor *temenna*"—the most respectful—began with touching the hand to the floor or ground, then the chest, then the forehead

TRAY BEARER   Servant whose major task was to carry meal trays from the palace kitchens into the harem, then back to the kitchens at the end of meals (*Tablakâr*)

ULEMA   The class of educated religious scholars, including judges and professors

ÜSKÜDAR   Suburb of Istanbul on the Asiatic shore of the Bosphorus, approximately opposite Dolmabahçe Palace

ÜSTÜFE   Cloth, or sections of fabric, an uncommon word probably derived from Italian *stoffa*, "cloth"; also spelled *ustufa*

USTA   Female supervisor of lower-ranking serving women in the palace harem

VALIDE MOSQUE   "Mosque of the Princess Mother," built in 1710 at Üsküdar

YÂ SÎN   Chapter 36 of the Quran

YAHYA EFENDI   Dervish convent and cemetery adjacent to the grounds of Yıldız Palace, along the Bosphorus; a primary burial site for the imperial family and palace household staff in the nineteenth and twentieth centuries

YAŞMAK   Women's head covering of thin white gauze consisting of two parts, one wrapped over the head, the other extended from ear to ear over the nose and chin, leaving the eyes exposed; the ends of the *yaşmak* were tucked into the collar of the *ferace*, so that the entire neck and head except the eyes appeared wrapped in white gauze

YILDIZ PALACE   "Palace of the Star," since the early seventeenth century the site of imperial gardens and, later, villas along the hills overlooking the Bosphorus slightly north of the city; named for the "Star Pavilion" erected by Sultan Selim III for his mother around 1800, the site was greatly expanded after 1876 into the residence compound of Abdülhamid II, consisting of villas set amid the palace grounds

ZAMZAM   Sacred well in the courtyard of the Kaaba in Mecca

Bibliography

Akbayar, Nuri (ed.). 1998. *Beşiktaş Past and Present*. Istanbul: Numune.

Alderson, A. D. 1956. *The Structure of the Ottoman Dynasty*. Oxford: Clarendon.

Arberry, A. J. 1974. *The Koran Interpreted*. New York: MacMillan.

Artuk, İbrahim, and Cevriye. 1967. *Osmanlı Nişanları*. Istanbul: İstanbul Matbaası.

Bardakçı, Murat. 1998. *Şahbaba: Osmanoğulları'nın Son Hükümdarı VI. Mehmed Vahideddin'in Hayatı, Hatıraları ve Özel Mektupları*. Istanbul: Pan.

Batur, Afife. 1994. "Yıldız Sarayı." In *Dünden Bugüne İstanbul Ansiklopedisi* 7:520–527. Istanbul: Tarih Vakfı.

Börekçi, Mehmed Çetin. 1999. *İkinci Meşrutiyet ve II. Abdülhamid Hakkında*. Istanbul: Bedir.

Çakıroğlu, Ekrem (ed.). 1999. *Yaşamları ve Yapıtlarıyla Osmanlılar Ansiklopedisi*. Istanbul: Yapı Kredi Kültür Sanat Yayıncılık.

Dodd, Anna Bowman. [1903] 2004. *In the Palaces of the Sultan*. Reprint, with introduction by Teresa Heffernan. Piscataway, N.J.: Gorgias.

Elliot, Henry G. 1922. *Some Revolutions and Other Experiences*. London: Murray.

Erginsoy, Abdurrahman. 1996. *Türkiye'de Masonluğun Doğuşu ve Gelişmesi*. Istanbul: Erciyas.

Esemenli, Deniz. 2002. *Osmanlı Sarayı ve Dolmabahçe*. Istanbul: Homer.

Georgeon, François. 2003. *Abdülhamid II, le sultan calife (1876–1909)*. Paris: Fayard.

Hassan, Hassan. 2000. *In the House of Muhammad Ali: A Family Album, 1805–1952*. Cairo: American University in Cairo Press.

İsen, Mustafa, and Ali Fuat Bilkan. 1997. *Sultan Şâirler*. Ankara: Akçağ.

Jeulin, Jacques (trans. and ed.). 1991. *Avec mon père le sultan Abdülhamid de son palais à sa prison*, by Aïché Osmanoglou. Paris: L'Harmattan.

Karateke, Hakan T. 2004. *Padişahım Çok Yaşa! Osmanlı Devletinin Son Yüz Yılında Merasimler*. Istanbul: Kitap.

Koçu, Reşad Ekrem. 1967. *Türk Giyim, Kuşam ve Süslenme Sözlüğü*. Ankara: Başnur.

Lewis, Bernard. 1969. *The Emergence of Modern Turkey*. New York: Oxford.

Lewis, Raphaela. 1971. *Everyday Life in Ottoman Turkey*. New York: Dorset.

Lieven, Dominic. 1992. *The Aristocracy in Europe, 1815–1914*. New York: Columbia.

Mümtaz, Semih. 1950. "İkinci Hamid'in damadı Kemalettin Paşa ile Beşinci Murad'ın kızı arasında bir aşk macerası." *Resimli Tarih Mecmuası* 1:343.

Ok, Sema. 1997. *Harem Dünyası Harem Ağaları*. Istanbul: Kamer.

Okay, Cüneyd. 1999. "Soku, Ziya Şakir." In *Yaşamları ve Yapıtlarıyla Osmanlılar Ansiklopedisi*, 2:548–549. Istanbul: Yapı Kredi Kültür Sanat Yayıncılık.

Ölçer, Cüneyt. 1987. *Sultan Murad V ve Sultan Abdülhamid II Dönemi Osmanlı Madeni Paraları*. [Istanbul?]: Yenilik.

Osmanoğlu, Ayşe. 1994. *Babam Sultan Abdülhamid (Hâtıralarım)*. Istanbul: Selçuk.

Osmanoğlu, Osman Selaheddin. 1999. *Osmanlı Devleti'nin Kuruluşunun 700. Yılında Osmanlı Hanedanı*. Istanbul: İSAR Vakfı.

Pamuk, Şevket. 2000. *A Monetary History of the Ottoman Empire*. New York: Cambridge.

Peirce, Leslie P. 1993. *The Imperial Harem: Women and Sovereignty in the Ottoman Empire*. New York: Oxford.

Sakaoğlu, Necdet. 1999. "Mehmed V (Reşad)." In *Yaşamları ve Yapıtlarıyla Osmanlılar Ansiklopedisi* 2: 93–97. Cited as "Mehmed."

———. 1999. "Murad V." In *Yaşamları ve Yapıtlarıyla Osmanlılar Ansiklopedisi* 2:247–250. Cited as "Murad."

Şakir, Ziya. 1943. *Çırağan Sarayında 28 Sene: Beşinci Murad'ın Hayatı*. Istanbul: Anadolu Türk Kitap Deposu.

———. 1950. "Enver Paşa ile Naciye Sultan Nasıl Evlendiler?" *Resimli Tarih Mecmuası* 1 (1950), pp. 376–378.

Saz, Leyla. 1994. *The Imperial Harem of the Sultans: Daily Life at the Çırağan Palace during the 19th Century*. Istanbul: Peva.

Şehsuvaroğlu, Halûk Y. 1947. "Çırağan Sarayına Dair Bazı Hatıralar." *Akşam* (26 November 1947). In Çelik Gülersoy, *The Çerâğân Palaces* (Istanbul: İstanbul Kitaplığı, 1992).

———. 1949. *Sultan Aziz: Hususî, siyasî hayatı, devri ve ölümü*. Istanbul: Hilmi.

———. 1951. "Beşinci Sultan Mehmet Reşat." In *Resimli Tarih Mecmuası* 2: 524–527.

———. 1956. "Sultan Beşinci Murat." In *Resimli Tarih Mecmuası* 7:64–67, 132–138, 206–216, 274–276, 332–335, 401–404, 462–464, 472, 519–523, 587–591, 651–655, 664, 710–718, 728, 766–774, 776.

———. 1960. "Baltalimanı Sahilsarayı." In Koçu, Reşad Ekrem, *İstanbul Ansiklopedisi* 4:2082.

Simavi, Lütfi. 2004. *Son Osmanlı Sarayında Gördüklerim*. Istanbul: Örgün.

Stitt, George. 1948. *A Prince of Arabia: The Emir Shereef Ali Haider*. London: George Allen & Unwin.

Toledano, Ehud R. 1998. *Slavery and Abolition in the Ottoman Middle East*. Seattle: University of Washington.

Türkgeldi, Ali Fuad. 1951. *Görüp İşittiklerim*. Ankara: Türk Tarih Kurumu.

Uluçay, M. Çağatay. 1992. *Padişahların Kadınları ve Kızları*. Ankara: Türk Tarih Kurumu.

Ünüvar, Safiye. 1964. *Saray Hatıralarım*. Istanbul: Cağaloğlu.

Uşaklıgil, Halid Ziya. 1940–1942. *Saray ve Ötesi: Son Hatıralar*. Istanbul: Hilmi.

Uzunçarşılı, İsmail Hakkı. 1944. "Ali Suâvi ve Çırağan Sarayı Vak'ası." *Belleten* 29:71–118. Cited as "Ali."

———. 1944. "V. Murad'ı Tekrar Padişah Yapmak İsteyen K. Skaliyeri-Aziz Bey Komitesi." *Belleten* 30:245–328.

———. 1944. "Doktor Mehmed Emin Paşa." *Belleten* 30:329–340. Cited as "Doktor."

———. 1944. "V. Murad ile Oğlu Salâhaddin Efendiyi Kaçırmak İçin Kadın Kıyafetinde Çırağana Girmek İsteyen Şahıslar." *Belleten* 32:589–597. Cited as "Kaçırmak."

———. 1946. "Beşinci Murad'ı Avrupa'ya Kaçırma Teşebbüsü." *Belleten* 37:195–209.

———. 1946. "Beşinci Sultan Murad'ın Tedâvîsine ve Ölümüne ait Rapor ve Mektuplar, 1876–1905." *Belleten* 38:317–367. Cited as "Tedâvîsine."

Vahdettin, Nevzat. 1999. *Yıldız'dan San Remo'ya: Nevzat Vahdettin'in Hatıraları ve 150'liklerin Gurbet Maceraları*. Istanbul: Arma.

Yıldırım, Tahsin. 2006. *Veliahd Yusuf İzzeddin Efendi Öldürüldü mü? İntihar mı Etti?* Istanbul: Çatı.

Index